BROKERING SERVITUDE

# CULTURE, LABOR, HISTORY SERIES

General Editors: Daniel Bender and Kimberley L. Phillips

# Brokering Servitude

*Migration and the Politics of Domestic Labor*
*during the Long Nineteenth Century*

Andrew Urban

NEW YORK UNIVERSITY PRESS

New York

NEW YORK UNIVERSITY PRESS
New York
www.nyupress.org
© 2018 by New York University
All rights reserved

References to Internet websites (URLs) were accurate at the time of writing. Neither the author nor New York University Press is responsible for URLs that may have expired or changed since the manuscript was prepared.

ISBN: 978-0-8147-8584-3

For Library of Congress Cataloging-in-Publication data, please contact the Library of Congress.

New York University Press books are printed on acid-free paper, and their binding materials are chosen for strength and durability. We strive to use environmentally responsible suppliers and materials to the greatest extent possible in publishing our books.

Manufactured in the United States of America

10 9 8 7 6 5 4 3 2 1

Also available as an ebook

*To the memory of my grandmothers,*
*Rose Rosenblum and Adelle Urban*

# CONTENTS

*Some figures appear as a group following page 202.*

# ACKNOWLEDGMENTS

The doctorate program in History at the University of Minnesota nourished me with a vital intellectual and activist community. I am grateful to Anna Clark and Doug Hartmann for all of their support and feedback. Kevin Murphy is a dear friend and role model. His commitment to the public humanities as a basis for critical social engagement continues to inspire me. My advisors Donna Gabaccia and Erika Lee put me on the right path, and their imprint can be seen throughout this book. I can only hope I have done justice to the education I received from them. To this day, I still count on both Donna and Erika for support and encouragement.

At Emory University, Leslie Harris's impact as a mentor cannot be properly qualified. The chance to work with the innovative Transforming Community Project was a formative experience.

There are so many colleagues and friends who helped me along the way. My apologies for any omissions. . . . I would like to thank Isra Ali, Bob Barde, Al Barrion, David Brecher, Candace Chen, Frances Chen, Janna Emig, Heather Fife, Lucas Klein, Nelson Lichtenstein, Allison Lorentzen, Heather Lukes, David Madden, Jeff Manuel, Molly McGarry, David McNeill, Brighde Mullins, Peter Philips, Eric Richtmyer, Maggie Russell-Ciardi, Liz Sevcenko, Michael Sullivan, Evan Taparata, Julia Thomas, Katie Tsuji, Sue Urban, Amity Wilczek, and Aaron Windel.

Nicole Heater deserves a special line of thanks for the years of patient support that she offered me. This book would not have been possible without her help.

I would like to thank Bill Creech and Angela Tudico of the National Archives.

I have benefitted from opportunities to present my book at a number of workshops and conferences. These include the United States in the World writing group at NYU, whose core members Justin Jackson, Augustine Sedgewick, and David Singerman were close readers and commenters. I was fortunate to have participated in two meetings of the International Conference of Labour and Social History, and I am grateful for the comments and feedback that I received from Dirk Hoerder, Elise van Nederveen Meerkerk, and Silke Neunsinger, who edited the volume *Towards a Global History of Domestic and Caregiving Workers*. I would also like to thank the contributors to the edited volume *Making the Empire Work*, who gathered at the University of Toronto. In addition, I acknowledge the James Weldon Johnson Institute at Emory, the Global Race, Ethnicity, and Migration workshop at the University of Minnesota, and Mae Ngai and the Weatherhead East Asian Institute at Columbia University. As an American Council of Learned Societies New Faculty Fellow, I had valuable time to work on this project.

Rutgers has been an incredibly supportive environment and an inspiring place to work. I would like to thank, in particular, Louise Barnett, Carolyn Brown, Kornel Chang, Dorothy Sue Cobble, Ann Fabian, Leslie Fishbein, Doug Greenberg, Allan Isaac, Kathy López, James Masschaele, Lou Masur, Meredith McGill, Andy Parker, Jamie Pietruska, Nancy Rao, Kyla Schuller, Ben Sifuentes-Jáuregui, Judith Surkis, Jimmy Swenson, Mark Wasserman, and Ginny Yans.

Support from the Rutgers University Research Council allowed for the inclusion of color images in this book.

Dan Bender and Kim Phillips have provided wonderful encouragement as series editors. Dan in particular has been a mentor to me in all aspects of my career. NYU Press has diligently ushered this book toward completion. Deb Gershenowitz and Constance Grady were my editors when I began, and offered important help getting things off the ground. Clara Platter and Amy Klopfenstein have been resourceful, candid, and insightful in seeing the book to its completion. Dorothea Halliday, NYU Press's managing editor, coordinated copyediting and production with precision and awareness of the various tenure-related deadlines I faced.

Last but not least, there are individuals whom I can never adequately thank. But I will try. Caley Horan offered editing help at a crucial juncture, and I am indebted to her for this timely intervention and for her support throughout. At Rutgers, Johanna Schoen read the book manuscript in its entirety and provided me with focused comments and suggestions. As my readers for NYU Press, Eileen Boris and Micki McElya provided two rounds of crucial feedback, each time pushing me to broaden the scope of my thinking. They have inspired me not only with their insights, but with their willingness to spend so much time helping a junior colleague. I can only hope that in the future I can replicate this commitment—and the generosity that inspires it.

My sister Claire, an immigrant rights lawyer, was a vital source of help in comparing past to present and in making sense of change over time. Where such change exists. . . .

My dad, Ted, has supported this project from day one. Whenever I seemed poised to lose it he helped with whatever needed helping, and brought me back down to earth. I am forever grateful.

This book would simply not be without my mom, Janet. Not only did she read the manuscript in its entirety and help to copyedit, she provided vital assistance in respect to cropping, formatting, and improving the resolution of the images that appear here. She has supported me with every aspect of this book—and in life—and I cannot thank her enough.

## A NOTE ON LANGUAGE

When referring to Chinese names in this book, I use the renderings that American journalists, missionaries, and immigration officials provided. English translations of Chinese names, however, are notoriously unreliable.

In English translations of Chinese, the family name appears before the given name. Accordingly, I refer to individuals with Chinese names by their first rather than second name. The exception here is when the first name is given as "Ah," which is used as a diminutive or nickname prefix added to a name in the Chinese language. Where white officials referred to a Chinese immigrant by Ah followed by a second name, I use the second name to refer to the individual, even if this is the person's given name.

In referring to Chinese place names, unless I am quoting directly, I use the current Hanyu Pinyin transliteration system.

# Introduction

Ye Gon Lun was eighteen years old when he succumbed to tuberculosis on June 23, 1874. Three days later, he was interred in Sacramento's Old City Cemetery in a plot purchased for him by Nathaniel Greene Curtis, who, along with his wife, Nancy, had employed Ye as a domestic servant for nine years. Walking around the various plots, visitors encounter Ye's tomb as an anomaly, surrounded as it is by grave sites memorializing the city's white, Anglo founders. In Western cemeteries, Chinese immigrant graves are often located in segregated sections.

Curtis, a transplant from Memphis, arrived in California in 1850 during the Gold Rush. He quickly gave up prospecting to practice law. While simultaneously holding public offices as an elected judge and Democratic state assemblyman and senator, he was also well regarded as a criminal defense attorney. Curtis worked, on a number of occasions, as outside counsel for the Central Pacific Railroad. In 1887, he testified before the Pacific Railway Commission in response to allegations that he had set fire to financial ledgers revealing that the railroad's executives and board members had fraudulently overcapitalized construction costs for their own personal profit. Reflecting on his relationship to California's advancements toward the end of his life, he would claim membership in the "noble band of pioneers who had brought order out of chaos and had laid deep and broad and lasting the foundation of the social fabric which led to the present and happy condition of the people."[1] Defending railroad officials from charges of financial fraud was indeed consistent with how "civilization" unfurled in the American West. In material terms, the lawyer-pioneer belonged to an expanding class of salary earners with disposable income in cities like Sacramento and San Francisco—professionals such as politicians, accountants, and business owners who wished to employ servants, cooks, laundry workers, livery drivers, gardeners, and other service workers.

The *Sacramento Daily Union* reported that Curtis "came across" Ye in 1865 while he was in San Francisco for business. Ye was a nine-year-old immigrant boy who, as the Presbyterian minister Ira M. Condit commented, was "fresh from his heathen home in China." How exactly Curtis encountered Ye, and what transpired between the two at that moment, was never disclosed, at least in public accounts. If Ye's story conforms to that of other Chinese immigrants, his family may have relied on a lender to borrow money to finance his transpacific passage. His young age meant that he would have struggled to compete with older workers to get hired in more physically demanding jobs, and it is reasonable to infer that the intent was to have him specifically seek out work as a domestic laborer. Alternatively, Ye could have been the orphaned or abandoned child of a Chinese merchant family—a theory that has some credence if later rumors claiming that wealthy relatives wanted to exhume his body for return to China have any factual basis. There is no evidence that Ye was indentured to Curtis or forced into this relationship against his will—although "will" is a concept that this book complicates. The Thirteenth Amendment, which was ratified in December 1865, outlawed "involuntary servitude" along with slavery, although Ye's age would have allowed for him to be fostered to a state-appointed guardian without his consent. "Being pleased with his appearance—for he was a bright, intelligent and handsome little boy, as white as any Caucassian [*sic*]," the *Daily Union* noted, without any additional detail, Curtis "took him into his service and gave him opportunities to learn."[2]

Under the supervision of Condit and a "native Chinese helper," Sit Ah Mun, Ye was baptized a Presbyterian when he turned fourteen. A member of Sacramento's Chinese Christian Association, Ye had aspired to train as a minister to his people, and as a dying wish, newspapers reported, he donated his savings to a fund that would allow other Chinese immigrants to pursue this purpose. In his eulogy, Curtis declared that his deceased servant was "an honor to Christian civilization, and an honor to the Church." Condit's bilingual lyrics to the Christian hymn "Happy Land" enabled Chinese immigrants attending Ye's funeral to solemnize his passing in song, alongside white mourners.[3] The inscription on Ye's tomb captures and conveys the possibilities for cosmopolitan and globe-spanning fraternity and equality that Christian universalism promised to the devout. It quotes Isaiah 45:22: "Look unto me, and be ye saved all the ends of the earth; for I am God and there is none else." Above it, two clasping hands are bordered by an impression of a ribbon with the term *fidelis*. While the loyalty referenced by the Latin word was likely meant to signify faith in Christ, given Ye's relationship to the Curtis family, it carried other valences as well. (A photograph of Ye's grave site is included as Figure 1 in the color image insert.)

The childless Curtises, newspapers noted, considered Ye to be a son and not just a servant. Journalists covering the funeral suggested that the boundaries that divided families from their hired servants, capital from labor, and white Americans from Chinese immigrants could collapse under the weight of the type of mutual affection that the Curtises and Ye had developed for each other. The extravagant cost of Ye's burial was cited as evidence to this point. The marble, granite, and brick tomb required the labor of three different stonecutting and masonry firms and cost Curtis twelve hundred dollars. It would have taken a Chinese servant in California earning typical wages of twenty-five dollars a month four years to make this sum. The elaborate expense also reflected the security features built into the tomb, which included a twenty-two-hundred-pound granite slab that required twelve men to roll into place. Curtis's efforts to keep Ye buried and underground became a central fixation of the media, which relayed rumors that the enormous stone lid was installed to prevent Ye's relatives from exhuming and returning his remains to China. The practice of having Chinese immigrants' remains sent back to China was frequently cited as evidence that laborers chose to be sojourners in the United States and were uninterested in assimilating.[4] In an 1869 speech he delivered in Boston, Frederick Douglass argued that Chinese immigrants' desire to return posthumously to China would change with time and was not a sufficient reason for denying them the right to citizenship—which the 1870 Naturalization Act would do one year later. Douglass predicted: "He will not be long in finding out that a country which is good enough to live in, is good enough to die in; and that a soil that was good enough to hold his body while alive, will be good enough to hold his bones when he is dead."[5] In Ye's case, his permanent incorporation into the earth that constituted American sovereign territory was ensured at great cost. It came, however, not as a citizen endowed with equal rights, but as a Christian servant guarded by his master. The intimate labor that Ye performed produced his racial identity and the terms of his inclusion, even in death.[6]

A North Carolinian by birth, Curtis would have been familiar with the commemorative narratives that white southerners deployed to extol the virtues of deceased "loyal" slaves and, in the postbellum period, free black workers they deemed compliant. The enactment of these rituals actively suppressed "market forces and economic exigency," historian Micki McElya observes, as well as the violence and inequality that were the very foundations of the master and servant relationship.[7] The framing of Ye's death enlisted similarly evasive tropes, refashioned, however, to commend not only his loyalty but also his spiritual conversion by way of the labor marketplace. Nevertheless, no matter how much the coverage of Ye's funeral emphasized the emotional and religious bonds between him and the Curtises, the other values produced through this relationship slipped out as well. The *New York Times*, for instance, informed readers that "the flowers which [Ye] had cultivated in his life are being transplanted to bloom over his grave."[8]

The political implications of Curtis's decision to employ a Chinese servant had different resonances still. By 1874, white antagonism toward Chinese immigration was mounting in California, and as a politician and public figure, Curtis had to be cautious about his hiring practices. The *Sacramento Daily Union* reported—without referencing its source— that Ye himself favored restrictions on Chinese immigration for religious reasons. Before his death, the paper quoted him as saying: "it was a disgrace to Christian civilization to permit the Chinese to live here, as the class of Chinese who come here were of the lower classes."[9] In 1877, only three years after Ye's passing, Curtis campaigned for a seat in the California Senate by asserting that he had "always been opposed to Chinese labor and in favor of white labor over Chinese competition." He added that he had no objections to proposals that called for "arresting Chinese immigration and sending the Chinamen out of the country." During the same campaign, Curtis tried to deflect attention away from his role in eliminating language from a bill that would have, if passed in its original form, prohibited California counties from issuing Southern Pacific Railroad construction bonds unless the company agreed to employ white labor exclusively.[10] The inconsistencies between Curtis's anti-Chinese pledges and his personal and professional actions failed to doom his campaign, and he emerged victorious in the election.

Curtis may have refused to see a contradiction in his love of Ye and his support for Chinese exclusion. He may have indeed believed that, as a Christian servant, Ye belonged to an entirely different class of Chinese altogether. More pragmatically, California's middle classes were reluctant to surrender the services that they had become dependent upon. It was one thing to rhetorically invoke "pioneer" days gone by when, as one memoirist recalled, even the governor of California tended his own garden.[11] It was another matter to enact this type of self-sufficiency in practice.

The hypocrisy of white employers who opposed Chinese immigration but continued to rely on Chinese servants did not go unnoticed. In October 1877, for instance, a cartoon in the *Wasp* attacked Richard Josiah Hinton, the editor of the *San Francisco Post*, who frequently penned columns castigating businesses that employed Chinese immigrants. In the cartoon, Hinton is shown eagerly awaiting the delivery of his meal from his Chinese cook, while a Chinese servant dusts in the background. (The cartoon, "A Hint-On the Chinese Question," appears as Figure 2 in the insert to this book.)

To those who heeded the *Post*'s advice, the cartoon offered (in what the editors no doubt thought was a clever pun) a "hint on" the complex realities of the "Chinese Question." In November 1882, six months after the passage of the first Chinese Restriction Act, the *Christian Advocate* derided the soon-to-be Democratic governor of California, George Stoneman, after it was discovered that he employed Chinese servants at his family's estate in the San Gabriel Valley. Eager to paint western politicians as engaging in the state's anti-Chinese furor for cynical, vote-hunting reasons, the *Advocate* observed that Stoneman's actions showed "the precise degree of sympathy which dwells in the bosoms of these politicians for the 'poor, down-trodden white laborer, who is ruined by Chinese cheap labor.'" Stoneman, meanwhile, defended his family's employment practices by claiming that his wife managed the family's household affairs without his input.[12] While Stoneman sought to reinforce a neat distinction between public and domestic affairs, it is clear that the politics of employing Chinese labor had eroded these boundaries.

How Ye viewed the social and economic relationship that he entered into with the Curtis family is impossible to determine with any certainty. His most immediate actions must be understood in the context of his need to plot for his survival as a nine-year-old boy apparently living alone in San Francisco. Accepting an arrangement that made him a dependent of the Curtises would have been an obvious move in the absence of kin or other Chinese immigrants willing to protect him. Orphans of all backgrounds were fostered out and brokered as labor, in order to relieve whatever costs that governments and social welfare institutions might otherwise have to assume for their care. As Ye aged, he seems to have developed a genuine belief in the Presbyterian faith that the Curtises exposed him to, to the extent that he was willing to identify with white restrictionists' goals for limiting "heathen" and unassimilable Chinese laborers. Then again, if he was indeed the son of more affluent Chinese immigrants, he may have been predisposed to such views anyway. Since he died when he was only eighteen, it is hard to forecast what the future might have held for him. It was not uncommon for Chinese servants to use white missionaries and Christianity, whether they were believers or not, to advance their own interests. Missionaries overwhelmingly belonged to the middle class and were valuable allies to Chinese servants who wished to open laundries, restaurants, or other businesses that allowed them to transition from household service to service work where they controlled the means of production. Whether he went on to pursue a career in the ministry or another vocation, it is doubtful that Ye would have remained a devoted servant for the remainder of his life. If the Curtises indeed saw him as a son, would they have wanted him to?

* * *

When I visited Ye's grave site in March 2014, it beckoned both as a monument to the historical subjects whose lives had already commanded my focus for years, and as a figurative portal through which to explore the larger issues and questions that *Brokering Servitude* addresses. At its broadest level, this book explores how different actors and institutions in the United States, between 1850 and 1924, brokered the placement of migrants in household positions, and what they hoped to accomplish economically, politically, and socially through these transactions.

Although this book is concerned with how race, gender, and nationality informed the day-to-day experiences of servants and how workers socialized off the job, worshipped, and participated in the cultural activities and practices of their communities, it is most interested in how these categories governed how workers were commodified and managed in respect to their purported capacity to serve. *Brokering Servitude* builds bridges between subjects that typically get studied in isolation. Household service defied conventional divisions between free and unfree labor, coercion and contract, protection and exploitation, and domesticity and work. *Brokering Servitude* delves into both sides of the often neglected commodity chains that households and migrant laborers participated in and were governed through. This book asserts that the study of the political economy of reproductive labor, usually confined to the static space of the home, cannot be properly understood without attention to labor migrations, and especially migrations of workers that were assisted, compelled, or contracted. Brokers tried to marshal opportunities that transatlantic, transpacific, and internal labor migrations posed. Their interventions responded to household employers who were eager to compare the merits of different labor sources, and to reinforce presumed differences by pitting workers against each other.

## Brokers

Matching supply to demand has always required intermediaries. In household service, brokers were responsible for identifying and making available supplies of domestic labor within their spheres of influence. They were also motivated to identify possibilities for transactions— through the promotion of migration—that did not yet exist. The "production of difference," historians Elizabeth Esch and David Roediger contend, has long been the key innovative force in American labor management, and, at the same time, a "contradiction," since "managers pretend to possess a knowledge of race and of human behavior that they could never have had."[13] Race is an imagined social and cultural construct. It is not a mechanical feature that can be found in workers and engineered for efficiency and maximum output. Brokers interpreted how race and gender were valued by employers, and constructed labor markets that produced racial difference anew. The robust and transatlantic free market economy that emerged around the sale and purchase of domestic labor in the 1850s ushered in the end of customary and fixed wages for servants performing general housework. Women could increasingly find work in manufacturing sectors of the economy, namely in the needle trades and in textile mills, and could move more easily between labor markets. Households with more disposable income and a willingness to pay more for servants with certain ethnic characteristics, or with skill and experience, also contributed to a competitive market.[14] From 1850 to 1870, the number of servants employed in the United States, not counting enslaved workers, nearly tripled from 350,000 to one million, outpacing the overall growth in population from roughly 23 to 40 million.[15] The emergence of an active and virtually unregulated market for domestic wage laborers in the mid-nineteenth century encouraged an environment where brokers and workers saw ethnicity, race, and religion as elements of character and identity that could be advertised. Whether a servant was black, white, Chinese, Catholic, Protestant, Irish, English, or German was a characteristic that employers factored into how they evaluated the potential benefits of a transaction and a trait brokers and laborers marketed. Writing in 1857, one woman diarist described her excitement upon learning that a German Protestant "girl" living on Carmine Street in Manhattan had posted notice, in English, that she was available for domestic work. Despite calling on her immediately, however, twenty-seven other women made it there before her, and the woman was already contracted to the highest bidder.[16]

When it came to placing individuals in household labor situations, the list of who functioned as brokers was capacious. Anglo-Irish gentry, Union army officers, abolitionists, commercial employment agents, steamship ticket agents, Protestant missionaries in China and the American West, ethnic community leaders, and immigration officials—to offer an incomplete inventory—all took part in brokering domestic servants. A broker could be someone like Curtis, who produced a servant from a Chinese boy he "discovered" on the streets of San Francisco, or the federal government itself. Nonprofit brokers were linked by the fact that they all strived and hustled to establish their worth and authority as intermediaries, and to prove the superior value of the exchanges they vowed to arrange. They championed their ability to identify potential migrants who could be reliably consumed due to the exigent or precarious circumstances under which they entered the labor market. Brokers promised to satisfy household employers' want for servants who were dependents, and whose lack of alternative options meant that they could be disciplined above and beyond what could be exacted through wage controls alone.

By the mid-nineteenth century, as political scientist Aristide Zolberg contends, "the massive procurement of foreign labor from a diversity of sources came to be firmly acknowledged as an essential feature of the country's maturing industrial capitalism, and hence an 'affair of the state.'"[17] During the Civil War and Reconstruction, how to deploy emancipated black labor generated similar calculations. The state was concerned not only with ensuring adequate supplies of labor, but also with keeping migrant laborers off of public assistance. For various government officials and private actors, the goal of keeping migrants off relief was often inseparable from the goal of provisioning servants to household employers.

Brokers of migrant servants not associated with the state—and, in the case of the Freedmen's Bureau, representatives of the state itself—had to contend with accusations that they were contributing to malevolent forms of trafficking, intentionally or otherwise. Trafficking, unlike assisted migration, carried sinister connotations and was presented as the unequivocal enemy of both free labor and free migration. In the 1850s, commentators focused on how trafficking preyed on new forms of transatlantic free migration and posed special dangers to single, unaccompanied white women vulnerable to recruitment as sex workers—a racial concern that would persist well into the twentieth century. From the 1860s onward, concerns about trafficking grew to encompass Chinese immigrants labeled "coolies," whom anti-immigrant activists accused of being unfree by virtue of being bound by debt and racial subservience to the commands of transnational bosses who dictated the contract of their labor. Denunciations of *padrones* who trafficked in Eastern and Southern European labor would elicit similar critiques.[18]

It was assumed that in the absence of explicitly coercive methods for moving labor, and where profit was not the apparent motive, brokers' restrictions on migrant workers' liberties maintained natural dependencies that were rooted in laborers' gender (in the case of white women) or in their race (in the case of black women and men and Chinese men).

Yet as historian Gunther Peck argues, "For the trafficked migrant, coercion begins not with one's legal status as a slave, but by the varied ways a migrant's transnational movement and political status en route become commodified and controlled by middlemen."[19] This holds true in regard to the brokerage of migrant laborers into domestic service, and is complicated further by the fact that the middle-class homes were not seen as market actors let alone potential destinations for bonded, deceived, or trafficked laborers, even though their consumer demand dictated that certain workers would be pressured or in some instances compelled legally to accept household employment. Middle-class households were often granted immunity—except from workers themselves—in respect to accusations that they might be sites of exploitation.

## Contracts

As legal scholars and historians have argued, a defining feature of the late nineteenth-century United States was the ground-shifting changes that took place in respect to how social relations within households were governed. Whereas slavery, master and servant relations, and family law were previously governed in accordance with the "natural" dependencies that they purportedly captured, and the belief that only white propertied men were fit for independent citizenship, this system clashed with and gradually yielded to the liberal belief that certain rights and protections were universal, regardless of an individual's race or gender.[20]

The liberty to contract has never implied a political commitment to social or economic equality.[21] Liberty of contract entitled individuals the right to freely determine the agreements they entered into without coercion, and protected them from the alienation of their personal property by granting them the autonomy to dispose of their labor power as they saw fit.[22] The freedom to contract or withhold labor power from an employer was a liberty that clearly mattered to formerly enslaved persons, but was of considerable importance to household servants and married women who were kept and governed as dependents as well.

Brokers' and employers' efforts to coerce workers into servitude they would otherwise avoid adjusted to new technologies that governed how labor was free to circulate. This is most evident in the ways in which the contractual arrangements that migrants entered into when promised transportation assistance, relief, or wages became devices for guarantee-ing third-party employers a captive supply of servants. The debates of the nineteenth century, focused as they were on the problem of slavery, inaccurately enshrined free versus unfree labor in a misleading, ideo-logical oppositional binary. The shifting and uneven topographies that the categories of "free" and "unfree" demarcate in respect to workers' liberties give these concepts their cultural and political potency.[23]

Employers and so-called charitable brokers conspired to strip house-hold labor transactions of their competitive dimensions. As sociologist Immanuel Wallerstein argues, one of the defining and ironic features of market capitalism, given proponents' vocal commitment to "free enterprise," has been its pursuit of monopoly positions and "profit-maximization via the principal agency that can make it enduringly pos-sible, the state."[24] Northerners committed to the sanctity of free labor routinely looked to private and public welfare institutions responsible for providing relief to the indigent, as well as to orphans and prisoners, to obtain a captive labor force compelled to work in servitude. Employ-ers tried to overcome this contradictory approach to consent by arguing that criminals, paupers, and vagrants forfeited liberal rights on the basis of having broken the law, or because they had become dependent on the state.[25]

Even when domestic workers failed to give cause for the abdication of their contract freedom, the availability of labor for use in household employment was predicated on the alienation of migrants from preexist-ing modes of social organization that were no longer viable, even if the pursuit of wages in service was ultimately rendered in liberal terms as a decision that was voluntary. This was the case both for Irish women forced to leave an Ireland spoiled by famine and British colonial land policies, and for black freed persons fleeing the horrors of war and slavery.[26] Employers also tried to undermine freedom of contract as it applied to the negotiation of wages. In their coauthored 1869 publica-tion, *The American Woman's Home*, Catharine Beecher and her younger sister Harriet Beecher Stowe asked readers to consider, self-reflectively, whether it was just to impose a "rule of rectitude" against servants who, coming from impoverished backgrounds, were perceived to be demand-ing "exorbitant wages." Punishing servants who sought to maximize profits from the sale of the property in their labor made employers complicit in violating "the universal law of labor and of trade that an article is to be valued according to its scarcity and the demand." In her 1873 memoir *Palmetto Leaves*, which she wrote while living on a former plantation in Florida, Stowe made the resignation of a talented black cook who left for a hotel job in nearby Jacksonville that paid forty dollars a month into a lesson on respect for the free market. That free people could "command their own price" was affirmative proof that what the North had fought for was working not just in principle, but in practice.[27] But these views made the sisters outliers.

Labor historians have suggested that by the twentieth century, the use of criminal and penal punishments rather than civil actions in the enforcement of labor contracts persisted as lawful devices for worker compulsion in only a few, select occupations. Merchant seamen, enlistees in the armed forces, and sharecroppers and tenant farmers in the American South are typically cited as workers who continued to be subjected to various forms of incarceration and detainment as penalties for leaving employment or lease contracts prior to their expiration. Service work exists as a neglected site of labor history because the workers who performed these jobs do not conform to the model of the liberal and national subject—the white, industrial worker—who was understood to be implicitly deserving of protections and liberties in the face of capitalist exploitation.[28]

As the latter chapters of this book conclude, facilitating the movement of migrant labor into domestic work became a priority enshrined in federal policies and their enforcement. One of the key ways that the federal government became a broker of servitude was by demanding that certain labor contracts be enforced as the status or condition by which a migrant was eligible to enter or remain in the United States. It did so by exempting Chinese servants from racial restrictions that would have excluded their entry into the United States as laborers and by carving out exceptions to prohibitions that would have barred European women as economic liabilities—as long as these subjects contracted to work as servants and remained in these positions. Whereas at the end of the Civil War contracts were heralded as essential to the guarantee of workers' freedom to consent to labor, by the second decade of the twentieth century—even if the decision to enter into contracts remained in theory voluntary—they had become devices for constraining immigrant laborers' liberty to move between jobs and employers. At the very moment when Progressive Era reformers were beginning to highlight domestic service as an occupation where labor remained governed by "feudal" rules, contemporaneous immigration legislation was creating new classes of laborers who were dependent on maintaining employment relations as servants in order to be allowed to enter or stay in the United States.[29]

## The Value of Domestic Labor

Household labor has often been neglected as a feature of capitalism. Domesticity's value to individuals and families, and how this gets calculated, defies a strictly monetary approach. Domesticity results from the production or consumption of tangible goods and services, but it is also a feeling and set of affective social relationships, and cannot be commodified or priced for purchase as a discrete "thing" to be obtained.

This does not mean that domesticity exists outside of capitalism. In *The Wealth of Nations*, Adam Smith famously asserted that the employment of servants could not be considered productive because their labor did not add real value to an economy. Some seventy years later, Karl Marx seconded this conclusion. Marx grouped together everyone from "whore to pope" as service providers who did not contribute to the production of capital.[30] Both classical and Marxist economic theories have been insufficient in grasping the significance of unpaid domestic and reproductive labor as well. Since the late 1960s, feminist historians and scholars have combated the view that unpaid labor performed for families and households could be dismissed, along with the work of paid servants, as unproductive in capitalist terms.[31] The performance of reproductive labor generated the very conditions under which men of all classes—and women burdened with second shifts as paid workers— were physically able to work for wages or other compensation.

Historians have failed to account for how capital gets generated through transactions that establish the social relations of production, and link supply to demand. As commercial intermediaries that profited from job placement, intelligence offices generated significant anxiety. Private intelligence offices or employment agencies as they were later called profited as middlemen (and often *middlewomen*) through fees and commissions. Through transatlantic, transpacific, and transregional networks, they not only managed migrants' placement in household service, but also provided loans and other forms of financing that enabled migrants' passage. As arbiters of borders, they instructed immigrants on how to maintain their eligibility to enter the United States and on how to avoid immigration officials who might declare their actions, and the assistance they had received, illegal. Intelligence offices were demonized by middle-class commentators and accused of making a mockery out of the principle of freedom of contract by seducing workers with the promises of riches and by convincing them that they had no responsibility to potential employers beyond the satisfaction of their own self-interest.[32] As an author complained in an 1868 *Godey's Lady's Book* article, lamenting the powers of contract that Irish servants had, the intelligence office "represents, in Biddy-dom, all the power of the State, and is moreover the Temple of Liberty." "The custom of other places is here reversed," she added, "and the servant is the mistress. She sits enthroned, waiting to receive the homage of dependent and tributary housekeepers."[33] Other middle-class commentators homed in on intelligence offices' predatory actions, which included trafficking women in sex work, holding their possessions as ransom, and eliciting exorbitant fees from the job applicants whom they were placing. While these practices no doubt occurred, employers seized upon their existence to try to eliminate commercial intermediaries altogether. This allowed them to evade a more nuanced analysis of how these brokers were imperative to labor migrations in the absence of other financing mechanisms.

Domesticity was also commercial, despite its long-standing associations with privacy and opposition to the values of the marketplace, in that it required employers—and middle-class women more specifically—to engage in the procurement, purchase, and training and management of labor.[34] Prior to the mid-nineteenth century, most Americans were only tentatively connected to an economy where wages predominated as the means by which to acquire goods and services. As historian Jeanne Boydston documents, in the antebellum period men and women participated in domestic production as relative equals, even if gendered divisions of labor existed in respect to the creation of goods for use and exchange. The divisions of household labor that accompanied what historians describe as the midcentury "market revolution" would segregate spiritual, mental, and reproductive work from domestic labor that wages rendered menial. The pursuit of comfort, contentment, and time to devote to intellectual, charitable, and religious matters became the surplus value that men and especially women might enjoy if their homes were well run.[35]

When commentators insisted that the typical Irish servant was "a more disquieting and unendurable ruler" than even the most "tyrannical" of workingmen's unions, as an article in *Putnam's* did in 1869, they also grappled with the extent to which domesticity might be perfected through the implementation of more conscientious and selective approaches to how supply chains could be assembled.[36] Too much was at stake for middle-class women to idly sit by and let supply and demand take its uncertain course. This explicitly commercial role aligned with middle-class Protestant women's self-appointed cultural responsibility to promulgate American domesticity to the indigenous people, immigrants, and colonial subjects who came under their jurisdiction.[37] A letter writer explained to the editor of the *New York Observer*, for instance, that her husband had encouraged her to act as the "Secretary of the Interior" over her domestic servants—a title that in 1865, when the letter was written, gestured toward the administration of "foreign" Indian populations within the domestic space of the nation—and that she was to convene the "cabinet" only when "great emergencies arose."[38]

## Competing Discourses of Empire

Consumer demand for services drove migration. The demand for domestic labor and other household services determined both regions' and the nation's demographic composition.[39] Servants, despite the needs they fulfilled, were considered by many to be impossible subjects for republican freedom. In the antebellum period in which this book begins, southern slavery provided the antithesis to white independence in racial terms, and contributed to the stigmatization of any work that entailed an individual to surrender sovereignty over hours, pace of production, and free movement. The cultural and social construction of what it meant to be a white American made rejecting the deference that personal and household service was supposed to require a gesture of almost mythical importance, and an act that was commonly cited in exceptionalist narratives about what set the United States apart—at least to white immigrants.[40]

As a matter of demography, the need for servants was framed in the context of how the human capital being imported to satisfy household labor needs might be redeployed—or not—in the social and cultural work of nation building. As E. L. Godkin, the founder and editor of the *Nation* argued in an 1869 editorial, Americans could not "go back to the early, happy time, when the mill girls wrote poetry and read French and the farmer's hired man could deliver a Fourth of July oration on a pinch."[41] Having abandoned republicanism for market liberalism, Godkin suggested, Americans could no longer limit what types of experimentations with the hire of wage labor might take place. This was especially true since white immigrant women and the Irish in particular resisted submitting to a social hierarchy within the household workplace. For this reason Godkin supported continued Chinese immigration. As free laborers classified as sojourners, whose unassimilable status allegedly limited them to menial labors, Chinese immigrants exemplified both new advantages to be gained from access to Asian labor markets, and the risks that purportedly came with remaking the United States as a nation that incorporated laborers whose inclusion was never intended to result in their possessing the full rights of liberal self-rule.

White servants' desire to control who got to participate in labor markets for domestic service and their attempts to exclude black and Chinese workers from job competition were emblematic of how they viewed white settlerism. In this book I use white settlerism, a complicated and multifaceted idea, as a concept that elucidates how white immigrant workers and their allies insisted that they had value as racial subjects that transcended how their worth was defined by labor markets. The goal here, as theorist Patrick Wolfe urges, is to grasp how white settler colonialism represented a "structure not an event."[42] Irish women's imagined transition, for instance, from wage-earning domestics to unpaid mothers and wives informed the larger philosophy that brokers of their labor professed to, genuinely or otherwise, when it came to intervening in how they moved along the various supply chains that fed household labor. It is possible to see racially inclusive settlerism reflected in the frontier embrace of Irish Catholic immigrant women sent in the 1850s to places like Illinois and Wisconsin, where emigration boosters advertised that wage-earning migrants would be treated as if they were daughters. At the same time, this did not preclude Irish servants from being embraced by white republicans and laboring classes as producers in their own right, whose breadwinner status, defined by the remittances they sent to families back in Ireland, made them independent contributors.

White settlerism also manifested in seemingly less obvious places, like Ellis Island. There immigration officials treated unaccompanied women arriving from Europe as future members of the nation's reproductive population who deserved protections and required control, but who were not to be treated as disposable labor or undesirable subjects. As the political scientist Aziz Rana argues, settlerism was one "face" of American freedom, distinguished by its democratic aspirations and desire to empower certain subjects, yet accessible only to groups and individuals of a certain skin color.[43] Horatio Seymour, the former governor of New York and the Democratic nominee for the presidency in 1868, captured this mind-set when he expressed the opinion that while "the Chinese have useful qualities" such as being "good servants, ready to do the work of men or women," these were not "traits which will build on this Continent a great and high-toned power."[44] In these contexts, when Irish servants usurped middle-class rituals as their own, by dressing and acting as if they were the rightful mistresses of the homes in which they worked, their actions represented both a power struggle between capital and labor and a conflict over who was eligible to lay claim to gendered citizenship. More generally, producing domesticity in the nineteenth and early twentieth centuries was dangerous and backbreaking labor in addition to being degraded in status. To make those who were defined in racial and class terms as favored representatives of the population live (and live splendidly if they could afford to) meant that the providers of menial services—those hewers of wood and drawers of water—could not be barred or exiled as unwanted subjects from the social life of the nation altogether.[45]

## Organization and Methodology

Throughout this book, I use the terms "domestic" and "servant" as interchangeable shorthand to describe hired laborers who performed work in and around private households. I also use these terms to describe employees who catered to the domestic needs of individuals and families in transit. My focus, with some exceptions, is on domestics who can be classified as general servants. Unlike domestic laborers assigned to specialized roles in more affluent households, such as chambermaids, butlers, and governesses, servants without these distinctions in title were expected to complete any and all work that they were assigned. Cooks and, to a lesser degree, live-in nurses do warrant attention here. Preparing meals often fell to general servants in households where only one hired worker was employed. But talented cooks with experience were highly coveted, and for many servants cooking was the primary route to higher wages, opportunities outside of private households, and situations that carried more prestige.[46]

Where necessary, I make specific reference to unpaid domestic labor to describe work that was conducted by female members of a household in the service of their own families. Because wives and daughters could be called on to perform the entirety of a household's labor when resources were lacking, this gendered division of labor kept wages for domestic work in check, and made debates about whether or not certain household services were a luxury commonplace. In addition, this book mainly examines servants working in private homes and not in boarding houses, hotels, or other commercial accommodations.[47] Where I depart from this focus it is to illustrate how commentators and policymakers perceived the service economy as an area for governance that extended beyond private homes.

This book addresses "live-in" servants who occupied the same dwellings as their employers. This reflects on the period it addresses, since "living out" would not really take hold until 1900 onward. Because live-in servants resided under the same roof as their employers, matters such as rooming arrangements and the right to visitors had to be negotiated contractually or, more likely, informally. Unlike factory jobs, where a shift—no matter how long—ended, servants and their employers constantly struggled to dictate when work began and finished. In November 1906, the social scientist Frances Kellor published in the *Ladies' Home Journal* a work schedule that a housewife had sent to her, which she announced was the second-place winner in a contest that she had sponsored to publicize the best management of servants' schedules. Despite being in a situation that Kellor deemed "favorable," the runner-up's servant was on call each day until eight in the evening and spent eighty-eight hours each week in service, with seventy-one and a half hours spent in active labor.[48] Wages for servants were paid weekly or monthly, not by the hour. Many employers dictated that their servants wear a uniform. They controlled the cleaning and cooking techniques they were permitted to use, and the affectations and mannerisms they were allowed to display. In some cases, employers' rules extended into other facets of their servants' lives, over where they could worship, for instance, or whom they were permitted to socialize with when outside the home. Sexual and physical abuse, although documented infrequently, were far more prevalent in domestic service than in other workplaces.[49]

In this book, I rely on novels, short stories, and other works of fiction in order to examine how American household employers—who were both the creators and audiences for these texts—interpreted the actions of their servants. Through fiction, authors narrated servants' choices, decisions, and habits in order to provide "evidence" that backed assessments about how different domestics should be brokered and employed as suppliers of labor. Where possible, I provide alternative explanations as to what servants would have done in practice, based on information gleaned from nonfiction sources. I also explore how representations of servants' actions did specific forms of damage when they refused to acknowledge workers' actual agency.

Why focus on black, Chinese, and Irish servants? Unlike German and Swedish immigrants, whose prominence in domestic work was more regional, Irish servants were employed nationally excepting only the rural South.[50] Anglo-American employers considered Irish servants, whom they captured in the stereotype of "Biddy," to be the primary obstacles to domestic peace and comfort. Irish servants were embraced by both the law and popular opinion as white subjects, but this racial construction did not spare them from attacks that were geared at fixing their place in both household and national hierarchies. Anglo-American household employers viewed Irish servants as members of an undifferentiated mass of poor immigrant labor flooding the United States. When Irish servants began to assert greater power over the domestic labor market, employers in cities like New York responded by presenting "Biddy" as the female prototype of the Irish rebel. In the same ways British imperialists argued that Irish subjects were not fit for self-governance and home rule, Anglo-American employers claimed that Irish servants were equally dangerous when it came to advancing their militant claims to sovereignty over American kitchens, parlors, and bedrooms.[51] In California, Irish servants were championed by the anti-Chinese movements that mobilized in the 1870s, as human capital that would drive Chinese immigrants out of domestic and laundry work. At the same time household employers of Chinese servants reviled Irish servants and accused them of using mob violence and populist calls for restriction to drive competitors out and further consolidate their monopoly over the occupation.[52] The prominence of Irish servants in the national domestic labor market allowed for these myriad interpretations of their racial, social, and political subjectivity.

The historiography on black women's domestic labor in the post–Civil War South and North is rich in detail and has done much to map out these workers' agency in the face of near constant structural discrimination and violence.[53] In this book, I add to this literature by examining how black women, men, and children were governed as displaced persons. I focus on the ways in which Reconstruction-era brokers understood the value that subjects classified as refugees presented to household employers, and how they viewed long-distance transactions of labor as an alternative to government relief. Depending on the context, the Freedmen's Bureau viewed the value of free black labor as either tainted or enriched by the experience of slavery. Progressive Era sociologists and the white middle-class public debated whether black migrants from the Jim Crow South were beyond the pale when it came to reforms that would bring them in line with how white women desired to see domestic labor transformed as an occupation, or whether this made them all the more exploitable for this very reason. In both instances, brokers' interventions and designs to capture migrant black laborers as a new commodity to be marketed to northern homes provided the backdrop for these evaluations.

This book dwells on the political economy of Chinese domestic labor more than it does on the other groups that are also its focus. As historian Mae Ngai asserts: "we know a lot more about what whites thought about Chinese labor than about Chinese labor itself." The study of Chinese immigration to the United States has consistently been plagued by what she describes as "orientalist historiography." "Orientalist historiography," Ngai argues, speaks to how many scholars continue to assume, despite evidence to the contrary, that Chinese workers were "indentured, bound by debt peonage, or otherwise enslaved by 'custom.'" Even though more recent scholarship has moved away from conclusions that conflate "coolieism" with all Chinese labor, misperceptions about Chinese immigrants' status and agency persist. Allusions to the allegedly sinister and secretive powers that Chinese labor bosses wielded to compel workers beyond the more universal pressures that were placed on individuals and families to satisfy debt obligations have prevailed in the historiography as well.[54] I flip these scripts by showing that the actor most responsible for keeping Chinese servants in a state of bondage or employment-based dependency was the U.S. government itself, through the federal policies it enacted.

The political history of what motivated white laborers and politicians to press for the passage of a Chinese Restriction Act in 1882 has often come at the neglect, historian Erika Lee argues, of "the six decades of the exclusion era itself."[55] This has obscured the sharp conflicts that persisted over how to utilize as servants the Chinese migrants who remained in the United States or continued to arrive as temporarily admitted labor. The extent to which the Bureau of Immigration should have the discretionary authority to determine eligibility for entry, as opposed to vesting this power in federal courts governed by due process standards, was at the center of debates concerning Congress's plenary power over immigration in the late nineteenth century. The landmark Supreme Court cases of *Ekiu v. United States* (1892) and *Fong Yue Ting v. United States* (1893) vastly strengthened administrative officers' sovereign power to determine whether immigrants had the right to be in the country, except in cases where errors in procedure could be clearly demonstrated. These decisions removed for all but a select few the grounds for habeas corpus appeal of their debarment or deportation, unless a blatant miscarriage of justice or "manifest wrong" could be proven.[56] With the 1906 Supreme Court ruling in *Ju Toy*, immigration officials' power to determine the validity of a potential entrant's claim to birthright citizenship was upheld, and individual inspectors' and supervisors' decisions "in effect became public policy," as Lee notes. When the bureau took measures to implement procedural uniformity and fairness in how it handled immigrant cases, it did so to preempt external critics who wanted to check the agency's power.[57] Governing the admission of servants created unique modes of governance in which productive forms of inclusion designed to favorably recognize the labor needs and interests of household employers had to be weighed against the threat that those same workers would become public charges, or, in the case of Chinese servants granted temporary admission under contract to a white employer, whether they would escape from the bonds of servitude and become unauthorized immigrants. These powers made the Bureau of Immigration a powerful broker of labor.

The geographic orientation of this book corresponds to the fluid labor market dynamics it analyzes. The brokers in this study specifically tried to defy spatial limitations on the supply of domestic laborers. Moments when brokers, whether in the form of private philanthropists or government agencies like the Freedmen's Bureau, took measures to collapse barriers to the placement of servants by offsetting the cost of their transportation receive special attention here. The ability to engineer movement represented a form of expertise that was both venerated and despised, and the production of knowledge on these practices developed in conjunction with the introduction of steamships, better railroad connections, and new methods for financing migration that were also heralded as ushering in a "modern" era of migration and immigration.[58] The major ports of Atlantic and Pacific entry, New York and San Francisco, and the hub for black refugees during and after the Civil War, Washington, D.C., receive particular focus here as nodes of distribution that supplied markets.

Finally, this book is transnational in multiple ways, and heeds the charge that historians of migration need to be attentive to how mobility gets governed at the point of departure as well as at the point of reception. Throughout this book, I shed light on the ways in which the brokerage of service relations, like migrants themselves, straddled the territorial boundaries that defined the nation-state. Individuals like the white Methodist missionary to China Esther Baldwin, for instance, made the availability of domestic laborers for hire by American household consumers a matter of foreign relations. This book also takes on how domesticity itself became transnational and no longer a spatially fixed social relation of production. Servants had to be mobile actors befitting U.S. overseas expansion and imperial aspirations.

\* \* \*

Beginning with immigration that took place in the decade following the Irish Famine, this book's initial focus is on how relief efforts marked as humanitarian steered and compelled recipients of assistance into domestic service. Servitude was viewed as an ideal means by which to salvage the laboring capacity of women whose sudden autonomy became potentially burdensome to the American and British states. Chapter 1 follows the enterprising activities of Vere Foster, a member of the Anglo-Irish gentry who funded the emigration of approximately 1,250 Irish women from post-famine Ireland during the 1850s. Foster's efforts serve as a case study that illuminates the ideologies of white settlerism and Anglophone imperial unity, and shows how they worked together in concert. Foster was convinced that the best way to govern rural Ireland's surplus population and inadequate lands was to finance and coordinate the integration of young migrant women into wage labor positions as servants in the United States, in areas of the country where the supply of white female workers was inadequate. In order to assuage concerns about the moral and sexual dangers that free markets and migration posed to young Irish women, Foster endeavored to establish transatlantic networks of migration rooted in what he presented as racial and familial values of protection and mutuality. Chapter 2 turns its attention to the period of the Civil War and Reconstruction, when formerly enslaved persons, classified as "contrabands" and refugees, were placed as domestic workers in northern households. The involvement of the Bureau of Freedmen, Refugees, and Abandoned Lands (the Freedmen's Bureau) in the placement of refugees as servants prefigured the federal government's expanded role as a broker of immigrant labor in the decades that followed, yet proved controversial. Designed to reduce government expenditures on the relief of refugees in Washington, D.C., and elsewhere, the Freedmen's Bureau's financing of black servants' migration was viewed with skepticism by detractors who claimed that it revived—under the thin veneer of "free" labor—a version of the slave trade. Due to insufficient federal funding, the reluctance of black refugees to relocate to uncertain job situations in the North, and constant questions about its efficacy, the Freedmen's Bureau—after contracting thousands of women and children to service positions—was ultimately forced to disband this initiative.

By the late 1860s, middle-class employers in eastern cities had shifted their attention to the labor supply of Chinese immigrants in California, and the possible importation of male servants who were portrayed as invaluable assets to western homes. In this period, Democrats seized upon abolitionism and free labor ideology, which were previously associated with Republicans, to critique Chinese laborers as "coolies" and push for restriction.[59] Chapter 3 argues that employers produced a version of Chinese servants' difference that referenced how they were naturally submissive and mechanically efficient—and therefore ideal as domestics. Employers overlooked the more complicated structural dynamics that relegated Chinese immigrants to service work through racial discrimination and legal marginalization as migrants barred from naturalizing. In these contexts, this chapter also explores the doubts that surrounded Chinese restriction as a policy and how proponents of allowing Chinese immigrants to do work labeled menial and unworthy of citizenship linked the continued employment of Chinese servants to the Pacific Coast's imperial advantages as the gateway to Asian labor supplies.

By 1882, federal immigration officials had assumed sole responsibility for determining who qualified as eligible to enter the United States. By the 1890s, they also wielded the power to deport immigrants—what legal historian Daniel Kanstroom has called "post-entry social control"—who violated the terms of their admission.[60] Building on Kanstroom's framework, chapter 4 grapples with the ways that government-appointed immigration officers and employment agents, first at Castle Garden and then at Ellis Island and the immigration station in Philadelphia, used the threat of barred entry and informal prohibitions on the release of unaccompanied female immigrants to compel these white women into taking jobs in domestic labor. Committed to the idea that young, white European women, when subjected to the right types of controls, remained a vital and privileged source of immigrants, officials devised and implemented practices and regulations that allowed for their foreign contract and for them to circumvent restrictions that would have otherwise prohibited their entry on the grounds that they were likely to become public charges.

Chapter 5 continues this thread, although it contends that in the context of Chinese servants exempted from the exclusion laws and granted temporary admission as laborers, officials implemented post-entry controls aimed at containment rather than protection. Following the passage of the 1882 Chinese Restriction Act, immigration officials brokered special arrangements that allowed white employers to continue to enter the country with Chinese servants in their employ, so long as they took out surety bonds that indemnified the government against the possibility that their Chinese servants might leave their service and remain in the United States on an unauthorized basis. How to gain access to foreign labor without having to dispense with the entitlements that would accompany more substantive or permanent incorporation has always made domestic work, along with agricultural labor, a salient area of concern for policymakers. The Chinese who entered as temporary laborers were governed as a legally captive supply of labor for select classes of imperialists working overseas—businessmen, military officials, and missionaries—and came to symbolize the compromise between the privileged, free mobility that imperial elites required, and, in a national setting, the need to shore up the sovereign boundaries of the nation against the permanent settlement of Asian laborers. In this respect, the temporary admission of Chinese servants and the bonded conditions that defined their stay offer examples of what I argue was an incipient guestworker program.[61] Chinese immigrant servants who lived in the United States legally—as well as birthright American citizens of Chinese descent—were also subject to various requirements by immigration officials that reinforced these workers' dependency on white employers. During exclusion, the testimony of white employers became a crucial factor in determining whether Chinese servants would be credentialed as authorized residents, even in cases where they claimed to be birthright American citizens. This was essential to avoiding deportation but also to being allowed to depart and reenter the United States.

Stymied by the refusal of "new" immigrant women from Eastern and Southern Europe to pursue work as domestic laborers at the turn of the century, middle-class employers reevaluated the fundamental utility of hired labor to the production of domesticity. Chapter 6 brings the book's different narrative arcs together by engaging public and expert debates about whether domestic service could best be reformed and made modern through changes to labor relations in the home or whether Chinese and black workers' alleged predisposition to servitude meant that looking for racialized sources of labor continued to be the best solution for "fixing" the occupation. Examining the start of the Great Migration, the 1917 Immigration Act, and the eventual passage of numerical restrictions on European immigration that the 1924 Immigration Act instituted, this chapter argues that the various exceptions built into immigration laws, which had exempted domestic servants from restrictions since the passage of the 1885 Foran Act, finally gave way to the conclusion that white women could no longer be counted on to do this work.

A basic but often overlooked question persists in the United States and other wealthy nations where service workers are drawn from the ranks of immigrants: under what terms and conditions are certain workers allowed to migrate in order to serve others? To not grapple with this question is to naturalize policies that, after 1924, have supplied middle-class households with labor in situations where servants, especially live-in ones, would not otherwise be procurable. The epilogue to this book touches on how U.S. internment of Japanese Americans and their supervised parole during World War II provided displaced persons for hire as servants. It also briefly explores the 1948 Displaced Persons Act, whose sponsorship requirements meant that European refugees could agree to work as live-in servants in exchange for asylum. More attention is devoted to the labor exceptions built into the 1965 Immigration Act, which provided Jamaican and other Caribbean women with a short-lived opportunity to enter the United States after taking advantage of immigration quota rankings that privileged domestic servants. Policies that continue to authorize migrant servants' temporary admission into the United States, contingent on their performance of domestic service to the employers they entered with, also garner focus here. Finally, the epilogue concludes by discussing how household consumers have exploited domestic and care workers classified as undocumented—and how the absence of state action has enabled this social relation of production.

* * *

The idea that the servitude of free laborers and free migrants had to be brokered challenges, on an epistemological level, how we view a past where liberty of contract allegedly triumphed against enslavement, indenture, and other forms of coercion that kept workers in a state of bondage. Accordingly, it is all the more important to delve into how intermediaries sought to justify interventions into labor markets and migratory processes, and to untangle why they presupposed the need to impose various controls. It is also essential, however, to keep in mind how servants' actions and employers' and brokers' perceptions of workers' agency influenced and obligated regulatory responses. As historian Walter Johnson has argued, historic agency is best understood in the nuanced circumstances in which it operated, and not through ahistorical maxims idealizing certain performances of liberal freedom. Independence and self-determination were not just ideological constructs of liberalism, but signifying concepts that whites used to maintain the exclusivity of their fitness for sovereign self-governance.[62]

Examples of this dialectic between resistance and control are myriad. When a white St. Alban's employer wrote to the Freedmen's Bureau in 1870 to complain that the two "black boys" whose rail fare he had paid absconded en route, we can assume that they were motivated to break their contracts by the lure of a better option that presented itself during their journey north. The Freedmen's Bureau, eager to maintain its reputation as a broker, sent two black refugee women instead.[63] When a correspondent for the New York Times reported from San Francisco in 1878 that Chinese servants demanded higher wages than their white counterparts, and that local employers were willing to pay the extra money, we can decipher that Chinese laborers were not the "coolies" that opponents made them out to be.[64] Rather, they were savvy market actors who knew how to leverage the very racial difference that employers produced and validated. In 1902, when Marie von Rhein, a twenty-year-old German immigrant, broke an oral agreement that she had entered into with a prospective domestic employer while in transit from Bremen to New York, we can conclude that she had good reason to change her mind upon landing. William Williams, the commissioner of Ellis Island, tracked her down nonetheless, after accusing a missionary and broker from the Lutheran Emigrant Home of conspiring to steal her labor. Had she been permitted to freely enter the United States unaccompanied, as male immigrants were, the matter of whom she needed to be contracted to would have been evaded altogether.[65]

If freedom is to be populated with real meaning, the purposeful abdications of its underlying economic and political principles must be diligently exposed.

1

# Liberating Free Labor

*Vere Foster and Assisted Irish Emigration, 1850–1865*

## Introduction: Assistance, Relief, Control

Assisted emigration accounted for less than 4 percent of departures from Ireland during the nineteenth century. Nonetheless, the roughly 275,000 people who left the island after receiving financial aid from landlords, the British state, or private philanthropists deserve attention as cases that demonstrate how the redistribution of underemployed surplus labor was governed and imagined as a resource for white, Anglophone settlements.[1] Bracketed by the Irish Famine and the beginnings of mass migration to the United States, and the Civil War, the period of 1850 to 1865 saw key developments relating to what it meant to be a free laborer and migrant if one was a young, unaccompanied Irish woman. By the end of the war, Irish servants were avidly pursuing the benefits that came with the ability to contract their labor freely, much to the dismay of Anglo-American employers. In conflict with the prescriptions that the brokers of their labor offered, which urged them to move west into the interior and marry, Irish servants crafted racial and political identities as independent, urban wage earners instead.

\* \* \*

Mary Harlon had strong opinions about wages, working conditions, and the respect she deserved as a domestic servant. Contrary to what might be expected of an Irish orphan whose emigration was paid for by charitable funds, Harlon was hardly a dependent. Between May 1862 and October 1865, she shared her perspectives on work and life in a series of six letters she wrote to Vere Foster, the man who sponsored her immigration. Foster was a member of the Anglo-Irish gentry. Using his personal inheritance and private donations solicited through his Pioneer Irish Emigration Fund, Foster financed the passage of approximately

1,250 Irish women between 1850 and 1857. During the early 1880s, Foster subsidized the emigration of an additional 20,000 women between the ages of eighteen and thirty, paying for half the cost of their steamship tickets.[2] The Foster family had been landlords in County Louth, Ireland, since the late eighteenth century, and most of the emigrants who applied for assistance in the 1850s came from the area around Glyde Court, the family's estate. Foster appears to have been an acquaintance of Harlon's parish priest, who probably connected the two. In her letters, Harlon asked Foster to relay to a Father Smyth that she was attending Mass every Sunday, and that she received communion whenever her work schedule allowed.

Foster was a critic of private and state-backed initiatives that dispensed charity without calculating what returns their investment might bring.[3] Influenced by the emerging social science of charity work in Britain, Foster's solicitations for financial support included the controversial proposal calling for prohibitions on the emigration of families, which landlords could finance as an alternative to paying taxes that supported local workhouses and outdoor relief. Foster believed that the migration of whole families increased the likelihood of pauperism, and that it was prudent to identify the most capable individual wage earners when administering emigration assistance.[4] Because the arrival of pauper families also aggravated nativist public opinion in the United States, their emigration endangered the trust on which more productive transfers of populations between nation-states rested. Framing migration as the trade in human subjects, Foster noted that his program was designed to minimize the possibility of "some trifling misunderstanding between the governments of the two most free and progressive countries on the globe."[5] The migrants Foster sponsored were asked to repay the assistance they received, although no data exist on how many actually did. In Harlon's case, she would have had no difficulty reimbursing Foster's "loan." In May 1862, Harlon's situation with the Carrigan family came to an abrupt end. To Foster, Harlon vented anger at having spent seventeen months working for the Carrigans only to be let go with one day's notice. She was upset that the Carrigans had provided no explanation as to why she was dismissed, since her service—to the best of her knowledge— had been exemplary. Her disappointment notwithstanding, Harlon had managed to put away eighty dollars in savings and found new employment, with the Taylor family, almost immediately.

In defiance of the thrift that Foster preached, Harlon communicated her plans to purchase a new silk dress.[6] This act of personal indulgence was perhaps intended to numb the sting of her sudden dismissal. It can also be read as an assertion of her continued autonomy. Clothing was a frequent flash point in conflicts between Irish servants and their Anglo-American employers. In the 1850s, middle-class employers were already complaining that Irish servants wasted their wages on unneeded and unbecoming consumer luxuries. When dressed in fine clothes, an Irish servant challenged the visible markers of class difference that separated capital from labor, and immigrants from the native-born. An 1863 cartoon in *Harper's Weekly* gave visual form to employers' anxieties, and the ways in which fashion and Irish servants' liberty of contract had become conflated. In the image, "Bridget O'Flaherty" wears a dress with a large bustle and sports an ornamental umbrella while she awaits hire in an intelligence office. The office's proprietor, Mrs. Blackstone, presents to O'Flaherty a "Mr. Jones," who is looking for a cook and assures his prospective domestic that he has a "fair character" and is "steady." *Harper's*

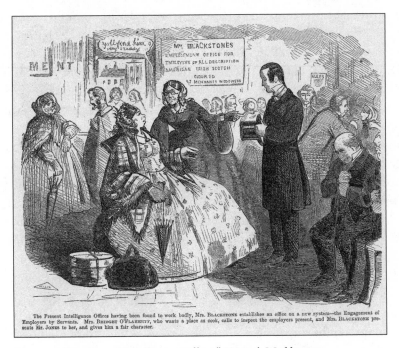

Figure 1.1. "The Present Intelligence Offices," *Harper's Weekly*, 1863.

readers would have appreciated the irony. It is Jones getting scrutinized rather than the other way around.[7]

The Catholic Church and middle-class employers were in agreement that Irish servants had no business concerning themselves with personal appearance, albeit for different reasons. Sister Mary Frances Cusack lectured in *Advice to Irish Girls in America* that the servant who bought "fine clothes, which are not suitable to her station in life," put "herself in danger both in this world and the next." Cusack was undoubtedly also worried that individual purchases would cut into the amount of remittances that Irish women were able to send back to Ireland. In this vein as well, Irish Catholic commentators sometimes dissuaded single women from marrying, since marital obligations—and the need to keep their own homes—hindered their ability to earn wages.[8]

There is an insular quality to Harlon's correspondence that gestures to ways in which immediate material concerns dominated the perspective of the immigrant wage worker. Written during the Civil War, her letters contain only passing mentions of the conflict. The New York City Draft Riots, which led some Anglo-American employers to allege that their Irish servants were plotting to loot their workplaces, merit no attention at all. The only biographical details Harlon provides in her letters are references to two brothers still in Ireland, and a one-line lament about the "loss" of her parents.[9] Harlon frequently prayed for Foster in order to express her "gratitude" for his "kindness," and concluded her letters with the valediction "your friend and servant." Deference coexists with an intimate and open tone in which Harlon appears almost indifferent to the chasm of social class between the two. Foster responded to the correspondence he received from Harlon—although the copies of his letters are unavailable—and she mentions in one of her letters that he called on her in person when he visited New York in 1864.[10]

Much more is known about Foster, unsurprisingly. Born in 1819 in Copenhagen, Vere spent his youth in Turin, before enrolling at Eton and then Oxford. His father, Augustus John Foster, was a career diplomat who served as minister plenipotentiary (the equivalent of ambassador) to the United States before vacating his position at the start of the War of 1812. Vere, if he set foot on Irish soil at all before 1847, left no record of having visited. Both he and his eldest brother, Frederick, pursued careers in diplomacy following their father, while the middle of the three brothers, Cavendish, became an Anglican minister. When Augustus committed suicide in 1848, Frederick took charge of Glyde Court. After touring famine-ravished southern and western Ireland in the autumn of 1849, Vere enrolled at the Glasnevin Model Farm School outside of Dublin, to study how to better manage his family's lands and tenants through modern farming techniques. He anticipated serving as his brother's estate agent.[11] While still enrolled at the Glasnevin School, Vere used a portion of his personal allowance to fund the passage of forty emigrants from County Louth, whose "character and industrious habits" he had vetted through interviews with police and clergy, a method that he would adopt as standard.[12] For reasons unknown, in 1850 he decided to abandon his plans to serve as estate agent in favor of pursuing assisted migration as a form of philanthropic social work, and, for the next decade, his primary vocation.

Foster was enamored of areas of the United States that existed beyond the Appalachian Mountains but east of the Mississippi River. In his opinion, these were the destinations where Irish migrants could best prosper. To Foster, the ideal course for an Irish woman he sponsored had her leave Castle Garden without delay for states such as Illinois and Wisconsin. Harlon disregarded this advice, although she did not reject job mobility outright. When she wrote to Foster in June 1864, she informed him that she was contemplating a move to California. Cheekily, she explained that she had decided not to go because he had once told her that the state was too distant for him to visit. A month later, Harlon again raised the possibility of relocating to California. She was no doubt tempted by the high wages for servants on the Pacific Coast, which averaged between twenty and twenty-five dollars per month compared to the ten dollars she could earn in New York City.[13] Still, the journey to San Francisco took a month or more and in 1864 could be accomplished only by boat and then railroad across the Isthmus of Panama. The trip was expensive and fraught with health risks, and ended in an unfamiliar place. Nor was there any guarantee that work would be as readily available and well-compensated as she had heard.

Irish wage laborers were understandably daunted by the upfront capital investment that secondary migrations required, and individuals like Foster, similar to commercial brokers, staked their authority on being able to intervene and help overcome this obstacle. Visiting California in 1867, Charles Loring Brace, the founder of the Children's Aid Society, estimated that female domestics in San Francisco made on average three times more than the monthly wages paid to their counterparts in eastern cities and that ambitious women could enter into contracts where employers paid the cost of their passage to San Francisco.[14] In 1869, the Dublin-based *Freeman's Journal* published an advertisement from an unnamed San Francisco company that offered to pay Irish women a hundred fifty dollars in gold for a year's work and to cover the expensive, lengthy journey. Receipt of the full sum was contingent, however, on the contracted servants' remaining at their jobs for a year.[15] As these offers indicate, Foster competed against other brokers who had commercial incentives to try to recruit white servants to areas where labor shortages existed. In New York, Harlon had the ability to earn steady wages while healthy. Not having to pay for rent or board, she kept her expenses minimal. She gave no indication that she supported her brothers with remittances. The city abounded with job opportunities for experienced servants like Harlon. In her June 1864 letter, Harlon inquired as to whether Foster had "herd of a place to sute me better."[16] She continued to view Foster as an intermediary who might be called on to assist her, albeit through references rather than immediate material support.

When the Taylors refused Harlon's request for a raise in August 1864, she responded to a newspaper advertisement seeking a servant willing to accompany a woman to Key West, Florida, and to work there at a salary of twelve dollars a month. Whether wanderlust or higher wages enticed Harlon to go "out South," as she put it, this was a speculative move on her part. In Key West, Harlon was employed by Walter McFarland and his family at Fort Zachary Taylor, a base in the Union's naval blockade. In a letter to Foster dated December 20, 1864, Harlon described falling seriously ill upon her arrival in Key West—malaria had long plagued the base—which had forced her to spend a long period convalescing. Whether or not she received pay while recovering was not stated; if she was not working, wages were not guaranteed. At the McFarlands' house, Harlon's only companion was a hired black freeman who did occasional work around the home. She lent him books and tried to teach him to read.[17] Melancholy permeates the letter. Relegated to the social margins of the household, Harlon felt "all alone." Her vulnerability is a subtext to the letter. If illness returned, who would look after her and ensure that she got back to New York City?

Harlon made it back to New York, her health intact. October 1865 found her writing from Litchfield, Connecticut, where her wealthy New York employers, the Whites, kept a second home. Upon returning to the city, Harlon had stayed with the Corcoran family, whom she described as her first employers in the United States. The Corcorans, their name suggests, were probably Irish Catholic. Whereas the McFarlands treated Harlon as a servant to be grouped with the rest of the hired help, the elderly Mrs. Corcoran viewed her as a member of the extended family deserving of free lodging while she looked for work in the city. Harlon's economic success as an independent wage earner led her to be disinterested in marriage. She turned down the engagement proposal of a suitor, telling Foster in her October letter—in a flirtatious tone—that a man of his class and intellect was the only type she wanted to wed.[18] This was the last letter from Harlon that Foster archived.

\* \* \*

From the colonial era onward local policies had required shipmasters transporting immigrants to indemnify municipalities and states against having to provide public relief toward the care of foreign paupers. The insistence of cities like New York and Boston on the need to restrict the entry of economically dependent migrants was instrumental in prompting Congress to act on its plenary power to regulate immigration, and offered the template for the first federal policies enacted in the early 1880s.[19] Despite the existence of such regulations, Foster's interventions are best understood not through the framework of exclusion, but rather as policies that modeled a particular form of integration for Irish women. He engaged in a mid-nineteenth-century version of "salvage accumulation," albeit without a personal profit motive, in which his assistance programs doubled as a transatlantic refugee policy. As anthropologist Anna Lowenhaupt Tsing notes, "salvage accumulation" refers to the processes in which actors "amass capital without controlling the conditions under which the commodities are produced."[20]

Foster viewed Irish women as human capital being squandered, since Ireland lacked both the land and employment markets for their labor and reproductive capabilities—as wives and mothers—to have real exchange and use value. The export of Irish women as sentimental commodities and republican mothers in the making was routinely cited by Foster as the attainable social reality that justified his endeavors. An ideological liberal when it came to his approach to political economy and markets, Foster was nonetheless aware that few Irish emigrants had the wherewithal to pay for their own passage. A self-styled entrepreneur, Foster routinely alluded to his charitable investments in the potential of the Irish people. Horace Greeley, one of the initial subscribers to Foster's Irish Pioneer Emigration Fund, editorialized in his *New York Tribune* that Foster's work represented a "systematic" approach to population transfers that was preferable to the "No-System" it supplanted. Foster's method of assistance, Greeley contended, meant the women could be relocated from Ireland to an interior state like Wisconsin for less than twenty-five dollars, and with an expediency that meant "they were hardly six weeks from work to work." These technical advantages did not even account for how Foster's supervision also impeded "the usual temptations to intemperance, lewdness and vagrancy, and the exposure to imposition, fraud and robbery."[21]

American public opinion most favored European immigration in the nineteenth century when immigrants were perceived as contributing to the continued settlement and development of regions marked as peripheral to the metropolitan core of the nation.[22] Foster's loans to emigrant women, whether he recuperated these expenses or not, enabled him to assert a type of coercive power—rooted in social debt rather than violence or formal legal guardianship—over the immigrants he sponsored. With varied success, as Harlon's case demonstrates, Foster tried to dictate where the Irish women he sponsored would settle. In the United States, he worked with third-party intermediaries such as priests to negotiate the contract of Irish women's labor to local employers in Canandaigua, New York, and Janesville, Wisconsin. Like most of the "friends" of migrants active in the cities of the Eastern Seaboard, Foster believed that urban settlement patterns left young Irish women vulnerable to sexual and economic exploitation, and that sprawling Irish slums were dangerous barriers to cultural assimilation. Foster's bias against eastern cities reflected the republican cast of his liberalism, and the deep-seated suspicions that he and others harbored against both "wage slavery" and, in contradictory terms, women wage workers who were content to forgo secondary migrations and marriage to male landowners in favor of maintaining their independence. Commentators framed immigrants' settlement choices as matters of personal character. An 1857 *Harper's Weekly* article, for instance, complained that since more ambitious German immigrant women were "shipped, on arrival, directly into the insatiable maw of the Great West," Irish women were able to monopolize domestic service in New York and demand wages incommensurate to their skill level.[23]

As Harlon's experiences demonstrate, Irish women had significant leeway in determining whether or not they would abide by Foster's advice. Although Irish women had to satisfy questions about their character and industry in order to receive his funds while still in Ireland, once they were in the United States, Foster's control over the migrants he assisted was indirect and based on persuasion rather than explicit coercion. Such were the perils of enabling free migration. Foster's work offers important insights into how gender and race factored into efforts that were designed to convince migrants to voluntarily surrender their independence. Irish servants were instructed to relinquish their liberty of contract in favor of assuming positions as wives and mothers—ideally in homes far removed from New York, Boston, and Philadelphia. Empirically, historian Cormac Ó Gráda suggests that midcentury Irish immigrant women, in contrast to their male counterparts, had few reasons to expect that upward mobility would result from secondary, westward migrations. Discounting interpretations that have attributed Irish women's entrenchment in urban areas solely to their lack of capital, Ó Gráda points out that it may not be "correct to see these Irishwomen as 'locked in' to the city and domestic service by poverty."[24] For young women, situations as servants in New York City were virtually guaranteed, even if the quality of available positions varied widely. Unclear as to what relocation and marriage offered them in concrete material terms, many Irish women resisted.

Foster was adamant that the Irish women he sponsored were free to leave the situations he ushered them to—often quite literally as a chaperone accompanying their secondary migrations—and that he would not seek to recover the funds given them.[25] But these were largely moot points for women who had already acquiesced to being sent to interior locations, without money or contacts of their own. In bad work situations, young Irish women were vulnerable to immediate exploitation. Their vaunted positions as future wives and mothers offered little in the way of protection against such abuses. As historian Clay Gish has argued, the disjuncture between discourse and material reality was a defining feature of many assisted migration programs created during the midcentury.[26] Legally, employers were permitted to dismiss household servants without cause. At best, servants might have a civil claim to their last month's wages, but only if they worked the majority of that period, had the time and resources to go to court, and found a sympathetic judge. In addition, employers had no legal obligation to provide character references to their servants even though, as the literary historian Bruce Robbins has noted, for nineteenth-century domestics this was akin to a "labor passport."[27] As was the case for all female servants, sexual harassment and rape were consistent dangers as well. Away from eastern cities, Irish immigrant women were far more likely to be isolated from networks of friends and family and commercial establishments such as intelligence offices, which provided resources—namely temporary housing—that allowed servants who left bad work situations to survive without public relief. During the economic crisis of 1857, Foster took a position with the Women's Protective Emigration Society and turned to unemployed women and widowed and abandoned mothers in New York as new targets for sponsored migrations to domestic labor jobs in the interior. As was so often the case in his work, these women (and their children) were the most economically vulnerable source of potential domestic labor. They were also the most susceptible to being coerced into taking jobs in unknown locations, where risks were highest.

After a fifteen-year hiatus from assisting emigration, Foster returned to this work in 1880. The situation, by then, was quite different. Whereas Foster's work in the 1850s was marked by his careful personal orchestration of the migration process, he assumed a more detached supervisory capacity in the 1880s that mirrored the corporate and industrial scale that had come to define global migration as whole. In the 1880s, Foster also had to contend with more formidable Irish nationalist resistance to emigration, and what the Irish Land League argued was the forced exile of young Irish women. He also had to navigate new federal policies in the United States that regulated and restricted assisted immigration. In this environment, Foster's work became divisively politicized. His claims to being a neutral, disinterested broker of migration—spurious to begin with—were no longer tenable.

## Surplus Irish Labor, White Settler Capital

Foster's involvement as a broker of assisted emigration originated in the ideological conflicts over population management that dominated post-famine Ireland. Foster believed that it was imperative for Irish tenants and their families to maximize possible returns on the sole commodity they possessed: their laboring power. Bluntly, he encouraged young men and women in rural Ireland to abandon any hope that there were sufficient natural resources or hiring opportunities—at least for the foreseeable future—that would allow them to remain on their island of birth. Foster characterized assisted emigration as the "most speedy and effectual present means" of aiding Ireland.[28] Like many British liberals, he blamed the famine on the failure of the British government to adopt reforms in the decades leading up to 1845. Throughout his career he would support legislation that promoted the sale of encumbered estates to landowners who were intent on introducing better practices. He also backed measures designed to facilitate landlords' voluntary sale of land as freeholds to successful tenants, which he argued incentivized prudent management.[29] On the other hand, Foster drew a hard line against compulsory estate sales. When the Land War racked Ireland during the 1880s, this was a position that squarely aligned him with members of the Anglo-Irish gentry who argued that private property—even though the land in question was obtained in the seventeenth century through colonization and conquest—was sacrosanct.

As a member of the local gentry, Foster was obsessed with his standing among the Irish Catholic tenant farmers who lived on his family's estate and on nearby lands. To this end, he worked to soothe the many anxieties that these communities had about inserting young women into the global market economy of the mid-nineteenth century. Emigration disrupted the protected status of gendered dependents. Racial and linguistic affinities that connected English-speaking migrants to each other at a familial level, Foster argued, could help offset the impact of these dislocations. Anglophone settler societies, regardless of their specific sovereign status, offered a field of opportunity for white migrants from all classes and were therefore essential spaces for perpetuating a form of democratic capitalism that might allay the internecine class and ethnic conflict that threatened social relations between whites in Ireland, Britain, and the cities of the Atlantic Seaboard.[30] In this respect, Foster's work is emblematic of the complex relationship that Ireland and the Irish people had to the British Empire.[31] Foster believed that the nineteenth-century "Settler Revolution," to use the historian James Belich's term for the explosive movement of capital, population, and cultural institutions from the British Isles and Ireland to settlements in lands seized by white, English-speaking populations, could be instrumentalized as a policy that included Irish men and women.[32]

Along with critiquing British state policies concerning assisted family emigration, Foster also lobbied government officials to be more proactive when it came to protecting emigrants' rights as transatlantic passengers. He pressured British parliamentary officials to protect Irish emigrants as full-fledged members of the Union with rights that transatlantic passenger ship companies were legally compelled to acknowledge. In 1850, for instance, Foster lobbied the British Colonial Land and Emigration Office to better enforce parliamentary measures that required captains to distribute a set amount of rations to passengers.[33] This was borne out of his personal experience as a passenger on the Liverpool-based sailing ship *Washington*. Foster observed that the already perilous five-week voyage was made even more brutal by the fact that the captain withheld the allotted provisions and medical services that he was legally mandated to provide. The *Washington*'s crew treated Irish steerage passengers with disdain and amused themselves by "drenching them from head to foot" when they used the vessel's water closets.[34] Upon the ship's arrival in New York, its passengers were discharged without supervision and left to navigate the "various fleecing houses, to be partially or entirely disabled for pursuing their travels into the interior in search of employment."[35] Foster's anger at the inhumane treatment that the ship's Irish passengers received was sincere, but he was also aware that Americans were more likely to embrace immigrants if the British imperial government affirmed their right to humane treatment. Technological change would end up having the biggest impact in ensuring Irish immigrants' healthy arrival. By the end of the 1850s, steamships had all but replaced sail-powered vessels, and cut the length of the journey to just ten days.

Foster's work shared many similarities with programs that targeted Irish and British women in workhouses for resettlement as servants in Australia and Canada. It was dogmatic for British imperialists to cast these migrations as bolstering settler colonies' labor supply, and their ability to grow their populations through reproduction.[36] To Foster, whether an emigrant was destined for Australia, Canada, or the United States, or came from Ireland, England, or Scotland, mattered only in respect to how these factors determined the bottom line when it came to the cost of moving a person—at least in theory. Assisted emigration to North America represented a more productive intervention because six emigrants could be sent across the Atlantic for every one emigrant financed to go to Australia. According to Foster, the United States held an advantage over Canada because the voyage was quicker, wages were higher, more public lands were available for sale at a cheaper price, and the federal 1847 Passengers Act better ensured that vessels arriving in American ports met a minimum standard of accommodations and sanitation.[37]

A free labor advocate, Foster promoted wage work as the transitional means by which Irish tenants could secure self-sufficiency and eventually put themselves in a position to become landowning capitalists in their own right. Wage labor tested individuals' fitness for self-governance and, when scaled to a group or people as a whole, fitness for national or collective self-rule. This philosophy informed both the position of liberal imperialists in Britain and, after the American Civil War, that of federal officials working with freemen and women.[38] Foster premised that the Irish population's fitness for liberal citizenship could not be gauged at home, since overpopulation and poor land were barriers that even the most industrious individuals could not surmount. The Irish demonstrated fitness for self-governance when they relinquished their attachment to Ireland and instead embraced opportunities to maximize the return on the sale of their labor power abroad. Foster forcefully condemned Irish tenant farmers whom he claimed ignorantly prohibited their daughters from seeking wage work abroad. In an 1857 letter to his local Irish newspaper, Foster promised that "the ensuing scarcity of labor" resulting from emigration would result in an "increase in wages and comfort," and "produce America in Ireland."[39]

America was less a distinct cultural and political realm than it was a set of advantageous market relations. Foster believed that access to "new" settlements was a vehicle that would allow immigrant wage laborers to compete equally in the primitive accumulation of capital—through land and property ownership—without the prohibitive economic, legal, or social barriers that doomed such endeavors within Ireland.[40] Following the passage of the Irish Poor Law Act of 1838, entry into workhouses became a mandatory condition for indigent populations seeking relief.[41] To Foster, this merely created an artificial and poorly run market for Irish labor that was reliant on the taxation of landlords rather than actual demand. It was harrowing to hear, he proclaimed in an 1851 circular, that more than 1,650 Irish men and women were alleged to have died from "neglect and starvation" while toiling in the workhouses of Ennistymon and Kilrush, County Clare, when a whole continent awaited their labors.[42] Even though economic conditions in Ireland improved from 1852 onward, Foster remained a vocal critic of the workhouse system's inefficiencies—a sentiment that many inmates of these institutions, who desired to emigrate, shared.[43]

Unlike many of his peers, Foster did not think that there was an innate backwardness and racial primitiveness to Irish Catholics.[44] In the United States, Foster critiqued nativism as a disingenuous stance that was bent on writing Irish labor out of narratives of American expansion and nation building. Even the most "arrantly bigoted know-nothings," he observed, were reliant on Irish servants and other laborers to perform work they saw as beneath them. Nativists falsely touted their republican self-sufficiency, yet were "so inconsistent as to pay others to work for them."[45] Ever the optimist, Foster claimed that this merely meant that ambitious Irish women faced less in the way of job competition. Foster praised Catholicism when it was useful to constructing the labor supply chains he envisioned. He worked closely with the Catholic clergy in both Ireland and the United States, and won the endorsement of the powerful New York archbishop, John Hughes, for his programs. Foster placated Hughes's concerns about the preservation of Catholicism in areas removed from Irish immigrant hubs by arguing that even if Irish women might temporarily labor in Protestant households as domestics, over the long run, they would eventually transition to new roles as married homesteaders in Catholic families.[46] Foster maintained contacts with Catholic clergy and bishops in major cities such as Detroit, Chicago, Cleveland, and Rochester, as well as in Hamilton and Toronto, Canada. He also worked with the Church in aforementioned rural town centers such as Janesville, Wisconsin, and Canandaigua, New York. Upon their arrival in these places, the "batches of girls" that Foster sent—as one Canadian newspaper described them—were transferred to Catholic authorities who brokered their local employment.[47]

When Foster did turn his attention to the cultural and behavioral stereotypes that surrounded Irish immigrants in the United States, it was mainly out of concern for laborers' marketability. To Foster, the Irish existed on the threshold of liberal modernity; they were, as he told the American Emigrants' Friend Society in 1851, "the poorest and most uneducated portion of what is termed the civilized population of the world."[48] During his first visit to the United States, he wrote to the *Irish Farmer's Gazette* to express his disappointment at having learned that Irish immigrants—"and even many of the girls"—had a reputation for being "drunken, riotous, and quarrelsome." This led American employers to prefer German immigrant labor when available. Rather than grapple with the stereotype, Foster instead argued that Irish immigrants were obligated to silence detractors by proving their industry and commitment to self-improvement. Respectability politics, this suggests, saturated the self-policing discourse of all groups where laborers' cultural backgrounds, whether defined in religious, racial, or ethnic terms, conflated marketability and social inclusion.[49] Foster himself subscribed to Father Theobald Mathew's stance on complete abstinence from alcohol, which he informed his readers gave him license to "preach to others to do so" as well.[50]

Foster denounced slavery and acts of racial discrimination and hatred carried out by individuals. The emigrants he sponsored, for instance, were required to sign a pledge that stated they would "love liberty and fair play for others as well as yourself, without distinction of race, religion or colour."[51] Foster had no problem accepting on a structural level, however, that Irish and British immigrants deserved to be, along with native-born white Americans, the beneficiaries of the federal policies that transferred land and natural resources to white settlers as private property. In an August 1851 letter to the *Irish Farmer's Gazette*, Foster compared the gaunt and poorly clothed Mdewakanton and Wahpekute Dakota women he observed at the signing of the Treaty of Mendota in Minnesota Territory to the "dishevelled Irishwomen" of Connemara, where two years earlier he had toured the devastation caused by the famine.[52] Whereas the Dakota women faced a precarious future due to dispossession, markets for the labor of Irish immigrant servants and their ability to win social inclusion as whites—despite a comparable expulsion from native lands—ensured them a more secure future. In his advice guide *Work and Wages*, which was distributed for free to more than a quarter million readers in Ireland and Great Britain in the 1850s (and to many thousands more who paid a penny in postage), Foster praised Minnesota's "judicious mixture of timber and pasture" as ideal for homesteading. Treaty lands that had belonged to the Dakota could be bought from the federal government at a standard rate of $1.25 per acre.[53] Foster's schemes were developed in concert with other state-backed settler colonial projects, such as the construction of railroads linking interior regions to markets. A farmer in Drury Creek, Illinois, for instance, wrote to Foster in October 1852 to dissuade him from sending Irish women to the region. A railroad connection would not arrive in nearby Carbondale until 1854. The farmer explained to Foster that when he was able to hire hands at all, it was only on a seasonal basis and the workers were compensated with cattle and surplus produce. These items were of little use to female migrants hoping to send remittances back to Ireland.[54] Irish servants' contributions to the project of long-term white settlement in the region would have to wait.

Railroads were crucial elements in how Foster designed for the efficient movement and placement of laborers. The networks that allowed agricultural producers in the interior to move commodities to eastern markets and distribution points also permitted these areas to import labor as a consumer good.[55] Janesville, Wisconsin, is a representative example of the type of settlement that Foster sought out. Founded in 1835 from treaty lands ceded by Sauk and Fox Indians after their defeat in the Black Hawk War three years earlier, the white settlement of Janesville was less than two decades old when thirty-nine migrants that Foster had sponsored disembarked there in 1857. The arrival of the railroad in 1850 not only contributed to Janesville's preeminence as a regional city, but also brought hundreds of male Irish laborers who laid the tracks. The Catholic infrastructure that Foster would later rely on in placing domestic laborers followed.[56] By 1860, the Janesville census would list 160 Irish-born women as live-in servants working in Anglo-American households.[57]

## Disciplining Free Women: Marriage and Labor

As historian Jeanne Boydston notes, brokers like Foster had to contend with fundamental suspicions concerning the marketing of women's wage labor, and the widespread belief that "femaleness was inappropriate to the public realm of commerce and trade and could exist there only as a personal degradation (seduction) and a public danger (prostitution), both of these being monstrous abnormalities."[58] Foster promised to protect Irish women from exploitation, and vouch for their reputations as prospective servants, so long as they accepted his advice to continue westward in their migrations. Foster resorted to the language of boosterism, even though he did not have a direct commercial stake in placing migrants. In *Work and Wages* he boasted that it was "customary" for American families in western states and territories to treat Irish servants as "daughters, sitting at the same table, dressing as well or better." Servants, Foster proclaimed, were likely to get married sooner than the daughters of their employers. He offered the story of one western homeowner who had lost nineteen of the twenty-three servants he had employed over the course of the previous eight years to marriage.[59] Foster appeared to relish the fact that assisted migration work made him both a labor and marriage broker. In 1864, during his first visit to North America in six years, he traveled to St. Joseph, Michigan, to see "two of my girls married," as he put it, and to sample the region's flour, which his friend Greeley had dubbed the best in the country. The same trip also brought him to London, Ontario, where his hostess reported that he had inquired and was pleased to learn that the "Irish servant girls" he had brought there were "married and doing well."[60]

These accounts, with their untroubled depictions of Irish women achieving equality, situated domestic wage labor on a progressive

AS I WAS.

Figure 1.2. and Figure 1.3. "As I Was" and "As I Am." Vere Foster, *Work and Wages; or, The Penny Emigrant's Guide to the United States and Canada*, 5th ed. (London: W. & F. G. Cash, 1855).

continuum toward motherhood and gendered republican citizenship. They invoked the popular and familiar republican trope of "help," and beckoned to a romanticized vision of peaceful social relations between labor and capital, where hired hands and mistresses worked side by side with no distinction in status. At a time when this very concept was under assault, with Anglo-American employers lamenting the disappearance of native-born women willing to enter into domestic service, Foster insisted that Irish immigrants could revive such arrangements in Western locales uncorrupted by hardened class and ethnic distinctions.

AS I AM.

Figure 1.2. and Figure 1.3. (*continued*)

Visually, *Work and Wages* included a "before and after" tableau that captured the domestic and economic transformation that migration allegedly portended to Irish (and British) paupers. At the beginning of the guide, a shoeless Irish emigrant wearing only rags is depicted departing his thatched-roof cottage, accompanied by the title "As I Was." Toward the end of the pamphlet, the same individual is shown sitting with his family before a well-stocked kitchen table. Although the protagonist is male, female readers would not have missed the detail of his wife being waited on by a hired domestic.

If marriage resided at one end of the spectrum as the most prudent course of self-governance for migrant Irish women, and the best long-term choice they could make when it came to the disposal of their labor power, then the sale of their sexual labor represented the opposite pole. Foster was no stranger to controversy in this respect. His work was enveloped in scandal when twenty-six of the one hundred twenty women whose passage he had paid for on the *City of Mobile*, which departed Liverpool in May 1857, spurned final destinations in the interior in order to stay in New York City. More scandalous, twelve of the women who remained in New York had snuck off the *Mobile* with sailors while the boat was anchored overnight off of Castle Garden. Two of those women, Susan Smith and Ellen Neary, eventually ended up at a brothel at 32 Water Street in Lower Manhattan, which was run by the notorious "sportsman" and Irish American gang leader Kit Burns. All of this came to light when Smith was found wandering aimlessly down Broadway, her face "covered with bruises and her body with rags." Police brought her before city officials to swear out a deposition on what had occurred, before sending her to the state-run Emigrant Refuge on Ward's Island.[61]

When the incident made newspapers in New York, Ireland, and Britain, Foster and his allies attacked the women for their excessive and dangerous pursuit of personal independence. They pointed toward the fact that the majority of women who arrived on the *Mobile* were in New York for less than a day, and that their socializing was limited to attending lectures delivered by a priest who had worked in the American West and by Greeley. They were instructed, in regard to travel into the interior, "the farther the better." In its coverage, the *New York Tribune* blamed Captain Marshall of the *Mobile* for failing to closely guard who had access to the women on the vessel, despite the fact that Foster had paid extra to sequester the migrants in second-class cabins. As the newspaper editorialized, during the transatlantic voyage, with Foster not present (he was already in the United States), it was the captain's responsibility to ensure that no harm came to the women. As their protector, he assumed the "same relation as a father to his children; his power is absolute and undisputed, and wherever he resolutely sets himself about it, he can always enforce obedience to orders." If the captain was to shoulder some of the blame, then the rest belonged to the twenty-six emigrants who had deceived Foster about their true character. Emigrants in the future, he warned, needed to "shew by their conduct on board ship and in America that they deserve the good recommendations on account of which they receive a free passage."[62]

Sensational incidents like the ones surrounding the *City of Mobile* cannot be attributed to Foster's particular method of sponsoring emigrants; all young women who traveled on their own faced the dangers of sexual assault and enticement. Without diminishing the ordeals of Neary and Smith, the moral panic that their enlistment as prostitutes fueled helped to rationalize the need for programs such as Foster's, and worked to keep Irish women in positions where they were more likely to remain subordinate.

The concerns Irish women raised as migrants went beyond dangers having to do with sex alone. As Foster learned, assisted migration invariably had to contend with the political economy of chattel slavery. Early on, Foster abandoned any plans he had to send migrants to the American South after hearing from a correspondent in Monticello, Florida, that the racial division of labor there was so fixed that white households refused to hire white servants, even when the cost of wages was less than what they would pay in leasing a black slave.[63] Moreover, whereas assisted migration to places like Illinois and Wisconsin referenced nationalistic images of maturing white settler colonialism, it was also framed in relation to the internal slave trade, and the inability of enslaved peoples to maintain family integrity and control their own mobility. Anxieties about Irish women's bondage infringed upon Foster's plans on both sides of the Atlantic. While transporting a group of women from County Louth to the port city of Drogheda in the 1850s, he was accosted by a mob of Irish farmers enraged by a rumor that he was readying Irish girls for sale to Mormons and black Americans. Years later, Foster would recall this episode to underscore the local superstitions that his work encountered.[64] Given that much of what constituted domestic work was still performed as involuntary and unpaid labor in the 1850s, these fears were more valid than Foster acknowledged. Local farmers had every reason to question what Foster stood to gain from sponsoring transatlantic migration. Population management, if Foster even bothered to explain the philosophy underlining his actions, would have come across as an ideological abstraction. Local farmers were more familiar with indenture and debt bondage as means by which migrations were financed.

## Seeking Out Precarity

The enticements of yeomen farming and republican marriages aside, Foster understood that the willingness of unmarried Irish women to migrate west corresponded directly to their economic and social vulnerability. The Panic of 1857, which began with bank failures in late August, led Foster to become involved in brokering and chaperoning the westward migrations of New York women receiving relief. During the winter of 1857–58, Foster served as an unpaid agent for the Women's Protective Emigration Society. Founded by women's rights advocates Elizabeth B. Phelps and Eliza Farnham, the society solicited funds to support the westward migration of women who had lost their jobs in the economic depression. In New York City, the needle trades in particular were hard hit by a shortage of capital, creating relief needs in excess of what city agencies could handle.[65]

Foster was an obvious asset to the Women's Protective Emigration Society. His preexisting network of contacts throughout the "Old Northwest" meant that he could identify employment possibilities in regions less affected by the collapse of the banks. Moreover, the society's agenda mirrored Foster's. Moving laborers to more favorable markets was seen as an efficient means to reduce public relief outlays and to stave off the temptation that unemployed women might have to engage in sex work. As Farnham and Phelps would stipulate in an appeal "to the Friends of the Helpless," the economic crisis had left thousands of women "cast upon the world—homeless, friendless, penniless—and who now, in the madness of desolation and want, are trembling on the verge of the dark stream of vice which pollutes our streets." An editorial in the *New York Tribune* estimated that there were seven thousand women prepared to take advantage of the society's assistance if funds could be procured. Referencing a proposal by the secretary of war that called for an increase in the military recruitment of unemployed men, Greeley lamented that the government had no plans but the "almshouse" for women. "Colossal prostitution" awaited, the newspaper warned, if New York donors persisted in their "elegant indifference."[66]

References to deserving paupers featured prominently in the society's rationalizations for why interventions into the lives of the women it hoped to relocate were justified, and worth supporting. Citing her partnership with Foster and what she had learned about "systematised" migration through their collaboration, Farnham argued that women who applied to be relocated automatically proved themselves to be of a better class than counterparts who chose to stay behind. Trying to counteract the negative associations that surrounded recipients of welfare, Farnham asserted that women seeking to migrate demonstrated that they were "energetic, pure, conscientious women" possessed with an "earnest resolve to help themselves honorably to a better lot." One might deduce that the women who sought the society's help acted out of desperation. Farnham was reluctant to acknowledge this, however, since it gave her relocation scheme a coercive rather than voluntary cast. More than six hundred women were placed in Illinois alone by Foster during the winter of 1857, and by the middle of 1858, the society had sent approximately a thousand women to points west. The cost of placing a woman in a new locale was between ten and twelve dollars. Farnham, a former resident of California, wrote to the *California Farmer* in March 1858 to encourage leading citizens to charter a steamer to deliver destitute women from New York to San Francisco, since the demand for servants remained unaffected "in our Golden State."[67] The society also followed Foster's lead by sending Irish Catholic women from New York to locations where Catholic parishes existed, in order to avoid accusations that they were using financial assistance to coerce conversions. In a letter to the *New York Tribune*, Farnham, like Foster, touted white mutuality. She included testimonies from farmers in Elkhart County, Indiana, where Foster had drummed up interest in the society's efforts, to illustrate the warm embrace that awaited migrant women. Farnham's enthusiasm notwithstanding, the testimonies she offered contained mixed messages. One writer noted that because male hired hands were so scarce, he and others planned on training the migrant women in "Western work," which apparently meant performing outdoor labor alongside household duties. Another writer depicted a bunch of bachelor farmers stalking the Elkhart railroad station, hoping that each arriving train might bear the cargo that Farnham and Foster had pledged.[68]

In addition to placing migrants selected by the society, Foster—working independently—also identified situations for women with children. Foster posted circulars in Chicago and other western cities soliciting employers who might receive one hundred women with children under the age of two for household service. He advertised that all of the candidates for situations had shown him marriage certificates that proved that they had been either abandoned by laggard husbands or widowed. None, he claimed, had given birth out of wedlock.[69] During the 1850s, the children of indigent women were often the subjects of placing out schemes, but rarely with their mothers. It is unknown whether this particular initiative met with any success, and Foster's foray into this work raises more questions than it answers. One wonders, for instance, whether any of the applicants for resettlement tricked Foster as to their marital status and whether their choice to accept his offer of assistance was made freely or came only after they were pressured by New York workhouses and orphanages—as was often the case—to migrate.

Always conscious of growing Irish nationalist resistance to assisted emigration, Foster never passed up the opportunity to broadcast the significance of his work. Whereas an Irish servant like Mary Harlon assessed domestic work in terms of material benefits and how she was treated, Foster was more willing to impart abstract social meanings to the meeting of American capital and Irish labor. Shortly after President Lincoln's assassination, Foster recalled meeting the future president and his wife Mary Todd while in Springfield, Illinois, during the winter of 1857, and recounted to Irish readers how the couple made a "promise to treat any girl we direct to them as one of the family, and to give her a home certain for a month, so as to give her time to settle in a place."[70] That the future martyr to the cause of free labor would embrace the Irish on such generous and egalitarian terms was freighted with symbolism. It was also perhaps fanciful. In other contexts, Mary Todd Lincoln voiced resentment at Irish domestics. She wrote to her half sister Emilie after the 1856 election that "if some of you Kentuckians, had to deal with the 'wild Irish,' as we housekeepers are sometimes called upon to do, the south would certainly elect Mr. Fillmore"—the nativist Know-Nothing candidate.[71] The placement of migrants in Illinois generated more serious incidents as well. The rape of a sixteen-year-old migrant girl that Foster had helped to place with a male employer provoked outrage and anger in newspapers throughout the state, and led to accusations that he was not properly screening the households to which servants were destined.[72] Again, the critique was not that Foster had used too heavy a hand in controlling migrant women as dependents; it was that he had been too lax in overseeing the contract of their labor.

## Whiteness, Nationalism, and Irish Servitude

In trying to channel the migratory course of Irish women away from the cities of the Eastern Seaboard, Foster was a small obstruction in a much larger stream. Between 1851 and 1921, 1.2 million Irish girls and women between the ages of fifteen and twenty-four arrived in the United States.[73] By 1855, Irish immigrants accounted for 74 percent of the approximately 31,000 female domestics working in New York City, at a time when slightly more than one-quarter of all households in the city employed paid servants.[74] Even though significant Irish communities formed in urban areas and towns in states like Minnesota and Wisconsin, and Chicago developed as an important hub for the Irish diaspora, in 1870 the Irish-born population remained concentrated in eastern states, with Massachusetts and New York leading the way. In 1900, 54 percent of all Irish immigrant women wage earners continued to be employed in domestic service, even as their waning significance to the occupation was being proclaimed.[75] Female Irish servants composed a distinct class in the cultural imagination of urban Americans and the national media. Their representation as laborers was an important touchstone in midcentury debates concerning the racial division of labor, wage slavery, the rights of free laborers, and the legitimacy of British colonial rule in Ireland. As much as Foster tried to redefine the terms of Irish women's incorporation, he could not escape these contexts. Irish servants—captured in the stereotype of "Biddy"—were caricatured as colonial threats to the sovereign domestic rule of their Anglo-American mistresses. These depictions of conflict circulated in sharp contrast to the revered republican mutuality that Foster and others claimed characterized American households. Yet they also gave Irish domestics an independent political identity that reaffirmed their status as free (and white) laborers.

During the 1850s, fierce condemnations of "wage slavery" provided proslavery commentators with a basis to compare the treatment of Irish servants to that of black slaves, and to argue that low pay made young Irish women more disposable than laborers owned as property. Racial slavery, they argued, was a more "natural" way of organizing the social relations of production that reflected innate and permanent differences in status. These same critics in turn highlighted the "unnatural" role that for-profit brokers played when they abetted commerce in white women's wage labor. While living in New York, William Bobo, a white South Carolinian, expressed shock at what he considered to be the degraded manner in which Irish women were forced to sell their labor power. Encountering "fifty or sixty" Irish girls waiting in the tenement basement of an intelligence office on Nassau Street, Bobo commented that the room's sanitary conditions and crowdedness were far worse than what could be found in Richmond's slave markets. Because "Yankees are generally very rigid in requiring their papers," Bobo added, it was not uncommon for employers to strategically withhold character references in order to keep favored Irish servants captive. Intelligence offices had such a bad reputation that even northerners opposed to slavery compared them to slave markets. In doing so, they ignored very real differences in how the labor of poor but free Irish immigrant women was marketed relative to involuntary transactions where enslaved persons were sold as chattel. In 1856, for instance, Frederick Law Olmsted described the facilities of the slave dealers he observed in Washington, D.C., as "much like Intelligence Offices, being large rooms partly occupied by ranges of forms."[76] Bobo concluded that the Irish would not achieve real citizenship until they went "where the country is in its maiden purity, among the forests of the far West." There Irish women could "rear a home and a family, build up a character and a reputation that their children will be proud of, and not skulk about the palaces of the wealthy."[77] Bobo unwittingly called attention to how the social construction of whiteness in the mid-nineteenth-century United States had both occupational and geographic dimensions.

The racialization of servitude was by no means an issue exclusive to the United States. The term "servantgalism," which American newspapers and magazines embraced, was first coined as the title of a cartoon series that John Leech drew for the English humor magazine *Punch* in 1853, during the height of the "wage slavery" debates. The ideology of "servant gals," "servantgalism" referenced a fictitious movement of domestic laborers who conspired to win greater sovereignty over their jobs, and to elevate their social position. In one cartoon, the joke hinges on the quip of an English nursemaid to a cook that they should refuse to

**SERVANTGALISM;**

OR, WHAT'S TO BECOME OF THE MISSUSES?—No. 7.

*Housemaid.* "WELL, SOOSAN, I'VE MADE UP MY MIND NOT TO STOP 'ERE NO LONGER TO WORK LIKE NEGROES AS WE DO!"

*Cook.* "NOR I, NUTHER! BUT JUST TURN THE MEAT, WILL YOU, PLEASE, THE WHILST I FINISH MY CROCHET?"

Figure 1.4. "Servantgalism—No. II," *Punch*, 1853. Courtesy of Rutgers University Libraries.

work "like Negroes"—an exchange that takes place as the two read and crochet before a fire.

Although Leech's cartoon appealed to employers who felt that white workers overstated their exploitation in comparison to workers who were actually enslaved, it also illustrates how servants disagreed with the notion that wages alone could make work dignified. In both London and New York, employers accused white servants of using race to justify laziness and bad work habits.[78]

Irish immigrant servants featured prominently in celebrations of white workers' labor republicanism and radicalism, and were venerated for their blunt resistance to the forces of capitalist alienation. Their steady earning ability often made Irish servants the most important breadwinners in transnational families, and upended conventional gender roles. Irish Catholic elites applauded Irish laborers' vigor and rejected the more fragile ideal of femininity that the Anglo-American middle class often fetishized. In an account published by the Catholic Sisters of Mercy, for instance, the physical strength and rural simplicity of Irish women were depicted as virtues that kept Irish women moored to the mutually reinforcing causes of family, religion, and community. Hanna Flynn, who received domestic training at the Sisters' House of Mercy on Houston Street in Manhattan, exemplified the type of migrant woman the publication found worthy of admiration. After securing a job, Flynn's thriftiness enabled her to send the bulk of her earnings to her brother and sister back in Ireland. The Sisters proudly described Flynn as "a woman of masculine strength and endurance" whose "utmost limit of travel was her crowded parish chapel." Flynn was illiterate and the "alphabet was to her as the hieroglyphics of Egypt," but this did not stop her from being "a heroine" who honored her parents and her faith, and who "was honest, upright, truthful, laborious and capable of self-sacrifice."[79]

Because the appearance of more aggressive forms of Irish servants' workplace resistance and their growing power over the labor market coincided with the rise of Irish nationalism, domestic employers had an immediate colonial framework through which to assess the social relations of production taking shape.[80] Addressing an 1872 speaking tour by English historian James Anthony Froude, who warned Americans not to be seduced to the Irish cause of independence by a naïve love of all republicanism, E. L. Godkin, the founder and editor of the *Nation*, added that "the memory of burned steaks, of hard-boiled potatoes, of smoked milk, would have done for [Froude] what no state papers, or records, or correspondence of the illustrious dead can ever do; it had prepared the American mind to believe the worst he could say of Irish turbulence and disorder." Indeed, Irish servants were political, and on occasion transformed their workplaces into sites of protest. When Froude lectured in Boston, the Irish servants employed by his hosts, the Peabodys, initiated a work stoppage rather than serve him. Dispatches from the *Times of London*'s foreign correspondents in the United States routinely updated English readers on visiting Irish politicians' appeals to the "servant girls" of New York and Boston for financial support.[81] In its account of a meeting of Irish nationalists that was convened in Philadelphia in 1883, the humor magazine *Puck* commented that "the Irish declaration of independence has been read in our kitchens, many and many a time, to frightened housewives, and the fruits of that declaration are to be seen in thousands of ill-cooked meals on ill-served tables, in unswept rooms and unmade beds, in dirt, confusion, insubordination and general disorder, taking the sweetness out of life."[82] An accompanying cartoon, which portrayed a muscular, ape-like Irish servant bullying her cowering Anglo-American employer, hammered home this point. (The cartoon appears as Figure 3 in the insert to this book.)

Violence was a common trope in Anglo-American employers' racialized portrayals of Irish immigrants as a people whose primitiveness meant that they had not yet evolved civilized gender distinctions. The Irish servant's masculinized aggression signified her distance from the refined qualities of the mistress and the restraint of "true women," whose more effeminate bearing made them the easy victims of Irish servants' bullying.[83] Irish servants were routinely accused of resorting to violence in order to get their way in disputes over the terms of their labor. Biddy's savagery, employers alleged, prevented her from accepting reprimand. She reacted with fury to even the slightest of criticisms, and "her mistress would as soon stir up a female tiger as arouse her anger." The Irish domestic's "strong arm and voluble tongue keep the most tyrannical housekeeper in such awe as to save her from all invasions of her prescriptive rights."[84]

Irish servants understood the social implications of doing domestic work even as they relied on the wages it provided. They realized that the racial groups believed to supply the "best" servants occupied a position at the bottom of the nation's social and racial hierarchy for this very reason. Hanna Flynn, despite all the praise she earned, was still described as "'slaving out' her life . . . among strange people, in strange places, for those she loved so well."[85] Among Irish nationalists, even violence could be justified when its goal was to preserve the baseline dignity that was considered the entitlement of all whites. In his 1867 account of Irish life in the United States, John Francis Maguire proudly recounted how Kate, an Irish servant working in an unnamed American city, dealt with the frequent harassment she received from a local Protestant minister.

Although Kate typically brushed aside his patronizing humor, which included calling her Bridget and taunting her Catholicism, when the minister announced during a dinner party at her employers' home that he was willing to pay her whatever "Father Pat" was seeking for her absolution, she lost her temper. With evident glee, Maguire described how "she flung the hot steaming liquid," a tureen of pea soup, at the minister's "face, neck, [and] breast."[86] No amount of money, Kate's actions implied, could convince her to renounce her faith, heritage, or racial birthright.

### Charity or Depopulation? Foster and Assisted Emigration in the 1880s

When crop failures and famine conditions struck the west of Ireland in 1879, Foster resumed work as a broker of assisted emigration.[87] He knowingly entered into a highly charged political debate about whether emigration, land reform, or home rule best served the island's interests.[88] While Foster claimed that his work was apolitical, this was unconvincing in light of how he set about announcing the revival of his assisted emigration campaign. In a public letter to Charles Stewart Parnell, the leader of the Irish Land League, Foster alleged that it was "unstatesmanlike and cruel to the poor to contravene the laws of nature by decrying emigration as some people do."[89] The more than twenty thousand women whom Foster sponsored in the 1880s were issued two-pound vouchers, and selected based on the recommendations of clergy. The vouchers were then redeemable at any of the Irish ports of departure or in Liverpool, with the steamship companies billing Foster. Together, passage and the mandatory outfit of food and clothing that emigrants had to acquire before sailing cost slightly more than four pounds, and assisted emigrants had to make up the difference on their own. In cases where prospective emigrants already had a prepaid ticket, yet lacked the funds to purchase supplies or to pay for the intermediate journey to a port, Foster donated one pound.[90]

In the eyes of home rule advocates and the Irish Land League, assisted emigration was at best a minor remedy that dodged the lasting question of Irish sovereignty and land reform. At worst, it was a scheme to depopulate Ireland and neutralize its resistance. The liberty of Irish women to forge their own destiny in Ireland, freed from pressure to leave, became a mantra to nationalists. If free labor in the United States often revolved around a narrow definition of what defined consent within specific employment relations, in the context of Irish emigration it became a more philosophical question about whether or not an individual's departure was truly voluntary. Public attacks directed at Foster regularly appeared in the nationalist press during the early 1880s. An editorial in the Dublin-based *Freeman's Journal* in May 1880, for instance, assailed Foster by name for failing to see how emigration led to "the sad life and sadder death of many an Irish girl in the slums of American cities." During a September 1880 anti-eviction protest meeting in Prouglish, County Leitrim, one tenant farmer familiar with Foster's work suggested to the laughter of the audience that he finance a boat to take landlords away instead. Foster received threats that promised violent retribution if he continued his work.[91] Even though the bulk of emigrants Foster sponsored made the transatlantic trip without ordeal, incidents to the contrary garnered significant negative attention. In August 1883, for instance, the *Freeman's Journal* reported on sixteen-year-old Margaret Moran, who had traveled on a voucher that Foster had provided only to be turned away by American immigration officials on the grounds that she was likely to become a public charge.[92]

The Irish nationalist media depicted Foster as a dotty, paternalistic figure who was incapable of adapting to changes in either Ireland or the United States. An 1884 editorial in the *Irish Nation* mocked Foster for clinging to the outdated notion that the American West was a region where any European immigrant, regardless of circumstances, could expect to be instantaneously rewarded. The West, the paper lectured, was no longer "the El Dorado of the European peasant." Foster's unconditional embrace of emigration had blinded him to the United States' economic woes during the tumultuous years of the 1870s and 1880s, and caused him to ignore the high costs of transportation to the interior, the industrialization of agriculture, and the railroads' monopolization of public lands.[93] Charlotte Grace O'Brien, the transatlantic Irish reformer and advocate for immigrant protections, wrote in the English periodical *Nineteenth Century* that although Foster was an "excellent man," and his desire to help the Irish genuine, his method of assistance was reckless and "a most dangerous experiment, if not a complete mistake." In response, Foster cited O'Brien's failure to provide any concrete evidence of abuses. Consistent with his liberal principles, he argued that since the women he supported pleaded for aid and consented to the assistance offered, it was unfair for them to be "denied the opportunity to emigrate in order to better their condition."[94] Still, by 1880 the Irish American community was more established and better equipped to receive immigrants than it had been in the 1850s. Accordingly, members were less reliant on elite intermediaries such as Foster for assistance. Many were no longer willing to support a market-oriented philanthropy that sidestepped the issue of Irish home rule and merely took for granted that young Irish women's labor was destined to be commodified abroad.[95]

During the 1880s, there was also mounting opposition to "pauper" immigration from the American public and elected officials. The United States experienced an economic depression that began in 1873 and lasted until 1880. The downturn would resume in 1882. The pro-immigration mood that had prevailed in the period that immediately followed the Civil War dampened considerably. Raising concerns similar to those that had surfaced during the post-famine period of the early 1850s, Congress accused the British officials of supporting the emigration of paupers from English and Irish workhouses so as to rid themselves of their care. The Select Committee to Investigate Foreign Immigration, convened by Congress in 1888, blamed the Tuke Society—the government-sponsored social welfare organization led by the Quaker businessman and philanthropist James Hack Tuke—for paying for the passage of more than forty-nine hundred immigrants to the United States since 1882. Many of these arrivals, the report claimed, "subsequently became inmates of charitable institutions in this country."[96] On at least two occasions in the 1880s, Foster's assisted emigration program was investigated by the American consuls in Cork and Liverpool. Although State Department officials concluded that Foster's vetting methods and reputation for calculated philanthropy meant that he was a low risk when it came to sending indigent migrants, many of his critics were uninterested in acknowledging such distinctions.[97]

Foster had also lost influence as broker. By the 1880s, migration was big business and the sale of steamship tickets an occupational pursuit for thousands of agents in Ireland and Britain. Steamship agents besieged Foster and tried to persuade him to steer the migrants he was assisting in their direction, so they would earn the commission. In November 1882, the Northern Police Court in Dublin fined Martin Gallagher fifty pounds after the local Board of Trade discovered that he was selling steamship tickets without a license. One of the violations Gallagher committed was the resale of vouchers that Foster had issued to a group of Irish women at the behest of a parish priest.[98] Steamship companies also took a more active role in steering prospective migrants to Foster's "discounted" rate of passage. After inaugurating steamship service from Liverpool and Queenstown to New York in 1881, the Beaver Line included in its Irish newspaper advertisements a notice that "female domestic servants of good character" could subsidize the cost of their passage by applying to Foster. A frequent recipient of free passes from both American railroads and the transatlantic steamship companies, these corporations adopted Foster as a broker who drummed up business.[99]

Finally, Foster could no longer rely on the Catholic Church for support. In July 1883, Catholic bishops in the west of Ireland ordered priests and curates to cease working with Foster altogether. They declared, under pressure from nationalists, that his assisted emigration schemes were a danger to the "faith and morals" of the Irish people.[100] On February 24, 1886, with his assisted emigration work at a virtual standstill, Foster again lashed out at political proposals that he believed would unnaturally stifle emigration. This time it was British Prime Minister William Gladstone, who had announced his support for Irish home rule a year earlier. Although Foster had been a supporter of Gladstone's Liberal Party, he joined many of his peers in defecting to the newly formed Liberal Unionist Party. In his letter to Gladstone, Foster insisted that he was not uniformly against state-backed land reforms. As for home rule, however, Foster expressed absolute opposition to any plan that would separate Ireland from the British Empire, and warned Gladstone that "the Loyalist population of Ulster may be expected to make itself unmistakeably and effectually heard in opposition to any such project." Home rule's "realization would be a bloody Civil War between different portions of the Irish people, and between Great Britain and Ireland." Foster's letter concluded with a postscript proposing a government office to formally promote assisted emigration—with him in charge. Disingenuously, Foster assured Gladstone that his work in the West and South of Ireland had been pursued "without encountering any opposition whatever."[101]

With the passage of the 1891 Immigration Act, Congress stipulated that "any person whose ticket or passage is paid for with the money of another or who is assisted by others to come" could be prevented from landing. Except in cases where immediate family members provided the funds, assisted immigrants were mandated to appear before immigration officials to determine whether they were likely to become a public charge. Officials were also tasked with evaluating whether the assistance immigrants received had left them in a state of debt bondage or violated the terms of the 1885 Alien Contract Labor Law (the Foran Act).[102] With the law's enforcement, Foster received letters from various steamship companies stating that they would no longer be able to accept his vouchers, since they did not want to risk having to bear the return cost of any immigrants who were rejected.[103] In response to a letter that Foster wrote to the State Department, Hermann Stump, the superintendent of immigration, informed him in May 1893 that the law's requirements could not be waived on behalf of his charitable designs, which brought his work to a halt.[104] Foster passed away on December 21, 1900, in the flat he rented in a Belfast lodging house.

## Conclusion

Foster's work anticipated many of the dilemmas that the 1864 Act to Encourage Immigration would encounter. Urged on by President Lincoln, the 1864 act empowered employers—primarily in the fields of agriculture, manufacturing, and mining—to enter into contracts with European immigrants. Although Congress provided only minimal funding to back the initiative, it placed the federal government's imprint on recruitment efforts already taking place in European ports of departure. Contracted for a term not to exceed one year, immigrants were to repay the cost of their passage from future wages earned. Ambiguously, the legislation prohibited indenture, bondage, and slavery as forms of compulsion that employers could use to recover sunk costs—even as they were prompted to extend credit. In 1868, after employers pushed to criminalize immigrants' breaches of contracts, thereby moving the matter out of civil courts, Congress repealed the act.[105] Capital investment in growing the labor supply and the maintenance of free migration and contract liberty, it seemed, were incompatible. In this context,

Foster's work was the exception that proved the rule. Because he did not seek to profit from his brokerage, and assumed costs in the name of philanthropy, he was not motivated to pursue harsh and punitive measures against the migrants whose passages he had funded.

The assisted migration of recently freed black women and children during and after the Civil War raised many of the same issues that Foster's work encountered. With the end of slavery, northern household employers became infatuated with opportunities to hire black refugees as servants. Private and government brokers flocked to meet this demand. Despite their newly won liberty to consent to work, in practice black refugees were a commodity whose dependency on relief meant that they might be deployed to wherever labor scarcities—or overly empowered Irish domestics—existed as a problem of household production. Unlike the Irish migrants whom Foster sponsored, black women and children would not be treated as potentially equal participants in national projects of expansion and white social reproduction. Nor would they be extolled for their labor republicanism, even though many displayed an independence that was just as fierce as their Irish counterparts. As the next chapter addresses, black refugees faced far greater constraints when it came to their ability to dictate the conditions under which they labored. Brokers of their labor banked on this very point.

## 2

## Humanitarianism's Markets

*Brokering the Domestic Labor of Black Refugees, 1861–1872*

### Introduction: "Destitute in Female Help"

On January 23, 1867, Josiah Crawford, a fifty-nine-year-old white farmer living in Skull Creek, Nebraska, wrote to the Washington, D.C., office of the Freedmen's Bureau. He had read in a local newspaper that thousands of black refugees crowded the nation's capital in a state of destitution. Calling himself a "true Union man," Crawford offered a solution that he claimed could remove at least one refugee family from public relief. The bureau would send him "a good woman" with "two or three children" who together would cook, keep house, and perform other domestic labor.[1] In exchange, he would gift the family a homestead consisting of eighty acres if they chose a plot ten miles removed from the railroad line or forty acres if they selected a location closer to transit. He would build and maintain a house for them on the property. Whereas land was abundant and surplus to white settlers in the area, hired domestic labor was a scarce commodity that even more affluent farmers could not acquire. Crawford explained that his part of Nebraska "was very destitute in female help" and could accommodate thousands of black women and children sent from Washington. If his neighbors did not wish to barter land for labor, as he was willing to do, they would gladly pay three to five dollars a week in wages.[2] As a farmer, Crawford may have been indirectly motivated by a desire to see the high tariffs on imported manufactured goods, which helped finance Reconstruction, reduced. Crawford may have also been affected by the newly implemented federal income tax; the 1870 census recorded his property holdings as one thousand dollars, which put him above the minimum threshold for those who had to pay.[3] Federal expenditures on the Freedmen's Bureau and refugee relief were charged topics that, for the first time in the country's history, made social welfare a matter of national rather than local politics.

Crawford's proposal shared a similar rationale to migration schemes that were advanced after the Panic of 1857. When surplus and unemployed female labor could not meet household demand due to geographic isolation, political economists consistently held that using state and private charitable funds to subsidize migration represented a practical investment in developing the nation's infrastructure. The race of those targeted for assistance, however, accounted for significant differences in how migration programs were implemented and understood, and the agency that individuals and families had to accept or reject the help being offered. Strict prohibitions against interracial marriages, covenants against black landownership, and the relative absence of single black men in places like Nebraska meant that the black women who agreed to resettlement were unlikely to move out of a position of hired servitude. The 1860 census counted 82 free black residents in the state, and in 1870 that number had increased to only 789. Antebellum army officers brought black servants with them to remote outposts on the Nebraska frontier, where workers' dependency rendered their status as free or enslaved—at least in an immediate material sense—inconsequential. Black refugees in Washington may have been aware of such legacies.[4]

Crawford's apparent generosity notwithstanding, his proposal failed to account for the long-term prospects or local reception of single black women sent to remote areas of the interior. What would his neighbors say about the arrangement? Nor did Crawford's letter address what would happen if the black family sent to him decided that the situation was not to their liking. Would he finance their return to Washington? Would the agreement granting the land to them be nullified? Would they be able to find alternative shelter, if the need suddenly arose? Crawford did not seek to eradicate the complicated dependencies facing recently emancipated black persons, as much as he wanted to enmesh them in new ones. Consent, independent contract, and wages—the hallmarks of the free labor system that the Union had fought for—are afterthoughts in his correspondence.

In the end, Crawford proved unsuccessful in convincing the Freedmen's Bureau to send him refugee laborers. In 1870, he shared his domicile with a man who appears to have been his nephew, but the census lists no servants in the Crawford household and there are no black female homeowners in the surrounding area. The distance from Nebraska to Washington, D.C., made Crawford's request an outlier to begin with—most black women and children were sent to locations in the Northeast or to places in the Midwest where free black communities had been established before the war.[5] Since the government had to pay the cost of transportation, and would not have paid for a chaperone to accompany a single family, fronting the money for this purpose would have also been viewed as a risky prospect. Numerous black refugees chose to abscond before arriving at their intended destinations if better employment options were presented en route. Whether or not any of the bureau's officials in Washington tried to persuade a family on relief to take Crawford's offer went unrecorded. Had bureau agents pressed the case, they could have threatened to remove from relief the refugee family to whom Crawford's offer was tendered. To white officials, the successful commodification of black labor relied on the ability to assert these types of coercive pressures.

\* \* \*

The end of slavery spurred experiments in how the provision of welfare, migration, and fulfillment of demand for household labor might be dealt with as imbricated social concerns. At a time when Irish immigrant women were increasingly perceived as wielding the menacing ability to win advantageous work contracts through their manipulation of northern domestic labor scarcities, the war provided employers with an opportunity to counteract this perceived threat through the brokered import of black labor. White northerners eagerly hypothesized about the potential value of black migrants' labor power, and how this supply of labor might be produced for market through various forms of state intervention. Brokers of refugee labor financed and controlled migrations from the South and Washington, D.C., by attaching numerous restrictions on how these funds were to be dispensed. In comparison to the assistance that was made available to white women, whether for transatlantic or internal migrations, black refugees interacted with a welfare program that was explicitly rather than passively disciplinary in the market behavior that it sought to effect. A question haunts this chapter: what would have happened if migration assistance was extended to black refugees without punitive conditions? Engagement with this counterfactual premise yields important insights into what forms mid-nineteenth-century white racial privilege took, and how servants' liberty to contract their labor power was shaped by private and state actions.

Northern households' covetous impulses inaugurated what would be, for the next half century, a near constant quest to colonize and expropriate new supplies of workers. From these new sources, employers and labor brokers aspired to create social relations in which hired laborers were less able to withdraw themselves from the production of domesticity, or to control the means by which it was performed. Northern households aimed to detach independence—as a formal status—from the ability to refuse or reshape job situations that workers deemed undesirable. Among proponents of free labor, wages and other benefits to workers were proxies for consent and more important than whether or not a contraband or refugee entered into a contract voluntarily.[6] Free market advocates urged displaced black migrants to forgo their own conceptions of what constituted economic and social security and to abandon the prerogative to choose where they wanted to live and work. Instead, they instructed refugee populations to consummate the commodified exchange of what was typically framed as their most valuable asset: their power to labor in servility. The Union Army's "liberation" of their enslaved labor, white northerners smugly declared, had made this possible.[7] There were fundamental paradoxes and myopic assumptions built into northern liberals' vision of how freedom would govern emancipated slaves. Literary scholar Saidiya Hartman uses the evocative phrase "burdened individuality" to signify the fraught position that freed blacks, deprived of the material and other resources necessary to self-sufficiency, occupied in society.[8]

Racial discrimination meant that it was more difficult for black men to claim a republican identity as heads of households and independent producers than it was for Irish women—even though both groups of workers performed service work. When it came to placing contrabands and refugees in northern homes, white employers analyzed and disputed whether or not blacks were innately predisposed to servile labor, or whether servitude was cultural behavior produced through the disciplinary regime of slavery and therefore an attribute that might be lost with free labor. (As chapter 6 returns to, this debate lingered into the twentieth century.) Observations of black laborers' work habits were transmitted from the Union front lines in the South back to northern households. Domestic labor's status as women's work, to be performed within the confines of homes, was upended by the exigent needs that the war created. When white officers and soldiers enlisted freed black workers, labor that had been gendered—such as cooking and cleaning— became racialized instead.[9] Although refugee women and their children command the bulk of attention in this chapter, the funneling of black men into positions of service work had a lasting impact on white Americans' perception of what a postwar racial division of labor might look like. Whether as porters, hotel workers, or waiters, black men—like Chinese immigrant men—were relegated to jobs in the growing service sector of the late nineteenth century, and denied employment opportunities in areas of the economy that would link industrial labor with manhood and citizenship. Union officials and their successors in the Freedmen's Bureau were concerned with refugee women, and especially single women with children, as subjects who they feared were most likely to fall into a state of permanent dependency.

An aim of this chapter is to refocus attention on American refugee policies and emphasize how government-run camps—whether created adjacent to the occupying armies of the Union or away from the front lines in Washington, D.C.—became sites of labor recruitment. In relation to the longer arc of federal policies governing displaced persons, internally or abroad, the Civil War–era plight of freed persons demonstrates that refugee sponsorship, while often cast as a humanitarian impulse, usually involved exploitative instincts as well.[10] To be critical and perhaps even cynical about it, refugee sponsorship has always been a form of labor brokerage, and where refugees have not been accepted for asylum, it is typically because demand has not been marshalled to justify the action.[11] White employers and brokers scavenged contraband and refugee camps for black bodies to enlist into wage servitude. Camps, in this regard, were places where emancipated slaves—resurrected from the social death of slavery—became sovereign economic subjects in a carefully orchestrated and limited fashion.[12] The Freedmen's Bureau was granted unique and unprecedented powers to regulate economic, political, and social behavior. From its commissioner, Oliver Otis Howard, on down, the bureau tended to employ self-styled Christian soldiers who viewed their work as a missionary intervention.[13] Black refugees, like

Catholic "soupers" in Ireland and "rice-Christians" in China, performed a version of want that responded to their very real material needs. In the context of American racial politics, refugees' reliance on relief, and what white missionaries demanded of them as part of this exchange, helped produce a safe and unthreatening black subjectivity.

Acknowledging the myriad obstacles the bureau faced as an administrative body under attack does not change the legacies of its particular approach. White northern officials required that displaced black persons accept their transformation from chattel to transportable "free" labor as a condition of their need. Anxieties about the mass migration of blacks conducted under more voluntary conditions fueled antipathy and opposition from northern whites who believed that blacks were incapable of being integrated as both laborers and citizens, except at the peripheries of economic and social life.[14] Even though assisted migrations were met with white resistance as well, the contractual conditions that such programs imposed were understood as important checks on wanton black freedoms.

## Servitude and Autonomy in the Antebellum Era

Prior to the Civil War, free blacks in the North struggled to balance their economic reliance on service work, as a source of wages, with the stigma that marked this labor. In New York, slavery was not completely abolished until 1827. By 1840, Manhattan's black community had grown to sixteen thousand people and accounted for roughly 5 percent of the city's total population. During the 1850s, the influx of Irish immigrants reduced the number of blacks employed as household servants to only 3 percent of the occupation's total workforce, even if the number of black men working as body servants remained proportionately higher—a reflection on the discrimination they faced in trades dominated by white laborers. Wages for black domestics declined as a result of the expansion of the labor supply. Black servants faced additional economic injury due to the fact that certain white employers seized upon Irish immigration to hire white servants exclusively.[15]

Even before European immigration spiked in the late 1840s, middle-class employers worried about their capacity to control how wage servants were hired, and to dictate how workers approached contractual obligations and loyalty to their employers. In 1826, New York elites led by Arthur Tappan, the abolitionist, chartered the Society for the Encouragement of Faithful Domestic Servants. Despite petering out of existence in 1830, the society's philosophy would be widely replicated in decades to follow. The New York Society was modeled after an organization by the same name in London, which had been active there since the eighteenth century. The New York Society offered bonuses (and free Bibles) to servants who stayed with a single household for longer than a year. As an employment agency, it promised employers that it would place only reputable, trustworthy women. While an estimated 60 percent of the women who used the service identified as Irish immigrants, the society also recruited black labor. Black workers used its services to obtain character references and win coveted placements in more affluent homes.[16] Even when organizations like the New York Society were not attempting to exercise direct influence over black servants' market and work behavior, as historian Kathleen Brown has argued, black domestics, cooks, and butlers in white northern households often practiced an extreme form of self-discipline and held themselves to trying standards of industry, hygiene, and loyalty. They understood that their value as workers would always be qualified in racial terms that made deference and comportment key measures of their worth above and beyond the caliber of their labor.[17]

Wage servitude haunted black families in ways that single Irish women, acting as transnational breadwinners, did not have to contend with. Historian Leslie Harris has shown how delegates at the Colored National Convention that took place in Cleveland in 1848 vociferously debated a resolution, which they ultimately passed, denouncing live-in domestic service as "a badge of degradation" to blacks. This position was vehemently espoused by black men who aspired to a form of republican citizenship and manhood that was defined by the ability of their wives and daughters to avoid having to work for wages.[18] Martin Robinson Delany, the intellectual and black separatist who by the 1850s would emerge as a fervent proponent of black emigration from the United States, played a key role at the Cleveland Convention advancing this position. In 1844, Delany was already articulating the difference between those who hired out as servants as a matter of "necessity," which he felt was the plight of black women with no choice but to pursue this work, and the white women who entered service because they had squandered racial privilege and opportunity.[19] Even though Delany's wife, Catherine Richards, was the interracial daughter of an Irish immigrant and black butcher, he did not parse where in-between Irish immigrants, who in cultural terms were not yet understood to be fully white, fit into this picture. He seemed to insinuate that white women's failure to marry landowners and tradesmen who could provide for them was a fault rather than a strategic choice. In his 1852 publication, *The Condition, Elevation, Emigration, and Destiny of the Colored People of the United States*, Delany more forcefully stipulated that when it came to free blacks, "We cannot at the same time, be domestic and lady; servant and gentleman. We must be the one or the other."[20]

Delany believed that prohibitions against black landownership, education, and commercial pursuits meant that free blacks would never find a community in the United States where their enlistment as servants would be temporary rather than permanent.[21] Instead he promoted black colonization of "uninhabited" lands in South America or Africa.[22] Not only did new opportunities for acquiring unclaimed (or conquerable) lands have to be forged, but labor markets, and the existing social relations of production that demarcated racial subject positions in the United States, had to be remade as well. Delany was but one voice in this particular debate. Although Harriet Beecher Stowe, upon the publication of *Uncle Tom's Cabin*, was criticized within the abolitionist community for imagining Liberia as the best solution to the problem of an emancipated, surplus black population, it is important to note that peers like Delany had similar reservations about whether racial divisions of labor—beyond slavery—could ever be overcome.[23]

## Wartime Patriotism, Contrabands, and Private Importation

With Union armies conducting the war primarily in Confederate territory, white northerners gained access to the labor power of runaways and refugees from slavery on a scale that few had predicted. The dispatches that Union officers and soldiers sent, in addition to the reports that northern journalists and missionaries filed, brimmed with enthusiasm about the productive value of contraband labor. The humanitarian crisis of sudden emancipation became an opportunity of political economy.

Before the war, northern states like Ohio had in place statutes that required free blacks to post surety bonds before entering as migrants, which they used to limit black settlement.[24] The war ended the enforcement of these laws and what had been, for all intents and purposes, more restrictive migration laws than what German and Irish arrivals to New York encountered. Writings from this period illustrate that many white northerners viewed emancipated slaves as a distinct species of labor whose value came from the fact that they were unacculturated to the free labor system. In July 1861, with the conflict only three months old, the *Independent* magazine proclaimed that the "troublesome experience of Northern households" was on the verge of being transformed. "The immigration of runaway slaves" with their "peculiar talent for service," the magazine noted, represented the spoils of war.[25]

The Emancipation Proclamation, which on January 1, 1863, decreed a formal end to slavery in the states of the Confederacy, generated excitement as well. Horace James, a Congregationalist minister from Massachusetts commissioned to serve as the superintendent of Negro affairs in North Carolina, effused in 1864 that the abolition of slavery had created a "nation of servants" awaiting employment. "The foolish prejudice against color which prevails . . . even among the best people of the North," James declared, "should immediately give way, that they may take their proper place in all our households." James underscored that proposals to send freedwomen and children to the North were not intended "to throw white laborers out of employment" but rather would "lift them higher in the social scale, and engage them in labors which require more skill." All of this was simply a natural function of how free labor markets operated, James insisted, even as he sought the federal backing that was necessary to orchestrate a massive population transfer. "In the successive orders or ranks of industrial pursuits," he concluded, "those who have the least intelligence must perform the more menial services, without respect to color or birth."[26] Irish immigrants who had paid their dues at the bottom of the free labor hierarchy were now ready to be elevated to more skilled pursuits, property ownership, and occupations that conferred upon them independence rather than dependence. During the 1870s, the theme of occupational succession and advancement would be picked up by proponents of Chinese immigration, who, in similar terms, insisted that Irish immigrants and other white laborers stood to be the primary beneficiaries of the introduction of nonwhite labor to menial positions. These new supplies of labor, they claimed, could be exploited by the white working and middle classes alike.

As historian Kate Masur argues, Major General Benjamin Butler's decision early in the war to treat runaway slaves who crossed over Union lines as "contrabands" meant that white northern officers and soldiers first interacted with emancipated slaves as service workers in military encampments, which framed their calculations on how free black incorporation was to proceed. Contrabands quickly became subjects of northern popular culture as well, appearing not only in journals and newspapers, but in minstrel shows and fiction. Masur notes that white northern missionaries exaggerated contrabands' status "as victims of a war they could not understand, [and] as illiterate, unworldly, and disorderly in their appearance and personal relationships." Paternalistic depictions such as these also helped to assuage white workers' fears that contrabands sent farther north were legitimate threats to take their jobs.[27]

In practice, contraband laborers were productive contributors to the Union war effort rather than dependents of largesse, especially since they could be compelled to perform gendered and racialized work that white soldiers disdained. Before freedmen became eligible to assume combat roles after the passage of the Emancipation Proclamation, they performed drudge work digging ditches, cleaning latrines, and chopping wood. They also supplied more intimate forms of labor marked as feminine and domestic, namely as personal servants to officers and as company cooks. Black servants were not just employed in camps behind battle lines. One military official estimated, for instance, that of the 10,000 freed blacks employed in August 1863 by the Department of the Cumberland Army in Tennessee, 3,700 worked as cooks and servants in active combat zones.[28] In a December 1863 message to President Lincoln, representatives from the Freedman's Aid Societies in Boston, Cincinnati, New York, and Philadelphia predicted that recently emancipated slaves were "destined to be the great want of the country over which we are extending our victorious dominion." In the interim, however, the representatives urged the president to respond on the record to complaints that federal money was being wasted on feeding and clothing contrabands. They pleaded with him to publicize how expenditures in this area represented an initial investment in the production of servants who were necessary to the war effort. Moreover, as other commentators argued, every adult male slave who escaped forced the Confederacy, in theory, to replace his labor with that of a white person.[29]

It was not until the middle of the war that the Union began to regularly pay black laborers, servants, and cooks. Equal wages for black workers remained a constant point of tension, even after the federal government made this official policy. At Fortress Monroe, where Butler had first initiated the Union Army's policy of refusing to return Confederate property in the form of enslaved persons, his successor General John Wool required army officers and civilians employing contrabands to deposit wages in a general fund, which was subsequently used to support refugees whose age or condition made them camp dependents. Refugee laborers' protests that this "Contraband Tax" was unjust and rife with corruption were met with imprisonment and whippings. The policy prompted some of Fortress Monroe's black workers to independently contract out their labor to civilians in order to circumvent the military's oversight altogether. A military commission appointed to investigate the situation questioned, in telling language, why "Irish souphouse" relief policies were needed at all, when the free market, its authors concluded, ought to suffice. Gainfully employed black laborers, the commission argued, could be charged with taking care of their fellow refugees without government oversight. (In 1863, undeterred Union officials introduced a Contraband Tax at the newly created Freedman's Village in Arlington Heights as well.)[30] The very existence of a refugee tax deserves comparative attention. It was not until the 1870s that American ports began levying a commutation tax on Irish and other European immigrants, and required them to offset the costs of providing public relief to fellow arrivals who became public charges. But even then, these taxes were not enacted under the same guise of inducing racial responsibility.

While blacks' martial service has received substantial attention from scholars as the means by which they proved, under fire, their worthiness for citizenship, the relationship between the performance of "unmanly" and menial servitude and social inclusion was more ambiguous.[31] Historian Micki McElya argues that the focus on free blacks' claims to citizenship through martial service has obscured struggles for rights that were organized around other contributions and actions.[32] Contrabands discovered that being relegated to menial and servile labor, even when they were granted the freedom to consent to work, represented a tortuous path to a form of economic and social citizenship that warranted respect in the eyes of white soldiers and officers. An article published in the *United States Service Magazine*, for instance, described how a contraband who had wandered into the camp of the First Iowa Cavalry in Tennessee was administered an oath by a Union corporal in which he had to solemnly swear to not only uphold the Constitution, but also "see that there are no grounds floating upon the coffee."[33] To counter perceptions that blacks were fit only for dependent service work, the American Freedmen's Inquiry Commission found it prudent to include in the report it submitted to Congress a letter to the *Galena (IL) Advertiser* from M. M. Miller, the white captain of the Ninth Louisiana Colored Regiment. Narrating the gory details of the recently fought battle at Milliken's Bend, Mississippi, Miller described not only the valor of the black soldiers under his command but also how "a boy" who cooked for him had "begged a gun when the rebels were advancing," so that he too could defend the Union position. The cook was "badly wounded with one gunshot and two bayonet wounds."[34] Testimonials such as this aimed to prove that black men and boys would proudly abandon service work and its emasculating status, if only given the opportunity.

Some Union officers treated contraband servants' labor as their personal property. As historian David Cecere has documented, Union officers secured their own differentiated status by having contraband servants complete tasks that enlisted men were required to do on their own. They also created impromptu brokerage networks to fulfill their civilian families' domestic labor needs. Enoch Adams, who hailed from a prominent New Hampshire family, invited his wife Sarah to visit him at Point Lookout, Maryland, where he oversaw the prisoner-of-war camp there, and promised she could hire a "black girl" to take home. Adams also wrote to his mother inquiring if she had any interest in laborers he described as "my contrabands," whom he pledged to deliver when granted leave. Union officers seemed to have little patience or tolerance for black servants who pursued independent goals. Cecere describes one officer who became enraged when he learned that his contraband servant had left without permission to search for his mother who had been separated from him during slavery.[35]

## Boycotts and Job Competition

The start of the Civil War had a varied impact on how Irish immigrants were viewed as a resource. On one hand, white immigrant labor gave the Union a distinct advantage over the Confederacy in respect to manpower, and the wartime recruitment of immigrants flourished in many European ports of departure even before the 1864 Act to Encourage Immigration was passed into law.[36] On the other hand, there was backlash against Irish immigrants accused of being disloyal to the Union cause and overly supportive of antiwar Democrats.

Campaigns denouncing the employment of Irish servants peaked in the aftermath of the July 1863 Draft Riots in New York City. It became popular for Anglo-American household employers, especially those who identified as staunchly Republican, to declare that they were boycotting Irish domestic labor altogether. A persistent rumor alleged that Irish domestics were involved in a citywide arson plot against the homes and families of those who had supported the Union conscription policy that had set off the disturbances. The *Tribune* published an editorial shortly after the riots, leaking a note that one of Democratic Governor Horatio Seymour's assistants had—allegedly—forwarded to the White House. In this note, Seymour was depicted as asking President Lincoln to end conscription due to the "gravest apprehension that the Irish servant-girls will, in case the draft is enforced, turn incendiaries in a body, and burn down their masters' homes." The paper chided Seymour for exaggerating the threat of civil disorder, which played into his calls to end the draft, while simultaneously mocking him for being a coward in the face of this feminine menace. Whether the missive was real or not, the *Freeman's Journal*, the leading Irish nationalist newspaper, felt obliged to issue a response denouncing the accusations.[37]

Northerners' elevated antipathy toward Irish servants remained palpable for some time after the riots. A representative of the Pennsylvania Abolition Society's employment office wrote to the Union superintendent at Fortress Monroe, Virginia, in September 1863, for instance, to request that refugee women and children be sent to Philadelphia, where demand for black servants had been stoked by the events of the previous summer.[38] After the war's end, the Freedmen's Bureau would continue to receive correspondence from northern employers urging the agency to redouble efforts to deliver black women and children as domestics, since, as one writer noted, a "general disgust with Irish help" prevailed. A white woman from East Bloomfield, New York, petitioned the bureau for a job as a broker of black domestic labor by explaining how she would use the position as "the means of getting in a class of laboring people who are not Irish." In Worcester, Massachusetts, an intelligence office promoted its ability to procure black servants by highlighting how this meant that middle-class women no longer had to degrade themselves with visits to Irish slums, where competing institutions dealing in Irish labor operated.[39] Back in New York City, although the Draft Riots did lead some white employers to boycott Irish labor, the threat of further violence against Manhattan's black community accelerated an exodus to Brooklyn and places farther afield. The riots, as they were designed to do, strengthened the position of white workers in the labor market.[40]

Stories were also realms where employers disseminated comparisons of servants' attributes, and produced racial difference as market knowledge. Literary fiction provided an important venue for airing wonder and anxiety about the integration of contraband domestic workers into northern homes. Mary E. Dodge's story "Our Contraband," published by *Harper's New Monthly Magazine* in August 1863, centers on a white narrator's interactions with Aggie, a young black woman. The story begins with Aggie being dropped off at the Ladies' Soldiers' Aid Society by two Union soldiers passing through New York City on leave. Her removal to the city follows her failed stint as a servant in a Union camp in Virginia, where she and her father fled after escaping slavery. The narrator explains that Aggie's "insubordination and impishness" were too much for her previous employers to handle. Her Union escorts hoped that domestic supervision, provided by middle-class white women, would prove more successful.[41]

In her analysis of "Our Contraband," historian Kate Masur reasons that Aggie symbolizes northerners' fears that emancipated blacks were indelibly marked in attitude and behavior by the institution of slavery. Aggie ultimately fails as a servant after being placed by the society in the narrator's household. She is prone to talking to herself, sneaking down at night to steal food, and breaking household objects. In the end, her care and employment pass to a Quaker woman, who discovers Aggie wandering the streets with the narrator's child.[42]

Although Aggie's character is used by Dodge to probe the question of black laborers' effectiveness, she is equally emblematic of white employers' speculative belief that black migrants might rescue the system of free labor as it related to household service. In "Our Contraband," the narrator at first withholds Aggie's race and background from her husband, and describes her only as a "raw girl; one that is not hopelessly set in other people's ways." His assumption is that she means "a fair Hibernian . . . newly landed, or a blushing Huytur-spluyter fresh from the Vaterland." When the truth is exposed, the narrator reassures him that Aggie is not "one of those deceitful, half-and-half yellow kind that are neither one thing nor the other, but a genuine negress." The narrator's description attempts to draw equivalencies between unassimilated European immigrant women yet to have acquired a disdain for being ordered around, and black women whose history of slavery has accustomed them to such controls.

Dodge's treatment of the narrator's three Irish servants is also worth parsing beyond calling attention to their stereotypical animus toward blacks.[43] The Irish servants in the story stake their claims to whiteness both within and against the work that the production of domesticity entailed. Ann, the cook, exercises "local supremacy" over the kitchen, and bars unwanted persons from this space at her whim; Nora gathers coals wearing a "crinoline twice as expensive" as her employer's; Ellen, the family's chief waitress, vainly believes in her "impeachability" as an employee. The three Irish women announce that they refuse to "slape and ate wid nagers," but it is the narrator—after claiming that she has no other choice—who sends Aggie away. The narrator brags that the new racial division of labor that she introduced, despite failing to take, has appropriately disrupted her Irish servants' confidence in their guaranteed employment and preference as workers.[44]

In other contexts, employers feared that insolent Irish servants, rather than being properly chastened, would instead corrupt black coworkers new to free labor. In an 1866 story that Harriet Beecher Stowe wrote for the *Atlantic Monthly*, for instance, one of her characters complains that whatever laziness black domestics might come to display, it would not be due to innate racial traits, but rather to their mastery of "imitation."[45] The need to isolate Chinese servants from the bad attitudes and habits of Irish coworkers was promoted as a wise managerial strategy as well.

With Irish servants themselves, Anglo-American commentators empha-sized hiring immigrant laborers in their "raw" state, before they became acculturated to market behavior in a democracy. In Patience Price's 1868 story "The Revolt in the Kitchen," the narrator earns the praise of her husband after she designs a scheme where she plucks Irish immigrant women from Manhattan's streets as she spies them about to enter into intelligence offices.[46]

## Moral Markets: Missionary-Run Intelligence Offices

During the Civil War, recently emancipated slaves' choices and actions were cause for special concern. Even liberals who believed that there were no inherent racial limitations to blacks' fitness for freedom still felt that the experience of slavery had left black workers perfectly igno-rant of the rituals and practices that marketing their labor necessitated.[47] Oliver Otis Howard, shortly after being appointed commissioner of the Freedmen's Bureau, issued a circular in May 1865 affirming that one of the agency's main goals was "to correct the false impressions sometimes entertained by the freedmen, that they can live without labor, and to overcome that false pride which renders some of the refugees more will-ing to be supported in idleness than to support themselves."[48]

This was no empty dictate. The records of the bureau abound with examples of this philosophy being implemented in practice. When black men and women chose to care for their own children rather than work for wages, local white officials punished them with expul-sion from relief rolls. Ann Brown, for instance, a freedwoman living in Fairfax Court House, Virginia, was forcefully escorted by Union soldiers to a six-dollar-a-month job as a servant in the house of a white neighbor after local officials discovered that she had been draw-ing rations of firewood and straw. Local bureau officials also sought to discipline black recipients of relief who were not appropriately humble, or hatched their own plans to migrate. Bureau officials in Chestertown, Maryland, petitioned to exclude from relief a group of free black house servants who, unemployed in the aftermath of the war, had taken to "constantly gadding about the streets," as the report described, and relaying to each other their "great desire" to relocate to Baltimore, which the author attributed to their childlike wonderment with the big city.[49] As historian Eric Foner has documented, Freedmen's Bureau agents in the South dismissed questions concerned with whether or not the involuntary year-long contracts that they mandated between freed people and white planters were legal—despite the ratification of the Thirteenth Amendment in December 1865—since maximizing production and obtaining full employment were the most salient priorities. In states like North Carolina, legislators found ways to circumvent the constitutional prohibition on keeping workers in a state of bondage by making it illegal for employers to entice or harbor servants who were already under contract, thereby denying black domestic laborers the right to take advantage of competitive hiring.[50]

The discipline urged upon free black laborers in these contexts rarely took into account the structural legacy of slavery, and what blacks defined as freedom. The bureau's willingness to naturalize wage labor as the sine qua non of postwar liberalism moved the Republican Party further away from the "free soil" mantle that had been a crucial component of the party's ideology in the decade leading up to the conflict.[51] Despite the attempts of Radical Republicans in Congress to create a Freedmen's Bureau bill that would have extended measures for Confederate land confiscation and redistribution to freed black men—a version of the famous "Forty Acres and a Mule" provision that General William Tecumseh Sherman implemented on a more local basis in the Sea Islands region of Georgia—these efforts were blocked by President Andrew Johnson and other opponents who argued that such a policy was too generous in the entitlements it proposed meting out. From the very beginning of the war, black newspapers, such as the New York–based *Anglo African*, lobbied for policies that made land confiscation and redistribution the basis for Reconstruction.[52] When Congress did pass the Southern Homestead Act in 1866, it allocated only the poorest lands to black settlers and was underfunded and lacking in enforcement. Even so, it was still met with fierce resistance by local whites.[53]

In the absence of policies empowering blacks as autonomous economic producers and landowners, markets and wage work were the means by which the bureau governed freed persons as economic actors. It is ironic though that Howard, in his December 1865 report to Congress, would propose having the Freedmen's Bureau's agents "adopt a system like the ordinary intelligence office" to "procure good places" for freedmen and women unable to find work. As a member of the middle class Howard would have been all too aware of the scorn these institutions generated, and the lack of confidence that they inspired among employers.[54] Northern employers blamed intelligence offices for corrupting the principles of a free market rather than assisting in their realization. As historian Brian Luskey observes, intelligence offices "defined wage labor relations in the era of slave emancipation with far greater precision than the hopeful narratives of free labor ideology that have taken precedence in the historical literature."[55] They were problems in practice.

Most of the intelligence offices involved in placing black refugees traced their origins to the missionary-run freedmen's relief agencies, which shielded them—at least to some degree—from the opprobrium that their commercial counterparts received. To offset anxieties about how long-distance transactions in black labor might replicate the slave trade—which would continue to dog intelligence offices into the twentieth century—missionaries presented their work as free of commercial motives. Oliver St. John, a Dutch Reformed pastor and the corresponding secretary for the New York and Brooklyn Freedmen's Employment Bureau, wrote to the general superintendent of freedmen's affairs for the Army's Department of Virginia and North Carolina in November 1864, claiming that New York and New England could absorb at least ten thousand freedwomen and children in domestic service positions. St. John stipulated that "residence of only a few months in our free states will be of very great service in lifting them up into a higher civilization than they have ever known." St. John arranged for the transport of fifty freedwomen to Brooklyn in August 1864, and bragged that "not *one*, so far as we know, have [*sic*] failed to find a good home through our Agency." If money could be raised to hire a vessel to depart Norfolk with a "load of 200," prospective employers could be brought down to the docks to meet the vessel and hire servants on the spot.[56]

Mission-inspired intelligence offices were not concerned with whether the interests and needs of employers were made legible to the laborers they recruited. In contrast, employers using the New York and Brooklyn Freedmen's Employment Bureau were treated as consumers who needed to be provided with information about the goods they were obtaining. Employers were required to pay a subscription fee of five dollars, deductible from their servant's future wages, as a down payment

toward lasting employment. Children aged ten to fifteen could be procured without wages, as legal dependents, so long as employers pledged
to comply with the New York statute dictating that fostered orphans
receive "the advantages of a common school education." Prospective
employers were asked to indicate whether they needed a chambermaid
or a cook, in addition to marking off whether they wanted a child or
an adult.[57] St. John, despite his public enthusiasm about the ability of
northern markets to absorb black labor, expressed private concerns
about whether large-scale refugee resettlement would result in pauper-
ism in northern cities caused by an oversaturated market. To safeguard
against this possibility, his bureau's program was designed to ensure that
only women and children with jobs contracted prior to their departure
were sent.[58] Unlike commercial intelligence offices, missionary agencies
were not willing to provide resources to unemployed laborers, which
would have allowed them to test the market.

Other missionary labor brokers concentrated on how to remove black
mothers with children from relief while keeping families together. The
free market, they discovered, contained few incentives for keeping these
families intact. A letter in the February 1865 issue of the *Pennsylvania
Freedmen's Bulletin* called attention to the reluctance of white employers to provide room and board to refugee children who were too young
to work. The author noted that even though most women with children
being placed in household service were widows or the common-law wives
of black men serving in the Union Army, communicating their respectability did not overcome employers' reluctance to hire them. Northern missionaries, including the author of the letter, worked to open foster homes
where black children could be cared for while their mothers lived out in
service.[59] By socializing child care, local and federal officials avoided having to pay relief on able-bodied adults. Later, when the bureau was forced
to suspend paying for the transportation costs of refugees contracted to
domestic jobs in the North, funds continued to be available for the transportation of women with children so as to incentivize their hire.[60]

## The Refugee Community as Labor Supply: Washington, D.C.

During the war and its aftermath, Washington became a crucial node in
the movement of black migrant labor and a city defined by its refugee

# THE NEW YORK AND BROOKLYN FREEDMEN'S BUREAU.

Persons residing at a distance from Brooklyn, and wishing to avail themselves of this Agency, will please fill in the following blank, place it (with five dollars and the price of a travelling ticket from Brooklyn to the Applicant's residence,) in an envelope, and remail it.

On the receipt of it at this Bureau, the certificate appended to this sheet will be signed by the Corresponding Secretary, and returned by mail immediately. As soon as the person described can be brought from the South, he or she will be forwarded as designated.

Your own name and Post-Office address.

For what employment and capacity do you wish a servant?

About what age?

What compensation or wages do you propose to give?

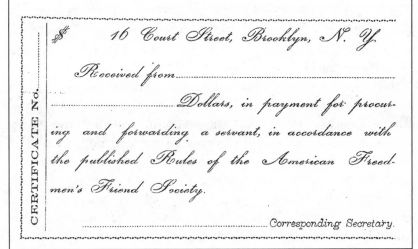

Figure 2.1. "The New York and Brooklyn Freedmen's Bureau, Application Blank." Courtesy of the Collection of Brooklyn, NY, Civil War Relief Associations Records, Ephemera, and Other Material, ARC.245, box 5, folder 7, Brooklyn Historical Society.

population and relief needs. In 1860, Washington included 3,185 slaves among its population; by 1867, it was home to 38,663 free blacks, two-thirds of whom were newcomers to the city.[61] Before it was ordered closed in December 1863 for lack of adequate sanitary conditions, Camp Barker—located adjacent to what is now the intersection of R Street and Vermont Avenue—was the largest refugee camp in the city. Although fifteen thousand people would pass through Camp Barker, most refugees resided there for only a brief period. Even if many refugees were dependent on some form of relief, they preferred, whenever possible, to live independently. For freedmen with families, this was paramount to establishing patriarchal authority over their households. Across the Potomac River in Arlington Heights, Union officials created what would become known as the Freedman's Village on the estate—now part of Arlington National Cemetery—that had belonged to Robert E. Lee and, before that, the adopted grandson of George Washington. The community was founded as a model village that would demonstrate the progress that black persons were making in their transition to freedom, but its administration raised serious questions about what rights refugees had to mobility and liberty of contract. White officers used a system of passes, for instance, in order to limit the ability of black laborers to travel into the District. In 1864, Union officers heightened restrictions on refugees' movement after they reported being overwhelmed by complaints from Freedman's Village residents about the poor working conditions and withheld wages at the jobs they were compelled to take as a condition of receiving housing.[62]

After Congress passed a bill creating the Freedmen's Bureau in March 1865, the agency took over relief efforts in the city and surrounding areas. Charles Henry (C. H.) Howard, Oliver's brother and the bureau's assistant commissioner in Washington, ordered that black refugees refusing situations offered to them—whether in the District or elsewhere—would be removed from relief rolls and prohibited from government-run camps.[63] This policy prevailed even though a considerable number of local white employers, conditioned to slavery, which was abolished in Washington in 1862 with the Compensated Emancipation Act, refused to pay the black laborers they hired. Officials at Camp Barker reported that civilians regularly used its employment agency to hire black women as domestics, then denied them wages on the grounds that they had been paid in room and board.[64] Although the bureau did establish primary education for blacks in the District, and opened seven industrial sewing schools, programs designed to enhance the long-term prospects of the city's black population often took a backseat to more immediate concerns of shrinking relief expenditures.[65]

The policies directed at refugees bore resemblance to the treatment of Irish women in the 1850s. Both black and Irish women were faulted for displaying agency that went against what third parties had determined constituted their greatest good, when they chose to remain in Washington or New York, respectively. In June 1865, Assistant Commissioner John Eaton ordered bureau agents in Washington to scout for work opportunities that might allow for refugees' removal from "abodes of filth," "idleness," and the "social peril" that makeshift and overcrowded dwellings cultivated.[66] Although such efforts were already under way before Eaton's order, the growing size of the refugee community in Washington, and difficulties finding employment, made the matter more pressing. On occasion, the reality of labor market conditions in Washington did cause bureau officials to reconsider their opinions about the factors contributing to black unemployment. In May 1867, for instance, Howard wrote to the Industrial School in Cambridge, Massachusetts, which trained and placed black refugees from Washington in service positions in the Boston area, to negotiate an agreement where the bureau would pay the salary of the school's matron and rent on its building in exchange for the institution accepting, unequivocally, any of the migrants the bureau sent. Although Howard admitted that he had previously pledged that "no paupers should be sent" to the school, he hedged by explaining that Washington was "so overcrowded it is impossible for all to be employed."[67] In the context of Washington's large refugee population and the surplus labor it created, one could be—Howard suggested—a deserving black pauper. An individual surrendered this status, however, if she refused to relocate for work.

Bureau officers dealing in the placement of black domestic laborers were regularly approached by individuals interested in winning what they understood, incorrectly, to be a federal subsidy that would allow them to expand and diversify their supply. The supply chains furnishing Eastern Seaboard cities with unskilled European labor were well established by the 1860s. When intelligence offices recruited women still in Europe, as they sometimes did, it was usually due to the fact that they also had financial interests in the sale of steamship tickets, and not because they thought they could profit directly from inducing further migration. (The situation in California, as the last chapter explored, was an exception in this regard.) These factors discouraged private and commercial brokers from independently seeking out southern sources of labor during Reconstruction, since the capital costs of recruiting and relocating labor were not likely to be recovered.[68] The Freedmen's Bureau openly acknowledged this reality when it intervened to create new markets through subsidized commodity chains. As J. M. McKim, the corresponding secretary for the New York branch of the American Freedmen's Commission, observed, facilitating refugees' migration to places in the North was akin to trying to "make water run up stream."[69]

While the Freedmen's Bureau wanted to finance or broker migrations that reduced its relief expenditures, it was not empowered to subsidize private businesses. Had it pursued this course of action, the postwar demographics of northern cities might have been more significantly transformed. John Grines, a commercial agent in Boston, described to the bureau how he received upward of thirty callers a day looking for "colored girls." He was eager to have the government assume the capital costs of transportation that his business would otherwise have to underwrite, but the bureau lacked the resources to support brokers like Grines on the scale they desired.[70] Instead, small numbers of women were sent north when funds were available, and only after situations had been secured. When E. A. Merrell of Springfield, Massachusetts, wrote to the bureau in the winter of 1867, inquiring about how to get licensed as a government broker, so that he could more actively arrange for refugee women to be transported north and earn commissions on their local hire, he was informed that federal agents were prohibited from charging fees as intermediaries. The reason given was concerns that fees would then be passed on to the servants themselves, and taken out of their wages, which was a common practice among intelligence offices. Merrell was instructed to join with a missionary association already involved in placing refugees, and to conduct his business for charity rather than profit.[71]

In April 1866, a lack of funding forced the Freedmen's Bureau to stop paying migrants' transportation costs. These costs were transferred to employers instead. In an April 1866 interview he gave to the *London Times'* American correspondent, President Andrew Johnson, an unrelenting opponent of Reconstruction, attacked the transportation program as nothing more than a trafficking business that northern missionaries and affiliated carpetbaggers profited from through their monopoly over the black refugee population. By way of demonstrating the bureau's bias, Johnson cited a white planter in Virginia who allegedly tried to hire three hundred former slaves that he had owned—who were sent to Washington during the war "for security"—only to be denied. In contrast, Johnson noted, referencing the free transportation that the bureau provided, "the Government railroads were placed at the service of other speculators." The *Times* correspondent paraphrased Johnson's dismissal of the agency with a curt summary: it was "little better than another form of slavery, only that it was solely conducted by Abolitionists."[72]

Johnson's ungrounded accusations, hyperbolic and political though they were, struck a chord with white northerners who distrusted the appropriateness of using government money to contract refugees to distant employers. Bureau officials continued to view the government's expenditures on transportation as a worthwhile use of federal funds that allowed agents to send refugees to labor markets that could adequately absorb them, but they fought an uphill battle to secure regular appropriations for this purpose.[73] In December 1866, after Radical Republicans in Congress pushed through the July passage of the second Freedmen's Bureau Act, officials in Washington again had money to pay for transportation costs. To keep expenditures down, agents in the North were instructed to recruit and contract domestic servants in groups of ten to twelve individuals, and to apply for discounted, bulk railroad fares. This policy also made it more efficient for the bureau to send chaperones to accompany the migrants and compel them to their intended destinations.[74]

In larger northern cities like New York, a commercial employment infrastructure specializing in black domestics was already in place. Occasionally commercial agents were contracted to broker the employment of black refugees and received a salary from the federal government to perform this work, despite the bureau's reservations. Sarah A. Tilmon, the black proprietor of an intelligence office at 104 East 13th Street in

Manhattan, had established a business placing black servants in the antebellum period. During the war, she became involved in contracting contrabands for relocation to northern households, a role she adapted to placing refugees during Reconstruction. In 1867, she was employed by the bureau at an annual salary of nine hundred dollars, in exchange for rendering services receiving, boarding, and placing black refugees sent to her from Washington. This was more than double the average salary that Americans, men and women, earned, and did not include any profits she made from her nongovernmental business.[75] Tilmon exemplifies the ambiguous position that commercial intelligence offices occupied in the bureau's brokerage program, and the concerns that often surrounded such figures. In February 1867, she was forced to respond to allegations that she had been sending refugee children under her supervision out on the streets to beg. She was also accused of withholding food from migrants in her care, and housing them in a room with no ventilation. She vehemently denied all of the charges, and the matter was eventually dropped. Regardless of whether Tilmon was culpable or not, the existence of these charges speaks to the uncertainties surrounding her responsibilities. While she was not supposed to send children out to beg, actively preventing them from doing so was another matter. Her job was to broker their hire.[76]

Many of the migrants placed in northern households did not remain in the jobs they were originally contracted to.[77] Given the unknown circumstances that black migrant laborers faced when pushed to migrate, it is not surprising that a sizeable number chose to abandon the destinations assigned to them while en route. Even if this was behavior common to all assisted migrants, in the case of black refugees their actions heightened white northerners' stereotypes about the fitness of black laborers to honor their contracts. When L. L. Dutcher, a druggist in St. Albans, Vermont, failed to receive "two boys" whose transportation costs he had paid for by sending the bureau ten dollars, Josephine Griffing (whose role is discussed in more detail below) explained that the two young workers had probably been enticed away by a better job offer during a stopover. Dutcher was incensed. He questioned why Griffing had bothered to send "unreliable" laborers to begin with, although he did agree, if a refund was not forthcoming, to try female servants instead.[78] Griffing insinuated that women were more easily controllable and therefore more likely to arrive at their intended destinations. If these black refugee women did indeed get sent to Vermont, by 1870 they were no longer in Dutcher's employ. That year's census listed four white servants in his household.[79] The abandonment of bureau-arranged jobs always carried the risk of permanent expulsion from relief rolls if alternative working arrangements did not pan out. In April 1867, a Freedmen's Bureau agent in Baltimore wrote to the Washington office that he had deported from the city five black women previously reported to have been "lost in transit" on their way to domestic jobs in New Jersey. Not only were these women barred from receiving relief in Baltimore, they also became ineligible in Washington.[80]

White employers were certainly not above deception and exploitation, which also explains why refugees did not feel obligated to remain in contracts. Demonstrating their liberty of contract was an act of freedom, but more importantly, it could also be an act of self-preservation. Before the bureau was established, Union officials in Washington described an incident in which Daniel Makel, "a colored boy" from Freedman's Village, had traveled into the District with the intent of working as a servant for a local white man. Upon arriving at the man's home, however, Makel was told that he was to go and work for the man's mother in Pennsylvania instead. Unwilling to relocate, Makel was able to leave the man and go to Camp Barker, where presumably he felt safe.[81]

Even when northern employers did not lose their own money in failed attempts to recruit black refugees, they still found occasion to call out bureau officials for wasting government resources. James O. Bloss was representative of the type of informal domestic labor broker who, despite having seemingly no experience in this line of work, imagined that all that was lacking when it came to placing black women in northern white homes was competent intermediaries.[82] Bloss wrote to the bureau's Washington offices from Rochester, New York, in March 1867 and included a letter that had been sent to him requesting servants, a sample of the correspondence he claimed to receive "almost daily." Noting that much of the demand for domestic labor originated from Quaker families, Bloss asserted that if he "had a 1000 of your Paupers here I could procure them all good places in a week's time." Bloss received ten migrants from Washington, but apparently this did not satisfy him. He angrily wrote that he was advising applicants for servants who continued to flood him with requests for domestic labor to "understand that the

Gov't agents of the Bureau have paupers to hold and feed not to send away to places where they can support themselves." Bloss accused bureau officials in Washington of wanting to keep refugees in a state of idle indigence since this guaranteed the preservation of their government jobs. He concluded with the promise that his future complaints would go to his congressman instead, with instructions to investigate the matter.[83] The Democratic newspaper in Rochester, the *Daily Union*, seized upon the spat in order to both discredit the bureau's employees and denounce the government's role in promoting the import of "cheap labor" that the paper claimed would ultimately be to the detriment of local white workers.[84] Federal politicians and officials may have also provoked ire when they treated Washington's refugee population, as officers in the Union Army had done, as their own private hiring pool. Francis Elias Spinner, the secretary of the treasury, for example, wrote on behalf of a family friend in 1870 to request a black female servant who he claimed "will have a good home, if you let her have the 'pikininny.' "[85]

In the end, public opposition, funding shortages, and flaws with how the bureau's assisted migration program was structured proved too much to overcome. In October 1867, by order of C. H. Howard, the bureau ended its transportation and placement program for unemployed refugees. For an additional year, northern employers could pay for transportation costs if they wished to receive refugee laborers, before this too was stopped. Historian Robert Harrison tabulates that between July 1865 and September 1868, 7,629 freed persons were sent to work outside the District, which was roughly a quarter of Washington's total refugee population. Agents placed 2,673 refugees in jobs south of the Mason-Dixon Line. A majority of the contracted refugee workers sent to the North were agriculture field hands and domestic workers employed by white households. In his October 1867 circular announcing the termination of the bureau's job transportation program, Howard claimed that the city's problem with "surplus labor" had been sufficiently alleviated.[86] Those in the know realized that this was wishful thinking.

## Structure and Sentiment: Josephine Griffing

After being installed as the general agent of the National Freedman's Relief Association for the District of Columbia in 1864, Josephine

Griffing became one of the main agents coordinating freed persons' job placement. During her tenure, she distinguished herself as a conscientious advocate for a realistic approach to when refugees could be expected to become economically self-sufficient, a position that often led to her being criticized as overly sentimental.[87] Born Josephine Sophia White in Hebron, Connecticut, in 1814, and raised by a staunchly Protestant Yankee family, Griffing was active in William Lloyd Garrison's abolitionist movement and, in the decade before the Civil War, worked on behalf of the Western Anti-Slavery Society in Ohio. Like many of her abolitionist peers, Griffing also supported women's rights and temperance. Garrison, in an obituary he penned upon Griffing's death, credited her "heart and brain" as the source of "inspiring thought which gave life and being to the Freedmen's Bureau." This was not just posthumous embellishment. A confidant and friend to Senator Charles Sumner, President Lincoln, and other leading Republicans, Griffing wielded real influence.[88]

Although Griffing was employed by the Freedmen's Bureau for a brief period from July to November 1865, most of her work placing refugees was done on a subcontracted basis, autonomous of direct government oversight. Griffing had been removed from her position with the bureau after other agency officials claimed that during a fund-raising speech she had too transparently detailed the relief crisis in Washington, to the embarrassment of local elites. Despite her dismissal and return to her position as the Washington agent for the National Freedman's Relief Association, the bureau helped to cover the rent on the intelligence office she operated on North Capitol Street, and intermittently paid her and her assistants' salaries.[89] (The bureau maintained its own labor bureau that Griffing also worked with, at the corner of Fourteenth and M streets.)

Griffing, in contrast to many other missionaries who staffed and subcontracted with the Freedmen's Bureau, did not tend to trade in abstract universal claims about what liberal rights should mean to blacks as free persons. She could be unflinching when it came to asserting how welfare had to be calibrated in respect to the social and economic obligations that the federal government owed to the recently emancipated, and in respect to what blacks desired from their freedom. She and her colleague William Henry Channing, the president of the National Freedman's

Relief Association of the District of Columbia, outlined a "plea for humanity" urging patience and context. As the association observed in its *Third Annual Report*, published in 1865:

> It has been suggested in some quarters that measures should be taken to compel their removal, in large bodies, to the several States, where their labor could be made available. Whatever may be the judgment of others, we are decidedly of opinion that the instinct of these freedmen should be respected in this matter, and that the adoption of any coercive means should be discountenanced as a measure of extreme injustice to those whom Providence has emancipated, as well as of tyrannical assumption of authority on the part of all who should attempt to carry it into execution.[90]

Black laborers' consent was not a mere formality to be breached. In an October 1866 letter to C. H. Howard, Griffing—whose daily work entailed meeting with and listening to scores of black refugees—patiently explained to the assistant commissioner why many black women in Washington were hesitant to take domestic jobs in northern cities and towns. Griffing reminded Howard that slavery had been defined by white masters' prerogative to violate blacks' domestic relations and family integrity. She pointed out that the northern climate was unknown and intimidating to black refugees.[91] While Griffing backed the placement of black women in northern domestic service positions to reduce relief expenditures on the Washington refugee population, she did not believe that this strategy should be imposed against their will.

By the early 1870s, Griffing had to contend with emboldened critics of Reconstruction, who, while often praising her personal dedication, questioned whether black refugees in Washington deserved to continue receiving relief and job placement services. Horace Greeley, for instance, despite initially supporting Reconstruction, communicated to Griffing his disillusionment with what he believed was freed blacks' racial inability to seize upon the opportunities that emancipation had allegedly offered them. In a September 1870 letter, Greeley upbraided Griffing for her naïveté, and lectured that blacks were "an easy, worthless race, taking no thought for the morrow." Greeley added that Griffing's best move was to retire from her work, and to publically discourage further black migration to Washington lest she inadvertently strengthen "the argument that slavery is their most natural condition."[92] One must recall that in the 1850s, Greeley had backed the assistance programs of individuals like Vere Foster as effective tools for managing the resettlement and distribution of pauper Irish and native-born white women. In 1870, he did not believe that black refugees were worthy recipients of similarly structured forms of assistance. The northern media also took to portraying black refugees as the unfair beneficiaries of relief, whose lackadaisical work ethic existed in contrast to that of the hardworking, deserving white poor. A correspondent for the *New York World*, a major organ of the Democratic Party, argued that a white resident in Washington had "to put burnt cork on one's face and pass for a darkey" in order to receive benefits.[93] These rumors and rebukes circulated in spite of the fact that the bureau served white refugees from the states of the former Confederacy as well.

By the spring of 1870, Griffing could no longer rely on funding from either Congress or the local District government. On April 22, 1870, she wrote to Lucretia Mott to explain how politicians, including many who formerly bore the mantle of Radical Republicanism, had concluded that the "basis" for "self-support and citizenship" had been sufficiently "furnished" to free blacks. Seeking Mott's assistance, Griffing pointed out that she remained responsible for the daily care of approximately eleven hundred elderly freed persons who were physically unable to work and, unlike whites in similar positions, were deprived of family support networks due to their displacement. On this and other occasions, Griffing invoked the plight of Anna Ferguson and Ann Sanxter, two elderly freedwomen who had labored as slaves at Mt. Vernon with the Washington family and were among the "one hundred and fifty broken-down slaves" who crowded into her office each day. Griffing tried to engender the public's empathy for her work by portraying Ferguson and Sanxter as living links to the nation's founding who had demonstrated their worthiness for relief by having cared for the first president and his family. Griffing angrily described the elderly freed persons who sought help from her as "paupers . . . whom nobody owns." She denounced a society where individuals lived or died based on their ability to sell their labor power on a daily basis; this was language that the white working classes would have appreciated had they been able to look beyond their own racial biases. Mott's response was undoubtedly discouraging to Griffing. Although Mott collected fifty dollars at the New York Women's Suffrage meeting she was attending, she also made it clear that she was done aiding Griffing's cause. Mott claimed that stopping individual and private donations would spur the federal government to renew its commitment to this purpose. She too was willing to lie about impending reality.[94]

\* \* \*

In the year that preceded her death in 1872, Griffing adopted the strategy of referencing the American nativity of the black women whom she was helping find employment. Exposing the complicated regional dynamics of nativist politics in this period, Griffing's assertions that blacks had a greater right to wage-earning opportunities mirrored the sentiments that Irish, European, and native-born working-class white women deployed in western states when trying to encourage middle-class white employers to boycott Chinese household labor. What was different was the racial and national coding marking who was most deserving. As Griffing argued to northern audiences, white middle-class women bore special blame for turning their backs on the plight of freedwomen whom they might hire as servants, since domestic labor shortages showed no sign of abating in the early 1870s. Instead, she lamented, they "call for the Irish and German."[95]

During the Civil War, resistance to the "special" treatment Griffing proposed for blacks had already begun to percolate. In January 1864, members of the House of Representatives' Select Committee on Emancipation issued a minority report that cautioned against the creation of a Freedmen's Bureau vested with too many powers. The power to aid free black laborers in contract negotiations and job selection, the dissenting voices on the committee argued, would invariably lead other groups to demand corresponding agencies to look after their interests. As the report's authors stipulated:

> A proposition to establish a bureau of Irishmen's affairs, a bureau of Dutchmen's affairs, or one for the affairs of those of Caucasian descent generally, who are incapable of properly managing or taking care of their own interests by reason of a neglected or deficient education, would, in the opinion of your committee, be looked upon as the vagary of a diseased brain.[96]

An institution like the Freedmen's Bureau, they claimed, could only harm aspirations for liberal self-governance by drawing attention to the inability of certain groups to realize such aspirations on their own. What these opponents of the Freedmen's Bureau failed to acknowledge was the fact that public assistance, through New York State government appropriations, was already being provided to Irish and "Dutch" (German) immigrants arriving at Castle Garden. As chapter 4 documents in more detail, by 1867 the Irish and German societies at Castle Garden, which had been authorized by New York State to provide services, dispensed various forms of relief and assistance to 44,966 destitute immigrants. These included the provision of meals, money for travel, and job placement services. In contrast to the many controversies that surrounded comparable relief activities supervised by the Freedmen's Bureau, the commissioners' assistance programs were backed by powerful white ethnic elites well embedded in the city's and state's power structures. While middle-class employers in cities like New York attacked Irish and other white immigrants' entitled liberty of contract, they accepted as a matter of commonsense policy that arrivals from Europe were an inevitable and necessary source of labor for the growing nation, and deserved regulation and protection.

## Conclusion: Looking West

By 1870, white employers' comparative exercises, which they used to determine the competencies of different subjects for both labor and citizenship, had shifted in geographic focus. Free labor advocates, whether they identified with the liberalism of middle-class employers or the social democracy and republicanism of workers, fixated on how Chinese immigration would contribute to the development of the American West. They vigorously debated whether or not Chinese subjects—whose right to live and work in the United States had been brokered by the 1868 Burlingame Treaty—deserved to be granted the right to social and legal citizenship as well.[97]

In this transitional moment, black and Irish servants proved to be enduring and national figures in the myriad texts that debated and discussed how Chinese immigration might impact household economies and domestic employment. Margaret Hosmer's short story "Mary

Ann and Chyng Loo: Housekeeping in San Francisco," published by the Philadelphia-based magazine *Lippincott's* in 1870, typifies this point. The story investigates in fictional form a topic that had come to captivate household employers across the country: the engagement of male Chinese immigrants as cooks and servants. Born in Philadelphia in 1830, Hosmer moved to San Francisco with her family shortly after the Gold Rush, before returning east in 1875.[98] Her writings relied on black, Chinese, Irish, and Native American stock characters whose imagined actions provided a body of intra- and intertextual comparisons that highlighted the changing social relations of domestic production.[99]

"Mary Ann and Chyng Loo" is, among other things, a commentary on the perceived failures of Irish immigration and the post–Civil War migrations of freed persons to produce a workforce capable of meeting the demands of middle-class households. It begins with the narrator, a native-born white woman, meeting Mary Ann Mahoney, an Irish immigrant who has been hired to replace her family's recently departed black servant. The unnamed "Ethiopian," as she is labeled, garners only two paragraphs in the story. She has left after deciding that cooking for her employer's frequent guests was an unfair obligation that she had not agreed to when taking the job.[100] Hosmer's portrayal of the black servant's haughtiness, manifest in her unwillingness to take on greater responsibilities, signified the uncertainties that middle-class white households had about whether blacks were reliable free laborers. Whether or not the "Ethiopian" was previously enslaved goes unstated in the story. Regardless, Hosmer's depiction exemplifies the racialized assumptions that white domestic employers had about postwar black workers acclimated to individual liberty: idleness was the freedom they most ardently guarded. This was not the first time that Hosmer questioned the resolve and loyalty of black servants. Her 1868 novel *You-Sing: The Chinaman in California* portrays a dutiful Chinese servant whose heroism saves a white Sacramento family from drowning in the floods that struck the city in 1861. His behavior is juxtaposed against the hysteria of the household's black servant, who is paralyzed with fear by the rising waters.[101]

In Hosmer's fiction, Irish servants epitomize the brazen and unwarranted boldness that white supremacy has granted European immigrant labor. Mary Ann, the new Irish servant, is "gigantic in stature and of great bone and muscle." She is the antithesis of self-control, yet faultless in her own eyes. On her first day, hearing a loud clatter from the kitchen, the narrator assumes she is busy at work, but discovers instead that Mary Ann has broken a number of cups and dishes. When supper is served, the meal arrives burned beyond recognition. Mary Ann blames the "nagur" who preceded her for leaving her a malfunctioning stove. When the narrator confronts Mary Ann about whether the skills and experience she recited applying for the job were in fact embellished, the situation deteriorates further. Enraged by this suggestion, Mary Ann brandishes an "awful iron spoon as a sort of scepter," forcing the narrator to retreat. The narrator tries to reprimand Mary Ann but is forced to flee in "cowardly haste" upstairs, after which a drunken Mary Ann celebrates her triumph with "peals of crazy laughter."[102]

The narrator's entrapment in her own home provides an analogy for the plight of household employers nationally. In both cases, it is Chinese immigrants who offer an opportunity for rescue. When Mary Ann leaves the house the next day, hungover and oblivious to the events of the previous evening, the narrator moves to replace her. Enlisted to help with the search, her cousin pledges to find "a good girl" but returns instead with Chyng Loo, a male Chinese immigrant. The reference to procuring a "girl" is both a linguistic slip and a subtle symbol of the radical changes under way. The narrator admits that Chyng's arrival fills her with thoughts of the "smell of stale oil, opium, and sandal-wood," and a "vision of stewed rats," but she grudgingly agrees to give him a chance. Chyng scours and repairs the kitchen. He prepares the afternoon tea service without breaking a cup or saucer. In cleanliness he is superior to both the black and Irish servants who have preceded him. Although Chyng impresses in all aspects, the narrator notes that the family still "had our prejudices, and the Chinaman's pigtail, whether dangling behind him or wrapped round his clay-colored brow, like a queer coronet, was objectionable to us." Fixating on his body, she further highlights "his blue night-shirt and long finger-nails." She is unable to "repress a shudder when he brought his slits of eyes and cavern of mouth into full play in receiving directions for breakfast" the next morning. When Mary Ann returns and is infuriated to learn that someone even "worse than the nagur" has taken her job, Chyng again springs into action. When Mary Ann again threatens violence with her spoon, it is Chyng who saves the day by throwing it in a pot of boiling soup.[103]

* * *

The reservations that Hosmer's narrator struggles to overcome mirror the doubts that Americans had about the assimilability of the Chinese— even in instances when employers confirmed their value as laborers. As formal Reconstruction came to an end, debates on how to best govern the economic and social integration of Chinese labor became ascendant, with domestic service again at the forefront of political attempts to discern what constituted a group's racially defined utility. When the federal government asserted sovereign authority over immigration in the 1870s and 1880s, it assumed the power to enable or stifle the supply of Chinese workers as a source of servants. This is what the next chapter explores.

3

# Chinese Servants and the American Colonial Imagination

*Domesticity and Opposition to Restriction, 1865–1882*

## Introduction: "No Questions Asked"

Two months after President Chester A. Arthur signed the Chinese Restriction Act into law on May 6, 1882, a cartoon titled "The Servant Question" appeared in the San Francisco–based political humor magazine the *Wasp*. Set in the kitchen of a middle-class home, the cartoon shows a woman and her two children besieged by an aggressive and seemingly infinite parade of job candidates, who come streaming out of an employment office and into the dwelling. (The cartoon appears as Figure 4 in the insert to this book.)

In the image, the boundaries between commerce and the private space of the home collapse so as to be nonexistent. Although employers in cities like Boston and New York constantly lamented what they considered to be their own problems with labor shortages that emboldened white servants to demand wages incommensurate to their experience, in San Francisco, far removed from the point of arrival for European immigrants, the issue was exacerbated.

"The Servant Question" assigned a familiar Irish cast to the problem of obstreperous white servants, and implied that with Chinese immigration restricted, the difficulties that these laborers posed would only grow. The broad faces and pug noses borne by the job applicants mark them as Irish, in contrast to the aquiline facial features of the woman evaluating them for hire. The text in the lower left-hand corner of the cartoon, which is presented in a solecistic written version of the Irish dialect, is titled "The Shorter Catechism," an allusion to Irish immigrants' Catholicism. Rather than respectfully submitting their qualifications, the applicants initiate a ruthless interrogation designed to vet the household's personal, political, and economic standing. Nothing is off-limits. The cartoon's fictional employer must divulge her husband's work schedule, the hours he keeps, and whether the couple will be having more children. She is asked if she will be hiring additional servants to further divide the labor. To readers' likely amusement, "The Servant Question" also alludes to some of the more idiosyncratic demands that Irish servants were accused of making. As the "catechism" ponders, could a married servant's husband use the kitchen to nap during the daytime? Would it be acceptable if a servant's sister's pig rutted and foraged in the garden on Sunday? Would the employer prepare breakfast for her servant on the days when the latter attended confession?

Its humorous intent notwithstanding, the more serious message that the "catechism" conveyed was that market dynamics forced employers to contemplate family planning, alter their schedules, and welcome suspect, working-class Irish Catholic practices into their homes. The emphasis is that in a labor market where supply failed to satisfy demand, Irish servants quickly became unchecked rulers. In the background of the cartoon, servants are portrayed reading on the job, attending Mass in extravagant outfits, entertaining male guests with the household's food and alcohol, and snoozing while a Chinese launderer busily works. Empathy toward servants who lacked their own homes to socialize and relax in is nowhere to be found in the picture.

White employers lent rhetorical support to proposals to restrict the entry of Chinese laborers. In practice, however, they passionately defended their freedom to hire and contract with whomever they chose, regardless of race. They blamed Irish servants for a cynical form of anti-Chinese activism that employers claimed was intended to help Irish women further monopolize the domestic labor market. As the *Wasp* explained in satiric fashion, "at first the cry [for Chinese exclusion] came from the Irish servant-maid who found in John a rival who prevented her from insolently bouncing her mistress." While the *Wasp* qualified that supporters of restriction had come to also include the "intelligent middle class" that did not "desire to see a landed aristocracy and a pauper peasantry spring up in this country," its argument was representative of the middle-class critique of the all-or-none approach to Chinese labor that characterized exclusionist politics.[1] In November 1877, the *San Francisco Commercial Herald* claimed that the anti-Chinese movement had originated with a "servant girl faction." In case the newspaper's readership felt guilty about employing Chinese men over white women, the editorial reminded them that prior to Chinese immigrants' entry into the labor market for domestic service, many Californians had been forced to put off marriage, since profiteering Irish servants had charged so much in wages that it was impossible for families to hire domestics.[2] Commentators also blamed white servants and the Irish in particular for making Chinese labor seem desirable in the first place. Chinese immigrants embraced this critique as well, and in some cases tried to redirect nativist sentiment toward the Irish. In 1878, the *Argonaut* published a poem composed by Sing Lee, a secretary for a Chinese wholesaler, which mocked Irish servants' impertinence before concluding: "if they don't behave themselves—'the Irishman must go!' "[3]

In California, the cartoon insinuates, the problems that defined the "servant question" were especially vexing since a solution haunted the question. In the cartoon, a male Chinese immigrant hovers, as an apparition, over the chaos. He is framed by the accompanying text: "no questions asked." The phrase references the automatic servility and willingness to subordinate their own interests that white employers assigned to Chinese servants as innate traits. As Frederick Bee, the outspoken white attorney for the Chinese Six Companies proclaimed, Chinese servants "were the balance wheel which protects the mistress and housewife from imposition, and relieves her of the idea that servant and mistress are on an equality. He holds the balance of power against Bridget."[4]

Chinese servants did, in fact, ask plenty of questions about the situations available to them. They negotiated for better pay and working conditions, and time off. After the 1882 Restriction Act, Chinese servants and cooks had even greater agency in the workplace, a consequence of labor shortages that federal legislation helped create. Writing in the *Californian* in 1892, as Congress debated renewing the initial act, John Bonner attacked the persistent myths of "coolieism" and "cheap labor" that restrictionists continued to expound. "Though the Chinese are supposed to live upon rice," Bonner noted, "Chinese servants in San Francisco expect hot meat twice a day, and have a pretty taste in pork chops and wings of duck."[5] If Chinese servants had ever been the passive recipients of their employers' orders, this was certainly no longer the case.

\* \* \*

Household labor consumption raised complicated questions about what the United States might gain by conditionally embracing Chinese immigration. Unlike other configurations of global and imperial free trade, such as access to export markets, which white residents, regardless of class, championed as integral to California's growth, there was no consensus about the benefits of a Pacific trade in human labor.[6] When Henry George warned members of Congress in 1876 that Chinese immigration would transform California's demography and local social relations of production until the state was like British India, "where the few white men who are there ride in palanquins, and are waited on by dozens of servants," he was invoking a principle of white settler colonialism that resonated around the white Pacific, from Sydney to Vancouver. "White man's countries" shared policy expertise as well as cultural and racial affinities, and were linked by the collective goal of shoring up Anglophone Pacific settler societies against an influx of Asian migrants and the perceived perils of multiracial democracy.[7]

White, middle-class households, however, advanced a different perspective. In their opinion, Chinese servants represented the physical embodiment of the new possibilities that globally integrated labor markets could allow, and, as figures in commercial exchanges, were animate symbols of the United States' newfound imperial access to Asian labor markets. Exclusionary policies designed to guard against Asian migration and settlement ignored dependencies on Chinese labor that supported Pacific territories and states' service economies. In the United States between 1870 and 1910, the number of workers performing service jobs quintupled, a growth rate that was more than double that of industrial occupations.[8] Household consumption of services was fundamental to the articulation of bourgeois domesticity after the Civil War, and a lasting dearth of service workers—defenders of Chinese immigration argued—could have drastic ramifications on the development of the American West.

White employers hoped that politicians, locally and nationally, would have the fortitude to resist anti-Chinese politics that they deemed shortsighted and harmful to the economy. The loss of additional Chinese immigrant labor was no small inconvenience. In testimony before the U.S. Congress's Joint Special Committee to Investigate Chinese Immigration in the fall of 1876, witnesses and officials estimated that seven thousand Chinese servants, almost exclusively men, worked for white households in California. A minimum of three thousand Chinese domestic laborers were employed in San Francisco alone. The 1880 census tallied San Francisco's population at 233,959, with 21,745 residents enumerated as members of the Chinese race (this figure does not distinguish between Chinese immigrants and American-born Chinese residents), meaning that roughly 15 percent of all Chinese residents in San Francisco worked in domestic service. These estimates may have been low. An author in *Scribner's Monthly* speculated in 1876 that the number of Chinese immigrants employed as domestics statewide was closer to fourteen thousand, while one witness at the congressional hearings placed the number of Chinese servants in San Francisco at five to six thousand, based on what he stated was a more accurate sampling.[9] When domestic service is grouped with other forms of paid work directed at enabling households' social reproduction, and expanded to include occupations such as laundry work and gardening, Chinese immigrants' importance becomes even more evident.[10] The depth of Chinese immigrants' contributions to the service economy was revealed in 1886, when the Trades and Labor Council of Los Angeles and the Knights of Labor circulated a list of white establishments that subcontracted Chinese labor to be boycotted alongside Chinese-owned businesses. The list included white-owned hotels that sent out guests' clothes to Chinese laundries, realty offices that used Chinese janitors, and restaurants that purchased produce cultivated and vended by Chinese "vegetable men."[11]

How Chinese immigrants fit into existing dichotomies of free versus unfree labor, and how they might also remake these categories in the post–Civil War period, elicited widespread discussion. Capitalism, as it transitioned away from slavery, was especially reliant on what English professor and social theorist Lisa Lowe calls the "plasticity" of the "coolie" figure. Historian Moon-Ho Jung has argued in similar terms: "Coolies were never a people or a legal category. Rather, coolies were a conglomeration of racial imaginings that emerged worldwide in the era of slave emancipation, a product of the imaginers rather than the imagined."[12] In the colonial fantasies of household employers, Chinese servants consented to their employment without the qualifications, negotiations, and abuses of contract that made Irish and white domestics volatile and unreliable economic actors. Chinese servants purportedly submitted to certain types of exploitation naturally, yet in ways that were fully compatible with the strictures of free labor.

The social constructions of race and gender that white employers invoked allowed them to imagine their Chinese servants as machines who were not preoccupied with humanistic concerns. At the same time, and more realistically, a number of employers did acknowledge that the relegation of Chinese immigrants to domestic labor had little to do with biology or culture, but was instead the result of discrimination. Chinese immigrants' permanent alien status, bachelorhood, and confinement in certain occupations compelled their servitude by making it the structural basis of their inclusion as a designated class of service workers.

This chapter recovers, where possible, the more material and empirical record of how Chinese domestic labor was brokered, employed, and compensated. In contrast to existing social histories examining Irish and black servants, this is for the most part uncharted scholarly terrain. Chinese servants' liberty of contract was constrained—but typically no more or less than that of other domestic wage workers. Like all servants, Chinese domestics used intelligence offices and mutual and familial networks to market their labor. Europeans were more likely than the Chinese to rely on family members' remittances to finance their emigration, reflecting their longer and better established settlement in North America. But many white immigrants were reliant on commercial credit as well. The need to walk through these somewhat prosaic realities underscores the deeply seated racial prejudices that denied the very possibility of free Chinese labor. This conceptualization has permeated the historiography on Chinese immigration and labor as well.[13]

Opportunities to broker Chinese labor migrations made a regional issue a national economic concern. With the transcontinental railroad's completion in 1869 and anti-Chinese sentiment on the West Coast gaining ground, domestic employers in cities like New York shifted their focus away from black refugees and began speculating instead on California as the geographic source of labor that would allow them to replace "Biddy." Emboldened by what they believed was their right to access and utilize the global labor market, middle-class American employers celebrated the railroad's completion—not only as the foremost marker of whites' conquest of the continent but as the "laying down of a service-pipe to an immense reservoir brimming over with labor." "To thousands of people in this country, Irish labor makes housekeeping a prolonged misery," noted a New York employer in *Putnam's Magazine*. "If the

Chinese shall come to compete with it here, as we are promised that they will, we, for one, hold out hands of cordial welcome to them." Irish dominance of the kitchen, another author claimed, had "done more to hinder our social growth than all other causes combined."[14]

While scholars have called attention to Protestant missionaries' vocal stance protesting restrictive immigration legislation and their arguments that exclusionist policies would irreparably damage their stature and efforts in China, the cultural and social histories of servants' unique contributions to these arguments have gone largely unexplored in these mainly diplomatic and political accounts.[15] Whether stationed in China or the United States, missionary employers framed their liberty to hire the servants of their choosing as a social relation of production that produced value in ways that far exceeded the immediate wages and received services that constituted the superficial currency of the exchange. After the Civil War, Protestant missionaries embraced an ideology of Christian universalism that was liberal in its outlook, and saw religious devotion and the performance of faith—rather than race—as the benchmarks that defined an individual. In this respect, they departed from white contemporaries who considered race to be the grounds for immutable biological and cultural difference.[16] Missionaries' universalism, however, was not so radical as to call for the elimination of racial divisions of labor. In practical terms, missionary schools and other church settings were spaces where market integration began for young Chinese men. Protestant hymns and homilies doubled as lessons on how servants were to interact with their employers as masters, and ministers functioned as brokers with access to middle-class networks for job placement.

Chinese immigrants were reliant on strategic allegiances with employers to win protections that they could not gain through the exercise of suffrage or from the rights that were afforded to citizens. In this respect, the colonial relations that Chinese immigrants were embedded in created specific forms of governance *and* specific forms of agency.

Finally, among an important subset of white employers and allied interests, the immediate reaction to Chinese restriction was to begin exploring the possibility of guest visas and special entry permits as state policies that could control Chinese labor while also finding spaces for its inclusion. By the end of the nineteenth century, employers, chambers of commerce, and middle-class commentators could all be found calling for incipient forms of what would evolve into the system of labor visas and guestworker programs still in use today. They targeted Chinese servants as a special class of migrants whose entry would be conditional on their contract to certain occupations, yet detached from the right to permanent settlement. In 1890, Judge Lorenzo Sawyer from the federal Ninth Circuit Court of Appeals bemoaned the demographic "misfortune" of slavery and emancipation, which had resulted in a population of free black Americans who he claimed were undeserving of citizenship yet impossible to remove. According to Sawyer, Chinese immigration could be governed in such a way that "we would never have more than we can make useful." Chinese immigration "lifts a very large class to a position superior to what they would otherwise be able to attain," he added, "and so long as the Chinese don't come here to stop, their labor is highly beneficial to the whole community."[17] Though still some years off in terms of their realization, these early conceptualizations of guestworker programs demonstrate how Chinese exclusion conveyed a lesson to policymakers about the problems that unqualified restrictions on labor could cause when the pursuit of white supremacy trumped all considerations of consumer demand.[18]

## Producing a Chinese Servant Class

White employers imagined that Chinese immigrants to California had an innate, racial disposition to servility. This assumption overlooked how these laborers were actively shunted into areas of the economy where service work predominated. Chinese laborers were driven from occupations that white men claimed as their racial and gender birthright.[19] Opposition to male Chinese servants emerged more gradually and only when the economic depression of the late 1870s made white women's wages more essential both in California and across the country.

The praise that American commentators heaped on Chinese servants alluded to the ingrained and inherited aptitude that the Chinese had for deferring to social superiors. These accounts misinterpreted the relegation of Chinese men to service jobs as a natural rather than political division of labor. White employers rarely considered what drove Chinese emigration to begin with. Restrictionists viewed Chinese immigration as involuntary, and attributed the movement of labor to transpacific traffickers' pursuit of profit. In actuality, Chinese laborers' emigration had origins in an array of factors. The Siyi or Sanyi (Sze Yup and Sam Yup) counties of the Guangdong province, the sources for nearly all of the Chinese migrants who arrived in North America during the nineteenth century, were coastal areas involved in the global market economy as early as the sixteenth century. Even before the 1842 Treaty of Nanking at the end of the First Opium War forced China to establish free trade ports, the Qing state had already designated Guangzhou (Canton) for this purpose. A large number of residents in the surrounding countryside produced commodities such as silk, sugar cane, tobacco, and hemp for international markets as well as for interregional trade and, compared to residents in other parts of China, were far more likely to import foodstuffs rather than engage in subsistence farming. As a result, the region was susceptible to global fluctuations in the prices of commodities. After 1842, the establishment of the British colony in nearby Hong Kong, which was not subject to Qing restrictions on emigration, made departure from Guangdong more feasible. The majority of emigrants relied on lenders to finance their transpacific passages, which cost between forty and fifty dollars. Lenders came from a range of backgrounds; ship captains, Chinese merchants, labor brokers working for mining companies and later railroad companies, as well as native-place mutual associations (*huiguans*) were all involved in this business. While a small number of early male Chinese migrants to California were indentured to specific employers, most arrived indebted to a creditor but without formal contractual obligations.[20] Although Congress passed an 1862 "Anti-Coolie Law" barring American citizens and vessels from participating in the transportation of Chinese migrants "held to service or labor" as "coolies," in the decade prior some Californians expressed concern that the main problem was not an influx of unfree labor, but rather the opposite: Chinese laborers had too much liberty. In 1852, for instance, a California state senator introduced legislation that would have criminalized Chinese migrants' breach of contracts.[21]

Like all migrant groups arriving in California during the early years of the Gold Rush, the Chinese were caught up in the pandemonium that accompanied the opportunity to strike it rich and escape wage dependency altogether. Accordingly, employers found it difficult to procure servants of any background. Thomas O. Larkin, the U.S. consul to Mexico, described in a June 1848 letter to Secretary of State James Buchanan how a Chinese merchant newly arrived in San Francisco was immediately abandoned by the servants he had brought with him, who absconded to the Sierra Nevada foothills to search for gold. Joseph Folsom, the first collector of the Port of San Francisco, observed that he "could not employ a good bodyservant for the full amount of my salary as a government officer" and was only getting by due to an "Indian boy" he kept in bondage.[22]

Lo Chum Qui, who had learned English from a missionary in China, wrote to the *Alta California* in June 1853 to mock an editorial that the paper had published, complaining that Chinese immigrants had "entirely

Figure 3.1. Cham (Amédée Charles Henri de Noe), "Actualités. Arrivée d'une famille en Californie." Robert B. Honeyman, Jr. Collection of Early Californian and Western American Pictorial Material, BANC PIC 1963.002:0001–1886, Bancroft Library, University of California, Berkeley. A French cartoon comments on a common California Gold Rush–era scenario. Upon arriving in the state, a middle-class family is "abandoned" by servants no longer willing to work for wages, and who seek their own fortune instead.

failed to answer the ardent expectation of becoming domestics." As Lo quipped in response, it was "a pity" that the Chinese were "not of a pliant nature enough to become household slaves." Continuing the dialogue, the *Alta's* editor stipulated that Lo and his countrymen were "too 'democratic' by half"—an assessment at odds with the racial stereotyping of Chinese labor that prevailed during the years when restriction began to be actively debated.[23] California experienced acute shortages of servants in the late 1850s, which meant that domestics in the state earned twenty-five to thirty dollars per month compared to the six to ten dollars per month that servants in New York made on average. Shortages in the domestic labor supply allowed servants to engage in collective bargaining actions that were novel and threatening to employers. In 1859, the *Sacramento Daily Union* reported that "boarding houses have been opened in San Francisco where domestics who are out of work and money are boarded by the joint contributions of those who have places." The paper attributed the collective endeavor to an organizing campaign by Catholic priests, which "would be a pious and humane arrangement, if the object was not, unfortunately, to prevent indigent persons from accepting service at lower than the market rate of labor." To counter the servants' collective action, the newspaper proposed that mistresses form their own union of employers and initiate a hiring freeze.[24]

Chinese immigrants were no less susceptible to the consolidation of capital in the American West that displaced independent producers of all backgrounds. But they also had to contend with overt hostility and the violent seizure of their property by white workers. In the Sierra Nevada, some Chinese miners were able to establish collective enterprises that they financed by pooling their resources. Others mined as wage laborers.[25] Chinese immigrants turned to laundry work and cooking food in mining camps only after they were driven from claims at knife- and gunpoint. As historian Susan Johnson has documented, white miners begrudgingly accepted in camps Chinese men who were willing to take on service work, whereas they remained opposed to their presence in the gold fields.[26]

In the other major area of the California economy employing Chinese immigrants, the completion of the first transcontinental railroad in May 1869 left thousands of workers—at least those who did not return to China—unemployed.[27] Railroad managers primed the way for the absorption of their former workers into urban service economies by frequently referencing the tractable nature of Chinese labor relative to white workers accused of being troublemakers. This meant engaging in a type of collective amnesia that ignored Chinese workers' participation in work stoppages and, in June 1867, a massive walk-off that ended only when railroad boss Charles Crocker threatened to leave them stranded without food or supplies in the middle of the High Sierra.[28] A. W. Loomis, a Presbyterian missionary, opined that Chinese immigrants working on the railroad, unlike the Irish, had not acquired "a taste for whisky, they have few fights, and no 'Blue Mondays.'" Writing in 1869, Loomis predicted that the Chinese laborers without work after the completion of the railroad would be welcomed as servants back in San Francisco.[29]

Congressional passage of the 1870 Naturalization Act barred Chinese immigrants from obtaining legal citizenship and meant that the ballot—the vehicle that European immigrant men had used to help win political favor and commensurate opportunities for social mobility—would not be available to them.[30] Even before the question of Asian naturalization was resolved by the passage of the 1870 statute, public figures like Agoston Haraszthy, the Hungarian-born viniculturist, lectured on the unique resource that residents of California had in Chinese laborers barred from advancing their interests through civil rights. Chinese immigrants, he proclaimed, "will at all times make us good servants, and as the law excludes them from citizenship, no matter how many come they can have no dangerous influence on our domestic institutions."[31] Free labor, at least when it was understood as representing nothing more than the right to consent to work and to earn wages, was perfectly compatible with structural discrimination.

In San Francisco, brokers of Chinese domestic labor were subject to the perception that they trafficked in unfree labor, even though intelligence offices in the city were no more or less transparent than commercial agencies responsible for placing white women. Chinese intelligence offices, as they were specifically designated, were a visible and enduring feature of the San Francisco landscape and by no means part of an underground economy—even if they were portrayed as such. Middle-class publications regularly alluded to scenarios where Chinese servants magically appeared for hire at their employers' homes, after being procured through shadowy networks inscrutable to white observers. Fanny

Stevenson, wife of the Scottish author, spun a tale about how her first Chinese cook was delivered to her home by a Wells Fargo agent, who "lifted a small mummy swathed in blue cotton from the wagon and stood him upright against the wall," as if he was no more human than any other package.[32] Orientalist portrayals of mysterious labor networks notwithstanding, offices that specialized in Chinese domestic labor were run by both Chinese and white proprietors and openly advertised their services in the city's directories.[33]

Even when Chinese domestic laborers demonstrated their independence by leaving jobs or refusing to work in certain situations, their agency was still subject to racialized interpretations by whites. Like domestic workers from all backgrounds, Chinese cooks and servants exchanged information on working conditions and employers' temperaments. According to various accounts, they did this by hiding inconspicuous notes or wood carvings in spaces that their employers were not likely to frequent. An article in the *Boston Daily Advertiser* described this method as a "secret society way" of communicating, while a piece in the *San Francisco Evening Bulletin* claimed that this system was representative of innate Chinese "shrewdness." The *Bulletin* article portrayed Chinese servants as both individually selfish and clannish at the same time. The author alleged that she had discovered a message from a former Chinese servant, which read: "Man in this house kill Chinaboy and bury him in the backyard!" The note, she claimed, had allowed him to take a vacation and reclaim his job, since his potential replacements had refused the position in horror. The *Bulletin*'s author explained that Chinese servants avenged "unprincipled employers" who withheld pay by blacklisting them, which she somehow found "treacherous." The author was also shocked to learn that Chinese-run intelligence offices earned multiple commission fees on placements involving the same individuals, and conspired with servants by having them leave situations shortly after being hired. Her revulsion belied the fact that white servants using intelligence offices were repeatedly accused of engaging in the exact same tactic. Less biased sources than the *Bulletin*, which was a strong backer of restriction, offered different accounts. An 1869 article in the *Atlantic Monthly*, for instance, praised employment agencies run by the "Chinese Companies" (a reference to the Chinese Consolidated Benevolent Association in San Francisco) for guaranteeing the servants they furnished for up to one year. Comparable to agents at high-end intelligence offices in New York and Boston, Chinese agents sent out replacement servants, free of any additional charge, when previous employees did not work out.[34]

Because Chinese immigrants' position in the American economy was especially precarious, they were more likely to rely on brokerage networks that, at least on the surface, eschewed commercial motives. In particular, they forged relationships with white Christians who imagined that Chinese servants would benefit from exposure to the values that middle-class domesticity embodied. Chinese servants entered into work situations that appeared to sustain a version of the master and servant relations that white Americans increasingly derided as antithetical to modern methods of labor management. Missionary employers misinterpreted Chinese laborers' continued involvement in domestic service as evidence of their enduring devotion and a commitment to their own uplift, which set them apart from other classes of laborers who approached household work as an uninspiring, menial job.

From another angle, one can also comprehend how Chinese servants used Christianity to counterbalance discriminatory labor markets. Huie Kin, who in 1885 became minister of the First Chinese Presbyterian Church in New York, provides in his autobiography a rare account of domestic service from the perspective of the Chinese worker. At the suggestion of James Eells, a transplant from the East who was pastor at the First Presbyterian Church in Oakland, Huie agreed to be baptized. When Eells took a position as professor at the Lane Theological Seminary in Cincinnati, he invited Huie to join him as a student there, which he did in 1880. In 1889, Huie Kin married Louise Van Arnam, a white woman from a prominent Troy, New York, family whom he met while doing missionary work.

Huie's later work as a pastor and missionary allowed him to cross racial and class boundaries to a much greater extent than many Chinese immigrants, and undoubtedly shaped his recollections.[35] Nonetheless, his narrative complicates the one-sided and biased accounts of white employers. Huie arrived in San Francisco in 1868, chaperoned by a representative from his village's mutual aid association, and stayed there until relatives from Oakland picked him up after paying off the cost of his passage. In all likelihood Huie, only fourteen at the time of his arrival, found work through family connections or other word-of-mouth networks, and was steered to domestic work due to his age. His first job was in a position providing "general help" and earned him $1.50 a week in wages with room and board—an entry-level pay rate. In his autobiography, Huie provides a vivid description of the homesickness caused by the "ubiquitous apple sauces" he had to eat while working in white homes. Chinese servants and cooks did not determine what meals to prepare, and most white households automatically opposed ingredients or meals that they associated with Chinese cuisine.[36] After working in a number of domestic positions in Oakland, in 1874 Huie took a job with the Gardiner family. The Gardiners were wealthy enough to employ multiple servants, and Huie and the family's cook, an older white woman, bore mutual antagonism toward each other. Huie learned that the best way to avoid conflict was to leave her "alone in her own domain of influence." Mr. Gardiner served as an elder in the Presbyterian Church, and his daughter-in-law taught Huie to read and write in English. Initially, Huie attended Sunday schools not only at the First Presbyterian Church in Oakland but at the Broadway Congregational Church and a local Baptist church as well.

For Huie and his classmates, "our motive, at least the conscious one, was not religion, but language."[37] This was a common arrangement. The Presbyterian missionary Ira Condit published an *English and Chinese Reader* that specifically included lessons for Chinese immigrants working as servants, so as to provide a practical backdrop to their language training. For example, lesson 42 translated and phonetically sounded out the phrases "Can you wash and iron?," "How man-y per-sons are in your fam-i-ly?," and "How man-y meals do you take each day?," while lesson 43 included "Sweep the floor clean" and "Wash the win-dows."[38]

English-Chinese language phrasebooks circulated in California as early as 1867, and were distributed at rail stations and other transport hubs where Chinese migrants might acquire them. Later texts in this genre would be published in New York and other eastern cities, and were marketed to white employers rather than Chinese laborers. The change in intended audience reflected ongoing household labor scarcities and the perception that Chinese servants were luxuries to whom employers had to actively adapt.[39]

The ability to speak, read, and write basic English also allowed Chinese servants to bargain for higher wages, to guard against deceptive

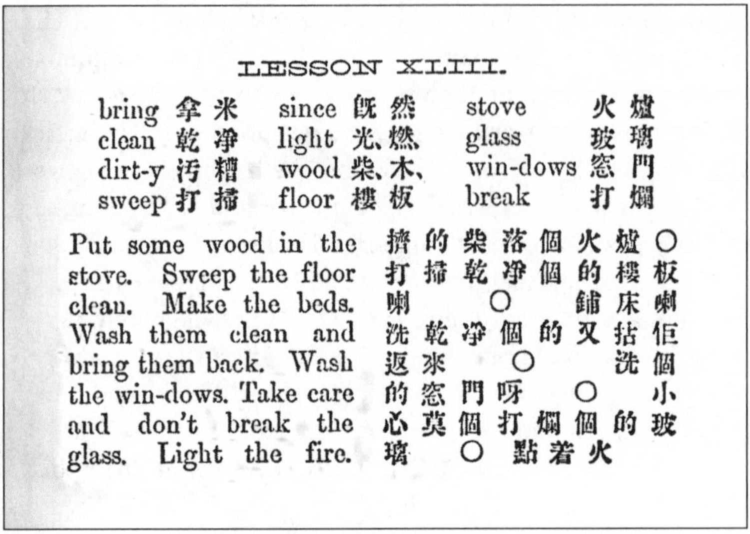

LESSON XLIII.

| bring 拿 米 | since 既 然 | stove | 火 爐 |
| clean 乾 净 | light 光、燃、 | glass | 玻 璃 |
| dirt-y 污 糟 | wood 柴、木、 | win-dows | 窓 門 |
| sweep 打 掃 | floor 樓 板 | break | 打 爛 |

Put some wood in the stove. Sweep the floor clean. Make the beds. Wash them clean and bring them back. Wash the win-dows. Take care and don't break the glass. Light the fire.

擠 的 柴 落 個 火 爐 O
打 掃 乾 净 個 的 樓 板
喇 O 鋪 床 喇
洗 乾 净 個 的 又 拈 佢
返 來 O 洗 個
的 窓 門 呀 O 小
心 莫 個 打 爛 個 的 玻
璃 O 點 着 火

Figure 3.2. Lesson 43 in Ira Condit's *English and Chinese Reader, with a Dictionary* (New York: American Tract Society, 1882).

job offers, and to more easily navigate labor markets where postings for situations appeared in newspapers or other printed sources. Most of the Chinese servants working in and around San Francisco who were interrogated by immigration inspectors after 1882 described attending English-language classes at various mission schools, at the age when they were preparing to enter the wage labor market. For example, the brothers Wong Mun Yuck and Wong Mun Dun both attended the English School at the Congregational Mission in San Francisco from the age of twelve to fifteen (while also attending the Wong Gar Mon Chinese School), until they left to work as cooks in private residences.[40]

The pews of missionary churches doubled as hiring halls, and it was common for Sunday school teachers and other church officials to recommend students for domestic work in private homes. J. M. Oviatt, pastor of the Presbyterian Church in San Leandro, California, testified in 1876 that all of his twenty Chinese Sunday school students earned wages as house servants.[41] Religious affiliation also provided Chinese servants with de facto character references. Servants procured through religious networks offered a symbolic check on the dangers associated with "heathen" Chinese labor. There were Chinese servants—like Huie—who came to identify and worship as Christians as a matter of personal faith. "Ah" Quin, for instance, worked for an Alaskan mining company as a cook in 1878. Despite having to wake at four thirty in the morning in order to complete all the tasks assigned to him, he still found time between his labors to translate hymns and read Bible verses.[42]

## "Bred in Servility": Producing and Commodifying Race and Gender

Chinese immigrants' perceived transgressions of gendered labor roles were not a predetermined cause for their exclusion—even though federal lawmakers eventually justified their actions by referring to this alleged aspect of racial difference. Many white employers were enthused about opportunities to capitalize on Chinese queerness. This is not to suggest that male Chinese immigrants collectively identified as queer in either their sexual identities or practices. Rather, the goal is to explore how Chinese workers' contravention of established and gendered labor roles—often because they had no other choice—inspired a political economy bent on exploiting this fluidity.[43] Although historians and other scholars have acknowledged the significance that social constructions of gender had in creating the discursive figure of the Chinese "Other," household employers viewed perceived differences in these areas as qualities that gave Chinese men implicit advantages over white female competitors.

While historian Karen Leong is correct to note that anti-Chinese discourse insisted that "without a home, a 'Chinaman' had no reason to defend the country; without a family, a 'Chinaman' had no reason to invest in the future well-being of the nation; without a wife, a 'Chinaman' was simply barbaric and uncivilized," this framing neglects the plastic and opportunistic agenda of capital.[44] Employers of Chinese servants did not see their "sojourner" status as a dangerous quality. Because Chinese immigrants were marked as nonsettlers, servants were more easily detached from the competing dependencies and bonds that might otherwise demand their loyalties and labor. Unlike single white women who were constantly leaving service to assume unpaid domestic labor as married women in their own homes, a Chinese bachelor—often a misnomer, since many immigrants had wives in China—could be counted on to stay in a situation for a longer period of time.[45] Chinese men did not pose the same liability therefore when it came to time spent hiring and training. Given employers' frequent complaints that white female servants appropriated their fashion, it is unsurprising that Chinese men were celebrated as additions to the household who eliminated this particular concern. As one Californian employer observed, the male Chinese servant would "not outshine his mistress in attire." Domestic advice author Harriet Spofford praised Chinese veterans of railroad work for being "strong enough to carry a weight of four hundred pounds among difficult mountain passes for twenty days together." She added that this was the type of "strength" that mistresses did not have to "be afraid of overworking."[46]

The exploitation of Chinese men was also framed by the 1875 congressional passage of the Page Act, which restricted almost entirely the immigration of Chinese women to the United States. The Page Act required Chinese women to obtain visas from American consular officials stationed in Hong Kong and other ports prior to emigrating. (Officials were also authorized to prohibit the emigration of Chinese men to the United States who they determined were not "free and voluntary" labor.) Consular officials were predisposed to judging all single Chinese women as likely to work in prostitution upon their arrival in the United States. Historian Adam McKeown disputes whether or not the Page Act had any dramatic impact on the gender ratio of Chinese immigrants arriving in the United States, since men were expected to leave China on their own and then return with their earnings. Even if this is accurate, the role that the law played in shaping white Americans' perception of Chinese men as tireless workers unconcerned with family should not be dismissed either.[47] In Henry Grimm's 1879 anti-Chinese immigrant drama *The Chinese Must Go*, for instance, a Chinese servant remarks that white men were "damn fools" for having wives and children who "cost plenty money."[48]

Some commentators claimed that Chinese men's successful employment as servants proved that biologically they belonged to a "third sex," and were devoid of typically masculine sexual desires. "Young ladies who have grown up with Chinese servants in the house all their lives," an author claimed in the Quaker *Friend's Review*, "tell me they never regard 'John' as a man."[49] Arguments of this sort helped white women justify allowing Chinese domestics' access to their bedrooms and other spaces where the presence of men not their husbands was considered indecent. Accusations concerning male Chinese servants' predatory lust, however, also circulated. In an 1876 article in *Scribner's Monthly*, for example, Sarah Henshaw noted, "No matter how good a Chinaman may be, ladies never leave their children with them, especially little girls."[50] As a cartoon from the nativist publication *Thistleton's Jolly Giant* illustrates, Chinese bodies were also depicted as sinister presences in domestic spaces. In "Innocent John," the apparent asexuality of the Chinese servant is a ruse that allows him intimate access to white women's bodies. Contradictory positions on Chinese sexuality coexisted. Chinese men working in domestic service were both modern-day eunuchs, unfit for independent manhood and queerly content to perform women's work, yet also lascivious agents of sexual violence and miscegenation.

In order to explain why Chinese immigrants were specifically suited to domestic labor, employers traded in cultural and racial explanations that took them further away from the structural reasons close at hand. They depicted Chinese workers as mechanical in their efficiency and unimpeachably devoted to saving money for the households that employed them. Chinese servants, Spofford claimed, were,

> people of simple habits, content with simple diet, people with so few wants that small wages answer their purpose, people so bred in servility that they will not fail in respect, people accustomed to scrupulous economy and untiring labor, people of kindly manners and gentle dispositions, people trained, as it has been said, by forty centuries of manual dexterity—people of that description are exactly what it appears to her would fill the aching void in the American kitchen.[51]

Spofford's description of Chinese immigrants' competencies as servants was rooted in her simplistic reading of Chinese history. Lacking a tradition of democracy and self-governance, she argued, the Chinese masses could be expected to remain serfs to whomever employed them, even when granted individual liberties.[52]

In this vein, one of the most frequent explanations used to characterize what made Chinese immigrants superior servants was their talent for imitation. Restrictionists maintained that the rote fashion in which

Figure 3.3. "Innocent John," *Thistleton's Jolly Giant*, November 3, 1877. Courtesy of the San Francisco History Center, San Francisco Public Library.

Chinese laborers performed work made them machines, and, like their inanimate iron counterparts, they were a comparable threat to alienate white laborers from wage-earning jobs.[53] Employers, however, argued that Chinese servants' aptitude for imitation carried special merit in the context of domestic work, where methods of cleaning and washing, not to mention cooking, left ample room for destructive improvisation. Before vacuum cleaners, dishwashers, and other household appliances were heralded as helping to routinize domestic work and wrest these tasks from careless servants, Chinese laborers were touted as purportedly allowing for the same type of standardization. The idea that the Chinese servant was a mirror, who reflected both the positive and negative traits of the individual who instructed him, led to dramatizations of the dangers of contaminating the "good" Chinese through negative influences. In the domestic advice literature of the period, authors advanced the notion that the Chinese servant, like a machine, still needed a thoughtful "operator." A story in *Scribner's Monthly*, for instance, presented a series of disastrous consequences that followed an employer's decision to assign Kitty, the reigning Irish servant in her East Coast home, with the task of training Fing Wing, a Chinese immigrant newly arrived from California. When Fing Wing is caught stealing sugar and tea from his employers, he explains that he has learned this behavior from Kitty's example. The illustration accompanying the article shows

Figure 3.4. "Fing Wing and Kitty."

a similar theme. Fing Wing faithfully follows the lead of Kitty as she carelessly (or perhaps maliciously) lets fall a tray of plates and bowls.[54] Employers were warned that "when you catch this Celestial domestic treasure, be sure that the first culinary operations performed for his instruction are correctly manipulated, for his imitativeness is of a cast-iron rigidity." "Burn your toast or your pudding," the author explained, "and he is apt to regard the accident as the rule."[55] An article in the *New York Post* relayed the story of an employer who was forced to dismiss her Chinese servant because he was too frugal. So closely did he police the amount of butter and bread that the family used after being instructed to do so, they could no longer stomach the shame his continual reprimands inspired.[56]

The Chinese community in the United States contributed to how the Chinese servant's racial identity was constructed, by invoking stereotypes about Chinese industry that aligned with the praises of white employers. It is not surprising that Chinese immigrants, denied allies in the white trade unions, turned to capital for assistance instead. Chinese immigrants singled out white workers and European immigrants in particular, and accused them of being lazy. White workers, they argued, were privileged and protected by their race. Lee Chew, a Chinese cook interviewed by the *Independent* in 1903, stated that, were it not for racial solidarity, "no one would hire an Irishman, German, Englishman or Italian when he could get a Chinese, because our countrymen are so much more honest, industrious, steady, sober and painstaking." In his opinion, "Chinese were persecuted, not for their vices, but for their virtues."[57]

This view was echoed in the middle-class media, which used Chinese men's perceived domestic utility to chastise the idleness of working-class white men depicted as having failed in their duties as heads of household. The August 1, 1881, issue of *Puck* magazine featured a cartoon titled "Why She Married Ching-A-Ling." In it, a Chinese man, "Ching-A-Ling," performs various domestic tasks in the different panels, his queue, robe, and slippers calling attention to his foreign characteristics. He serves tea and cradles an infant in his arm; he launders muslins; he irons while a small boy "plays" by pulling at his hair. As he labors, his white wife is shown profiting from the surplus value that his industry produces: time for leisure. As a caption explains, "She can go out when she likes." Another frame shows her arm in arm with a white suitor, with the caption: "She can be polite to former admirers." Wales's final panel introduces an alternative yet at the same time more conceivable vision for readers to consider. The same woman is shown as haggard, disheveled, and bent over a sewing machine. Her white husband reclines in a chair, sipping a drink. The caption to the final frame, referring back to the imagined union with "Ching-A-Ling," reads: "Better than a lazy American husband—whom she might have to support."

Whatever the cartoonist J. A. Wales felt about the willingness of Chinese men to perform jobs marked as "women's work," his more immediate target was to call out working-class white men as breadwinners. The final frame of the cartoon insinuates that drunkenness, idleness, and the willful exploitation of loved ones plagued men of this class, and doomed their wives to working a second shift on top of their unpaid labor. The woman sews a dress, which it can be assumed has been subcontracted

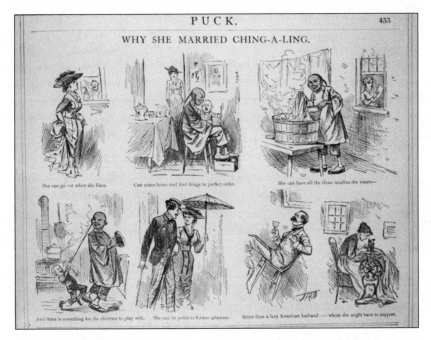

Figure 3.5. J. A. Wales, "Why She Married Ching-A-Ling," *Puck*, August 1, 1881. Courtesy of the Library of Congress.

to her through the putting-out system, her home transformed into a factory.[58] Although Wales was surely aware that his suggestion that white women might prefer Chinese men as husbands could be construed as inflammatory, his argument for interracial relationships is sarcastically conveyed as a matter of convenience rather than desire. The woman uses the relationship merely to preserve a more carefree social life; the children pictured do not have the visual cues of being the products of "miscegenation." Wales's take is quite different from those that could be found in images from the antebellum period, which focused on interracial couplings between Irish immigrant women and Chinese men in New York's Five Points neighborhood, but to highlight local "exoticism."[59] In the *Puck* caricature, Wales is less concerned with taboo and more bent on offering a humorous yet cautionary take on how Chinese men might factor into American households' economy if white men could not prove themselves to be more responsible.

## "John Chinaman to the Rescue"

In the colonial imagination of American employers, the West functioned as a laboratory where the social relations of domestic production were actively being reinvented. From the West, accounts of Chinese domestics and their positive attributes flooded eastward and inspired middle-class employers to dwell even more sharply on the perceived deficiencies of Irish servants. Household employers rapturously imagined future scenarios in which they were no longer reliant on white laborers arriving from across the Atlantic, who were imbued with false conceptions of how republican equality informed the contract of their labor. In contrast to Western commentaries on the "Chinese question," Eastern authors had no reason to try to reconcile their strategies for procuring household labor with support for white settler colonialism, which to them was a regional and narrowly self-interested political project that was intent on promoting California's white workers at the expense of everyone else. They were unapologetic in their pursuit of Chinese servants, and made loyalty and deference the only meaningful criteria in hiring. Eastern authors frequently referred to the Chinese immigrant servant in evolutionary terms, as "the coming man" who would eliminate the stresses that white servants imposed on the free labor system.[60] Spofford, a regular critic of Irish domestic labor, posited that the "resolve" of middle-class women, which had been tested in struggles with Biddy, might finally see its moment of triumph. "If the Irish girl will still give her no rest, and the American girl refuse her succor," Spofford noted in her 1881 book *The Servant Girl Question*, "she will find out some honorable way to bring John Chinaman to her rescue!"[61]

The rescue that Chinese servants purportedly represented, despite the elevation of this theme to a full-fledged consumer fantasy, had only a nominal impact in actual numbers. Like black and Irish servants targeted for assisted migration schemes, Chinese workers were equally reluctant to participate in commercial transactions that reduced them to pure commodities transportable to any community where their labor was demanded. Nor were there financing mechanisms in place to cover the costs of large-scale recruitment of Chinese laborers, since the ability to recover this capital investment—or to raise it in the first place—was limited.

With the abolition of slavery, labor recruitment schemes crisscrossed the nation as employers and brokers looked to generate new supply chains. Outside of the West, initial interest in Chinese labor emanated from the South, where planters were eager to experiment with Chinese immigrants as replacements for emancipated slaves, whom they felt could no longer be relied on to regularly contract to labor. In July 1869, agricultural and commercial interests in Memphis hosted a Chinese Labor Convention headlined by Cornelius Koopmanschap, a Dutch-born, California-based labor broker who bragged about his access to a limitless supply of Chinese workers. In its coverage of the convention, the *New York Herald* stipulated that southerners would soon learn that Chinese immigrants not only excelled in agricultural labor, but could be used to "fill the household duties of cooks, laundrymen and male servants," while the *Philadelphia Press*, inspired by southerners' proactive recruitment efforts, encouraged local intelligence offices to "revolutionize their own business" by importing Chinese servants. In practice, the original Chinese workers contracted to labor on sugar plantations in Louisiana and other southern states were not the idealized supply that white planters envisioned. They routinely left jobs or refused to work when they felt that the terms of their contract had been violated.[62]

Shortly after the Memphis Convention, a select number of manufacturers in northern states embarked on their own initiatives to import Chinese labor. When shoemakers belonging to the Order of the Knights of St. Crispin organized a strike in North Adams, Massachusetts, in June 1870, Calvin Sampson, the factory's owner, contracted Chinese immigrants from the West Coast to replace them. Although Sampson had no compunctions about using Chinese laborers as replacements for the striking French Canadian Crispins, he was adamant in the interviews he gave to local and national newspapers that the Chinese workers who had migrated to Massachusetts did so voluntarily. In fact, due to the unique circumstances of their arrival, and fears that they would be assaulted and boycotted by the local population, the contract that Sampson entered into with the Chinese workers included provisions for lodging, firewood, and water, and required the manufacturer to pay the cost of their transcontinental rail fares and return trips if demand for their labor slackened.[63] In 1871, Chinese labor brokers in San Francisco entered into an arrangement with the Passaic Steam Laundry Company in Belleville, New Jersey, and by July of that year had supplied the plant with 175 Chinese workers. Again, these efforts generated an angry backlash from white laborers, who accused industrialists of seeking to drive them out of jobs through the use of "coolies." While the New York Tribune praised the scheme for its ostensible role in pressuring "Bridget and Mary Ann" to work harder, its coverage suggested that the Chinese laborers contracted from California lacked individual freedom and answered to a Chinese foreman who commanded them as slaves. Responding to these depictions, James Hervey, the plant's owner, felt obligated to state that he was "forced to resort to Chinese labor by no 'strike' or disaffection on the part of his former hands." His main motivation, he claimed, was the high turnover caused by white women leaving to get married.[64]

Eastern labor brokers imagined that meeting household demand for Chinese servants could also be profitable. In the fall of 1870, shortly after Chinese laborers arrived in North Adams, Julius Palmer opened an intelligence office at 11 Pemberton Square in Boston. Palmer had originally launched the bureau to supply Chinese "workmen in colonies" to area manufacturers, but "was so beset with applications for Chinese servants" that he changed his plans. He charged ninety dollars gold to bring a Chinese servant from San Francisco to the city, although that price decreased if multiple workers were transported together. On top of upfront costs, employers in Boston could expect to pay English-speaking Chinese servants eighteen to twenty dollars per month in wages, while non-English-speaking Chinese servants could be had for ten to twelve dollars per month. This latter figure was less than the average wages paid to an Irish servant, the *Christian Union* pointed out. Chinese servants' wages would decrease further if more Chinese came to the East Coast from California, Palmer promised, and there was greater competition. The article in the *Christian Union* concluded that the superior work ethic of Chinese servants made the investment in the cost of their transportation worthwhile. There was no discussion as to whether or not employers could try to recoup the cost of transportation through withheld wages—or whether Chinese workers would accept these deductions or the going wage rates that intermediaries promised.[65]

Palmer's bureau ultimately failed. Although he seems to have been able to generate some interest from prospective Boston-area employers, it was insufficient to justify the expense of the venture. The willingness of Chinese servants to migrate also proved to be a problem. "Ah" Young, the Chinese labor broker in San Francisco with whom Palmer had intended to partner, explained that most Chinese laborers had an "aversion . . . to going so far, under the difficulties they would encounter." Difficulties here could mean any number of things: social isolation, discrimination, or employers who might hold them in debt bondage. The *Advertiser* stipulated that New England households would have to wait until the factory in North Adams no longer needed its Chinese labor force or until a large hotel contracted Chinese servants who could subsequently be lured away.[66]

By and large, relatively few Chinese servants ended up in cities such as Boston, New York, and Philadelphia during the nineteenth century, and Chinese domestic laborers remained concentrated in the West. Writing in 1875, Francis A. Walker, the superintendent of the 1870 census, acknowledged in *Scribner's Monthly* that the "great domestic revolution" that newspapers and magazines had promoted earlier in the decade had failed to become manifest. Walker estimated that fewer than four hundred Chinese immigrants were employed as domestic servants outside of Western states.[67]

In the early 1880s, events in California momentarily renewed hope that there would be a mass migration of Chinese laborers east, and that refugees of anti-Chinese sentiment could be offered asylum and living accommodations through employment in domestic service. As had been the case during the Civil War, household employers postulated that a labor force for undesirable service work could be salvaged from the fallout of a distant humanitarian crisis. At the end of 1879, the Workingmen's Party of California and Mayor Isaac Kalloch formally declared Chinatown a "public nuisance" and threatened to remove the entire Chinese population from the city.[68] Employers in cities like New York expressed their willingness to "save" Chinese immigrants from persecution by finding them jobs as servants. In contrast to the Workingmen's Party and white restrictionist depictions of Chinese servants as vectors of disease who endangered white homes, the New York Times documented the arrival of thirty Chinese refugees by describing how "all were scrupulously neat and clean."[69]

A Times article that appeared on March 6, 1880, claimed that no fewer than a half dozen women from "Madison-avenue and other fashionable up-town quarters" had journeyed to Mott Street in Manhattan's Chinatown seeking servants. A week later, a New York employer wrote to the Herald to inform readers that an intelligence office dealing in the new Chinese arrivals would be opening shortly.[70]

The humor magazine Puck, true to form, interpreted the events as precipitating what it suggested would evolve into a bicoastal struggle between Chinese and Irish immigrants over who controlled the labor supply for domestic service. A cartoon, "The Chinese Invasion," published on March 17, 1880, invented what this scenario might look like. The title itself was a play on the myriad articles and books that prorestriction authors had published documenting what they claimed would be the inevitable conquest of the United States by China if Chinese immigration was allowed to continue unimpeded.[71] In the center of the image, Chinese immigrants, whose queues are drawn to make them look like rats, flee the sinking ship of California for the island of Manhattan. Their arrival is cheered by middle-class white women eager to employ them. (This panel appears as Figure 5 in the insert to this book.)

Shifting to the future, the cartoon shows Chinese policemen beating up on the Irish and evicting them from trains, while Chinese servants,

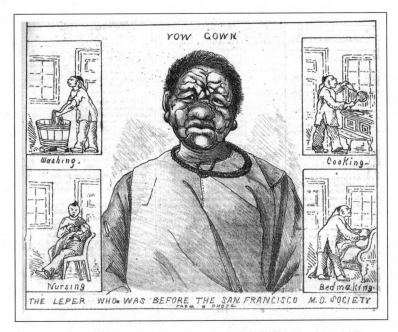

Figure 3.6. "Yow Gown—The Leper Who Was Before the San Francisco M.D. Society," *Thistleton's Jolly Giant*, February 23, 1878. Courtesy of the San Francisco History Center, San Francisco Public Library. *Thistleton's Jolly Giant* regularly provided coverage of alleged health threats that Chinese servants posed to white bodies and families. An illustration in the magazine depicts Yow Gown, a leper rumored to have hidden his medical condition while working as a servant for white families. "This is the kind of servants some of our aristocratic people hire to nurse their children, cook their food, make their beds, and wash their clothes," an accompanying article lectured, "while our white men and women starve for the want of employment." Although a man by the name of Yow Gown did appear before the San Francisco Medical Society and was diagnosed as a leper, despite the cartoon's sinister implication, there is no evidence that he was involved in nursing, cooking, or any other type of domestic labor. In the *Southern Medical Record*, where Yow's case was published, he was described by San Francisco doctors as a merchant (see "A Case of Leprosy—Elephantiasis Græcorum," *Southern Medical Record: A Monthly Journal of Practical Medicine* 9 [1879]: 126–27).

enscoced in the city's middle-class brownstone dwellings, usher their Irish competitors to the door. In the cartoon's first panel, a white mob in San Francisco is portrayed attacking Chinese immigrants, and is captioned with the phrase "The Chinese Must Go," the slogan popularized by Workingmen's Party leader (and Irish immigrant) Denis Kearney. In a later scene, the phrase is repurposed to declare that "The Irish Must Go" instead. Neither condoning nor condemning Chinese labor, the cartoon giddily anticipates how future contests for service jobs, pitting Irish women against Chinese men, would be a spectacle to be enjoyed regardless of the outcome.[72]

By the end of March 1880, the *New York Times* reported that despite the earlier hype—for which it was partly responsible—only an additional sixty to seventy new Chinese migrants had arrived in the city.[73] In San Francisco, Kalloch's eviction plans were shelved.[74] Many of the Chinese migrants who did eventually migrate to eastern cities, after first settling in California, did so to open their own businesses, such as laundries and restaurants, from savings they had earned working as laborers.[75] They had no interest in taking the risk of moving just so they could remain servants.

Chinese servants continued to be symbolic figures in the rallying cries of eastern proponents of Chinese immigration, who decried restriction as a policy that was detrimental to the nation as a whole—a point they claimed was lost when the Democratic and Republican parties fought to appease white workers in California and win the swing state's Electoral College votes. In an 1883 article published in the *Gospel in All Lands*, the Methodist missionary Esther Baldwin claimed that "if half the energy expended by the Californians in persecuting the Chinese had been kindly used in distributing them in little companies over the country (they are open to reason and kindness), we would have been saved a *very dark* page in our history, and many a home would have been blessed." The *Christian Union* posed a similar question: "Why should she [California] demand that New York shall not employ Chinese servants because she does not wish them?"[76]

Missionaries working in China represented a distinct class of household employers. They had a transnational stake in Chinese servants, and envisioned domestic labor relations as a crux for spreading the gospel. Chinese servants were not just commodities made available through new access to China; they were also subjects and agents of evangelization.

Esther Baldwin, quoted above, is a telling example in this regard. Less than six months after her marriage to the widower Stephen Livingstone Baldwin in 1862 at the age of twenty-two, she and her new husband departed from New York for the American Methodist Episcopal Mission in Fuzhou, in China's Fujian province. The 140-day trip by sail allowed ample time for the recently betrothed to better acquaint themselves. The American missionary enterprise in China was still in its nascent stages and rife with challenges. Stephen, who had been in China since 1858, knew this intimately. His first wife, Nellie, had contracted chronic diarrhea and died at sea while returning to the United States for treatment.[77] Esther recalled that when she arrived at the missionary station in Fuzhou her first task was to translate Bibles, hymns, and Sunday school books into Chinese, which she was still learning, in order to supply a body of Christian literature that could then be distributed. Early missionaries like her, she stated, "had to be not only preacher and teacher, but translator and bookmaker."[78] In nineteenth-century China, historian Jane Hunter observes, "Christian and servant communities overlapped substantially, since obliging servants often became Christians and needy Christians, servants."[79] Undoubtedly, some of the first recipients of the texts the Baldwins labored assiduously to produce were their hired servants. According to Stephen, in Fuzhou it took American Methodist missionaries a decade to win their first official convert, although by the end of the century the local Christian community had grown to approximately seven thousand individuals.[80] Armed with the gospel, servants were expected to radiate the faith and tenets of Christianity outward as so-called "native agents" and "helpers."

Due to her failing health, the Baldwins left China in 1880. Upon her return to the United States, Esther took a position on the board of the New York branch of the Women's Foreign Missionary Society of the Methodist Church, where she earned the nickname "the Champion of the Chinese" from her peers, in recognition of her advocacy on behalf of open, unrestricted Chinese immigration. In *Must the Chinese Go?*, a pamphlet that Baldwin wrote and first distributed in 1881 in support of this cause, and subsequently reprinted in 1882, 1886, and 1890, her servant Fong Ka Ku features prominently. He is "a Christian, gentle, kind, and most courteous to all." Ka Ku, as he is referred to by Baldwin, volunteers to remain in the family's service when they decide to leave Fuzhou. While the pamphlet is undeniably told from Baldwin's perspective, it is not fictional in a strict sense; at the time of the 1880 census, a forty-three-year-old Chinese immigrant servant by this name was employed in the Baldwins' Newark, New Jersey, home.[81]

In *Must the Chinese Go?*, Baldwin appraises the United States as a Christian nation through Ka Ku's eyes, and his observations become the basis for a series of questions about what it means to be a civilized nation. Shortly after their party lands in San Francisco, Ka Ku, on a Sunday walk to church, observes numerous fruit and vegetable peddlers ignoring the Sabbath and comments that "it is just about the same here as in China" (21). In Newark, where the Baldwins are initially stationed, Esther's hopes that residents of the East Coast will prove more tolerant and accepting of Ka Ku are dashed when, on a carriage ride, he is harassed and followed by an "unsightly, dirty, hooting rabble" (63). On another occasion, Ka Ku and Baldwin wait for a car to go downtown, admiring an "elegant church, with steeple pointing heavenward." Their reverie is disrupted by a drunken white immigrant who "deliberately circled round and round, with eyes bent full of hate upon the Chinaman" (63). While shopping with the family for shoes, Ka Ku has to be escorted out of the back of the store in order to avoid a contemptuous mob of "ragamuffins" that has assembled at the door. Baldwin, in a statement intended to chasten and shock readers, expresses a "longing for the *freedom* of China" (64). White laborers' violations of Ka Ku's right to live in the United States in peace, and their infringements on Baldwin's liberty to consume and govern his labor, are framed in the pamphlet as equally dangerous threats. The family is reassigned to Brooklyn, but Ka Ku and the Baldwins are persecuted there as well. Baldwin describes how a routine trip to Prospect Park turns into a daunting excursion. When her son is almost hit by a stone hurled at Ka Ku, the attack becomes a trespass against the enjoined bodies of white capital and Chinese labor.[82] Baldwin's narrative collapses the distinctions between foreign and domestic, just as it conflates master and servant into one unit. The streets of San Francisco, Newark, and Brooklyn become more alien and threatening than those of Fuzhou, where the imperial pairing of a white master and Chinese servant is tolerated.

Baldwin instructed readers to devote special attention to the notion of what constituted a "*Christian* land," which in her estimate was measured not only by devoutness but also by the willingness of the state to protect individuals' private property in the form of labor, and to honor the exchanges they entered into. Employers in the United States, she argued, should suppose "at least as much comfort and safety here as in heathen China and India or papal Europe." Baldwin noted that had similar attacks occurred on an American stationed in China, State Department officials would have immediately pressured the Chinese government to redress the situation and protect the rights of American citizens abroad. Even if China lacked the power and influence to demand similar rights for its subjects, this did not mean that middle-class American Protestants were sanctioned to sit by and do nothing. She argued that Chinese immigration and the labor question were inseparable issues and that it was cowardly for "good Christian men" to take a stance against anarchic Europeans only when capital was directly threatened. "The same element that persecutes and murders the Chinese," she asserted, "is just the very element to make this nation wail in revolution and blood" (65–68).

Baldwin did not limit her critiques of Chinese exclusion to punditry alone. Her activism demonstrates how middle-class women's involvement in household management evolved from trying to reform individual laborers under their control to political lobbying, a move that began with the introduction of the Freedmen's Bureau, and deepened with the establishment of federal immigration policies.[83] In the preface to the second edition of *Must the Chinese Go?*, Baldwin expressed dismay over the fact that its publication was funded by Sunday school donations made by Chinese immigrants, whereas anti-Chinese interests—she cited anecdotally—had raised five hundred thousand dollars to support their efforts. She would add in the preface to the third edition that if "American Christian sentiment" was to exercise real influence over policy, then evangelicals were going to have to put their money where their mouths were.[84] In 1886, Baldwin petitioned Congress for permission to bring a Chinese servant into the United States, presumably to join Ka Ku. The *Congressional Record* contains a one-sentence reference to Baldwin's petition and notes only that Senator George Hoar, a prominent Republican from Massachusetts who had opposed the 1882 Restriction Act, was responsible for its introduction. The petition was passed on to the Committee on Foreign Relations, where it languished without further debate. In 1901, Baldwin continued her advocacy by writing to President Theodore Roosevelt (who forwarded her letter to Terrence Powderly, the commissioner general of immigration) to weigh in on the "open door" policy with China and its connection to the soon-to-be-extended

Restriction Act.[85] Her crusading in support of unrestricted Chinese immigration did not wane.

## Brokering a Compromise with White Supremacy

In California and throughout the West, a cohort of political economists dismissed the exclusion of Chinese immigrant labor as unsound economic policy. They encouraged white workers to embrace rather than resist racial divisions of labors, and to exploit the possibilities that Chinese labor offered them to advance socially. The difference between a thrifty, industrious, and upwardly mobile white wage worker and his unambitious peers, proponents of Chinese labor contended, could be seen in a laborer's willingness to strategically employ Chinese labor. To embrace mastery over Chinese service workers was to command an imperial subjectivity. In light of the prohibitive transportation costs blocking white migration, a significant number of politicians and public figures took steps to reassure white laborers that Chinese labor, until California was better connected to the eastern United States and Europe, was best understood as a temporary fix. George Frederick Seward, who held the position of U.S. ambassador to China in the years leading up to the 1882 Restriction Act, predicted that until transportation costs declined, and the "class" of white women likely to work as servants could afford to travel to California and the other Pacific territories, there would invariably be labor shortages that Chinese immigrants could fill. "It is to be remembered that the State is not only young," he instructed, but that "it is distant from the sources of supply."[86]

Minimal though it is, there is evidence that white female workers on the job acknowledged—in more practical terms—the benefits that they accrued from the state's access to Chinese labor. In 1879, for instance, Ann Jane Sinclair wrote from San Francisco to her cousin in Ireland that she had "not much work" to do for the family that employed her, since "all the Cloths is washed out" and "the China men do all the washin."[87] Apparently the cost of dividing domestic labor into specific jobs was not too prohibitive, even at the tail end of the economic depression. The perspective of an individual like Sinclair offers an important counterpoint to the arguments advanced by white women orators at the myriad anti-Chinese rallies of the 1870s and early 1880s, who argued that

Figure 3.7. "The Chinese Must Go! But, Who Keeps Them?," *Wasp*, May 11, 1878. Courtesy of the Bancroft Library, University of California, Berkeley. White laborers are depicted conducting business with a Chinese laundryman, fishmonger, and cigar manufacturer, while Denis Kearney—appearing in the center of the cartoon as a braying donkey—advocates for exclusion. Targeting the divide between rhetoric and action, the cartoon implies that the services wage earners utilized would be either unavailable or no longer affordable if their attempts to bar Chinese immigration proved successful.

Chinese laborers denied female white workers opportunities to support themselves and their families.[88]

There were legal barriers in place that prevented local governments from introducing laws that barred the employment of Chinese labor already in the United States. When federal courts intervened to redress boycotts, expulsions, and discriminatory legislation directed at Chinese communities, their rationale for doing so was to uphold workers' and employers' right to freely contract without state infringement or private coercion. This was first demonstrated in an 1880 case involving Tiburcio Parrott, the president of the Quicksilver Mining Corporation, who refused to dismiss his Chinese laborers in defiance of the newly ratified California Constitution and state statute that had made their employment illegal. The federal Ninth Circuit Court ruled in Parrott's favor and found that the constitutional amendment and statute violated both the privileges and immunities granted to Chinese immigrants by the 1868 Burlingame Treaty and the Equal Protection Clause of the Fourteenth Amendment. The constitutional liberty to be hired rested specifically on the Fourteenth Amendment's protection of property as something that could not be denied without due process. In line with the liberal doctrine of the period, the court held that labor was a form of private property, possessed by the individual, whose sale could not be prohibited on racial grounds.[89] In 1886, the U.S. Supreme Court ruled in *Yick Wo v. Hopkins* that an 1880 San Francisco statute that subjected all laundries operating out of wooden buildings to municipal licensing was unconstitutional, on the grounds that it too violated the Due Process Provision of the Equal Protection Clause since the city enforced the law against Chinese businesses only. By recognizing noncitizens' right to their property, whether in the form of their labor or capital, and the rights of consumers and employers to purchase or conduct business with this property, federal courts checked the ability of anti-Chinese activists to exclude Chinese immigrants from employment altogether.[90]

For many critics of the United States' categorical restrictions on the entry of Chinese laborers, the problem was a lack of creativity in imagining how governance might be refined to protect the interests of both white employers and white laborers. They expressed frustration about the way that the question of Chinese labor had been approached as an all-or-none scenario, and the fact that the United States had proved incapable of tailoring immigration policies to meet both economic demand and the social imperative of ensuring white supremacy. In an article that appeared in the *Methodist Review* in 1892, the San Francisco–based Methodist minister A. J. Hanson praised the Exclusion Act for keeping out "undesirables" from China. At the same time, however, he found fault with the law's role in reducing the number of available Chinese servants to work in white homes. Reflecting on the debates of the previous decades, he argued that all parties were guilty of oversimplification when it came to Chinese labor, and that the individual immigrant could no more easily be reduced to "industry, economy, docility, inoffensiveness, reliability," than he could be to "ignorance, depravity, churlishness, heathenism, duplicity, and general worthlessness." For Hanson, both sides missed a more practical truth. The Chinese immigrant was not a Christian brother deserving equality, as proponents had made him out to be, but a perpetual "alien and foreigner." On the other hand, any threat of an invasion and takeover by Chinese immigrants amounted to hysteria that ought to be embarrassing to any confident, self-respecting empire. Rational Americans could appreciate that Chinese immigrant labor could be useful in certain occupations—notably domestic service.[91]

This view emanated from official corridors of power as well. Senator John Tyler Morgan of Alabama, a Democrat, staunch restrictionist, and vocal critic of "race mixing," felt that denying reentry to Chinese laborers who had dutifully obtained a return certificate prior to departing the United States, which was accomplished with the passage of the 1888 Scott Act, went too far even for his politics. On the Senate floor, he declared his ethical qualms about witnessing "gentlemen, who may themselves, as far as we know, have Chinese servants in their own houses," betray the law-abiding laborers who had faithfully served them.[92] This stance aligned with Morgan's white southern heritage, and the "Jim Crow" position that control and subordination rather than exclusion could constitute the basis for white supremacy. In more local contexts, in the first decade of the twentieth century the chambers of commerce in Portland and Los Angeles advocated for occupation-specific exemptions to the exclusion laws and listed domestic service as work where additional labor was desperately needed.[93]

The theme of managing and containing Chinese laborers, while reaping their benefits, would provide ample material for policymakers and commentators throughout the era of exclusion. Hubert Howe Bancroft, the renowned historian of California and the West, argued for an American empire that maintained free trade and labor, while doing away with political liberalism that insisted on the fitness of all subjects for self-governance. As he wrote in 1900, the goal was not to exploit unfree labor. "Though a servant," the Chinese immigrant was "not a slave."[94] Servant in Bancroft's usage took on both a literal meaning, referring to household labor, and a metonymic function that alluded to the type of worker who could be enlisted to do anything considered menial.

In 1912, thirty years after the passage of the initial Chinese Restriction Act, Bancroft published his *Retrospection: Political and Personal*, in which he argued that "a true story of the Asiatics in America" would emphasize "the amazing gullibility of the American people." "The white race proposes to control the earth," Bancroft noted, yet "when that time comes the working-man of to-day will want men to work for him; will he employ all white labor or use Asiatics for some things?" Although millions of European immigrants had arrived in the United States since 1865, their "aspirations"—Bancroft cynically noted—had resulted in labor radicalism and ingratitude. "We want some men in the United States for work alone," Bancroft emphasized. "We do not need them all for governing or for breeding purposes, least of all low grade foreigners, Asiatic or European." Bancroft estimated that a hundred thousand Chinese servants would be needed to adequately satisfy contemporary demand. Bancroft proposed keeping restrictions on Chinese immigrants in place, and instead creating a "system of passports" so that "needed Asiatic laborers could be admitted as required, and sent away when no longer needed."[95] As invocations of the state's role as a technocratic agent in the development of consumer services, in which its power could be deployed to both ensure white supremacy and allow for racial spaces of inclusion for those committed to servile labor, Bancroft's plans mapped a new vision for how migration might be governed in the future.

Resolute exclusionists maintained their willingness—in rhetoric if not always in action—to secure the American West as a white man's country. By demanding white employers display racial solidarity in their hiring practices, anti-Chinese activists advanced an economic vision where race was central to how labor markets functioned on a day-to-day basis, and to longer-term issues of supply. This vision was both nostalgic for preindustrial republican labor relations and forward-looking, at least in terms of what it demanded of the state. D. S. Cowan, a special agent hired by the U.S. Department of the Treasury in 1888 to investigate the smuggling of Chinese from Canada into the American Pacific Northwest, waxed biblically on how the Chinese laborers found in the region's homes, laundries, and hotels were "hewers of wood and drawers of water," adding that "there are no whites on the coast to take their places."[96] Like many immigration officials, Cowan did not see Chinese immigration as a mere matter of supply and demand, and he remained adamant that conditions on the ground did not necessitate the reform of restrictive legislation. Instead, he pined for a day when the region would be able to recruit white women from the East and Europe, who could then claim these service positions. His vision of settler ownership extended well beyond control of land and political institutions, and into the realm of labor markets and their very constitution.

## Conclusion

The passage of the 1882 Chinese Restriction Act represented a watershed moment in immigration history. Congress asserted its sovereign authority to forbid a whole class of people—Chinese laborers—from entering. Shifting its attention to Europe, in the 1880s and 1890s Congress passed new legislation that established the grounds for debarring and deporting individuals on account of their economic status, health, and political ideology. The 1891 Immigration Act authorized a federal bureau to govern the nation's borders. The next two chapters of this book peer inside the emergent state apparatus created to govern immigration in spaces such as Castle Garden, Ellis Island, and, out west, Angel Island. When it came to enforcing new immigration laws, virtually nothing was certain. As the following chapters argue, with federal sovereignty over immigration in place, the state also entered into the subjective realm of brokering how immigrant labor was to be consumed for domestic purposes and under what conditions. The authority to regulate entry made the state a key actor in steering immigrant labor to domestic service jobs and, in the case of Chinese servants granted temporary admission into the United States, forcing these workers to remain under contract and bonded to their employers. The inability to compel servants to remain in jobs was a major limitation to the feasibility of assisted migration programs that targeted Irish, black, and Chinese laborers for domestic service during the middle part of the nineteenth century. The authority that federal immigration officials had to make immigrants' entry contingent on accepting service work changed this dynamic in dramatic ways.

4

# Controlling and Protecting White Women

*The State and Sentimental Forms of Coercion, 1850–1917*

## Introduction: "She Could Work!"

Among the newspaper clippings that William Williams chose to archive is an excerpt from an article that appeared in the March 5, 1910, issue of the *Saturday Evening Post*. Since Williams was often accused of being insensitive to the plight of immigrants trying to enter the United States, it was perhaps set aside to demonstrate his compassion to future historians. Williams, after a career as a Wall Street attorney, served as commissioner of Ellis Island from 1902 to 1905 and, during a second appointment, from 1909 to 1914. He was responsible for overseeing the station's daily operations. Among contemporaries, he had a reputation for being a hard-liner when it came to interpreting the statutory grounds that authorized officials to bar individual European immigrants from landing. Of the estimated 1,041,570 immigrants who arrived in the United States during the 1910 fiscal year, only 24,270 people, or approximately 2 percent, were rejected. An additional 2,695 individuals were deported that year after developing or revealing a cause for exclusion following their landing. Despite the low percentage of inadmissible and deported immigrants relative to the total volume of entrants, these numbers do not account for how regulations informed steamship companies' decisions to refuse emigrant passengers—they were responsible for covering the cost of immigrants' return if they failed to be admitted—or for how the laws dissuaded attempts to come to the United States altogether. During his tenure as commissioner, Williams introduced an unofficial and intentionally vague requirement that immigrants arriving at Ellis Island had to have the equivalent to twenty-five dollars in currency to be admitted. In actuality, the statutes stipulated only that immigrants had to prove that they were not likely to become public charges. This and other actions earned him enemies in the ethnic communities and foreign-language presses of New York and beyond.[1]

Williams was practiced in dealing with public scrutiny and curiosity. Visits by members of the media were commonplace at Ellis Island, and the station provided an unlimited font of anecdotes for journalists to relay to readers. Social scientists were drawn to Ellis Island as a laboratory where the processing of human subjects was occurring on an unprecedented, industrial scale. Members of the public and officials of all stripes came to the station to observe the character, appearances, and habits of the newest arrivals that the United States was supposed to absorb culturally and employ with its capital.[2]

Arthur Train, the author of the article in the *Post* that Williams clipped, left Ellis Island with a favorable impression of the commissioner's work and the resourcefulness that station officials displayed in handling the diverse range of scenarios they encountered. In the section of the article that Williams isolated for preservation, Train described how a "handsome, clear-eyed Russian girl of about twenty years, the daughter of a farmer," had posed, in the commissioner's words, a "'puzzling case.'" A young man from her village, who had immigrated to the United States two years earlier, had invited her to join him with the promise of marriage. When she arrived in New York, however, her fiancé was a no-show. Immigration officials located him in New Jersey, and although they were able to convince him to visit his bride-to-be, this only reinforced his opinion that "he wasn't sure whether he wanted to marry her or not."[3]

Unaccompanied women were held in limbo at Ellis Island as wards of the state. They were detained until immediate relatives, their husbands, or another guardian that officials deemed suitable called on the station to accept them. Weddings were sometimes performed on steamships or at the station. In 1914, for instance, a British journalist traveling in steerage described being asked by an inspector who boarded the docked vessel if a nearby woman standing alone was his "sweetheart," so as to marry the two.[4] Fears of "white slavery," the racially coded language used to describe trafficking for the purpose of prostitution, meant that officials guarded against the release of unaccompanied European women to parties who might be using falsified credentials.

Immigration officials could be cavalier about pushing single women into dependent labor relationships, so as to resolve their unaccompanied status. Her marriage postponed indefinitely and without immediate kin, the Russian woman in the *Post* story was detained at Ellis Island at the expense of the steamship company. The woman did not want to return to Russia but could not be landed either. Breaking from his ostensibly bureaucratic, letter-of-the-law role, Williams inquired whether Train knew of "any lady who wants a servant." "She could work!" he confidently asserted, beckoning the journalist to "look at her arms" and inspect her body. Williams took for granted that Train and any acquaintance he might recommend as an employer were respectable persons and therefore trustworthy when it came to assigning work and housing to the young Russian woman. And indeed, a significant number of unaccompanied women accepted similar arrangements since this allowed them to land in the United States. Still, one wonders what Williams's antagonists might have thought of this. The commissioner often clashed with ethnic and religious "missionaries," as social workers at Ellis Island were called, who were also responsible for brokering the labor of young, single women. Williams reprimanded them for allegedly being careless in screening for exploitative situations.

Train's visit with the Russian woman concluded with Williams stating that he would write the procrastinating fiancé and "fool" one last time to inform him that "he'll never have such a chance again." And then the journalist and the commissioner moved on. When stories involving stranded immigrant women were publicized to a national audience, it was common for Williams to receive letters from men looking to acquire female companionship and the domestic labor that came with it. The case of the young Russian woman was no exception. A forty-six-year-old male correspondent from Oakland, California, wrote Williams asking whether she could be released to his custody if he paid for her train fare and agreed to her "care" as his wife. He gave references that Williams could consult and promised that his "offer was bona fide."[5] Like that of many Ellis Island subjects who captured the media's fleeting attention, the conclusion to the detained woman's ordeal is unknown.

* * *

This chapter addresses the role that representatives of the U.S. government played as brokers of European immigrant women's domestic labor. It focuses on women facing detainment, denied entry, or unemployment that might put them at risk of becoming a public charge, and the measures taken to prevent these outcomes.

The federal government made the defense of free labor a major policy imperative, at least on the surface. The introduction of "unfree" contract laborers, organized labor and other restrictionists argued, threatened whatever material gains that "free" workers stood to make through their ability to stave off unfair competition from strikebreakers and debt-bonded workers who could be compelled to replace them on the cheap.[6]

Gender complicated these more generic intentions of immigration policy. How to govern and control the domestic labor of white immigrant women raised an entirely different set of questions. Paternalistic and sentimental views about the need to keep white immigrant women subordinate to household employers, as a matter of formal status, extended into the modern era of immigration regulation. Rather than liberating white women from dependency rooted in servitude, the state asserted its authority to intervene in and produce these relationships.

As earlier chapters in this book address, state-level actors were involved in the governance and brokerage of migrant labor even before the federal government averred its plenary power in this area. From 1850 to 1891, the labor bureau at Castle Garden was one of the most important and active agents in this process. Backed by New York State, it was allegedly uninterested in the pursuit of profit, and therefore solely concerned with facilitating rational and efficient transactions, without bias, that benefitted the sellers and purchasers of labor alike.

This proved to be far from the case. The Castle Garden labor bureau was the object of significant and lasting controversy. The German Emigrant Society and Irish Emigrant Society, two mutual associations that were formed in the first part of the nineteenth century to protect immigrants arriving in New York City, were in charge of the exchange. The societies' method for managing transactions between labor and capital was anathema to the priorities of the New York State–appointed officials charged with overseeing immigrants' entry at Castle Garden, which was a separate area of responsibility. The two parties disagreed over whether immigrant women's liberty to contract their labor was to be cultivated and protected, as the societies claimed to be doing, or, in contrast, whether state officials had the right to set strict conditions and rules governing the use of the placement services that the exchange offered.

Whether immigrant women were mandated to take the first domestic labor position offered to them, or whether the Castle Garden labor bureau might serve as a haven for new arrivals seeking to test the market, ignited a much larger debate about the role that the varied guardians appointed to oversee immigrant women's entry were to play in disciplining their market behavior. The competition between ethnic associations and the state as to who controlled immigrant labor revealed divergent ideologies of what constituted exploitation and protection respectively, and whether the state and those whom it charged to carry out its business were beholden to the producers or consumers of domestic labor as middlemen.

At the turn of the century, European immigrants were most frequently denied admission on the grounds that they were likely to become public charges, a provision introduced by the general 1882 Immigration Act but carried over from earlier state-level regulations.[7] The 1882 act instituted a fifty-cent head tax on all immigrants and prohibited the entry of convicts, lunatics, and "any person unable to take care of himself or herself without becoming a public charge." With the 1891 act, the language of the last provision would be changed to any person "likely to become a public charge."[8] The evaluation of who was "likely" to become a public charge was by definition subjective, as legislators' use of this adverb intended.[9] The issue of who was at risk to become indigent and the determination of why this was "likely" fell on immigration inspectors stationed at each port of entry. Although New York officials and members of the German and Irish societies continued to manage Castle Garden for another decade, with the 1892 opening of Ellis Island the federal government and its employees became the sole arbiters of decisions concerning immigrants' admissions. By the mid-1890s, as a result of a series of U.S. Supreme Court decisions that limited Chinese and Japanese immigrants' right to file writs of habeas corpus when denied entry, immigration officials' discretionary powers were confirmed as both broad and, for the most part, not subject to appeal.

The statutory basis for the detention of unaccompanied women was even more opaque, and developed as a rule that the federal immigration bureaucracy deemed was custom. This practice inferred that women arriving on their own were at inherent risk of falling into various restrictive categories, which, after 1907, were expanded to include having committed crimes of moral turpitude.[10] Officials claimed the authority to detain unaccompanied women indefinitely.

The controls that immigration officials placed on unaccompanied immigrant women's freedom of movement and contract referenced two overlapping concepts of protection. Concerns about "white slavery" and international trafficking in migrant women's sexual labor were central to the expansion of the immigration bureaucracy's mission, historian Gunther Peck has shown, and legitimated its authority.[11] While moral protectionism has tended to garner the most attention, immigration officials were also protectionist in an economic sense: they wanted to aid household employers who felt undermined by free market conditions. Officials like Williams deployed the risks of "white slavery" as a bugaboo that could be called on whenever the bureau's powers were challenged. Delving into the intricacies of women's commodification as domestic laborers entailed far more nuanced assessments of how certain types of brokerage benefitted or endangered women workers, which immigration officials were not willing to pursue. Denied the ability to contract their labor freely, unaccompanied immigrant women lost the chance to exercise a more strategic and deliberate agency over the terms of their domestic employment.

A desire to maintain gender-based dependencies explained why there was widespread support for federal immigration policies that restricted Asian and male European contract labor migrations and, at the same time, backing for policies and regulations that kept white women under close control. In respect to the latter, immigration officials gave no indication that they considered their actions to be improperly coercive.

The 1885 Alien Contract Labor Law, or Foran Act, prohibited the entry of immigrant laborers already under contract with an employer, but exempted domestic and personal service as occupations. Whereas the Foran Act sought to protect native-born laborers' wages and capacity to organize against a labor reserve that industrialists would assume the costs of transporting to American shores, unions and policymakers were unconcerned that the labor market for domestic service would be imperiled by the same vulnerabilities. With these exceptions to the Foran Act, Congress demonstrated its reluctance to interfere in a labor market where supply shortages, even during times of economic depression, were frequently cited as a glaring problem that threatened to sabotage middle-class domesticity and therefore the nation. Moreover, Congress was disinclined to regulate labor contracts that originated from private homes, at least when the employers involved were unaffiliated with any coordinated recruitment scheme that went beyond fulfilling their own consumer demand. Policymakers helped to further blur the line between wage-earning domestic laborers and familial dependents by treating pre-arranged contracts as protective and steadying influences over a migrant labor force composed of young white women. When confronted with attempts to expand interpretations of how the domestic labor exception built into the 1885 Foran Act might be deployed, the bureau took steps to ensure that only individual households and employers would be able to capitalize on the loophole, and not middlemen seeking to profit commercially. White women, immigration officials determined, were not to be treated as commodities to be transferred under contract, in bulk.

Rarely mapped unless it was made subject to accusatory investigations, the transatlantic brokerage of servants reveals an intricate, multipart commodity chain that moved young immigrant women from Europe to middle-class American homes. As the last section of this chapter addresses, early twentieth-century reformers, led by the sociologist Frances Kellor, directed attention to the role employment offices played in prompting undesirable migrations of both European immigrants and southern blacks. Kellor charged commercial brokers with failing workers and employers alike. She accused employment offices of coming up with devious methods for breaking immigration laws. Labor agents exploited women whose "primitive" backgrounds meant that they were both easily manipulated by intermediaries and tricked into debt bondage, or, in the best-case scenario, ill-equipped to perform the domestic work they were being recruited to do. With demands for Congress to introduce numerical restrictions on European immigration mounting in the first two decades of the twentieth century, Kellor's view would gain increased purchase in convincing legislators—as chapter 6 of this book returns to—to put aside whatever anxieties they might have about restricting European supplies of domestic labor.

## Domesticity's Marketplace at Castle Garden

Although commercial intelligence offices catering to the placement of domestic servants date back to seventeenth-century England, in the

United States it was the mid-nineteenth-century influx of wage labor-ers from new transatlantic and rural sources that put these institutions in what employers considered to be a state of crisis. Intelligence offices operated on a fee or subscription basis, and typically required both employees and employers to pay fifty cents to a dollar to use their ser-vices for a term of one to three months. During this period, a domestic employer could choose among job candidates that the office sent to her home on a trial basis. In some instances, a domestic was given simi-lar leeway to explore options in different households. Applicants' fees did not cover the room and board that unemployed servants required, which intelligence offices provided directly or subcontracted to boarding houses at additional cost. The primary motive driving the establishment of privately run intelligence offices was profit. Their visible presence as part of the urban employment landscape offers a reminder—and challenge to both liberal and Marxist economic theory—that the ser-vice sector economy generated value in the form of capital, even if this capital did not go to service workers' immediate employers. By the mid-1850s, there were more than twenty intelligence offices operating in New York City that specialized in domestic servants, and undoubtedly many more informal ventures that escaped count. Although some servants sought employment by placing newspaper advertisements, intelligence offices plied their services in the media just as frequently. Employers also used help-wanted notices, but many disdained the resulting parade of working-class women who came to their homes to interview for the situation being offered.[12]

Spatially, intelligence offices required mistresses to travel from middle-class enclaves to the immigrant neighborhoods where these offices operated, and to bargain over commissions, fees, and employ-ment terms in cramped tenement storefronts or basements where unemployed women, awaiting work, gathered. Employers argued that one of the gravest offenses commercial intelligence offices committed was helping servants be too free. By offering rental accommodations and a base for the conduct of business, intelligence offices relieved servants from immediate housing needs and upset employers' interests in com-pelling their labor.

Of course, there were intelligence offices that were predatory and had no compunctions about trying to profit in any way they could from the chaotic market for domestic labor. Employers cited, for instance, having to pay for untrained servants whose marketed skills were clearly embellished. Other tricks that intelligence offices used, such as paying domestics to leave jobs in order to get employers to renew their subscriptions, drew similar rebuke.[13] Still, intelligence offices' shady activities were more likely to harm the laborers who used their services than employers. Servants, especially newly arrived immigrants, had to be wary of fraudulent and exploitative agencies that sought to rob them of the entirety of their meager savings. A *New York Times* editorial accused intelligence offices of being parasitic "blood suckers," whose runners swarmed arriving vessels and seized applicants' luggage as collateral. Intelligence offices also lied to immigrant women about available work, in order to have them continue to pay rent on their boarding house rooms. Occasionally the city rescinded the licenses of intelligence offices that committed blatant acts of fraud.[14] However, this was a rare occurrence until turn-of-the-century statutes strengthened the regulations that intelligence offices had to comply with.

Given the reasons that both workers and employers had to be suspicious about commercial intelligence offices, it was perhaps inevitable that the state became more directly involved as a broker of immigrant domestic labor. The establishment of a job placement office at the point of immigrant arrival offered, in theory at least, a means for rationalizing exchanges between native employers and immigrant labor. Between 1855 and 1892, more than eight million immigrants were processed at Castle Garden. In 1847, at the height of famine immigration from Ireland, the New York State legislature created the Commissioners of Emigration and authorized the agency to bar immigrants from landing if they were deemed "likely to become permanently a public charge." Alternatively, a shipmaster could indemnify the state against this possibility. While ports of entry had long required shipmasters to take out bonds on passengers suspected of being indigent, the rise in the number of pauper immigrants made the effective capture of these revenues more urgent.[15] After the U.S. Supreme Court's decision in the 1849 *Passenger Cases* confirmed the federal government's exclusive power to collect head taxes on immigrants, New York adopted a "voluntary" system where shipmasters could either take out a refundable three-hundred-dollar bond on each immigrant they sought to land, or pay a far less expensive commutation tax on each passenger instead. This prevailed until 1876, when the U.S. Supreme Court, in *Henderson v. Mayor of the City of New York*, declared the revised system to be a regulation of foreign commerce in practice, and therefore unconstitutional.[16]

In addition to policing entry, Castle Garden was also intended to help impose order over the post-landing commodity trade in immigrant labor. Humane concerns about the need to protect immigrants from theft, deception, and extortion intersected with proactive efforts to coordinate their employment. In December 1849, the Commissioners of Emigration opened employment agencies in two warehouses near the Canal Street docks. In 1867, a new labor bureau—as the exchange came to be officially called—would be built adjoining the landing facilities at Castle Garden, which opened in 1855. In its 1851 report, the labor bureau reported placing 10,203 immigrant women in job situations in only its second full year of operation. This was compared to 8,001 men placed in jobs, during a year when 289,601 immigrants arrived in New York in total. Between 1860 and 1866, despite the temporary reduction in immigration caused by the war, bureau officials still placed 40,222 women in positions as servants—a staggering number that made it the busiest intelligence office in the world.[17] The bureau maintained its own boarding houses. When immigrants could not afford to pay for a room, the bureau coordinated with officials on Ward's Island to have them lodged in public facilities while awaiting employment.

The state laws that dictated how immigration was to be governed made differing agendas at Castle Garden inevitable. The Commissioners of Emigration Board was composed of six unsalaried officials appointed by New York's governor, and four ex officio members: the mayors of New York and Brooklyn, and the presidents of the German Emigrant Society and the Irish Emigrant Society.[18] The board's makeup reflected the changing demographics of New York, and the state's recognition that Irish and German immigrants were powerful voting blocs whose interests had to be represented. The board's composition also acknowledged that the German and Irish societies, as mutual aid associations that ran banks, transferred remittances, and monitored both immigration and emigration conditions on the ground, possessed a type of expertise that had value beyond political pragmatism.

Nonetheless, the formula determining who sat on the Commissioners' Board was volatile. Officials divided not only along party and ethnic lines, but as competing representatives of producer and consumer interests. Like private intelligence offices, the state-commissioned labor bureau discovered that it was impossible to remain neutral as a broker, a realization that contravened the office's ostensibly philanthropic purpose. Even though the labor bureau's directors came from the Irish and German societies, its staff qualified as civil servants of the state of New York. They adhered to the philosophy, passed down from the Emigration Commissioners, that it was their duty to limit aggressive and disreputable manifestations of immigrants' liberty of contract. Over time, this policy would create a large rift between state officials and the ethnic politicians and power brokers who understood Castle Garden to fall under their domain. The seeds of this conflict, however, were there at the beginning. Shortly after the bureau commenced operation, Mike Walsh, an Irish-born Democratic state senator, professed outrage after witnessing Irish women being turned out on the streets because they had refused a position.[19] Observers acting on behalf of New York's employer class divined opposite conclusions. In July 1857, a reporter from *Harper's Weekly* complained that it was a travesty that "raw" Irish immigrants were demanding wages of five dollars a month as entry-level maids of all work, despite the same class of workers earning only three or four dollars a year earlier. The author praised the labor bureau's chief officer (described only as a "Frenchman") for expelling immigrant women who had rejected job offers at the lower rate. He was right to do so, the article proclaimed, since the holdouts had no basis for bargaining for higher wages due to their "total ignorance of the very elements of housewifery." In 1865, the *New York Times* extolled the bureau's meticulous record keeping as a measure that prevented immigrant domestic workers already residing in the United States from passing themselves off as new arrivals. The newspaper explained that this tactic was deployed by laborers who wanted to avoid having to acknowledge negative or withheld character references from disappointed previous employers. The exchange, the newspaper acknowledged, still struggled to sequester its "fresh" supply of Irish immigrants from family and friends already working as servants in the United States, who passed along instructions on how to exaggerate their experience in order to command better pay.[20] But otherwise it was to be commended for serving the interests of consumers.

After the Civil War, the labor bureau gained clout as the hub that coordinated both the local and national distribution of immigrant labor. *Bradstreet's* business weekly noted in 1882, for instance, that "the receptive power of the United States, industrially speaking, may be well gauged at the Castle Garden labor bureau."[21]

All was not copacetic within the bureau, however. Castle Garden was run by appointed and salaried civil servants who, in an era when bureaucratic professionalization was still gaining a foothold, varied enormously in respect to their dedication, experience, skill, and commitment to job-related ethical behavior. Although many of the bureau's employers sided with the commissioners' pro-consumer stances, others pledged loyalty to the Irish and German societies. Patronage was practiced by both political parties. While Republicans tended to constitute the majority of the commissioners, employees affiliated with the German and Irish societies were usually Democrats and Tammany Hall loyalists. Commissioners, whether appointed by the governor to a six-year term or serving in an ex officio capacity from the German and Irish societies, took advantage of their influence by assigning valuable concessions. Because Castle Garden was served by baggage handlers, railroad ticket agents, and food concessions, whoever the commissioners appointed had ample opportunity to profit. An 1872 investigation of Castle Garden unearthed numerous examples of how the facility had become a valuable source of patronage and kickbacks for Tammany Hall and the Tweed Ring.[22] In July 1871, an anonymous letter writer to the *New York Times* alleged that officials staffing the labor bureau were complicit in the corruption taking place. They were accused of holding immigrant women who might be hired immediately, in exchange for bribes from the "emigrant runner and other pests that are permitted to infest the locality."[23]

When state legislators again investigated Castle Garden in 1875, Tweed and his associates were no longer in the picture, and the resulting report noted only isolated incidents of corruption. More ambiguously, the investigation also shed light on the bureau's persistent ideological conflict over what liberty of contract ought to mean to immigrant women. The investigative committee focused on a dispute between Edmund Stephenson, who was first appointed as a Commissioner of Emigration by Republican Governor John Dix in 1873, and James Lynch, the president of the Irish Emigration Society. Stephenson denounced Lynch for using his influence to pressure the exchange's staff into

THE LABOR EXCHANGE AT CASTLE GARDEN—CHOOSING A GIRL.—[DRAWN BY MISS M. L. STONE.]

Figure 4.1. "Choosing a Girl," *Harper's Weekly*, January 25, 1873. An illustration depicts the hiring of a servant at the Castle Garden labor bureau. Despite the internal conflicts taking place within the labor bureau, outsiders remained fascinated with its role as the preeminent broker of immigrant labor.

allowing immigrant women, especially those from Ireland, to repeatedly avail themselves of the agency's placement services. Secretly, Stephenson instructed a clerk to compile a list of women who could be classified as serial offenders to be barred from using the bureau altogether.

The list—and the clerk's accompanying annotations—seemed to confirm what Stephenson was arguing. Kate Boyle was accused of using the exchange to land eleven different situations and was a "notorious fraud." Jane Morrison, the recipient of eight placements, was a thief who used Castle Garden as her base of operations. Bridget Coffee and Kate Slattery were Castle Garden "bummers," content to drift in and out of jobs knowing they would soon be placed again. Mary Boyers's offense was calling one of the clerks "an English son of a bitch." Stephenson was so concerned with the reputation of the bureau that he instructed one of the clerks to furtively hand out a version of the list that they had assembled, rather than insult respectable employers by pushing on them what he claimed were tainted goods. Even though the bureau at Castle Garden was intended to be a neutral actor, Stephenson was still strongly beholden to his class interests, which he conveyed as a matter of preserving his reputation among his peers—the household employers who used the service. He claimed that Lynch, upon discovering Stephenson's instructions to the clerk, had tried to have the employee dismissed. When Stephenson and the other state-appointed commissioners intervened to prevent this, Lynch reduced his salary instead. Stephenson concluded his testimony to the assembly's investigative committee by appealing for the authority to expel women from the bureau without interference.[24]

The defenders of the bureau admitted that the pure volume of business that the exchange handled meant that there were, inevitably, some dishonest users. At the same time, they championed in populist terms the bureau's role as a sanctuary and base of power for immigrant servants treated as disposable wage earners by exploitative employers. John E. Develin, a Democratic assemblyman, cross-examined Stephenson on behalf of the investigative committee. Although Develin identified with the reform wing of the national Democratic Party, and was not a Tammany man, he still offered a different interpretation of why the bureau was engaged in repeat placements.[25] Develin was the child of Irish immigrants, which likely shaped his perspective on the German

| Names. | No. of places. | Remarks. |
|---|---|---|
| Bridget Barry | 13 | Notorious character. |
| Kate Boyle | 11 | This girl landed in May, 1874; she is a notorious fraud; never keeps a place. |
| Kate Chute | 10 | This woman has had over 25 places within a period of one year and a half. |
| Jane Morrison | 8 | A notorious character; she is charged by Mrs. Austen, of Great Neck, L. I., with having broken open a chest, and taking therefrom articles of great value. |
| Mary O'Brien | 9 | Since the 1st of September, 1874. |
| Mary Petit | 8 | |
| Mina Reid | 7 | Fraud ; never keeps a place. |
| Mary Murphy | 6 | Since the 1st of September; she is a hard drinker; has been expelled a number of times. |
| Hannah Coyni | 6 | She has been expelled from this bureau twice; she is a gay deceiver. |
| Alice Dolan | 4 | This woman is a notorious imposter; she was expelled for giving impudence to Mrs. Moody, and a constant expense to the commission. |
| Bridget Coffee | .. | Never takes a place ; she is a Castle Garden bummer; she has been to Ward's Island a number of times; a constant expense to the commission. |
| Jane Conroy | 3 | Never takes a place; she is a notorious imposter. |
| Mary Anglem | 5 | |
| Ann Ahern | 4 | Within a period of twenty days. |
| Mary Ahern | 3 | |
| Ellen Brady | 4 | |

Figure 4.2. Excerpted list of serial abusers accused of dishonestly using the Castle Garden Labor Bureau complied by order of Commissioner Edmund Stephenson. New York State Legislature, *Documents of the Assembly of the State of New York, Ninety-Ninth Session, 1876* (Albany: Werd, Parsons, 1876), 134.

and Irish societies and what mutual assistance entailed. According to Develin, it was employers who were to be blamed for violating the spirit of honest contract by abusing the "employment at will" doctrine. Develin asked Stephenson whether he or the clerks loyal to him had ever bothered to ask why Irish immigrant women "left their places where they were employed." When Stephenson responded that he had not,

Develin eagerly provided a theory. "There are a good many people in New York," Develin explained, "that employ women and keep them a couple of weeks and then say they misbehave themselves and discharge them so as to save paying their wages." It was common knowledge, he continued, that many employers discharged domestics after two weeks of service—right before they became eligible to sue for *quantum meruit* damages in civil court.[26]

Even if Develin was trying to win a specific argument with Stephenson, his theory was not baseless. While all American wage laborers were to a degree disposable, domestics who constantly came and went without written employment contracts remained among the most vulnerable.[27] One indicator of the precarity that servants faced was the amount of litigation they brought to courts, in attempts to recover wages denied to them. In New York State, legislators introduced bills in 1858, 1860, and 1876 that were drafted to expedite and reduce costs for legal proceedings in laborers' small claims cases, since court fees and the loss of working hours meant that "in most cases servants who are unable to procure payment of a small balance of wages, having neither time nor money to spare, let the matter rest." The *New York Times* supported statutory reform because these types of suits were delaying the administration of justice throughout the civil court system.[28] None of the bills, however, became law. The Legal Aid Society, which was founded in 1876 by the same German mutual aid society responsible for overseeing the labor bureau, dedicated significant resources to representing servants involved in lost wage suits. In 1900, the society reported two thousand cases where domestics had reported wage theft, and that 75 percent of the cases had merit in its opinion. During the 1880s, the Women's Educational and Instructional Union in Boston also reported providing legal assistance to servants who, upon losing their jobs, turned to the courts to help recover possessions that boardinghouse operators owed rent had seized.[29]

For domestic laborers, the evidentiary and practical challenges to recovering withheld wages were formidable. In one telling case that was heard by the New York Court for Common Pleas in 1880, Bridget Daveny, whose name suggests that she was an Irish immigrant or first-generation American, testified that she had entered into an express contract with her employers, the Shattucks, guaranteeing summer employment. Since demand for servants slackened in cities during the summertime, when the Shattucks changed their mind about needing Daveny in the late spring, leaving her unemployed, she filed for damages based on the loss of earnings that the withdrawal of the offer, which she considered a breach of contract, had caused. Her suit was dismissed on the grounds that the promised job had not risen to the level of an enforceable contractual obligation. As the legal historian Jonathan Fabian Witt notes of Daveny's case, even when employees tried to formalize contracts beyond oral agreements, "the difficulty of knowing the magic words required to do so successfully often defeated their attempts."[30]

Undoubtedly both sides of the dispute between Stephenson and Develin were correct to some degree. All capitalist exchanges encouraged the buyers and sellers of labor to pursue their interests in ways that were by definition incompatible. The attacks on Irish servants that were such a common feature of middle-class discourse during the 1870s contributed to an environment where employers were reluctant to see Irish immigrants as a long-term investment. In her 1873 book *Motherly Talks with Young Housekeepers*, Eunice White Beecher, the wife of the Brooklyn minister Henry Ward Beecher, summarized what she claimed was the prevailing wisdom about the Castle Garden labor bureau: "Not one in a hundred . . . of all the Irish that come to our country can by any amount of care, patience, or indefatigable teaching, be transformed into a neat, energetic, faithful, truth-telling servant." Servants hired from the bureau who did prove capable of learning, Beecher lamented, quickly used their experience to obtain better paying positions. Viewing the bureau as nothing more than an open, unregulated exchange, Beecher advised prospective employers to bypass its facilities and inquire with steamship captains instead. How an Irish woman handled herself on the voyage across the Atlantic, Beecher claimed, would provide a better measure of her character.[31]

The 1875 investigation recommended that the governance and finance of the Castle Garden labor bureau be entirely transferred to the emigration societies, so as to separate the warring parties. The commissioners would continue to pay for the lease of the space, but would otherwise have no role in the bureau's management or staffing.[32] Stephenson resigned his position in 1875 due to his frustration with the societies' influence, although Republican Governor Alonzo Cornell would reappoint him to the board in 1880. (In the absence of civil service rules requiring him to forgo other employment, Stephenson also held the position of president of the Home Bank.) Although historian Charlotte Erickson argues that the legislature's decision to vest authority over the bureau in the German and Irish societies ultimately limited its capacity to reach newer immigrants arriving from Eastern and Southern Europe after 1880, in respect to domestic labor markets in New York City the bureau remained a vital exchange.[33] In 1877, despite the onset of an economic depression, the exchange was responsible for placing 4,952 female immigrants, or 9 percent of the total number of immigrants who arrived that year. In 1883, of the 8,384 women the bureau served, only 97 were hired for jobs outside of domestic service. That same year, 70 percent of the women placed by the bureau were Irish, with German women accounting for another 22 percent of the total. Employers in New York, New Jersey, Connecticut, and Pennsylvania hired 97 percent of all the women placed.[34] The bureau received so much in-person demand for domestic labor that it did not bother to even try to fill orders from outside the region. In 1881, William Connolly, the bureau's superintendent, reported having nearly seven hundred unanswered out-of-state requests for female servants on file.[35]

The reports filed by Connolly and his colleagues from the German Emigrant Society during the late 1870s and early 1880s painted a rosy picture of the work the bureau performed. The reality was more complicated. After 1886, the annual reports filed by the commissioners would no longer include a section on the labor bureau, in response to allegations that the numbers the bureau provided were inaccurate, since they counted repeat users as multiple individuals.[36] With anti-immigration attitudes on an uptick with the return of economic hard times in 1882, the state-appointed commissioners renewed their attacks on the labor bureau, blaming the exchange for indulging idleness and criminality. Stephenson remained the bureau's most vocal opponent. In February 1888, the four appointed commissioners voted for a resolution that called for abolishing the bureau altogether. As the *New York Times* reported, the commissioners alleged that in line with other labor bureaus where fees were not required, the exchange at Castle Garden had "become a sort of loafing place for lazy persons, who, under the guise of being immigrants, manage to find shelter under its roof." In an interview with the *Times*, Stephenson called the bureau a "pest house," and shared his own personal anecdote of hiring a German servant who ten days later revealed that she was pregnant, an experience he claimed was common. In his capacity as the bureau's superintendent, Connolly responded that if this was the case, then it was the commissioners' fault for landing an unaccompanied pregnant woman in the first place. Stephenson also relayed that he told his friends to "go to the workhouse" in search of labor rather than rely on Castle Garden. The commissioner claimed that there was no reason for the German and Irish societies to continue to receive preferential treatment, and that they could run—as Italian mutual associations did—their own free bureau separate from Castle Garden. This would allow for Castle Garden to use the space to house immigrants whose eligibility to enter was pending, and were therefore "necessarily detained" unlike the "bummers" who came to the bureau on a voluntary basis.[37]

Although the *Times* gave Stephenson ample space to espouse his views, it backed the German and Irish societies' position that the Castle Garden bureau was essential to protecting immigrant women "from outside runners of disorderly houses" and prostitution. The societies also hinted to the paper that Stephenson's antipathy toward the bureau was the result of a specific incident in which the exchange had successfully placed two Irish immigrant men he would have had deported as individuals liable to become public charges. Testifying before the House of Representatives Select Committee on Immigration and Naturalization in 1890, Connolly would repeat the substance of this charge. He claimed that Stephenson was unreasonable when it came to wanting to see the public charge provision more zealously enforced. Such measures were unnecessary since the labor bureau could almost always guarantee farm work to able-bodied immigrant men and domestic work to women.[38]

When the Board of Commissioners met in February 1888 to vote on whether or not to abolish the bureau, at the urging of New York Mayor Abraham Hewitt the motion was suspended pending further investigation.[39] In June 1888, the motion to abolish the bureau lay dormant. The board could barely even tolerate meeting given the open hostility that existed between Charles Hauselt and James Rorke, the presidents of the German and Irish societies, and the appointed commissioners. At an August 1889 meeting, the commissioners defended measures designed to prohibit employees of the labor bureau from accessing other parts of Castle Garden. Stephenson argued that the ban was necessary since employees of the bureau "made a good deal of money" accepting bribes in exchange for the promise of employment, which led Rorke to call him a liar.[40]

When not engaged in in-fighting with his fellow commissioners, Stephenson found other forums in which to campaign against the pernicious effects of an unregulated market for immigrant domestic labor. Before the Select Committee of the House of Representatives that convened in New York in 1888 to investigate Castle Garden, Stephenson introduced the case of Josephine Homelian, a Finnish immigrant. After Stephenson placed her in detention at the Emigrant Refuge on Ward's Island, Homelian was brought before the committee and testified that she had been sold a steamship ticket by a man named Peito in her native town of Gamlakarleby, Finland. Peito had promised Homelian that he would provide her with placement assistance upon her arrival in the United States, and that he could guarantee her a desirable job in domestic service at high wages. He also offered to loan her money to pay for her passage if she could not raise the full fare, which Homelian refused as unnecessary. Peito worked in partnership with his cousin Martin Souva, who operated an employment agency specializing in servants at 130 East 32nd Street in Manhattan. Souva had planned to meet Homelian at Castle Garden, but Stephenson got to her first. Subpoenaed by the committee, Souva revealed under interrogation that he and his cousin bought tickets from the steamship companies in bulk, at $18 a ticket, and then resold them individually for $27.75. Melbourne H. Ford, the Democratic Congressman from Michigan who chaired the committee, asked Homelian whether she would "have been willing to have landed in the city of New York with $2 of money" if she "had not supposed that Mr. Souva would give [her] work," to which her response was no.[41]

Myriad facets of Homelian's case irked Stephenson and sympathetic allies on the congressional committee who backed his calls for the heightened enforcement of restrictions on immigration. Rather than viewing Souva as helping to ensure that young women like Homelian did not become public charges, officials insinuated that figures such as him encouraged the wrong classes to immigrate in the first place. Representatives of the committee repeatedly tried to get Souva to confess that he and

Peito promoted the emigration of paupers by selling tickets to whom-ever they could find, which Souva denied. The implication was that Peito and Souva would have been well positioned to recoup whatever loans they tendered to Finnish immigrants, through arrangements with household employers where they garnished the wages of the servants they placed.

The ambiguity of the situation derived from the fact that Souva was well equipped to place immigrants who were penniless or indebted to him, since demand for domestic servants was inelastic. Stephenson felt that the commercial intelligence offices recruiting unskilled and untrained European immigrant women did more harm than good to the market for domestic labor; a quality they shared with the Castle Garden labor bureau. Poor women with no knowledge of middle-class house-hold management, he suggested, were so disposable that whatever labor scarcities they filled were not of any lasting significance. But this was a different matter than saying that a woman like Homelian was realisti-cally a risk to become a public charge. Peito and Souva's roles as ticket agents and brokers were inseparable from the capitalist innovation that the unceasing demand for immigrant domestic labor encouraged.

Bickering between the factions remained incessant until the commis-sioners' role in regulating immigration was ended altogether with the federal takeover of immigration inspection in 1891. The labor bureau run by the German and Irish societies briefly continued to occupy the Barge Office next to Castle Garden, and would remain in business into the twentieth century. No longer afforded its prime real estate and gov-ernment monopoly, however, its powers were vastly diminished and it became just another no-fee intelligence office run by charities. Even Rorke was forced to note while testifying before Congress in 1888 that much had changed over the course of the past four decades. As he put it, agents of his society no longer spent much of their time helping "Irish servant girls" post letters to the correct addresses.[42] In 1890 Connolly would express similar views. The commissioners suffered from a "want of kindness," he claimed, and the inspectors under their command were pressured to meet rejection quotas. As a result they invented pauper-ism where it did not exist and barred immigrants the labor bureau was capable of assisting.[43]

## Constructing Servants at the Border

Despite Connolly and Rorke's laments, the German and Irish societies' real grievances had to do with their loss of a guaranteed place at the table. No longer would these ethnic interests be assured representation, even if individual members from these communities continued to feature prominently within the new bureaucracy.[44] When restrictions on Chinese immigration were first introduced in 1882, customs collectors from the Department of the Treasury served as the original inspectors. In respect to European immigration, the federal government continued to rely on state-level officials for close to another decade. In New York, the federal government contracted with the Commissioners of Emigration, who continued to fulfill the same functions they had since the late 1840s at Castle Garden. It was not until 1891 that Congress designated funds for the creation of a federal immigration service, and in 1895 that office received the title of Bureau. In 1903 the Bureau of Immigration was transferred from the Department of Treasury to the Department of Labor and Commerce, and in 1906 its jurisdiction was expanded to cover issues pertaining to naturalization as well. The two bureaus would remain there until 1940, when they were transferred to the Department of Justice.[45]

Picking up where state-level enforcement efforts had left off, early federal policies directed at Europeans were most concerned with the entry of immigrants who might end up on public relief. The 1891 Immigration Act stipulated that any immigrant who became a public charge within a year of arrival could be deported. In 1903 the period in which an immigrant could be deported as a public charge was extended to up to two years after their arrival, and in 1907 to three years. In respect to being labeled likely to become a public charge, an immigrant could avoid deportation if it could be demonstrated that the need for public relief—whether by illness, injury, or another condition—was the result of an incident that happened subsequent to the individual's landing.[46]

Whereas the discretion that was granted to immigration inspectors negatively affected Chinese immigrants and encouraged their harassment, young white women were often the beneficiaries—at least when it came to being permitted to land—of those same subjective powers.[47]

White immigrant women, especially those who came from Northern Europe and "old" sources of immigration, could in many cases count on a gendered embrace that acknowledged middle-class households' unrelenting demand for domestic labor. Immigration inspectors shared the middle-class belief that domestic service was a safe occupation for young, unaccompanied women. They even made domestic work an involuntary sanctuary for white immigrant women who could have been rejected on account of questions about their past behavior.

The preservation of immigration records was not comprehensive. Board of special inquiry transcripts from New York were generated when an immigrant was flagged for additional investigations and inter-rogations, but these records were not saved unless a decision on entry posed administrative or legal issues that prompted officials at Ellis Island to forward these materials to Washington. Special inquiry records are available for Philadelphia, covering the period of 1893 to 1909. The 1893 Immigration Act established these boards in order to provide immi-gration officials with a means to more thoroughly investigate whether or not immigrants belonged to the growing number of categories that marked them as inadmissible. The boards conducted more in-depth inquiries into the backgrounds and destinations of immigrants flagged as suspicious during initial inspections that took place on ships and in the stations.[48] Reflecting the far greater scrutiny that attended decisions concerning Chinese immigration, inquiry records in the form of exclu-sion case files can be found for nearly all of the Chinese immigrants who entered or departed the country after 1891.

The fourth largest port of entry in the country, Philadelphia processed slightly fewer than ten thousand immigrants in 1899, and in 1913, its peak year, handled sixty thousand. Prior to federal government assumption of immigration enforcement, the state of Pennsylvania maintained a medi-cal quarantine station in the Delaware River and, like New York and Mas-sachusetts, required sureties from ship captains against the possibility that immigrants might enter onto public relief. In 1873, the Washington Avenue Immigration Station opened to accommodate the introduction of regular steamship service from Europe on the American and Red Star lines, which the Pennsylvania Railroad, the owner and operator of the pier and connecting trains, had helped finance. While Philadelphia never came close to equaling the volume of traffic to New York, by the end of the century all of the major steamship lines serviced the port weekly if not more frequently.[49]

The board of special inquiry records, documenting as they do the minutiae of back-and-forth conversations between European immigrants and inspectors, demonstrate the contradictions that were built into the dual and sometimes dueling missions of protecting both the nation and the immigrant. The sentimental border that federal officials constructed and policed was a place where the prevailing ideologies about liberty of contract and autonomy—the characteristics attached to the idealized free migrant—could be suspended on account of gender, age, and sexuality. While officials' emphasis on protecting white women harkened back to earlier concerns about unaccompanied women traveling on their own, they can also be read in the context of defending middle-class homes from free market competition, at a time when household employers were finding it increasingly difficult to compete against industrial occupations for women workers.[50] Women whose admission might be denied were at their most vulnerable, which in turn made them ideal candidates for domestic work. White women laborers who came with resources or traveled with families could more freely explore their options, and often procured industrial jobs instead. When potential debarment was at stake, immigrant women routinely stated that they were domestic servants even if they had no experience doing this labor.[51]

If Williams's intervention that began this chapter seemed staged for the benefit of the *Post* and its readers, consider instead the case of Kate Kerghrin. On May 18, 1896, the twenty-year-old Irish woman arrived in Philadelphia aboard the S.S. *Indiana*, having departed from Queenstown (Cobh), Ireland. Kerghrin arrived with only fifty cents and a prepaid train ticket to New York City. She told the inspector who questioned her that she was supposed to travel north to meet a married cousin, Bridget Rogan, but had misplaced her address. Her unaccompanied status, minimal funds, and confusion about her destination generated skepticism, and following administrative procedure, she was brought before the board of special inquiry.

The Philadelphia board's discretionary power, like that of Williams and other high-ranking officials, was deployed to commodify and broker immigrant women's labor power. The consumption of immigrant women's labor as servants rendered them "safe" in the eyes of the state, in both economic and moralistic terms, since their assignment to middle-class households protected them as dependents while also making them self-sufficient as wage laborers. In Kerghrin's case, inspectors in Phila-delphia first wrote to a friend who she claimed knew Rogan's address, but they received no reply. Kerghrin spent four nights in the boarding house that the Philadelphia office used to house European detainees awaiting a decision on their admission.

As with all things relating to the governance of immigration, race mattered in respect to how a young Irish woman was treated relative to other immigrants. Chinese immigrants, for instance, did not receive the form of parole granted to Kerghrin, who was allowed a room outside the facility and not kept in a holding cell. Until Angel Island opened in 1910, Chinese immigrants being held for further investigation were sent to the Pacific Mail Steamship Company's detention shed, a build-ing notorious for its poor sanitary conditions and crammed quarters.[52] When Chinese immigrants arriving in Philadelphia were held pending further investigation into their eligibility to enter, they were confined to the station's facilities. On May 22, by unanimous vote the three members of the board released Kerghrin to Frederick Karlthoff. No information about Karlthoff's occupation, background, or familial status is included in Kerghrin's file, just a brief note stating that the situation was arranged by the steamship company.[53] Since the Red Star Line, the owner of the *Indiana*, paid for her room and board—and would have been responsible for the cost of her passage back to Ireland if she had been deported—facilitating this connection was in its material interest. Kerghrin wit-nessed her plans, however inchoate to begin with, remade at the border.

In Philadelphia, inspectors repeatedly worked with steamship per-sonnel to find mutually beneficial solutions to cases where detention or deportation might burden their companies' bottom lines. Such was the case with Nellie Sullivan, a twenty-six-year-old Irish woman who arrived on May 10, 1896, with only eighty cents. She listed no friends or relatives living in the United States. Her release came at the hands of a stranger whom she suddenly found herself bound to, if not by formal contract, then by word and promise. After being detained by the board she was landed when a man listed only as Mr. Buchard, a steamship company employee who appears to have sat in on Sullivan's hearing, "guaranteed a position for her." The odd circumstances of Sullivan's arrival, which included her lack of funds and declaration that she had no family or acquaintances in the United States—a rare occurrence for Irish immigrants by the 1890s—suggests that she may have been in flight. Sullivan may have seen Philadelphia, a secondary port of arrival, as a safer option for evading the type of rigorous inspection that could have led to debarment. During the 1895–96 fiscal year, the Philadelphia station received 25,036 immigrants and barred only 59, 0.24 percent of the total, from entry.[54] While Sullivan could not be legally forced to remain in the position in which Buchard placed her, any period of unemployment during her first year put her at risk for deportation if she was caught as a public charge.

The involvement of the steamship companies in ushering a migrant through inspection began at the very moment an individual decided to leave her country of origin. In Sullivan's case, in her local Irish town, the agents providing her a ticket—whether procured through remittances or purchased with her own money—would have conducted at least a cursory evaluation of her eligibility for admission. Repeated sales to ineligible immigrants resulted in the steamship companies dropping agents who cost them revenue. When she departed from Liverpool, British officials would have subjected her to a medical inspection and further questions about whether she might fall into any of the excludable categories. During the trip across the Atlantic, crewmembers and fellow passengers returning to the United States would have been available to coach her. Undoubtedly, many of these parties would have been able to advise her that demonstrating a willingness to work as a servant would have offset her more questionable qualifications for admission.

Immigration inspectors also possessed the power to use the public charge provision to compel arrivals into taking jobs where wages were below the prevailing rates, and impeded immigrants' freedom to compete for positions where higher wages might be found. In the cases of Lizzie and Maggie Farrell, who appeared before the Philadelphia board in November 1900, inspectors prevented the two Irish sisters from testing the market by detaining them. Lizzie and Maggie, who were twenty-three and nineteen, respectively, were "bound to New York on speculation" with $17 between them. Rather than permitting them to continue in unaccompanied transit to New York, the Philadelphia inspectors relied on a steamship company representative to redirect the sisters to local employers. Lizzie was contracted out to the Kensington Hospital at $12 per month and Maggie was sent to a woman named Mrs. Jacoby at $3 a week. In Maggie's case, her placement was eventually annotated with a comment that she had relocated to another home at $2.50 a week. This suggests perhaps that things with Jacoby did not work out, or that the position was not as secure as the steamship agent had claimed.[55] In the case of Mary Waterhouse, a twenty-one-year-old English immigrant who arrived in December 1900, officials intervened when she stated that she did not wish to go to the address of a Mrs. Douglass (whether Douglass was a relative, friend, or employer was not clarified). A steamship company agent found a position for her as a live-in servant with a family in Devon, Pennsylvania, for $2 per week. Farrell's and Waterhouse's wages appear to have been below the occupational average. In a report commissioned by the U.S. Industrial Commission in 1900, Gail Laughlin noted that laborers classified as inexperienced "general servants" earned $3.09 per week as the Pennsylvania state average. Based on these numbers, it appears that immigration officials and their steamship company accomplices were contracting domestic laborers at a discount. Citing interviews with employment agencies in Philadelphia, Laughlin noted that women willing to work as general servants were especially hard to come by. As a result, officials at the immigration stations were uniquely positioned as suppliers.[56]

It is not difficult to imagine the unrecorded backstories that were also part of these various incidents. Perhaps the steamship company agents placing women made a small commission in exchange for brokering the arrangement, or won some other favor from an employer whom they helped to find domestic labor in a tight market. The Philadelphia immigration station also occasionally reached out to private employment offices, although the details of these collaborations were not recorded. In the annual report for the 1895–96 fiscal year, for instance, the Philadelphia station reported that 334 immigrants came to the office seeking relief after having landed either in the city or in another port, and that immigration officials found jobs for 126 of these individuals through employment offices at no cost to the government. This suggests that officials had some arrangement where they were able to get waived the fees that a job applicant using an employment agency owed.[57] Moreover, these incidents reveal the extent of the assistance that officials were will-ing to offer to able but unemployed European immigrants to spare them deportation.

Officials in Philadelphia were more conservative when it came to admitting older women, and less likely to attempt to spontaneously contract them out as servants. Mary Rolands, a fifty-year-old Welsh woman who had traveled back and forth between the United States and the United Kingdom working in domestic service jobs in both countries, was denied entry in October 1899 when she arrived with only $4.60. The friend she claimed to be going to in Philadelphia refused to accept care of her or to even receive the telegram that Rolands had sent her. No response was received from Rolands's brother, who was also contacted. The board of special inquiry ordered her deported. It noted the public health officer's comment that she seemed to be of a "frail constitution," and dismissed her contention that she "worked by the day among her friends and many ladies" while living in England, and was therefore capable of finding work in the United States.[58] As Rolands's case and others involving older and unaccompanied single immigrant women reveal, women could lose both their status as dependents deserving pro-tection and help finding work upon reaching a certain age.

The perception that a European immigrant woman possessed youth-ful vitality and could start over in the United States could lead officials to ignore histories that might otherwise be read as evidence of poor moral judgment and character. Twenty-one-year-old Adeline Porter, for instance, lost a child to premature birth in the Philadelphia Alms-Hospital in September 1897. Having arrived at Ellis Island from Scot-land, unmarried and alone, only four months earlier, she was eligible for deportation as a public charge. In Porter's case, however, the physician treating her was able to convince immigration officials to allow her to stay, and arranged a domestic position for her in a colleague's home.[59]

The experiences of Kerghrin, Sullivan, the Farrells, and Porter show the sentimental state at work, and the privileges and compulsions that informed how migrants defined by their whiteness, gender, and youth were governed. As young unaccompanied immigrant women, these women's ability to determine whom they worked for was always going to be constrained by pressures, whether from the family guardians required to receive them, or from government officials. It is impossible to discern whether they made a conscious choice to try Philadelphia as their port of entry, and therefore had their decision validated when immigration officials relented and let them in—despite the fact that they represented cases where they might have been deemed likely to become public charges. Within a year's time these women would no longer have to worry about being deported if they ended up on public relief, and, as soon as they had another job offer, they could leave the situation that immigration officials had compelled them to take as a condition of their entry. Being forced to relinquish freedom at the border could pay longer-term dividends.

## Ellis Island, Revisited

As the nation's largest port of immigration, New York remained the main laboratory for determining how federal officials could best insert unaccompanied white women into local domestic service situations, thereby circumventing intermediaries accused of exercising a negative influence over the labor supply. Ellis Island officially opened on January 1, 1892. Geographically, the new facility was designed to segregate immigrants from the predatory actors who had surrounded Castle Garden and made it their base of operations. Ellis Island was accessible only by ferry, and federal officials required missionaries and social workers to obtain licenses before they were permitted to visit the station and offer assistance. Station officials also had the power to expel those who violated their terms.[60] A labor bureau was not included as part of the new complex.

The federal government's attempts to present Ellis Island as a symbol of modernization belied a more troubling start to its work. During its early years the new station was a dangerous place for single women. An 1899 Treasury Department investigation into how Ellis Island was managed under the administration of its assistant commissioner, Edward F. McSweeney, revealed that the hazards posed to immigrants came not from outsiders bent on exploiting them but rather from the bureaucracy itself. The chief of the Registry Division at Ellis Island, John Lederhilger, investigators reported, was known to be a "serial groper" whose actions were "mortifying" to his colleagues. In particular, Lederhilger abused his discretionary authority to keep women in Ellis Island's "pen," the name for the space where unaccompanied women were held while awaiting the arrival of a guardian to whom they could be released. He then pressured these women in the pen to bribe him with sexual favors or money, investigators alleged, to expedite their discharge.[61]

While Lederhilger offers an especially nasty example, the subjective nature of discerning an immigrant's eligibility to enter frequently made women vulnerable to sexual entreaties and trafficking that were tied to promises of helping them gain admission. In 1897, J. H. Senner, the commissioner of Ellis Island, dismissed a gate man at the station after receiving a tip that his employee was also a proprietor of a hotel and bar that doubled as brothel. Edward A. Steiner, who wrote about his experiences traveling with steerage passengers, witnessed a young Czech woman being propositioned by an inspector, who warned her that she might not be allowed to enter otherwise.[62]

President Theodore Roosevelt appointed William Williams to the commissioner position in 1902 as a "good government" advocate who would clean up the corruption already pervading the station's administration. Williams embraced the role. He disciplined minor infractions of the station's rules and punished employees for a host of violations ranging from absenteeism to unprofessionalism with a stringency that made many of his colleagues resent him.[63] Determined to fully control operations at Ellis Island, Williams also introduced measures that were designed to check the powers of intermediaries who might interfere with the federal government's authority. In 1903, for instance, Margaret Ellis and representatives from the Women's Christian Temperance Union (WCTU) convinced President Roosevelt to permit them to conduct a ninety-day experiment where women would work as onboard ship inspectors alongside men in New York harbor. The WCTU premised that female inspectors could more effectively detect women who were bound for prostitution. They could also win their trust and persuade them to discuss the circumstances of their trafficking. Williams opposed the idea, and tried to halt the program before ninety days had even expired. He argued that women threatened the professional reputation of the service as a whole, and that they were ill equipped to take on the physical demands of the work. To the exasperation of the WCTU, Williams claimed that dresses and petticoats were obstacles that female inspectors who had to climb ladders to board ships could not surmount.[64] Although all of the major immigration stations employed female matrons responsible for supervising detained female immigrants, until the 1920s female employees of the service were limited to this work.

When it came to adjudicating the "likely to become a public charge" clause, Williams—like many of his peers within the immigration service— was openly biased toward Northern and Western Europeans. If immigrants from these groups arrived without money, officials were more likely to give them the benefit of the doubt since the bureau adhered to a racialized understanding of how these immigrants' character, aptitude, and physique better positioned them to overcome poverty and thrive. In contrast, inspectors and officials dismissed the ability of comparably indigent Southern and Eastern Europeans to improve their condition through gainful employment. In 1902, Frank Sargent, who had just replaced Terrence Powderly as commissioner general of immigration in Washington, wrote to Williams to confirm that he was "in hearty accord" with his fellow appointee's opinion that the boards of special inquiry had to be trained on how to judge an immigrant's cultural and racial background in the context of interpreting the public charge provision. This meant instructing inspectors to admit "Scotchmen, Irishmen, or Germans" Sargent wrote, and not rejecting them "simply because they do not have a certain sum of money in their possession."[65]

In regard to unaccompanied white women, Williams did not stray far from the line that had been invoked by patriarchal authority figures since the days of the Irish Famine migrations: women were dependents who did not possess full natural rights to free mobility and contract. With unaccompanied women, the distinctions that immigration officials used to categorize the capabilities of different groups of European men to succeed, based on their national backgrounds, had less significance. Because all women were viewed by male officials as dependents, the goal was to direct the contract of their labor in a manner that reaffirmed this status. The Immigration Bureau, demonstrating the wide consensus that this idea enjoyed, was never forced to legally justify its basis for detaining unaccompanied women even when they were otherwise eligible to enter. The rule mandating that single women had to be received by guardians who could vouch to immigration officials that they would ensure the arrivals' welfare and protect them from sexual trafficking could be found nowhere in any of the statutes regulating immigration, and was enacted purely as an administrative directive. There is no evidence that women held in such a fashion ever posed legal challenges to demand their release, and therefore this policy was never tested before a judicial body. In 1914 the secretary of labor proposed adding language to House Resolution 6060 that would have made unmarried immigrant women under the age of twenty automatically excludable unless they were "accompanied by or going to a parent, a respectable and responsible female relative, or a respectable and responsible male relative and his wife." But the bill was vetoed by President Woodrow Wilson in 1915. Instead, the policy continued on an ad hoc basis.[66]

Williams also made it a priority to further routinize how the release and subsequent monitoring of unaccompanied women took place. In September 1903, he issued a memorandum to Ellis Island's inspectors instructing them in the new procedures. He ordered the chief of the Registry Division to "see to it that all *unattended female immigrants* are, in any event, required to telegraph their relatives or friends before leaving Ellis Island, and in all proper cases such immigrants will in addition be temporarily detained until they have received a reply to such telegrams."[67] By 1912, Williams had refined this system to include a basic identifying tag, which was used alongside the chalk markings made on immigrants' clothing to signify presumed physical or mental illnesses. The marking was meant to help prevent unaccompanied women awaiting a relative or friend from slipping by the gatekeepers unnoticed. In addition, unaccompanied immigrant women wishing to make train connections to locations outside the region were affixed with a piece of paper that read "Telegraph," which indicated that these women should telegraph the parties they claimed were going to receive them in the presence of an inspector, who could then assess the legitimacy of the arrangement. Callers coming to secure the release of detained immigrant women remaining in New York City and surrounding areas were required to bring paperwork satisfying officials as to their identity.[68] Even before these last measures were implemented in 1912, Kellor, who monitored how Ellis Island handled immigrant women, praised Williams for creating a system of supervision that was superior to the methods being used at other ports. Her only complaint was that the railroad companies making fortunes off the immigrant trade had managed to shirk any accountability for the welfare of the female passengers they handled. She proposed that they be mandated to hire matrons at each of the major transit hubs handling immigrant traffic, to ensure that women departing Ellis Island for points west remained under supervision.[69]

One reason Williams gave to explain the bureau's policy of detaining unaccompanied immigrant women was the need to protect them from predatory missionaries. Williams got into numerous spats with ethnic and religious agencies performing social work in New York City, and on multiple occasions withdrew the offending parties' licenses allowing them to visit Ellis Island. Again, there is no denying that corruption occurred and that charitable workers were sometimes involved. Many instances involving young women's placement as servants, however, were rife with ambiguity. In these cases, federal officials wanted to suppress the actions of intermediaries so that they could exercise more absolute forms of control over how the labor supply was provisioned to households.

Williams's insistence on seeing corruption as the fault of bad individual actors made it difficult for him to appreciate how Ellis Island's policies could also cause problems. In 1903, for instance, he issued a memorandum explaining why the Austro Hungarian Home, a benevolent society supported by the Habsburg state, had joined the ranks of agencies banned from doing business on Ellis Island. As was often the case, the alleged abuses that the home had committed centered on its treatment of women. Only rarely did the treatment of men spark similar controversies, which also reflected the fact that many social agencies had a policy of aiding women exclusively. Williams maintained that the home had "prevented immigrants from reaching their friends," and had sent women into domestic service "against their will." He also alleged that it charged exorbitant rates of rent and prevented visitors from checking on the female residents it housed. In further violation of their charitable status, Williams claimed that agents of the home received commissions from the households they placed servants in. On top of all of these inappropriate actions, Williams noted that representatives of the home had also allegedly told immigrant women that they had the power to compel them to take jobs as domestics because the immigration bureaucracy had ordered them "subject to its control for a period of one year."[70] While it is impossible to know what exactly was said, "a period of one year" was the time frame in which immigrants could be deported as public charges. It appears that both officials at Ellis Island and missionaries understood that the threat of deportation was a means by which they could assert legitimate and illegitimate power over immigrants.

Williams preferred to see immigrant women placed in jobs—which immigration officials could vet—prior to their release to missionaries. Williams's intention was to minimize the uncertainties related to placement, which he believed corrupt missionaries preyed on. This policy also reduced the number of immigrant women sent to boarding houses, where even if missionaries were honest and diligent, Williams claimed their charges were still vulnerable to being lured into disreputable lines of work.

Missionaries who worked at Ellis Island interpreted the matter differently. They viewed Williams's efforts to place women in domestic jobs prior to their release as a policy that undermined women's economic agency by forcing them to rush the contract of their labor. In a letter to Williams, a representative of the Hungarian Relief Society observed that in his experience, contracts arranged prior to departure from Ellis Island were counter to the interests of the immigrant women being discharged. Revisiting many of the themes that had prompted so much contention within the labor bureau at Castle Garden, the representative noted that when women sought out work as servants, they had to contend with the fact that every employer had idiosyncratic needs and tasks they wanted fulfilled. If already under contract before they ever entered their employer's household, immigrant women were denied an opportunity to freely negotiate what they would or would not do, which in turn made the officials complicit in reducing their autonomy. An immigrant worker was fearful to leave a situation if it meant risking deportation. The subjective nature of the public charge provision led to confusion where unemployment and the receipt of public relief could easily be conflated in the minds of immigrants as causes for their potential removal.[71] Confident that he was a positive, patriarchal influence in immigrant women's lives, Williams brushed this and other advice aside.

## "Very Respectable Girls, but Girls That Are Likely to Get into Trouble . . .": The Foran Act and Exceptions for Domestic Labor

The 1885 Contract Labor Law, also known as the Foran Act, after the bill's Democratic sponsor, was the first federal immigration legislation aimed at defending American labor from European sources of unfair competition. The Foran Act prohibited American employers from paying for the transportation costs of an immigrant living abroad, and from contracting with foreign workers prior to their arrival. In the wording of the original 1885 act, domestic and personal servants were exempted from these prohibitions. Servants hired abroad still had to pass the medical and other tests that statutes mandated in order to gain entry. The 1891 Immigration Act bolstered the Foran Act by barring immigrants from receiving financial assistance for passage, even in the absence of labor contracts, except in cases where funding came from family or friends residing in the United States who did not have a direct stake in the assisted immigrant's future employment.[72]

The economic recovery that followed the end of the long depression of the 1870s was short-lived. By 1882, railroad construction, which was accompanied by overly optimistic and often corrupt financial speculation, had collapsed. Capital disappeared and downsizing followed. In this environment, white laborers in the West, who were especially reliant on employment from the railroads and attached industries, attacked Chinese immigrants and what they argued was the lax enforcement of the extant restriction acts. In the rest of the country, organized labor and allies cited immigrant men from Eastern and Southern Europe as the new source of cheap and bonded labor that capital would use to undermine their position.[73]

In passing the Foran Act, Congress yielded to the argument of the law's main advocates, the Federation of Organized Trades and Labor Unions and the Knights of Labor, which argued that the statute was necessary to protect American workers from corporations that would otherwise be able to mobilize contracted foreign workers to break strikes and replace unionized workers. Nonetheless, legal historian Kitty Calavita describes the Foran Act as a "symbolic law," enforced with largely "symbolic action." At the time of its 1885 passage, private labor exchanges clustered around Castle Garden supplied newly arrived workers to break strikes, but, crucially, dealt in immigrant labor that had already landed. The official labor bureau located *in* Castle Garden was also accused of supplying strikebreakers, although its directors denied these accusations. In contrast, the import of foreign laborers under contract was not practical since they could not be brought in quickly enough to meet employers' antiunion needs. In addition, until the initial act was amended in February 1887, it was unclear as to whether federal officials could deport immigrants found to be in violation of the law or bring criminal charges against contractors. In 1901, a congressional investigation uncovered that only eight thousand immigrants had been barred by the law. And, despite the addition of statutory provisions that made violations of the Foran Act a criminal offense, only one in every thousand employers charged with the offense was ever convicted.[74] The impact that the Foran Act had on how emigration was approached is less clear. Even if its regulations were rarely enforced within the United States, the act did have the unintended consequence of helping to further empower steamship company agents as migration boosters and creditors, since corporations and land agents in the United States could no longer openly perform these roles.

Congressional debates leading up to the passage of the Foran Act placed racial and gendered constructions of dependency front and center, albeit as the hypothetical counterpoints to the autonomy and independence that free white men were supposed to embody in their actions. Prohibitions on the importation of contract laborers posited that white men could be "coolies" too, and, like Chinese immigrants, had to be monitored as dependent subjects incapable of acting autonomously. Republican Senator Henry William Blair from New Hampshire, one of the principal backers of the Foran Act, explained that the legislation was "aimed at slavery rather than freedom," and that it was "designed to prevent substantially the cooly practices which have been initiated and carried on to a considerable extent between America and Europe." That European immigrants could be classified as such was controversial, and many of Blair's colleagues rejected the equivalency he put forth. Morgan, the Democratic senator from Alabama, was one of only a handful to vote against the Foran Act. He argued that it would be a "disgrace and dishonor" to the character of Irish, English, Welsh, German, and even Italian workers—whose "whiteness" in the public's mind rested on less solid ground—to be lumped together with the Chinese.[75]

How the exemption for personal and domestic servants wended its way into the legislation is itself revealing. On February 13, 1885, a verbal amendment to the bill (H.R. 2550) that would become the Foran Act was proposed by Blair. There was no debate on the amendment,

which outlined the exception, and it was agreed to by a floor vote.[76]
How and why the Foran Act came to include an exception to the contract labor migration of servants was divulged only years later, in 1913.
This occurred when John L. Burnett, a Democrat from Alabama and
the chairman of the House Committee on Immigration and Naturalization, presented a general immigration bill (H.R. 6060) that would have
required all immigrants over the age of sixteen to pass a literacy test in
their native language before being allowed to enter. During the debate
on H.R. 6060, the exemption of servants from contract labor restrictions
was raised since the new bill proposed carrying over this provision.

Sarcastically, J. Hampton Moore, a Republican member of the House
representing Philadelphia, argued that it was hypocritical to continue
to allow the contract of servants from abroad while at the same time
proposing to bar with the literacy test the immigration of women who
might otherwise enter the occupation. "The wealthy lady or rich man,"
drolly described by Moore as a hypothetical "Mrs. Astorbilt," "can make
a contract with 'James' of England or with 'Francois' of Paris. [She] can
bring any one of those servants into this country under contract and
they will not be excluded under this law." At the same time, Moore
claimed, a literacy test would "bar out 84,000 females," his estimate of
the number of illiterate immigrant women who would be prohibited
from entering annually, "many of whom would make excellent servants
and bring positive relief to the American housewife." To laughter, Moore
concluded his comments with a bipartisan appeal: "I do not think the
Democratic Party will vote James the Butler in by this bill."[77]

With this imagined contrast, Moore implied that the ability to contract domestic labor from abroad represented elite market behavior
and an impractical option for the middle class as a whole. Moreover,
his point appealed to gendered and racialized tropes that depicted butlers and male valets as emasculated. In the same way that the racial stereotypes of "Sambo" and "John Chinaman" were deployed to represent
black and Chinese men as servile subjects who were willing to care for
other men and their families, while abdicating their own roles as heads
of households, "James the Butler" sacrificed his manhood in order to
perform a function that had no social utility beyond the frivolous value
it provided to decadent employers. Whereas "James the Butler" was a
luxury item reserved for the few, Moore portrayed the potential loss of

thousands of female servants—whose literacy was not a requisite skill for their employment—as an affront to middle-class households desperately in need of additional laborers.

Despite being passed by both the House and Senate, H.R. 6060 was vetoed by President Woodrow Wilson in 1915. During the first session of the subsequent sixty-fourth Congress, however, Burnett introduced a new bill, H.R. 10384, which was closely modeled on its predecessor. Again the issue of exempting servants from the contract labor restriction arose in debate. On March 27, 1916, George Young, a Republican member of the House from North Dakota, proposed amending the language of the bill to allow for the importation of farm laborers. Young's constituents, North Dakota farmers, wanted to pay for the transportation of contracted seasonal laborers from nearby Canada. When Young's amendment was rejected, to express his disappointment he introduced an additional amendment that would have barred the import of servants by eliminating their exemption from the pending legislation. Resentful that his constituents' interests had been denied, Young claimed that "the only consistent course we can follow here . . . would be to strike out the clause that gives the privilege to the city dwellers to bring in the butlers, servants, and footmen without any restriction."[78]

In response, Augustus Peabody Gardner, a Republican from Massachusetts who supported increasing restrictions on European immigration, finally explained to the House—thirty years after the Foran Act was passed—how the original 1885 exception had come to be. According to Gardner, it was about "Martha and Mary, girls who do not like to come to this country on speculation." Again trading in hypothetical figures, Gardner argued that "Martha and Mary" were not elite-trained valets and butlers but young women who desired to contract with household employers prior to emigrating so that their safety and morality would not be compromised in transit. Blair's original rationale in 1885 was to assist "girls coming down from Nova Scotia, New Brunswick, and Newfoundland," who were "very respectable girls, but girls that are likely to get into trouble, as all girls are who come into a country where they are strangers."[79] (How Gardner knew Blair's reasoning was left unstated. Gardner did not enter Congress until 1902, some fifteen years after the Foran Act was passed. Blair had left Congress in 1895, although he was still alive in 1916.) This form of contract immigration, Gardner suggested, was acceptable because it was a natural reaction to the circumstances of young women who desired to enter into domestic service, whereas migrant farm laborers could not be viewed as vulnerable in the same way. In his debate with Young, Gardner did offer a compromise where the language of the bill would be changed to exempt only female immigrants employed as personal or domestic servants, thereby making it explicit that the legislation was designed to protect women wage earners. At the end of the day, both Gardner's compromise amendment and Young's proposal were rejected handily in separate votes.[80]

When H.R. 10384 was finally passed into law as the Immigration Act of 1917, with Congress marshaling enough votes to override President Wilson's veto, personal servants were no longer exempt from alien contract labor law while domestic servants maintained their special status. Servants were not exempt, however, from the literacy test. Why "personal" was struck from the final version of the bill is unclear and never specifically addressed in any of the congressional debates on the legislation. One possible reason is that the term "personal," as the populist arguments by Moore and Young demonstrate, was too closely associated with valet and butlers, and the types of domestic laborers that the public viewed as superfluous. While both the working and middle classes accepted domestic service as a necessary (if not particularly beloved) feature of the social relations of middle-class household production, they did not have a stake in supporting the contract migration of workers for elite households intent on maintaining an aristocratic division of labor. This change in language would nonetheless end up creating new and unanticipated issues of enforcement that the bureau and federal courts would later have to address, as chapter 6 of this book examines. Determining what constituted the difference between domestic and personal service was not a simple or self-evident task.

* * *

When opportunistic labor brokers and steamship ticket agents tried to deploy the domestic service exception to the Foran Act more proactively, they encountered rigid opposition from immigration officials. The bureau was suspicious of all commercial ventures that might import European women in bulk. In July 1907, the Department of Labor received a favorable ruling from the U.S. attorney general stating that the exemption to the foreign contract of servants did not extend to women destined for employment in "public institutions not of a domestic character," such as hotels.[81] Hotels were associated with sex trafficking, which explains why officials were reluctant to see women sent their under contract by third parties. In 1911, Daniel Keefe, the new commissioner general of immigration, ruled that "wholesale importation" in any form was not what the Foran Act had intended. Keefe's opinion was prompted by a letter from an American consular official in London who had received an inquiry from a local employment agency asking whether it could recruit servants and pay for their emigration. The servants' debts for the cost of their voyage would be deducted from their future wages. The employment agency's interest in this question derived from the fact that it was "frequently in receipt of requests from Americans to supply them with domestic servants."[82]

Although schemes such as the one proposed by the London-based labor broker had existed in the 1860s and 1870s—and were considered important to provisioning western states like California with white domestic labor—by the start of the twentieth century concerns about sex trafficking made them the subject of intense scrutiny. After 1911, when faced with additional inquiries about the importation of contracted servants, officials clarified that while the direct accompaniment of servants by their employers was not mandated, brokers and labor agents were not allowed to bring domestics across the Atlantic so that they might be hired out on a speculative basis to undetermined employers. This point was conveyed to the Board of Development for the city of San Angelo, Texas, for instance, after its secretary had written to the bureau inquiring about whether it might arrange for its "leading citizens" to be matched with a "large number of female servants," preferably of Scandinavian origin.[83] This was permitted but only if orchestrated by individual employers themselves and not a middleman, officials explained.

The contract of servants by intermediaries rather than direct employers was permitted only when a state agency took on the role of broker. In December 1915, the New York Bureau of Employment received permission to work with counterparts across the border in Canada in order to connect household employers in Buffalo, Rochester, and Syracuse with Canadian domestic laborers who had not yet entered the country. This brokerage was presumably allowed since the New York Bureau of Employment did not claim a fee or commission for the service it provided, and because the intermediaries involved were public officials.[84]

Outside of cases such as this, however, immigration officials' interpretation of the Contract Labor Law ensured that the main beneficiaries would continue to be affluent individuals and families whose connections and travels abroad allowed them to recruit servants directly. When E. W. Barnes, the chief engineer of the Grand Rapids and Indiana Railway Company, wrote to Washington with a plan to advertise for servants abroad, whom he would then bring into the country to meet local demand, he was warned that "any extensive importation of domestics under pre-arrangement for employment might result in a return to the former practice of allowing them to enter the United States only when accompanied by their employers" (even though this had never been the case in practice).[85] Similarly, when the New York banker Lionel Sutro wrote to the secretary of commerce and labor in September 1912 about whether he would be permitted to set up an import business bringing servants into the country, which he hoped to develop alongside a scheme to contract experienced Egyptian cotton growers to planters in the Mississippi Delta, not only was he denied permission, but his request for information prompted an in-person investigation. Upon visiting Sutro at his office on Cedar Street in Lower Manhattan, immigration inspector Edwin B. Woods lectured him that it was "contrary to law to import laborers into this country."[86]

The United States' prohibitions on agent-sponsored contract labor migrations differed in comparison to its northern neighbor's. Canada's position within the British Empire encouraged the transatlantic coordination of women's domestic labor migrations, whereas the United States emphasized individual migrations assisted only by private families. In 1906, Canada implemented a policy where the Office of the High Commissioner for Canada paid British ticket agents a one-pound bonus, on top of whatever normal commissions they stood to earn, if they convinced female servants and male agricultural workers to emigrate. Once servants arrived in Canada, they reported to local household employer organizations that placed the women in situations and recorded the British agents' bonuses—as long as the immigrant servants sent proved their "*bona fides*." The Ministry of the Interior, which oversaw immigration in Canada, also employed government agents dedicated to helping

immigrants find work as servants and farmhands. So as to avoid antago-
nizing organized labor, these same agents were barred from helping men
find work in industrial occupations. By 1919, Canadian immigration officials had grown frustrated with the loose selection criteria that commercial ticket agents were using, and the caliber of servants being sent.
Their response was to open their own screening offices in Britain and to
reduce their reliance on ticket agents mainly interested in drumming up
business.[87] As these various initiatives demonstrate, the Canadian government was willing to take a more active role in brokering household
employment in ways that were also more systematic.

From a different angle, what drove Gardner's "Martha and Mary" to
decide to enter into employment arrangements where they arrived in the
United States under contract? Because women who entered the country in
this manner were permitted to do so, they did not produce detailed interrogation records. From what evidence does exist, it seems that a number
of the immigrant women who entered under contract were first engaged
as servants by Americans traveling abroad, and then chose to accompany
their employers back to the United States. For wage-earning women,
this would have been a more secure and less speculative decision than
answering an advertisement from an unknown household employer, and
then agreeing to travel to work in a position sight unseen. Unless, that is,
a family member or friend of the immigrant being recruited facilitated the
connection and contract. This was a common occurrence when women
arrived in the United States looking for jobs in service and, if an employer
was willing to pay, could have been orchestrated with prepaid tickets and
contractual agreements as well. Servants who entered under the exception to the Foran Act would have been more beholden—economically,
emotionally, and psychologically—to the employers who paid for their
passage. Although servants were not mandated to remain with employers
who brought them to the country, it is not difficult to imagine that they
would have risked their sponsors' anger and desire to extract legal or other
revenge by leaving their employment shortly after arriving. Immigrant
women who arrived in the United States under contract would have been
especially reliant on their employers' references, not having any work history in the country. And, the threat of deportation for becoming a public
charge always loomed. Still, a free passage was a free passage. For some
immigrant women, this was surely enough of an incentive.

## Frances Kellor and the Struggle against Private Employment Offices

In the first decade of the twentieth century, more than eight million immigrants arrived in the United States. Frances Kellor was at the forefront of reform efforts designed to improve consumer protections for household employers, who relied on commercial employment agencies to ready recently arrived immigrant women for hire. To this end, she was also a leading voice on how immigration restrictions might benefit or undermine employers when it came to enhancing their power in market exchanges. Kellor was instrumental in reviving debates about whether commercial employment offices could be trusted. Her book *Out of Work* documented exploitative practices that employment offices had been accused of engaging in since the middle of the nineteenth century. Tapping into the same panicky suspicions about the "white slave trade" that immigration officials and politicians manipulated, Kellor highlighted the role that employment offices played as conduits for brothels, saloons, and theaters involved in the sex trade.[88]

As historian Ellen Fitzpatrick argues, Kellor's muckraking, while typical of Progressive Era activism, was distinguished by her emphasis on practical politics and "active intervention by the state."[89] After receiving a law degree from Cornell University, Kellor enrolled in graduate studies in sociology at the University of Chicago before moving to New York City in 1902. There she joined the New York School of Philanthropy and Civics before taking a fellowship and residency with the College Settlement Association, an umbrella organization for settlement houses that sponsored her in-depth study of unemployment. In 1904 she published *Out of Work*, the resulting text. That same year, Kellor, along with her life partner, Mary Dreier, and other leading women's reformers in the Northeast, created the Inter-Municipal Committee on Household Research, which pooled studies, surveys, and reports from organizations in New York, Boston, and Philadelphia. Kellor would also serve as chief of the New York State Bureau of Industries and Immigration, an office involved in workplace arbitrations between immigrants and their industrial employers, before heading the Progressive Service initiative of the Progressive Party, which was formed in 1912. Kellor's work bridged the concerns that middle-class Americans in northern cities had about "new" immigration from Eastern and Southern Europe with the like-minded apprehensions that they directed at the increased number of black migrants arriving from the South. Analytically, she viewed the employment challenges and dangers that new European immigrants and black migrants encountered as nearly identical. Kellor helped to found the National League for the Protection of Colored Women in 1906 out of concern that migrant black women were vulnerable to exploitative employment agencies and other actors. This organization would merge with other groups in 1911 to become the National Urban League.[90]

Presented as neutral, objective social science, *Out of Work* was received by the middle-class public as a consumer's guide. As one *New York Times* reviewer noted, after reading the book "careless house-wives" would "look more thoroughly into the subject of servants' character references."[91] Readers could neglect the book's detailed discussions of how migration was financed and brokered, but still have a handy and accessible guide on how to best spend their money when it came to hiring domestics. Kellor's methodology had her and her assistants pose as both job applicants and employers, and visit a range of different employment offices in Boston, Chicago, New York, and Philadelphia.

Kellor's work confronted a fundamental contradiction. On one hand, the American public, as she herself acknowledged, lamented the fact that immigrants hailing from places of origin like the Austro-Hungarian Empire, Italy, and Russia tended not to enter into service—as chapter 6 of this book addresses in more detail. On the other hand, Kellor wanted this same public to be distrustful of immigrants who did enter into service since labor brokers and the offices they worked for, she asserted, preyed on the most vulnerable, undesirable, and unqualified candidates for assimilation. Kellor believed that the federal government had to ramp up its enforcement of existing restrictions, in order to debar immigrants indentured to labor brokers and steamship agents. Alternatively, local governments could direct their attention to improved regulation of employment offices that contracted immigrant women's labor post-entry.

Kellor aligned politically with William Williams and other early twentieth-century reformers who, while not outright restrictionists, felt that federal officials were often stifled when it came to exercising the regulatory powers that they did have. Kellor pointed to the fact that employment agencies regularly found ways to evade the 1891 Immigration Act, which prohibited American businesses from running advertisements in foreign newspapers. The 1891 act was supposed to bolster the Foran Act by construing such advertisements as trying to "assist or encourage the importation or migration of any alien by promise of employment." Immigrants could be prohibited from landing if it was demonstrated that they had decided to come to the United States as a result of such inducements, which legislators stipulated were tantamount to contracts.[92] Kellor blamed foreign-language newspapers in the United States for posting employment offices' promises of domestic labor employment, which were brought to Europe by returning steamship passengers and circulated among prospective emigrants. She also attacked the methods that employment agents used to circumvent measures preventing unaccompanied immigrant women from leaving Ellis Island. Before departing Europe, Kellor observed, women were coached to pretend that the agents who greeted them at the immigration station were actually family members. (In this respect one imagines that she applauded Williams's policy, implemented after *Out of Work*'s publication, of having family members bring proof of their identity.) To hide evidence of direct assistance, which was also outlawed by the 1891 act, employment offices collaborated with steamship company agents—if they did not hold these dual positions themselves—to have fares advanced to migrants using a series of intermediaries. Kellor reserved special venom for employment agency runners who tailed missionaries shepherding newly arrived unaccompanied migrant women. "In this way," Kellor warned, "they get the address, visit them, and later the missionary finds her girls gone."[93]

What Kellor failed to note was that employment agencies dealing in domestic labor were transnational businesses by necessity rather than design, since native-born and already established immigrant women willing to enter into service were scarce. For all her critiques, Kellor did concede that employment agencies functioned as "essential clearing houses for immigrant women who could not otherwise find work" and that "restriction of the immigration of women who are household employees would have a disastrous effect upon homes." Calling for responsible brokers, Kellor cited "first-class" intelligence offices that profited off their reputation for quality, which made them the recipients of repeat business. She was less forthcoming with the fact that these agencies tended to focus on more specialized forms of domestic labor, and often limited their stock of workers to native-born women and "older" immigrants from Northern and Western Europe, who—by the start of the twentieth century—were now the most coveted domestics. Offices catering to the general entry-level market for servants had to deal in newly arrived European immigrants or black migrants considered less desirable. Even when these migrants possessed experience belying this classification, they were still often placed in the lowest-paying situations. Kellor discussed one case involving a black woman who after being offered a position as a nurse by a New York employment agency—work that she had been doing for years in the South—agreed to have her $12.75 train fare from Richmond deducted from her future wages by the office. Upon arriving in New York, however, she was placed as a general house servant. The office held her baggage and personal effects as collateral on her debt, which prevented her from breaking the contract.[94]

On April 27, 1904, New York State passed a new statute regulating employment agencies that Kellor and Dreier had authored and lobbied for with the backing of the Women's Municipal League. The new legislation required all agencies operating in New York cities with populations greater than fifty thousand to be licensed and bonded, with the latter meant to be a surety against rogue offices that might simply shutter and disappear if accused of violations. Agencies were also mandated to take transparency measures, such as keeping written receipts of fees and commissions, investigating and archiving character references, and registering all placements. The new law necessitated the creation of a commissioner of licenses in all cities where it applied. All employment agencies placing workers in remote situations were required to document the circumstances of these transactions out of concern that immigrant workers were especially vulnerable to being held in bondage when sent to rural areas. In 1906, the law was amended to introduce more stringent enforcement measures after Kellor mounted a public relations campaign that accused the newly appointed commissioner in New York City of being lax in her duties. The employment agency law caused some of the least profitable offices, run out of tenements and relentlessly attacked by Kellor and other reformers, to go out of business. They could not afford to pay the required fees. The law also prohibited employment agencies from operating out of spaces that doubled as living quarters for brokers, a practice that had long offended reformers as uncouth and unnerving to prospective employers. A corollary effect of the legislation was that it reduced the ability of job seekers to access spaces where they could exchange knowledge with fellow domestic workers for the purpose of fostering collective action.[95]

Despite her in-depth knowledge of how domestic labor markets worked, Kellor, for the most part, avoided questions about how servant migrations were to be financed in the absence of commercial brokerage. The success of *Out of Work* and the positive attention that New York's statute garnered led to Kellor being offered a column, cheerfully titled "The Housewife and Her Helper," in the *Ladies' Home Journal*. In response to Lily W., a self-described "country girl (colored)" who wrote to the column asking whether it was realistic to think that she would be able to repay the transportation costs and placement fees that a southern labor broker demanded, Kellor recommended that she abandon her plans on the grounds that "many agents who offer such an arrangement are unreliable, and cheat or misuse the girls who come to them." Instead, she suggested that she contact a social service organization in Philadelphia dedicated to aiding black migrants already arrived in the city.[96] While this may have appeared to be sound advice on the surface, the protective society that Kellor recommended did not pay for migrants' transportation costs. Lily W.'s basic dilemma of how to fund her trip was left unresolved. Employers among Kellor's readers sometimes called for greater powers of coercion, which they could then use to force reluctant workers into household employment. In the May 1906 edition of "Housewife and Her Helper," a letter writer noted that "laws against vagrancy, vice and larceny would help solve the 'employment problem,'" implying that penal institutions, which were already allowed to lease out female prisoners, could be more holistically involved in making up labor deficits. Kellor, if she disagreed with this specific stance, did not bother to state so. In her response, Kellor redirected the question to highlight—as was her wont—the ongoing involvement of brokers and agents who caused "immigrants, negroes and country girls," her trinity of migrant women laborers, to be "led astray."[97]

While Kellor eschewed the biological racism that many of her middle-class white peers embraced, her theories of cultural difference had a clearly defined teleology concerning where groups resided on an imagined spectrum of primitivism to civilization.[98] As she wrote in 1907:

> Two civilizations meet in intimate daily contact under one roof. The one often represents experiences, traditions, superstitions, and suspicions of a middle-age progress and opportunity, together with a different language and religion. The other often represents an advanced civilization which has little sympathy with or understanding of the other.

Like Williams, Kellor invoked a past where the "strong character" possessed by German, Irish, and Swedish immigrants was a cultural attribute that allowed individuals from these groups to triumph over "privations" and forge their own destinies as immigrants. She did not dwell on the copious domestic advice literature from previous decades, which had urged suppressing Irish women's "independent" character as dangerous. Earlier migration, which individuals had initiated on their own volition, had given way to a system where "the desire to emigrate is artificially stimulated" and was "more successful in countries from which undesirable workers come." There was no evidence to back this point, but such details did not matter. Kellor's romanticized version of the past even led her to praise Castle Garden as a model of efficiency when it came to placing immigrant domestic laborers—an assertion that middle-class reformers thirty years earlier would have chortled at.[99]

The lack of will and character that Kellor assigned to newer immigrants and migrants manifested as well, at least by her accounting, in their susceptibility to bondage. When a revised edition of *Out of Work* was published in 1915, Kellor's discussion of peonage—using this specific language—represented a notable addition. Following decisions in *Bailey* (1911) and *Reynolds* (1914), in which the U.S. Supreme Court ruled that the Thirteenth Amendment's ban on "involuntary servitude" applied to incidents involving indirect forms of debt bondage, Kellor weighed in on how these rulings resonated in respect to the practices of employment agencies. Although *Bailey* and *Reynolds* addressed black southern plaintiffs who were legally bound to white employers as a condition of debts owed or invented, Kellor saw similar forms of compulsion routinely occurring in the hiring of domestic laborers in the North.[100] Building on the campaigns against "white slavery" that immigration officials had introduced in the previous decade, she claimed that "no peonage among immigrant men is more binding than the slavery of the immigrant girl whose passage is prepaid by the office, or who comes from the country in answer to an advertisement and who is met by a runner—the essential factor in the system."[101]

In her 1920 book *Immigration and the Future*, Kellor argued that while the 1885 Foran Act was flawed in its implementation, there was nothing inherently wrong with labor contracts that held immigrants to strict obligations in respect to the work they were to perform. Rather, the dangers related to who did the contracting. She argued that the 1885 act's intentions would best be served by replacing its existing provisions with a guestworker program that had strict rules for deportation, and was flexible in respect to responding to labor shortages as they arose. This was the technocratic ideal for the governance of socially undesirable yet needed immigrant labor that had been put forth ever since the initial Chinese Restriction Act in 1882.[102] Although the 1921 Emergency Quota Act and the 1924 Immigration Act went in the direction of blanket reductions and restrictions on European immigrants, Kellor—like so many others who dwelled on the relationship between immigration and domestic service—arrived at a position that promoted the state-coordinated importation of servants who could conveniently be removed if they violated the terms of their entry.

## Conclusion

The various policies and regulations that governed unaccompanied European immigrant women should be read as measures that were intent on coercing certain forms of economic and social integration. They emphasized the safety of customary dependencies that officials felt could be found in household service positions. Following the passage of the 1882 Chinese Restriction Act, immigration officials instituted exceptions and exemptions for white employers who wished to enter the United States with their Chinese servants. Unlike the legislation and enforcement practices governing European women, immigration officials would rule that Chinese servants were bonded to the employers they entered the United States with, and were permitted to remain in the country only on a temporary basis. The different racialization of white and Chinese servants as laborers meant that the entry of Chinese servants, unlike that of their white counterparts, would be governed by a series of sureties that made employers financially liable for any personal or household Chinese laborers whom they were unable to detain in their employment. Whereas non-Chinese immigrants imported under domestic service contracts could be deported as public charges only during a probationary period, Chinese servants entered as temporary, bonded laborers beholden to the white consumers of their labor.

5

# Bonded Chinese Servants

## Domestic Labor and Exclusion, 1882–1924

## Introduction

On October 15, 1919, Lieutenant Colonel W. Garland Fay arrived in Charleston, South Carolina, with "Ah" See, his Chinese servant. An officer in the Marine Corps, Fay had been stationed at the U.S. Naval Base in Guantánamo Bay, Cuba, which American forces had occupied since 1898 and would continue to hold indefinitely under the terms of the 1903 Cuban-American Treaty of Relations. The base at Guantánamo played a crucial support role backing U.S. imperial aspirations in the Caribbean, including as a coaling station for navy warships. The Marines stationed at Guantánamo were deployed to Haiti, to the Dominican Republic, and within Cuba, where they assisted the government in quelling local insurgencies that targeted American-backed sugar estates.[1] Immigrants from Guangdong province in China had been arriving in Cuba since 1847, when they were first brought under contract to work on the sugar plantations. By the twentieth century, many Chinese immigrants and their descendants could be found working in service occupations, and the base at Guantánamo seems to have employed a number of Chinese laborers in this capacity.[2] See's father, Sing Lee, held a government concession to run a laundry business on the base. In 1915, at the age of fourteen, his son arrived at Guantánamo from China. When See was hired by Fay and his wife, he spoke no English. Four years later, he landed in the United States.[3]

As a Chinese laborer, See was ineligible to enter the United States. By 1919, however, the Bureau of Immigration had adopted a policy in which American military officials and white businessmen, missionaries, and academics living in China, Cuba, the Philippines, and Japan—and anywhere else where Chinese labor might be hired—were permitted to bring in Chinese servants as temporary, nonimmigrant entrants. Fay, prior to departing for Charleston, had corresponded with Anthony Caminetti, the commissioner general of immigration in Washington, who had responded with instructions on how to proceed. Caminetti informed Fay that he would be required to take out a five-hundred-dollar bond from a surety company, covering a period of one year.[4] Before the year expired, See's departure from the United States had to be witnessed and verified by immigration officials, at which time the bond would be canceled. If he did not depart within the stipulated period, the Fidelity and Deposit Company of Maryland, the issuer of the surety bond, would forfeit the full amount to the Department of Labor. If this happened, Fay, who up until then had paid the bond issuer only a percentage commission, would owe the company the remaining sum in its entirety.

Caminetti failed to communicate to Fay that although five hundred dollars was the standard bond required by officials and the minimum amount mandated by section 18 of the 1917 Immigration Act, individual officers at each port of entry had the discretion to set the amount on a case-by-case basis. When See was landed, officials in Charleston set the bond at a thousand dollars. As Fay would subsequently plead, he was so convinced that he could trust See that he "never raised any question concerning the amount of the bond," and failed to even examine the official paperwork that the surety company processed on his behalf.

Fay and his wife lived in Leonardtown, Maryland, and he commuted to the nation's capital for work. In August 1920, Fay petitioned the Bureau of Immigration to extend See's bond for an additional year, a routine courtesy that was typically granted. Shortly after the extension was approved, Fay gave See time off from work. As he had done on previous occasions, See used his "leave" to visit Washington. From this trip, however, he never returned. The details of what happened were narrated in a memorandum that Fay subsequently drafted as part of a campaign he mounted to avoid having to forfeit the bond. Fay explained that he and his wife "took [See] as a house servant and taught him to read and write English," and that when they were scheduled to leave Guantánamo, See "had begged us to bring him to the United States and seemed to enjoy the life with us in the country." Fay blamed "other Chinamen" for corrupting See during his trips to Washington, and for convincing him that "he could earn more money from other sources that [sic] we were able to give him." The Fays' erstwhile trust in See was perhaps exaggerated, since they also took measures to compel his continued service by making him dependent. "When Ah See came to this country he deposited in the bank $200," Fay noted, "and I requested the bank not to honor his checks except when countersigned by me." Fay blamed the bank for facilitating See's departure, since in his opinion it had erroneously let him withdraw his balance—one hundred dollars—prior to his flight. Fay omitted any discussion of how See was compensated and what he was paid, but it is evident that he believed that exposure to English and the affection that he and his wife imparted were forms of payment that his servant had callously abandoned.[5]

Following See's departure, Fay reached out to Sing Lee to try to ascertain his son's whereabouts. In May 1921, Sing informed Fay that he heard that See was in Chicago, where he was working for a local Chinese import firm. This was relayed to Fay, who then wired immigration officials in the city to apprehend him. Although bureau officials in Chicago belatedly issued an arrest warrant, by the time inspectors visited the store where See was allegedly employed, he was nowhere to be found. Desperate to avoid losing the bond, Fay implored Sing to take a more active role in trying to locate his son. Fay claimed that this was justified by the fact that Sing owed him a "debt of gratitude" as a friend. It is possible to infer that a complicated web of perceived obligations existed below the surface of this request. Fay's solicitation seemed to imply that if Sing did not find his son and prevent the forfeiture of the bond, his livelihood might be at stake. Sing, in any case, was convinced to temporarily transfer the management of the Guantánamo laundry to a partner, and in June 1921 embarked for the United States to look for See. (See and Fay's conjoined file does not explain how Sing was eligible to enter the United States.) At the same time, Fay recruited Maryland Senator Ovington Weller and Colorado Senator Lawrence Phipps to see if either of these politicians, with whom he had personal connections, could convince the Bureau of Immigration to forgive the bond. Theodore Roosevelt Jr., the assistant secretary of the Navy and oldest son of the former president, was also engaged to this end. As Roosevelt informed bureau officials, "The Colonel is not a wealthy man. The Marine Corps is not a place where one makes money." Although these appeals on Fay's behalf did not persuade officials to waive the surety altogether, Fay was allowed a series of postponements on the bond forfeiture to continue his search for See.

When the Fidelity and Deposit Company of Maryland was served a final notice by the bureau instructing them to produce See within thirty days of August 7, 1924, or to make the bond payment, officials instead received a letter from Fay indicating that both See and his father Sing were back at Guantánamo. So was Fay, who was assigned there for another tour. Whether or not the bureau had a federal marshal or other government employee verify this fact, as it usually did in such circumstances, was left unnoted.

At the base, one can assume that Fay tried to elicit from See a more detailed account of why he left employment. Or maybe Fay stuck to the explanation that he had provided immigration officials, in which See left because he was led astray by bad influences. Regardless, Fay's interpretation of See's actions deserves greater attention—not for what it claims as fact—but instead for what it suggests about race, free labor, and state regulation. When See agreed to enter into the Fays' service, prior to entering the United States, his options as a young man seeking wage work would have been quite limited, especially if he felt obliged to stay on the base near his father. In the United States, his decision to travel to Chicago and pursue work as a store clerk was an economic and social choice that thousands of servants from all backgrounds made. Fay's racial fantasies about his uplifting impact on See notwithstanding, few workers welcomed the surveillance, lack of free time, and around-the-clock availability that live-in domestic service continued to require. Had See been white and authorized to immigrate to the United States, it is likely that the Fays would have been briefly disappointed by his decision to leave and then dropped the matter. Servants left all the time. With racial mastery and financial liability at stake, however, immigration policy provided Fay with motivation to keep his servant bonded.

* * *

Following the passage of the 1882 Chinese Restriction Act, immigration officials struggled to develop an enforcement apparatus that could carry out legislated restrictions against the entry of Chinese laborers. The various statuses constituting the grounds for an individual Chinese immigrant's excludability or admissibility—as permanent entrants rather than visitors, as laborers rather than merchants, as immigrants rather than native-born citizens—were categorization schemes open to both interpretation and manipulation.[6] This was made evident by the passage of laws in 1884, 1888, 1892, 1902, and 1904 that amended and supplemented the original act in order to make it more effective and exclusive.[7]

The bureau's inability to secure the border against unauthorized Chinese immigration has garnered significant attention from historians.[8] Little to no scholarly light has been shed, however, on immigration officials' experiments with how they might effectively uphold the baseline principles of exclusion while at the same time finding ways to allow for temporary entries of Chinese servants deemed necessary adjuncts to the imperial and transnational transit of capital, missionaries, and government and military officials. The expansion of American power abroad necessitated intimate labor that was transportable.[9] By the end of the nineteenth century, American domesticity, as a set of services, routines, and comforts produced through the hire of labor, no longer represented a fixed geographic set of practices sourced by a nearby labor market.

Policies of selective inclusion—or "imperial openings" as historian Paul Kramer has called them—allowed Chinese students, who might have been excluded on account of their race and national background, to receive an education in the United States. Such policies were considered useful to American interests abroad and to easing diplomatic tensions with the Chinese state. Restrictionist politicians and officials were forced to make concessions to foreign policy goals when it came to students' entry.[10] The globalization of American consumer habits meant that immigration officials were also obliged to carve out regulations that allowed for the temporary admission of Chinese performers and lecturers.[11] Despite these parallel examples, Chinese servants were the only manual or unskilled laborers allowed entry for the purpose of working. Whereas Chinese seamen and other laborers in transit were also granted temporary entry into the United States, unlike servants they were not admitted to ply their vocations. The federal government demonstrated that it had no wish to interfere in the domestic labor relations of privileged, white transnational actors, so long as it had financial guarantees against the unauthorized permanent immigration of Chinese laborers.[12]

Chinese servants' admission to the United States under contract was subject to the racial discrimination that informed all aspects of immigration policy. When non-Chinese laborers were recruited to come to the United States by employers, as long as these immigrants did not violate any of the grounds for deportation or were not barred outright by the 1885 Foran Act, they were permitted to remain in the country permanently—even after they left the jobs they had initially contracted to perform. The ability to transition from temporary to permanent labor was never extended to Chinese servants. The category of temporary laborer governed Chinese servants as wards who could never be independent in the United States. Ironically, this was even more stringent than the demonized system of indentures and debt bonds that had allegedly enslaved Chinese laborers in earlier eras. Prior to 1882, Chinese immigrants were at least offered the opportunity to settle permanently as the eventual outcome of their contracts. By detaching work performed on American soil from the possibility of permanent residency, immigration officials created—even if they did not call it such—a framework for state-backed guestworker programs.

The terms under which Chinese servants were exempted from exclusion help to illustrate how certain dependencies—portrayed as untrustworthy and potentially conspiratorial when occurring between Chinese subjects—could be nullified as nonthreatening when operating within accepted racial and paternalistic hierarchies. The paradox of immigration officials defending native, "free" labor against the threat of job competition from Chinese labor—by rendering Chinese servants unfree in respect to their liberty of contract and movement—offers an important launching point for exploring how exclusion created entry statuses that were ripe for exploitation. Immigration officials' insistence on treating Chinese servants as a special category of temporary laborers invalidated due process protections that would have otherwise granted them the liberty of contract to pursue other jobs.[13] Immigration rules made Chinese servants captive to their employers. Deportation was the consequence of being caught asserting their freedom. For some servants, like See, this was a calculated risk to be made, and perhaps something that was understood even before a Chinese worker chose to enter into contract with an employer who would be traveling to the United States. With surety bonds, immigration officials instituted a system of indemnification that made employers financially liable for Chinese servants who violated the terms of their temporary admission. Surety bonds were never tied to actual administrative costs associated with capture and deportation. Their real purpose was to incentivize white employers to demonstrate racial mastery over workers deemed their dependents.

For Chinese servants already in the United States, as immigrants or birthright citizens, exclusion laws created other dependencies as well. Chinese servants often interacted with the state through white interlocutors and intermediaries, who in turn became responsible for brokering the authorized status of the labor supply that they wished to maintain. The verification of status that Chinese exclusion laws required gave white employers leverage over their workers, and an ability to regulate their right to be in the country and depart and return. Immigration officials relied on white witnesses, often the employers of servants, to vouch for an applicant's right to depart from the United States and reenter the country legally, since Chinese witnesses were disqualified from testifying in this capacity. In these respects, Chinese servants and their white employers jointly negotiated and at times even collaborated to frustrate the legal credentialing process that restriction laws laid out.

Immigration officials did not extend to Chinese merchants and students the same privilege to visit the United States with servants hired abroad. In addition, officials scrutinized Chinese middlemen as the issuers of sureties. In both of these cases, bureaucrats' discriminatory treatment functioned to ritualize race, as historian Adam McKeown describes it, as a feature of migration's global governance.[14]

Stretching into the third decade of the twentieth century, and focusing on the period in which the modern state apparatus of immigration control was formatively shaped through legal decisions and administrative action, this chapter brings with it myriad contemporary parallels. As the epilogue to this book explores further, the U.S. government continues to broker domestic service employment relations through its visa-issuing process, and remains willing to acknowledge that foreign businesspersons, diplomats, and other migrants entering the United States carry with them the privileged right to employ servants and other domestic workers hired abroad. As recent scholarship has documented, the transference of these types of employment relationships across national borders is permitted—in exception to restrictions on other non-quota labor migrations—as a vital concession to the needs of global capitalism and its elite agents.[15] Although undocumented immigrants remain highly susceptible to labor exploitation as a result of their status, the problems faced by legally permitted temporary laborers, bound to employers as domestics, show that vulnerability can be produced through inclusion as well.[16]

## Word as Bond: Vouching for Servants

From the very beginning of Chinese restriction, whether officials were to enforce the laws in absolute or pragmatic terms was a major source of division and confusion. Immigration officers, who were often recruited from the ranks of organized labor, clashed with politicians, businessmen, and missionaries who did not want to cause harm to American diplomatic, commercial, and religious interests related to China and its overseas population. When not engaged in direct disputes over what exclusion was meant to accomplish, these varied interests also confronted complex uncertainties having to do with the law and its amendments' intent and enforcement. The *Case of the Chinese Cabin Waiter*, the first case heard in a federal court following the passage of the 1882 act, revealed what policymakers had failed to consider. It adjudicated whether a Chinese sailor taking shore leave should be considered an immigrant. Commenting on what he offered as a reasonable and prudent interpretation of the statute's intentions, Justice Stephen J. Field ruled that while "it was deemed wise policy to prevent the coming among us of a class of persons, who, by their dissimilarity of manners, habits, religion, and physical characteristics cannot assimilate with our people," officials also had an obligation to "avoid an unjust or an absurd conclusion" about what the legislation covered. As Field outlined, it was imperative that officials distinguish between masses of Chinese laborers immigrating permanently, and the temporary entry and stay of select Chinese workers that global commerce necessitated.[17] Field may have been overly generous in his reading of Congress's wisdom in the matter. As legal scholar Kitty Calavita argues, "Congress, with its essentialist assumptions about the nature of race and class as intrinsic—even biological—categories, had largely overlooked the difficulties of operationalizing these concepts."[18] Officials would soon discover that categories taken as stable—such as laborer, student, and merchant—were anything but. Questions of temporality were equally perplexing to officials. Legislators had not bothered to define with any precision the boundaries between temporary and permanent admission.

Household and body servants of foreign diplomats and consular officials assigned to the United States possessed diplomatic immunity. This had been established by federal statute, following English custom, as early as 1790.[19] Article 2 of the 1880 Angell Treaty between China and the United States declared that Chinese students, merchants, and visitors—in addition to diplomats—were permitted to travel to the United States accompanied by their servants. The 1880 treaty was itself emblematic of the overlapping sovereign interests that were at play in regulating Chinese immigration, and had been pushed on China in order to legitimize anticipated congressional restrictions—which the earlier 1868 Burlingame Treaty between the two countries would have otherwise prohibited.[20] When the 1882 Restriction Act was passed, it contained subtle changes suggesting that in the intervening period, legislators had become wary that this right to employ domestic and personal labor might encourage abuses. Sections 8 and 13 of the 1882 act made explicit reference to the fact that restrictions did not apply to the servants employed by Chinese government ministers and official state emissaries. But the legislation no longer specifically stated that the servants of Chinese students and merchants had the right to enter as well.[21]

In December 1882, U.S. Attorney General Benjamin H. Brewster issued an opinion that Chinese immigrants who hoped to establish permanent residence in the United States and work as servants, as well as Chinese servants who accompanied employers seeking to establish (or reestablish) permanent residence, were to be considered laborers and barred from landing. A Chinese servant accompanying the temporary stay of a foreign national or American citizen living abroad, however, was allowed entry. The distinction, Brewster explained, hinged on whether individual Chinese servants would "ply their vocations in competition with our own people similarly employed," or whether they belonged to a class of laborers, contracted abroad, "in transit." Immigration restrictions, Brewster's interpretation suggested, were intended only to defend the position of native laborers competing to be hired within what was conceived of as the domestic job market, but could not be used to regulate global hiring practices. In 1887, addressing the issue again, Attorney General Augustus H. Garland repeated and affirmed his predecessor's earlier decision verbatim. Like Brewster, Garland made the temporary stay of Chinese servants the crucial matter in determining that they were not immigrant laborers. Both men failed to elaborate on how exactly the transitory employment of Chinese servants was to be defined or policed in respect to specifics.[22]

The two attorney general rulings did not provide any further clarification on whether Chinese merchants and students visiting the United States could bring their servants with them, although it would subsequently become evident that Chinese employers were not intended to be included in the exception gradually being carved out. When Garland first issued his 1887 decision, however, the public misinterpreted its potential application. Restrictionists were incensed by what they believed was the feeble enforcement of Chinese exclusion, and any loophole that allegedly enabled the continued immigration of Chinese laborers was subject to fierce denunciations. An article in the *Daily Alta California* published shortly after Garland's ruling stated that it established that "the Chinese Restriction Act does not apply to Chinese women who accompany other immigrants to this country in the capacity of nurses or servants."[23]

The newspaper's gendering of the issue—even though the majority of Chinese servants were male—suggests that one reading of the servant exception was that it might be used to smuggle Chinese prostitutes into the country. The *Alta*'s story prompted the Pacific Mail Steamship Company to inquire with the Department of the Treasury as to when consular officials in China would begin issuing Section Six Certificates—the official forms used to establish an immigrant's exempt status—to Chinese servants. If restrictionists saw a threat, the Pacific Mail Steamship Company saw an opportunity to expand business. Treasury officials wasted no time disabusing this notion. The department's response to the company pointed out that the *Alta*'s coverage had incorrectly failed to distinguish between "visitors" permitted to bring in servants, and "immigrants" barred from doing so.[24] The *Alta*, after being informed of the error, printed an editorial admitting the mistake the very next day.

The editorial expressed satisfaction with the federal government's actual position, since its readers could "see that a rule which excluded such personal attendants in transit would give rise to most vexatious controversies with the citizens of other countries besides China."[25] Reassured that the exception would benefit elite and privileged global travelers who were not Chinese, but employing Chinese servants, the newspaper gave its support for the measure. On March 9, 1887, the Department of the Treasury issued yet another circular, this time stating that the exception allowing servants to enter applied only to "visitors" who were "intending to remain here but for a short period." They still neglected to define, however, what was meant by a "short period."[26]

Confusion about whether Chinese merchants and other Section Six Certificate holders were allowed to enter the United States with their servants persisted. Technical misreadings of the law and its enforcement revealed how American authorities understood dependency. In the bundled cases of *In re Chung Toy Ho* and *Wong Choy Sin*, which the federal district court in Oregon heard in May 1890, Judge Matthew P. Deady granted the admission of the wives and children of Chinese immigrants in possession of Section Six Certificates, even when these dependents did not possess these documents themselves, based on his erroneous conclusion that Chinese merchants were permitted to bring servants into the country with them. As Deady asserted, unaware of the intervening clarifications that had been provided, it was "impossible to believe that parties to [the treaty of 1880], which permits the servants of a merchant to enter the country with him, ever contemplated the exclusion of his wife and children."[27] This would defy logic, he claimed, and the customary acknowledgment that men had the right to sponsor anyone in their household who for reasons of wages or familial or marital relations could be considered dependents.

Deady was wrong, both in fact and in his understanding of the principles at stake. Immigration officials refused to accept that Chinese merchants and students could be trusted to keep their Chinese servants in a state of dependent control sufficient to ensure that they would not become unauthorized immigrants. Moreover, immigration officials also doubted whether Chinese officials—who *were* permitted to enter with their servants—were properly motivated to keep these laborers in a state of bonded employment.

White Americans possessed long-standing biases and prejudices about the trustworthiness of Chinese immigrants, whose reputability and character they questioned along racial, religious, and national lines. In 1854, before restrictive legislation was even contemplated, the California Supreme Court ruled in *People v. Hall* that an 1850 statute barring blacks and Indians from serving as witnesses in cases involving white defendants was applicable to the Chinese as well—a decision that remained in effect until 1873.[28] The perceived dishonesty of the Chinese surfaced as a common stump position adopted by various exclusionist factions, and the credibility of Chinese immigrants routinely came under assault. After 1882, immigration officials introduced a host of safeguards against what they believed was the natural tendency of the Chinese to deceive. They refused to see Chinese immigrants' acts of subterfuge and illegal entries in the context of the discord that existed between exclusion and the enduring American consumer demand for the services and goods that Chinese labor produced.

Into the twentieth century, the Bureau of Immigration would continue to suspect that Chinese ministers and other government representatives were systematically using diplomatic protocol as a front to engage in smuggling operations. When it came to Chinese state officials, attachés, secretaries, and translators all qualified for designation as exempt. As the American consular office in Guangzhou (Canton) put it in 1911, these employees were to be treated as a special class of "salaried dependents."[29] Even though Chinese officials' right to enter with their servants and other attachés remained inviolable throughout the period of restriction, once these workers exited the employ of the Chinese government, they immediately surrendered their legal immunity. This was in line with the authority of the bureau to deport other Chinese migrants who had entered under exemptions, but were subsequently discovered violating the terms of restriction. In 1914, the federal court for the Northern District of California ruled that immigration authorities could deport Chinese immigrants who had entered as servants and assistants to officials using the same omnibus administrative warrants that were valid in other cases of unauthorized entry. The case in question involved Chun Woi San, who landed in San Francisco as the personal assistant to a Chinese bank official who had come to the United States to sell government bonds. Chun was arrested in Ensley, Alabama, two months after his arrival, after an informant reported his employment in a laundry there. Another assistant to the banker was found working on a Bakersfield, California, seed ranch.

Granting the accuracy of the details presented, it is possible to infer that Chun and the other man entered into a financial arrangement with the banker in which they paid him to pretend to employ them as servants so that they could enter the United States illegally. If this was the case, it would be in line with a host of other methods that Chinese immigrants used to deceive immigration officials. Chinese migrants were willing to violate immigration laws that they knew were racially discriminatory and unjust in targeting Chinese laborers alone.[30] Despite the bureau's victory in court in *Ex Parte Chun Woi San*, officials expressed frustration that they could do nothing to punish the bank official for his role in what they presumed was a smuggling operation.[31] Occasionally immigration officials did interrogate state-sponsored visitors about their attachés and servants, but this was mainly to assert their ability to harass, since barring their entry risked causing an international incident.[32] In June 1916, for instance, inspectors in Seattle chose to detain Wan Hung Fei, whose business for the Chinese state was to explore export markets for agricultural produce. Not only was Wan forced to explain why his hands were calloused, a routine line of questioning that officials used to try to discover potential manual laborers, but Lan Shing, his servant, was interrogated about his employer's stated family history and business activities. Inspectors elicited testimony from Lan stating that he fully understood that he was bonded to Wan as a dependent, and that he would undertake no work outside of serving him.[33]

\* \* \*

In contrast to the scrutiny that confronted Chinese employers, white employers were usually given the benefit of the doubt in matters having to do with authenticating or vouching for Chinese servants' immigration or citizenship status. White Americans were trusted to demonstrate a form of racial mastery that entitled them to speak on behalf of their servants as intimately known dependents, at least when it came to testimony. Immigration officials routinely called on white employers to verify their Chinese servants' personal migration histories and claims to birthright citizenship. Consonant with their precarious existence and membership in a targeted and suspect population, Chinese servants had no choice but to derive agency through the dependencies and personal relations that their employment as domestics, cooks, and other household laborers created. Employers offered legal advice and assistance in order to retain valued Chinese servants seeking to visit China and reenter the United States legally. The involvement of employers in immigration investigations added another layer to Chinese servants' labor contracts, and created dependencies that went beyond those that were already intrinsic to wage labor. The structural realities of Chinese exclusion discouraged Chinese servants from exercising their liberty to contract when leaving a job meant risking the loss of valuable allies in struggles to remain in the country.

In the early days of restriction, white employers had nearly unchecked personal authority to vouch for servants. A bureaucratic system for regulating the exit and reentry of Chinese domestics—as well as all Chinese laborers—evolved gradually. In the Pacific Northwest, where land and ocean border crossings were everyday occurrences linking the United States and Canada, American employers had become conditioned to bringing cooks and servants with them on transnational business trips. Often given leave on these trips, Chinese servants were able to visit with relatives and acquaintances living on the other side of the border.[34] Following the passage of the 1882 Chinese Restriction Act, white American employers showed no indication that they wanted to let go of favored Chinese servants. They were, however, forced to comply with new regulations. In July 1883, for instance, Moses Redout Maddocks, the builder and proprietor of Seattle's Occidental Hotel, swore out an affidavit stating that his Chinese servant "Ah" Hing had resided in the United States prior to November 1880, which under the terms of the 1882 Restriction Act made him eligible to depart the country and return. When restriction was enacted, Hing was in Canada and stranded lacking proof of his previous American residency. On Maddocks's word, he was permitted to return to the United States. J. W. Anderson of the Villard House in Seattle filed an affidavit on behalf of Lim Jim, his cook, stating that he met all the criteria making him eligible to return.[35] In these cases, the statements of the prominent white men involved were simply taken at face value and officials declined to investigate further how proof of these Chinese servants' residential history in the United States had been obtained.

When Congress amended the Chinese restriction laws in 1884, the revised legislation stated that only prima facie evidence of a return certificate, issued by customs collectors, would be accepted when it came to granting Chinese laborers reentry into the United States. This was in response to the fact that federal courts were overwhelmed by habeas corpus petitions submitted by Chinese plaintiffs, who attempted to use parole evidence to overturn their denied entry. Between 1882 and 1890, the U.S. District Court for the Northern District of California received approximately seven thousand habeas corpus petitions from Chinese immigrants denied entry. It was believed that the "no certificate—no entry" principle of the 1884 act would lessen their daunting workload. The 1884 act did not resolve how to deal with, however, the estimated twelve to fifteen thousand Chinese laborers who had departed the United States prior to the certificate requirement, under the assumption that they were eligible to return without any paperwork.[36] This came to a head on December 8, 1884, when the U.S. Supreme Court ruled that immigration officials could not deny entry to the plaintiff Chew Heong on the grounds that he did not have a return certificate.[37] A frustrated Congress intervened with the 1888 Scott Act, which barred all Chinese laborers from entering the United States—even if they held valid return certificates that the federal government had previously issued.[38]

After 1888, how to navigate restrictions was increasingly seen by white employers as a matter of employee retention. In October 1889, for instance, Mrs. J. G. Goddard of Manhattan wrote to the Department of the Treasury requesting a "passport" for an unnamed "Chinaman" who had been in the employ of her family for four years as a servant, and who wished to travel to China to visit his family. Goddard's advocacy on her servant's behalf was motivated, it seems, by her concerns that an equally competent replacement would be difficult to find. Her appeal was dismissed by the assistant secretary of the treasury.[39] An article by Marie Allen Kimball that appeared in the *Chautauquan* in 1893 complained that California families were being deprived of valued Chinese servants who, wishing to pursue "matrimonial intentions" in China, could no longer do so. Household employers had previously tolerated this practice on the condition that the departing Chinese servant provided a replacement pending his return, but now, she alleged, the restriction laws made the decision to travel abroad the equivalent of quitting.[40]

Figure 1. Photograph of Ye Gon Lun's grave site. Courtesy of Janelle Michel and Daniel Oen.

Figure 2. "A Hint-On the Chinese Question," *Wasp*, October 6, 1877. Bancroft Library, University of California, Berkeley.

THE IRISH DECLARATION OF INDEPENDENCE THAT WE ARE ALL FAMILIAR WITH.

Figure 3. Frederick Opper, "The Irish Declaration of Independence," *Puck*, May 9, 1883. Courtesy of the University of Minnesota Libraries.

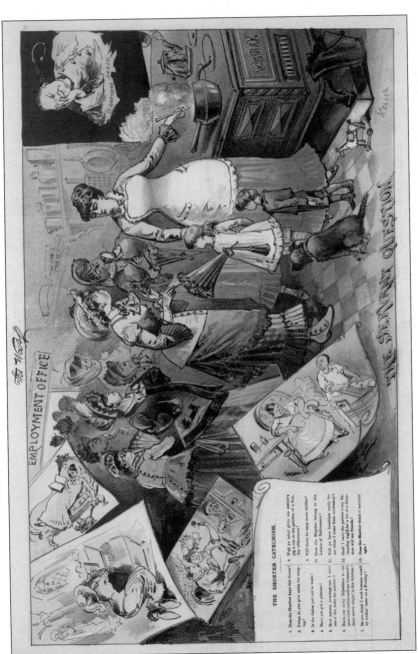

Figure 4. Frederick Keller, "The Servant Question," *Wasp*, July 15, 1882. Bancroft Library, University of California, Berkeley.

Figure 5. Panel from Joseph Keppler's "The Chinese Invasion," *Puck*, March 17, 1880. Courtesy of Princeton University Library.

Figure 6. Frederick Opper, "The Servant-Girl Problem," *Puck*, January 28, 1891. Courtesy of Princeton University Library.

The 1892 Geary Act and 1893 McCreary Amendment required all Chinese immigrants and American-born Chinese domiciled in the United States to register for certificates of residency that proved their legal right to be in the country. The new statutes—which the Chinese community referred to as the "dog tag" law—required two white witnesses to provide legal testimony verifying a Chinese resident's legal status. Some white commentators believed that as familial dependents, Chinese domestics could more easily be brought in line with the project of racial surveillance that the legislation initiated. Their employers, the theory went, could both command them to register with the federal government and, at the same time, vouch for their eligibility. According to the *San Francisco Morning Call*, which published a lengthy series on the Chinese "conspiracy" against the Geary Act's registration requirement, servants were the only members of the Chinese community in San Francisco who had registered punctually while the law's constitutionality was still being contested in court. In April 1893, with the initial deadline for registration only a month away, the *Call* claimed that a large number of white employers had arranged secret meetings between federal officials and their servants unbeknownst to Chinese opposition leaders.[41] In the *Overland Monthly*, Elizabeth Bales related the story of a Chinese servant whose mistress mandated him to register, even though he had pleaded not to, since it would allegedly put his life at risk for violating an order of the Chinese Six Companies. Bales's sensational account drew on the popular perception of the mutual association as a criminal consortium or "tong" with coercive powers over Chinese laborers. At the internal revenue office where registration took place, Bales described how

> such pitiful white faces some of the domestics presented when brought, unwillingly, by their employers to be registered. And no wonder that terror was depicted in their countenances, for had not the edict of their masters gone forth against their compliance with the law? Rarely could they be cajoled into coming the second time, and in some cases they even refused to sign the order necessary to procure their certificates.[42]

In Bales's fanciful account, the registration process provoked anguish among Chinese servants forced to choose between two sets of masters, each with conflicting laws and rules that they demanded be upheld.

She did not acknowledge that widespread resistance to registration had formed within the Chinese community before leaders announced their opposition, or the premise that the law itself was discriminatory and unjust.[43]

Some white employers were ambivalent about the need to comply with immigration laws, especially when the laws might have a negative impact on their own hiring needs. Occasionally they even abetted the entry of inadmissible Chinese immigrants when it directly benefitted their interests. One case that received substantial attention in the media and drew intense backlash from various anti-Chinese groups involved the immigrant Wong Mie. After receiving an anonymous tip, an immigration inspector dispatched to San Jose, California, had "virtually caught [Wong] in the act of making up beds" at the St. James Hotel. Wong had been permitted to reenter the United States from China in 1892 after Tyler Beach, the white owner of the St. James, had sworn in an affidavit that Wong was a businessman with a stake in an employment agency. Typical of the disparities in prosecution that persist to this day, Beach avoided any consequences as a result of his actions while Wong was deported.[44]

From what evidence exists, it appears that after 1893 white employers were mainly content to ignore whether or not the Chinese servants they hired were authorized to be in the country, and did not make proof of legal status a prerequisite for employment. In this respect their actions prefigured those of household employers in the present. Today, employers regularly choose to overlook whether or not an immigrant domestic worker is undocumented, thereby evading status questions.[45] Given the wave of boycotts that anti-Chinese labor leaders had tried to implement in 1885 and 1886, nineteenth-century employers of Chinese servants were already guarded against being told how to conduct their household affairs. Private homes, when it came to the enforcement of immigration laws, were usually considered off-limits.

In rare instances when white homes did come under the purview of enforcement measures and were investigated for unauthorized Chinese immigrants, the resulting uproar made clear that the middle-class public understood such practices to be excessive and intrusive. A series of articles that appeared in the *Call* recounted, with barely concealed amusement, how the San Francisco residence of the merchant shipowner

Samuel Blair and his family was reluctantly raided by a federal marshal on September 25, 1893, after District Court Judge William Morrow was persuaded to issue a warrant for the arrest of Sam Lo, a Chinese servant who had not registered for a certificate of identity. A local white gardener swore out the complaint and the erstwhile Workingmen's Party leader, Denis Kearney, accompanied the marshal on the raid as a monitor for the Anti-Chinese Law and Order League. After the two men entered the home—let in by Sam himself—and declared their business, they were met with hostility from Mrs. Blair and her daughter, who questioned their authority to be in a private residence. Marshal Long "found the proceedings decidedly embarrassing . . . [and] stammered something about being very sorry to have to perform such an unpleasant duty." Sam took advantage of the commotion to flee. Long and Kearney were unable to find the servant after searching all twenty-five rooms in the home. Back at Judge Morrow's office, while Kearney called for the pursuit to continue, Long threatened "to resign his office rather than try to arrest any more Chinese servants in private residences in the face of any feminine opposition." On September 30, when the *Call* last reported on the story, Sam remained a fugitive.[46] What makes the hesitant raid on the Blairs' home significant is the fact that it took place at all.

Where Chinese domestics and other service workers were able to obtain permission to depart or enter the United States without intense scrutiny, it was because they conformed to the representations of Chinese servility toward whites that marked them as safely submissive and therefore also trustworthy. When Lum Jun, for instance, conducted an interview in Fresno in June 1913 in order to obtain Form 430, the official reentry certificate that the bureau eventually adopted, he directly involved his employers so as to dispel any doubts about his identity. Lum's boss, S. W. Norton, owned the café where he worked as a cook. Norton explained to the immigration inspector that "everybody calls [Lum] by his American name, Charlie," which, along with Lum's English language skills, was presented as convincing evidence of his birthright citizenship—the grounds upon which he was claiming the right to leave the United States and return. Even though English fluency was an acquired talent, and American-born Chinese residents of Chinatowns could grow up without ever gaining command of the language, when Norton cited this as proof of citizenship it was given significant weight.

When asked if he believed "Charlie" when he claimed to be born in the United States, Norton testified that "Charlie is a good boy"—Lum was twenty-nine years old at the time—"and I would believe his statements in all cases."[47]

## Bonded Admissions: Regulating Temporary Labor

Since 1882, a small but significant number of American commentators had implored the federal government to experiment with visa programs that would allow for certain classes of Chinese laborers, including servants, to enter as guestworkers on a temporary basis. Because these proposals were never tried in practice, it was left unclear as to how immigration officials would remove guestworkers once their labor was no longer needed. When confronted with how to handle Chinese servants entering with their employers, the solution that officials devised was to require employers to take out a surety bond that provided collateral against a servant's failure to depart. In modeling a type of guestworker program, immigration officials determined that placing the onus of a Chinese laborer's removal on the employer rather than on the employee was crucial.

The willingness of the American state to bond Chinese servants as a safeguard against their unauthorized immigration was a novel method of governance that federal restriction laws necessitated, even if this method itself had antecedents in controls on other labor migrations. Bonding harkened back to older and more coercive ways of facilitating labor migrations, and indentured servitude in particular. Linguistically, "bondsman" or "bondswoman" referred to an individual who was under contract with an employer and denied the freedom to pursue other jobs until he or she had worked off an economic or social debt that he or she had entered into—often the cost of passage—or, in some cases, until the individual had satisfied punishment for a crime.

Bonds were also a form of insurance. Historically, the financial bonding of migrants to and within the United States, providing insurance against loss or liability, followed two distinct paths. Prior to the end of the legal transatlantic slave trade, surety bonds on enslaved persons were purchased by shipowners as insurance against the loss of property that might be incurred from revolts, natural calamities, maritime accidents, or sickness. In the years preceding the Civil War, actors involved in the internal slave trade and the redistribution of enslaved persons from the Upper South to cotton-growing regions took out insurance policies as well.[48] With respect to voluntary migrants whose passage was not explicitly coerced, from the early nineteenth century onward states like New York, Louisiana, and Massachusetts required vessel owners or captains to take out bonds in individual cases where migrants were identified as being at risk of becoming dependent on public relief through poverty or illness. Eventually states used the threat of requiring bonds for all immigrants to have ship captains pay a far less expensive commutation tax instead. After the Supreme Court's decisions in *Henderson v. Mayor of City of New York* and *Chy Lung v. Freeman* in 1875 and 1876, respectively, the authority to demand surety bonds on the entry of immigrants was transferred to the federal government, along with other enforcement powers.

Bonds, in yet another usage, were also deployed to free immigrants, held in detention, whose eligibility to enter the United States was pending. Immigrant detention bonds bore a close resemblance to the bail bonds available to arrested suspects awaiting criminal trials. Immigration detention bonds again raised issues of race, trust, and respect for the law. Chinese bail bondsmen were the primary issuers of the sureties required to release Chinese immigrants from administrative detention. Unlike the corporate insurance firms that white employers would later rely on, Chinese bail bondsmen were small and sometimes fly-by-night enterprises.

In both immigration and criminal law, white officials attempted to limit the ability of Chinese bondsmen to supply sureties. They denounced Chinese bondsmen for fraudulently conspiring with detainees. Chinese bondsmen were accused of issuing "straw" bonds and then dodging payment on those bonds when released detainees failed to show up for legal proceedings. In 1888, William Gavigan, special counsel for the City of San Francisco, argued that local criminal courts would be wise to adopt the categorical policy of refusing bail bonds proffered by Chinese bondsmen, unless a specially appointed expert certified in each and every case that a payment on forfeited bonds could actually be made. In the same report, Gavigan also listed numerous white bondsmen who had defrauded the San Francisco courts, although they did not provoke the same outrage. In 1890, the Superior Court of San Francisco declared that a ruling by a municipal judge requiring two Chinese defendants to pay their bail in cash was unconstitutional and in violation of the Equal Protection Clause of the Fourteenth Amendment. The judge, William Wallace, felt moved to clarify that even if he had to uphold the Constitution, under no circumstances would he compel lower courts to accept a bail bond from a Chinese source, since "it was a well-known fact that all the bonds heretofore given by Chinese were worthless." He recommended a version of Gavigan's proposal in which Chinese bondsmen had to prove to the satisfaction of the attorney general that they could back up the sureties they were issuing.[49] Since this requirement would have been applied in a racially discriminatory manner, it was perhaps unconstitutional in its own right.

In immigration cases where debarment was being appealed, authorities regularly complained that Chinese immigrants released on bond failed to appear before the federal judges and specially appointed commissioners tasked with rendering decisions on their entry. Once they were freed, officials argued, the threat of deportation was an insufficient deterrent since unauthorized immigrants already had nothing to lose by being on the wrong side of the law. In a February 1892 article the *Call* alleged that in recent cases where a total of 140 Chinese immigrants had been released on bond rather than being kept in detention, not a single one appeared at his scheduled hearing. Recovering the forfeited bonds, the newspaper suggested, was nearly impossible, since they were issued under the same dubious circumstances that criminal bail bonds were.[50] In response to these frustrations, the Geary Act explicitly prohibited bail in cases where Chinese immigrants were awaiting decisions on their entry.

There can be no doubt that these concerns and suspicions weighed on immigration officials tasked with policing temporary admission. Still, admitting Chinese laborers on a temporary basis posed new conundrums to authorities, since their voluntary departure rather than deportation was the end object of governance. In section 3 of the general 1882 Immigration Act, which applied to all immigrants, Congress gave the secretary of the treasury and his office the authority to "prescribe all forms of bonds, entries, and other papers to be used under and in the enforcement of the various provisions of this act." Language to this effect would appear in all subsequent immigration acts that followed. Section 20 of the 1907 act stated that surety bonds were to be set at a minimum of five hundred dollars per individual. These regulations were also concerned with establishing procedures for admitting European immigrants on a probationary basis. Their dual purpose—and the differing racial motives that informed immigration policy—meant that in addition to governing in-transit Chinese labor, surety bonds were also used for indemnification purposes in cases where immigration officials had to delay final judgment on a European immigrant's eligibility to enter or remain in the country. When it came to white immigrants, surety bonds were designed to give restrictive policies a more humane face and to avoid prolonged detentions.[51]

With the passage of the Scott Act in 1888, immigration officials focused attention on the unique issues that the transit of Chinese laborers posed. Because categorical restrictions on European immigrants did not exist until the 1920s, they would not present similar administrative issues until then. The first "in-transit" laborers that the bureau targeted were Chinese workers who met a more literal definition of this term than servants working in the United States for a temporary period of time did. These were laborers, primarily from Cuba, who were traveling via the Southern Pacific Railroad from New Orleans to San Francisco, and then by steamship to China. In the reverse direction, immigration officials were also suspicious that laborers from China, arriving in San Francisco, were falsely claiming that they were destined for Mexico or Cuba but instead staying in the United States.[52]

In July 1889, the U.S. solicitor general ruled that statutes prohibiting Chinese immigration did not apply to travelers passing through the United States, who as nonimmigrants had a different legal standing.[53] On September 28, 1889, Secretary of the Treasury William Windom began instructing customs collectors to require in-transit laborers to furnish paid tickets to their destination and to carry certificates with their physical descriptions. As a more significant deterrent, he also required all in-transit laborers to either take out a two-hundred-dollar bond pledged as a surety by a third party or to provide this amount in full themselves. When they arrived at their port of departure, the bond would then be canceled or the cash refunded to them. Windom explained to Secretary of State James G. Blaine that "to permit an unregulated transit of that class of Chinese subjects would be equivalent to inviting a practical nullification of the laws prohibiting [their] immigration." Registering a formal complaint, Tsui Kwo Yin, the Chinese minister, argued that the bond requirement would effectively cut off transit through the United States, since it would be impossible for the average Chinese laborer to find a bondsman willing to take a risk on an unknown person, and he could not be expected to possess such funds himself.[54] Tsui accurately interpreted federal officials' intent. Even when the required bond was raised to five hundred dollars, Chinese immigrants still found creative ways to get around the law. Chinese individuals already residing in the United States, who were permitted to depart the country and return, switched places with prohibited in-transit laborers not allowed entry. Merchants complicit in these schemes fronted the bond money that they hoped to recover when these substitutions went undetected.[55]

The regulation of sailors' shore leave also caused confusion and conflict. Like servants, Chinese seamen were seen as essential to the conduct of global commerce and necessary adjuncts to the establishment of American military and commercial power abroad. In particular, ship captains enlisted them to work as stewards, servants, and firemen responsible for stoking coal- and wood-fired steam engines. These were jobs that were racialized and gendered as unfit for white male mariners. American and British steamship companies, and their navies, often found it difficult to find non-Chinese laborers willing to perform this work.[56] When the habeas corpus case of *Ah Kee* came before the federal court for the Southern District of New York in November 1884, Justice Addison Brown was reluctant to rule against Chinese sailors in a way that might interfere with the fluidity of global trade. "Ah" Kee, the plaintiff, embodied the diffuse commercial reach of the British Empire and the cosmopolitan origins of its maritime workforce, despite his simplified racialization as a "Chinese" threat against American national and economic security. Born in post-annexation Hong Kong as a British colonial subject, he had most recently shipped on the *Richard Parsons* from Calcutta, on a contract that expired upon his arrival in New York. Held on board by the ship's master while the vessel's non-Chinese crew was discharged, Kee—angered at his confinement—decided to sneak ashore. He was caught and imprisoned by a federal marshal monitoring the East River piers. In a key passage defining the legal precedent that would predominate until 1917, Brown ruled that

> the persons prohibited by the act from coming within the United States are throughout described by the phrase "Chinese laborers." The well-known use and meaning of this phrase, and contemporaneous history, leave no doubt in my mind that the words "Chinese laborers" have no reference to seamen in the ordinary pursuit of their vocation on the high seas, who may touch upon our shores, and may land temporarily for the purpose only of obtaining a chance to ship for some other foreign voyage as soon as possible, and who do not intend to make any stay here, or enter upon any of the occupations on land within this country.[57]

Accordingly, Brown ordered Kee released. As a nonimmigrant, he could not be accused of violating immigration law.

Chinese inspectors, especially those in California, understood *Ah Kee* to be a precedent that could undermine restriction. In July 1886, John Hager, the vehemently anti-Chinese collector of customs for the Port of San Francisco, wrote to Daniel Manning, the secretary of the treasury, to protest the decision. Hager underlined in his letter that Chinese "seamen *individually* are recruited from the *very element* which the law prohibits from entering the country," even if the occupational category to which they belonged fell outside the scope of the legislation. To Hager, it was utter fiction to believe that Chinese sailors, if granted shore leave, would comply with the law and depart after a set period. "When ashore," Hager argued—raising a point that was to become standard among opponents of Chinese sailors' shore leave for years to come—"they are soon lost sight of in the vast throng of their countrymen in this city." According to numbers compiled by the San Francisco surveyor of customs, which Hager forwarded to Washington, between the passage of the 1882 Restriction Act and July 31, 1885, a total of 2,328 Chinese crew members had left port with valid return certificates permitting their reentry.[58] Each, his letter implied, might be a substitute for crew members who had taken shore leave and then remained in the country. Lost in all of this was the fact that Kee had initially demanded the liberty to go ashore in order to exercise his freedom to reship with another company at better wages—not because he desired to stay. Comparable to the ways in which regulations policed Chinese servants' liberty of contract by refusing them the freedom to seek alternative employment, officials sought to similarly constrain Chinese sailors' right to choose the vessel they wished to sail on under the auspices of blocking their unauthorized immigration.

Eventually, Chinese businessmen—immigrant and American-born— met the demand for in-transit and seamen bonds, for both legal and illegal purposes, and engaged with rail and steamship companies to provide this service. Chinese bondsmen attending to the sureties that allowed seamen to temporarily disembark in the United States continued to generate automatic suspicion. Chinese surety bondsmen were demonized for providing a service that allowed Chinese sailors to comply with a requirement that immigration officials themselves had instituted, and for facilitating the global networks of trade that American producers and consumers demanded.[59]

## Insuring against Free Labor

"Colonel" Cushman Rice was an archetype of the globe-trotting, early twentieth-century American imperialist. The son of a prominent Willmar, Minnesota, family, he fought as a soldier of fortune in the Honduran and Cuban revolutions before joining the American military to serve in the War of 1898, the Philippines War, and eventually the First World War. In his travels, he acquired a cattle ranch in Cuba and a townhouse in Manhattan's wealthy Gramercy Park neighborhood to go along with his family's vacation home in Green Lake, Minnesota. Rice was a well-known New York socialite, and it has even been suggested that he was the inspiration for Jay Gatsby in F. Scott Fitzgerald's *The Great Gatsby*.[60] In Cuba, Rice hired a Chinese servant, Foi Lem. Through his New York banking agents Rice established a standing thousand-dollar bond that officials at Ellis Island renewed every time Foi entered the country. Given Rice's reputation and public prominence, immigration officials abstained from interrogating Foi or taking any other measures to ascertain whether he could be trusted to remain in Rice's service—outside of the bond itself. Foi was even allowed to enter the country unaccompanied by his employer. In August 1926, for instance, Foi arrived in New York alone and traveled by train to Green Lake. At the time of Foi's arrival Rice was off on an African hunting safari, but upon his return he thanked officials for their courtesy in allowing him to find "my China-man . . . installed at my summer place."[61]

Dependent migrations did not disappear with the late nineteenth century's emphasis on free migration. Historian Adam McKeown argues that one of the challenges of modern nation-states was "isolating the individual as the agent of migration, possessor of rights, and object of regulation." He adds by way of a rhetorical question: "under what conditions could Asian migrants be understood as free when it was believed that tyranny and servility were the very conditions of their existence?"[62] With bonded Chinese servants, officials did away with this perceived racial conundrum altogether. In the case of Chinese servants admitted on a temporary basis, the threat of Chinese "illegality" outweighed any concerns officials had about placing foreign laborers in situations where they were forced to surrender their independence to contract freely. During the early twentieth century, the annual number of Chinese servants necessitating bonds was never very large. In 1922, for instance, immigration officials reported that only nineteen bonded Chinese servants were granted admission as temporary nonimmigrant laborers that fiscal year. There were no standard procedures for recording the issue of these bonds, so the number sent to Washington may have been underreported.[63] Regardless, the bonding of Chinese servants created an important precedent that subsequent regimes of immigration enforcement would further in spirit and specific tactics.

The indemnification of Chinese servants as subjects whose admission had to be regulated and monitored made white employers' mastery a formal obligation that they had to fulfill. Even though Chinese servants left employment situations for any number of reasons, their departure was seen by immigration officials as the fault of employers who had proved incapable of exercising a proper form of white mastery over their racialized dependents. By the twentieth century, the racial hierarchy captured in the vision of this social relationship between Chinese men and white male employers was firmly entrenched and celebrated in popular discourse.[64]

For other white visitors traveling through or returning to the United States, the ability to retain Chinese servants that they had hired before departing had to do with the continuity of domestic employment relationships that were widely understood, especially by members of the middle class, to be volatile and instable, and therefore worth preserving if at all possible. An American employee of Standard Oil's Shanghai branch, for instance, understood the ability to retain a valued *amah* (nurse) while on furlough in the United States as a friendly consideration that helped ameliorate the hardships of employment abroad and the difficulties that attended the hiring of reliable servants in China.[65]

In an era when minimum wage laws and other statutory protections for laborers were virtually nonexistent, and when the exploitation of Chinese immigrants was weighed mainly in respect to whether or not white laborers were negatively affected, no one appears to have considered how state-mandated dependencies between Chinese servants and their employers might be subject to abuse. Authorities paid no attention

Figure 5.1. Tung Yang Sze and the unnamed daughter of Paul Jernigan. Jernigan worked for the Shanghai branch of the Standard Oil Company and bonded his *amah* for admission and work in the United States during a six-month furlough that he and his family spent in the United States in 1920. File 54783/42, Subject Correspondence Files, NARA.

to how limiting the avenues in which Chinese servants could contract their labor power once in the United States created conditions of bondage. Surety bonds incentivized white employers to keep temporarily admitted Chinese servants under coercive forms of supervision and control. While Chinese servants consented to hire with employers prior to leaving for the United States, and therefore exercised liberty of contract prior to departure, after their arrival they had no recourse against wage theft or other forms of mistreatment—except to abscond from employment relations and become "illegal" immigrants. Employers were instructed to guard against this possibility. In one case involving the *amah* of a white British doctor, her employer surrendered his servant to immigration officials in San Francisco, after taking out a bond for her entry, when he became suspicious that she was plotting to leave him. Required to pay her passage back to China, he assumed this expense knowing that it was still considerably cheaper than a forfeited bond.[66] By and large, the methods that employers relied on to guarantee their sureties were not reported to immigration officials, who would have been nonplussed by these tactics anyway.

In the late 1910s and 1920s, immigration authorities did begin to coordinate with American consular officials in China as to whether or not travelers' needs for personal servants were warranted. As Acting Commissioner W. W. Sibray outlined in 1920, the general rule was that the temporary admission of servants could be approved when denying their entry "would involve special hardship" to employers.[67] What constituted need was of course a subjective assessment and informed not only by practical questions about travelers' medical health and the number and age of their children—if nurses were involved—but also by whether the visitors to the United States were prominent figures within China's foreign settlements meriting these privileges. Visitors seeking to enter with Chinese servants could be found providing immigration officials with testimonials about how they were "favorably known" and warranted "all possible courtesies."[68] Discussions of need also veered toward questions of racial suitability for the performance of certain types of service and care work, and whether or not American laborers could be hired by visitors as potential replacements. E. I. Ezra, the Shanghai-born son of Baghdadi Jewish merchants and a leading opium importer in the city, successfully petitioned immigration officials in 1920 to be allowed to enter the United States with three Chinese servants and an unstated number of children. Ezra was traveling to the Mayo Brother medical facilities in Minnesota to receive treatment, and, as a representative writing on his behalf explained to immigration officials, his children were "use[d] to only Chinese servants."[69] This statement went unchallenged, as did its implication that the care and attention that Chinese *amahs* and servants provided could not be replicated by (white) laborers hired for this purpose in the United States. Immigration officials may not have been confident that imperial labor needs, viewed as sumptuous, extravagant, and, in the eyes of republican-minded Americans, excessive, could actually be fulfilled by the existing service sector. Maurice Benjamin, a prominent British subject in Shanghai, was allowed to enter the United States with his wife and seven "house servants" in 1930 after brandishing his credentials as a key figure responsible for working with Chinese officials to guarantee the safety of the city's International Settlement during the upheavals of the 1920s.[70] In cases like Ezra's and Benjamin's, immigration officials afforded certain privileges to international figures whose dedication to advancing the goals of Western imperialism in China had been proven.

Even though the bonding process was a formality to some employers, other visitors—like Colonel Fay, discussed at the beginning of this chapter—grappled to maintain the necessary compulsion and surveillance that the sureties required. Racial stereotypes notwithstanding, Chinese servants sought out the best situations in which to maximize returns on the contract of their labor power. They were quite capable of defying their reputation for being compliant. When Dr. Hugo Hardy, the commissioner of the German East Africa exhibit at the 1904 St. Louis World's Fair and an attaché to the official German delegation, arrived in Hoboken, his Chinese servant Wang Su Tang was permitted to land and was inspected dockside with minimal hassle rather than being sent to Ellis Island.[71] Wang was landed without Hardy taking out a bond, since they were in the United States on official government business. Upon arriving in St. Louis, however, Wang's "innate" deference was apparently corrupted. As Hardy explained to a St. Louis newspaper, Wang fell under the negative influence of "the flippancy and independence of American servants." Hardy dismissed Wang, who was then deported.[72]

Bonded Chinese servants could also be denied entry when they were found to be ineligible to enter on medical or other grounds or if they were caught violating other criminal statutes pertaining to border controls. In one instance, U.S. customs officials in Toronto caught a Chinese servant, bonded to accompany a white Canadian family to the resort town of Kennebunk, Maine, with a trunk full of opium. He had been bonded for at least one other trip to the United States in the past, and, applying for the surety bond, his employer had cited ongoing domestic labor shortages in Toronto as the rationale for bringing him with her. Prior to his arrest, the servant may have thought that his employment status offered the perfect guise for drug smuggling.[73] The need to retain Chinese servants routinely appeared as a justification for bringing them into the United States. In 1920, for instance, an employee of the Dollar Steamship Company accepted the risk that he might have to forfeit the bond on his valued servant rather than have him remain in China and lose his services to another Westerner stationed there.[74]

The case of Army Lieutenant Colonel A. A. King and his servant Chan "Ah" Chang—also referred to as Jin "Ah" Chung and Jung "Ah" Chung in the immigration case file—details a case where a five-hundred-dollar bond, issued by the American Surety Company, was actually forfeited. Because the bureau did not keep records in this area, it is not possible to determine how frequently this occurred overall. Chan arrived in San Francisco on March 16, 1914, in order to attend to King's ill sister, who had apparently been living with her brother on an unnamed American base in the Philippines. In May 1915, the bureau allowed King, who by then had also returned to the United States, to rebond Chan for an additional period of two years. In 1917, King, who was stationed in Philadelphia as a recruiting officer, filed a request to take out another two-year bond. He explained to officials that Chan "relieves me of all anxiety in my domestic affairs and is a great factor in my efficiency to the government." This was also approved, meaning that Chan's "temporary" admission was officially prolonged to a five-year stay.

In December 1918, King instructed Chan to board an army transport ship in Philadelphia for the Philippines. Thinking Chan had followed his orders, he considered the matter closed. In March 1919, however, when immigration officials began proceedings to either cancel or collect the bond, which by that point had expired, they discovered no record

Figure 5.2. Chan "Ah" Chang, in one of the two photos that his employer King submitted to immigration officials, poses with what appears to be a puppy. File 53725/77, Subject Correspondence Files, NARA.

of Chan's departure. Faced with forfeiture, King employed a Washington law firm, which petitioned the bureau for relief from the financial burden. According to his attorneys, King was adamant that Chan, his loyal servant, would not leave him financially liable for his unauthorized stay in the United States. King instead believed that Chan either was dead or had embarked, undetected, on another vessel. The latter scenario was unlikely given the scrutiny that typically attended to the departure of Chinese migrants. Anticipating that this line of reasoning might not convince immigration officials, King's lawyers simultaneously requested that the bond be pardoned on the grounds that his frequent travel on behalf of the Army was a type of patriotic duty that excused the lax surveillance of his servant. None of these arguments succeeded, and the American Surety Company was forced to pay out to the Department of Labor.[75] In cases such as this, the fact that the bond came from an established and licensed guarantor meant that the government could eventually cut off communication with a recalcitrant party such as King. If he still refused to assume responsibility for the bond's forfeiture, the matter of who owed whom was now a civil one between him and the company.

Figure 5.3. Chan "Ah" Chang (on the right), with an unnamed colleague. File 53725/77, Subject Correspondence Files, NARA.

As King's failure to persuade immigration officials to waive the bond forfeiture shows, authorities monitored the departure of Chinese laborers in uncompromising terms as both revenue collectors and opponents of unauthorized immigration. When Chuen Yu Mei, a bonded Chinese servant, died in the United States while in the service of his employer, immigration inspectors were dispatched to the Oakland morgue to verify that the body in question was his.[76] Immigration officials were less likely to issue bond extensions when the reasoning behind these requests suggested that the employment of temporary Chinese laborers was trending toward labor that went beyond abetting employers' domestic and personal needs. Although the Hogg family of Delaware Water Gap, Pennsylvania, claimed that their two Chinese servants Liu Liln Fah and Gin Sung Tsii could not return to China due to ongoing civil strife in Tientsin, this did not stop them from employing the two men in a Chinese-styled tea house that Mrs. Hogg operated in a resort community in the Poconos. Officials were skeptical and denied the bond extension after an investigation was conducted, although they relented when the former U.S. Attorney General A. Mitchell Palmer intervened on the Hoggs' behalf.[77] Another plea for an extension that would have allowed an *amah* to remain in the United States to tend to the needs of her employer's dying mother-in-law, who had become attached to her Chinese nurse, was rejected. Immigration officials were suspicious that the employment relationship had been uprooted from its temporary status and was on the verge of making the *amah* a permanent rather than temporary migrant laborer.[78]

In regions where the United States shared borders with Canada and Mexico, immigration laws had always been enforced in ways that reflected the necessity of frequent traffic back and forth across international lines. Local residents resented government impositions on cross-border travel understood as customary.[79] Railroad companies, whose routes and capital holdings straddled land borders, offer a unique example of how immigration inspectors, when faced with enforcing restrictions that could make the conduct of daily business arrestingly onerous, found ways to accommodate employers. Anticipating the passes currently used to permit the daily, employment-based migration of Mexicans into the United States and Americans into Mexico, early twentieth-century businesses were privileged with similar credentialing.[80] Given the importance that the U.S. government placed on the railroad companies' endeavors abroad, immigration officials were inclined to view this work as taking place in the national interest and therefore immune from the more stringent enforcement of restriction laws.[81]

In a 1928 letter from the bureau's regional office in El Paso, Texas, to the commissioner general of immigration in Washington, the officer in charge noted that "it had been the custom for several years for our

Department to issue, as a matter of courtesy, certificates of identity to the Chinese servants of certain high officials of the Southern Pacific Railroad Company in Mexico, which would permit the said servants to accompany the officials to the United States on their private cars, *merely for temporary stay*, upon the understanding of course that the said Chinese laborers would not remain in this country but would return to Mexico" (emphasis in original). The El Paso officer felt obliged to reiterate that the certificate system did not represent any larger aberration from official policy: "These certificates were issued merely for the purpose of facilitating the ingress and egress of the Chinese servants." The letter was drafted in response to the arrest of Alejandro Fong in Nogales, Mexico, after he was allegedly caught smuggling goods into the United States without paying required duties. Fong was accused of using the certificate of identity that he was issued in his capacity as a servant to J. B. Finley, vice president and general manager of the Southern Pacific's operations in Mexico, in order to travel back and forth across the border without scrutiny.

The labor passes issued to railroad executives were comparable to the bond system, in that immigration officials believed that the responsibility for monitoring and controlling the mobility of Chinese servants belonged to their railroad employers and could not be delegated to servants themselves. Officials in El Paso contended that the blame for Fong's actions rested with the railroad, and suggested that lacking the proper guardianship such behavior was to be expected from Chinese laborers who possessed little respect for the law. When Finley and the railroad initially applied for the certificate, they were instructed that the certificate should "remain in the possession of some American person in charge of the car."[82] Assigning railroad officials responsibility for their Chinese servants' labor passes was not confined to the southern border. Louie Lee, a Chinese servant who worked for James Blair, the division superintendent for the Canadian Pacific Railway along the Québec and Vermont border, was allowed to enter the United States as a cook in a private car that made cross-border trips to Newport, Vermont, twice a month. Lee's certificate of identity was issued with the provision that Blair was responsible for the possession of the certificate and "agrees to make certain that the cook will not leave the car while it is in the United States." When Lee's service was terminated, his certificate was revoked.[83]

## Conclusion

The scholarship examining the regulation and exploitation of nonimmigrant, temporary laborers has proceeded in a largely ahistorical manner. It implies that the vulnerabilities that these groups face are the novel and contemporary byproducts of the new modalities of globalization.[84] This is clearly not the case. A focus on how enforcement measures got constructed during Chinese exclusion, in ways that emphasized inclusion as well as exclusion, offers a more precise genealogy of how labor exploitation and bondage got built into practices geared at integrating—with contingencies—a workforce deemed necessary to American global interests. This focus also reveals how ideas of race, mastery, and trust were present in the formation of incipient guestworker programs at a structural level.

The bonding requirements used to permit the entry of Chinese servants on a temporary basis, despite being relatively limited in their application, represent an important precedent as well. During World War II, the use of bonds in indemnifying the United States against the unpermitted stay of temporary guestworkers swelled with the introduction of the *bracero* program. Under the provisions of this program, employers had to post bonds on contracted guestworkers from Mexico, which, in the postwar continuation of the program, amounted to twenty-five dollars per worker. The desire to see their posted bonds recouped upon a laborer's departure contributed to an environment where employers were motivated, beyond the need to maintain a sufficient workforce, to prevent farm laborers from leaving their contracts.[85] In the present, immigration officials juggle an array of bonding requirements that are used in a wide range of scenarios. The federal government continues to find ways to insure against the possibility of certain classes of migrant workers freely contracting their labor while in the United States, even though it has never satisfactorily demonstrated what "costs" this unauthorized liberty would incur against the nation.

# 6

## Race and Reform

*Domestic Service, the Great Migration, and European Quotas, 1891–1924*

Readers perusing the January 28, 1891, issue of *Puck* would have encountered, tucked in among the publication's back pages, a full-page cartoon inset on "The Servant-Girl Problem." Frederick Opper, the artist, made a career out of drafting cartoons that portrayed Irish women as savage figures and the bane of middle-class households (see Figure 3 in the insert to this book for an example).[1] By 1891, however, employers' obsession with the specific problems that "Biddy" allegedly posed had waned. Labor scarcities, always a concern, had become the touchstone issue employers fretted over. In the cartoon's upper left-hand panel, "a family man" casually mentions to his friend that his cook has left. This results in pandemonium as he is besieged by competing employers trying to learn of her whereabouts. In another panel, a wizened old man recalls the past from the vantage point of 1991—a century after the cartoon's publication—and regales a group of children with a story about the bountiful surplus of servants and surfeit of intelligence offices that once existed. *Puck*'s readers would have been amused to see intelligence offices, reviled by the middle classes, posited as a subject of fond remembrance. Opper still manages to sneak in a dig at the Irish in the image. A servant named "Miss Whalen," drawn with simian features, is the recipient of "a theatre-party" that her employers have organized as her reward for completing three weeks' service. The joke is that retaining servants, even problematic Irish ones, had become so difficult that despairing employers were willing to go to absurd lengths to keep workers. A real-life analog could be found in the program of the German Housewife Society of New York, which pooled members' contributions in order to pay out bonuses to domestics. Uninterrupted employment with a single family for a period of two years earned servants a twenty-dollar bonus;

five years' service earned them a forty-five-dollar bonus; and ten years, one hundred dollars.[2] A panel in the lower right-hand corner of the cartoon presents an inventor and social "scientist" who has come up with a solution that has eliminated the servant problem once and for all. A hero, he is festooned with accolades, public commendation, and riches. Teasingly, no indication is given as to what exactly he figured out.

All of these smaller panels frame the cartoon's central scene. The focal image, titled "The Intelligence Office of the Future (as Things Look Now)," portrays a middle-class white woman shopping for a servant. Her options are a "Sioux Squaw," an "Esquimaux Lady," "One of Stanley's Pygmies," an "African Amazon," and a "Turkish Lady." The exoticism of the agency's "stock" is conveyed by their sensationalized physical appearances and clothing. At the same time, these details are juxtaposed against the banal tasks that the prospective servants are being marketed as willing to do, which conform to their perceived racial traits. The Sioux woman is willing to take on all domestic tasks but washing; the pygmy wants to work only for a small family. The indigenous "Esquimaux" woman does not object to living with her employers in a distant suburb; the servant from Africa will take a position in Brooklyn. With the servants hailing from remote places on the outskirts of "civilization," the joke is that they can be convinced to work in comparable distances from the Manhattan metropole. (This cartoon appears as Figure 6 in the insert to this book.)

Opper's attempts to mine for easy laughs notwithstanding, the main panel of the cartoon broaches imperial expansion and settler colonialism in a manner that sets aside the typical rationalizations for these actions. It instead ruminates on what access to new supplies of workers might mean when white workers had become even more forceful in rejecting domestic labor burdened with stigmas of racial servility. If an intelligence office were to monetize the brokerage of these new sources of colonial and racialized labor, Opper insinuates, it might very well reap a handsome profit.

The "Servant-Girl Problem" references two political strains of American imperialism that were being reshaped at the end of the nineteenth century, and looks to both as factors in the potential creation of new labor supplies. With the cartoon appearing in *Puck* only a month after the U.S. Army massacred between 150 and 300 Lakota Ghost Dance participants at Wounded Knee, the inclusion of the "Sioux" woman takes on a macabre and ugly meaning that goes beyond the immediate racism that the joke about her cleanliness displays. The massacre at Wounded Knee would accelerate the federal government's shift in its Indian policies that had begun with the 1887 Dawes Act. American settler colonialism in the West would now emphasize the division of native lands into private allotments. At the same time, the federal government intensified its efforts to steer native women into boarding schools and other fostering systems, in order to prepare them for wage work as domestic servants. This was the most effective means, federal agents argued, to free these women from dependencies on government welfare.[3]

The "Servant-Girl Problem"—in indirect fashion—also anticipated how household employers would come to speculate about the potential that the newly acquired U.S. overseas colonies had as sources for servants. This would grow in intensity by the end of the decade. An article that appeared in the *Brooklyn Eagle* in 1900, a year after hostilities between the United States and Spain had ceased, described a plan to import female servants from the Philippines, Puerto Rico, and Cuba. This was ultimately scrapped, but only after immigration officials ruled that the wholesale importation of domestic workers violated contract labor laws. In 1904, the U.S. Supreme Court would rule in *Gonzáles v. Williams* that Puerto Ricans, as colonial subjects, were not aliens when it came to immigration—even if they were not American citizens—and were not subject to restrictions. But in 1900 this decision was still forthcoming. By the mid-twentieth century, private intelligence offices and the Puerto Rican colonial government were involved in brokering contract migrations for Puerto Rican women to job sites in New York and Chicago, and the island had indeed become another source of household labor.[4]

Opper's "Servant-Girl Problem" did not include black women from the South as job applicants in his intelligence office of the future, even though the migration of these laborers to the North would double in the 1890s. Lucy Maynard Salmon, the Vassar historian whose history of domestic service was published in 1897, observed that white Americans had lost faith in the servile capacities of black servants from the South, and that their migration to the North could not be trusted to provide a solution to the domestic service problem. While some of the employers

Salmon surveyed claimed to be satisfied with their black domestics, others felt that "younger negroes are too lazy to be of much use" and lacked the "natural" training that slavery had previously bestowed upon them. Taking these white southern perspectives at face value, Salmon believed that free black laborers lacked the discipline to make them modern workers. "It has proved such to those who know the negro best," she summarized, "[that] there is little hope that Northern employers would gain more than new and perplexing complications by introducing as domestic servants large numbers of negroes from the South."[5]

The 1900 article in the *Brooklyn Eagle* demonstrated that this was not a uniform view. After noting how immigration officials had intervened to cut off contract servants from U.S. colonies, the same article discussed how an employment agent working out of Albany had plans afoot to pay for the migration of black servants from the South. This had "caused a sensation in local domestic services, and likewise no small amount of indignation." According to the newspaper, news of the scheme had made its way to the city's Central Labor Union, whose members planned a protest. Although the male members of the union had no intention of competing for these positions themselves, and had shown no prior interest in organizing white domestic workers, they apparently did not like the idea of labor brokers searching the South for contracted labor.[6] Like Salmon, they too thought that this was an ill-conceived plan for improving conditions in the occupation.

\* \* \*

Whereas previous chapters in this book addressed different groups of servants in the discrete contexts in which employers understood their brokerage and governance as sources of labor, this chapter converges these histories. It begins by examining how both sociologists and works of popular fiction—namely Mary Stewart Daggett's novel *The Yellow Angel*—argued that Chinese servants were content to remain in master and servant relations where employers' sentimental investment in laborers' moral and social uplift was a sufficient reward. In isolation, the representations that white employers advanced about Chinese servants' willingness to remain "premodern" in their aspirations were just another assumption about how imagined racial differences determined workers' capacity to tolerate (and even welcome) certain types of labor. In relational contexts, however, this discourse suggested that any reforms that did modify working conditions in domestic service would be to the benefit only of white laborers who actually desired these changes. By the turn of the century, progressive reformers were increasingly advocating for routinized contractual relations in domestic service that resembled those found in manufacturing work. They pushed for professionalization and emphasized that the relationship between household employers and their laborers was best understood as a contractual transaction—with wages for services rendered the sole form of compensation. Representations of Chinese servants' religiosity and unwavering loyalty appeared as vestigial features from an earlier period of labor relations. In cases where Chinese servants' allegiances to white employers were encouraged by discrimination and marginalization, they ended up being reinterpreted as natural.

Many of these same assumptions would haunt black women laborers arriving in the urban North. The support that white and black progressives gave to the free labor and mobility of black workers was far from unconditional. Leading sociologists and reformers of the period, both black and white, viewed European immigrants recently removed from the peasantry in places like Italy and Russia, and black southerners recently removed from "Jim Crow" rural life, as akin in their needs. Both groups were purportedly ill prepared when it came to adjusting to the modern world of northern cities like New York, and therefore at high risk in terms of engaging in behavior that compounded their social marginalization. Historian Andrew Zimmerman argues that members of the so-called Chicago School of sociology and their peers in Europe, such as Max Weber, have mistakenly been understood as less concerned with race in their approach to the study of urban ecology and the place of different social groups in an industrial economy, since most members adhered to a view that race was sociological rather than biological. "Unlike biological conceptions of race," Zimmerman points out, "sociological conceptions left room for reformist corrections to the perceived failings of supposedly inferior races."[7] Their belief in the malleability of race and confidence that certain groups' cultural traits and work ethic could be adjusted to the needs of political economy prompted reformers to intervene in the attempted assimilation of migrant laborers in the early twentieth century. When it came to black women entering into domestic service, this required constraints on their liberty of contract. While domestic service was to be reformed as an occupation so that it would be more attractive to white women workers, black women workers were to be reformed as individuals and members of a group—to make them better servants.

The final sections of this chapter return to the issues that white immigrant women encountered after the 1917 Immigration Act introduced a literacy test for immigrants seeking entry into the United States, and revised exceptions to contract labor laws. How immigrant servants contributed to the public and social good framed whether or not their illiteracy and arrival under contract might be overlooked by policymakers determined to expand restrictions. The conundrum that domestic service represented within the movement to restrict European immigration mirrored the situation in California during the 1870s, when members of the white middle class—while ostensibly in favor of halting the immigration of Chinese laborers—singled out servants for different governance. In 1907, Frances Kellor attributed nativists' relative silence on the subject of domestic service to the fact that it "has influence unlike that of any other occupation." The economist I. M. Rubinow concurred. He observed that anti-immigration activists tended to evade whenever possible any discussion of whether restrictions would exacerbate shortages of servants, since this might cause them to lose middle-class allies.[8] Even if many white immigrant women were rejecting domestic service, as an occupation out of line with advances made in industrial fields of labor, the ones who did enter into household employment became, in effect, more valuable. Nonetheless, calls for numerical quotas on European immigration proved too strong for policymakers who had previously built in exceptions for domestic servants to defeat. The spike in black migration to the North by World War I helped make restricting European servant migrations a safer political bet and a move less likely to raise the ire of middle-class employers.

By 1920, there was a marked decline in the number of households that continued to employ live-in workers designated as servants. In Boston, in 1880, 219 families out of a thousand employed servants, whereas by 1920 that number dropped to 74. In New York it went from 188 to 66 per thousand, and in Philadelphia from 183 to 70.[9] Joseph Hill's 1929 census monograph, which was commissioned by the Department of Commerce, observed that the drop in the number of households employing servants could not be attributed entirely to women's job selection. "Women are not leaving the occupation," he argued, "so much as the occupation is leaving them." In 1870, 60.7 percent of all women wage earners in the United States worked as servants, a category that included household waitresses, charwomen, cleaners, porters, and cooks. By 1900 that number was down to 33 percent. In 1920, it was only 18.2 percent.[10] Improvements in household technology in the forms of vacuum cleaners, dishwashers, and other capital equipment encouraged households to do without full-time workers, as did the greater availability of domestic services that non-live-in service workers provided commercially.[11] These factors, combined with the eagerness with which "new" immigrants from Eastern and Southern Europe opted out of domestic labor for factory work, finally laid to rest the belief that European immigrant women committed to working as servants warranted exceptions from restrictions.

## The Yellow Angel: Chinese Servants as Antimodern Figures

Armed with the tools of social science, turn-of-the-century reformers framed domestic service as an atavistic occupation. It was resistant, they claimed, to modern improvements that could make labor relations between servants and their employers more efficient, rewarding, and tolerable. Household labor remained untouched by the changes in cultural attitudes and legal regulation that had transformed most other industries by the end of the nineteenth century. Unlike industrial workers, servants were expected to demonstrate deference that went beyond the completion of the duties assigned to them, and to serve at the beck and call of the families who hired and housed them. Because domestic servants were required to wear uniforms, eat alone, and forgo socialization during the many hours of the week when they remained on the job or on standby, the work was also emotionally and psychologically taxing.[12] In 1896, Jane Addams argued in the American Journal of Sociology that for these reasons, domestic service was "A Belated Industry" that social change had left behind. It was governed by "feudal" relations based on status. Efforts to standardize how domestic workers were to be treated had for the most part failed. Until domestic service became transactional rather than feudal, Addams warned, it would continue to attract the least ambitious and desirable workers.[13] As historian Vanessa May argues, commentators who emphasized domestic service's "feudal" and "anachronistic" nature contributed to the public's perception that the occupation could not be remade by "labor reform agendas and state and federal labor laws," and that household labor was somehow impervious to technological and social change.[14]

Social scientists armed with empirical data began to argue what workers already knew—that the flight of women to industrial work was a rational decision, even if it meant sacrificing certain material benefits in the short run. Women wage earners wanted regular, set times off from work, rather than being granted free time based on the capricious scheduling needs of their employers. Many also wanted to be freed from the emotional labor and performance of deference that domestic service required of them beyond the completion of the tasks they were assigned.[15] Accounting for the greater diversity of job options open to white women at the end of the century, Addams concluded "that on the whole the enterprising girls of the community go into factories, and the less enterprising go into households." In *Newer Ideals of Peace*, which was published in 1907, Addams argued that since white women and immigrants were leaving the occupation for good, Americans were "obliged to consider the material for domestic service which a democracy supplies."[16] Although she did not come out and say it, one can infer that she meant black women with few other options.

Arguments about domestic service's innate antimodern character led some social scientists to conclude that the ambition to escape service was best understood in racial terms. Because white women were racially predisposed to seek out modern individual liberties, if domestic service failed to evolve as an occupation, their involvement in this work—at least as paid laborers—would decrease commensurately. On the other hand, Asian and black workers might be counted on to remain at this work since they were allegedly less sensitive to having their autonomy infringed upon. Social scientists did not pause to consider their own role in defining certain types of work as racial in character, which in turn validated job discrimination. In 1899, the sociologist Mary Roberts Smith Coolidge argued in *Forum* that domestic service posed different governing concerns in regions of the United States where Chinese and, increasingly, Japanese laborers were available. Her intention was to highlight how reformers' calls to impose modern industrial labor relations upon domestic service had to take the available supply of servants into account. As she noted:

> A new ideal is inevitable,—a standard which shall harmonize with the tendencies in other industries, which shall share the democratic spirit developed in this country and which shall take into account the race constituency of the American people. The social standard of domestic service in the Far West, where Chinese and Japanese domestics are employed, or in the Southern States, where the Negro is the only help available, must differ widely from that which should prevail in the Eastern and Central Northern States.[17]

Ten years later, Coolidge's publication of *Chinese Immigration* earned her a reputation for being a staunch defender of the Chinese. In her academic study, domestic service is referenced numerous times as an occupation where Chinese immigrants had proven their worth. "The laboring Chinese have found defenders in the housewives and farmers whose straits for lack of domestic and agricultural labor have made the virtues and the scarcity of the Chinese doubly conspicuous," Coolidge argued, adding that "the irony of [restriction] is emphasized by the wholesale and exasperated condemnation of their vari-colored successors."[18]

As historian Louise Newman notes, Coolidge's willingness to view Chinese immigration through an "assimilationist paradigm" set her apart from many of her contemporaries.[19] What purpose Chinese incorporation served in Coolidge's mind, however, needs to be parsed further. Coolidge's peers in academia attacked her definition of assimilation as elitist and out of touch with what "modern" non-Chinese workers wanted from their liberty of contract.[20] In his review in the *Political Science Quarterly*, John R. Commons, the noted labor historian at the University of Wisconsin, argued that Coolidge's "ideals of race harmony seem to resolve themselves into an adequate supply of mobile labor for fruit growers, ranchers, railroads, households *etc.*"[21] Commons implied that for Coolidge, assimilation was not about social democracy, citizenship, or loyalty to American ideals. Rather, it was about ensuring that there would be an adequate supply of surplus labor willing to submit to its exploitation as menials. For Salmon, the question was not whether the Chinese were excellent servants, but rather if they could be supplied in sufficient numbers to stave off the need for more holistic reforms. Despite the fact that "much has been said of the superiority of the Chinese as household employees and not a few housekeepers would be glad to see the [Exclusion] act repealed," Salmon reasoned that such a reversal would function only to harm the occupation further. "Superior and inferior labor cannot exist side by side," she asserted. "The introduction to any considerable extent of Chinese servants would drive out European labor as that has in a measure driven out native born American servants."[22] Salmon's use of "superior" switches from one sentence to the next. As "superior" servants, the Chinese belong to an "inferior" class of laborers whose greater integration into the labor force outside of the West Coast will only prevent the reform and improvement of domestic labor's occupational status.

In California and other western states, authors' romanticized laments about the loss of Chinese domestic labor through exclusion increased in frequency in the early twentieth century. While earlier backers of Chinese servants had also proffered testimonials to their reliability and loyalty as workers, with social scientists' reform agenda for domestic service gaining ground, these representations took on new meanings. Relatively few biographical details exist about Mary Stewart Daggett, a fictional purveyor of "the way things were," and her career as an author. According to a brief profile published in the *Los Angeles Times*, Daggett was born in Ohio and lived and wrote in Pasadena after moving to California. Sue Chang, the Chinese servant at the center of Daggett's fiction, first appeared as a character in 1899 in a short story published by the *Los Angeles Times Sunday Magazine*. Daggett's various short stories featuring Sue were eventually compiled in a book she titled *The Yellow Angel*.[23] In this book, Daggett offers a collection of separate but interrelated stories narrated from the perspective of the unnamed white woman, and wife and mother, who is in charge of the house at Temple Hill, a ranch located outside of Los Angeles. When *The Yellow Angel* was published in 1914, it received national attention and was reviewed in the *Boston Globe* and *New York Times*.[24] In *The Yellow Angel*'s dedication, Daggett wrote that the book was for her husband and for "friends of earlier California days who deplore with me the passing of the 'Yellow Angel.'" In this usage, Daggett referred to the loss of a certain concept of service rather than to the death of an individual.[25]

Daggett's material for *The Yellow Angel* came from her personal experiences as an employer. The 1910 census record for the Daggett household lists Wan Quong, a forty-year-old Chinese immigrant who arrived in the United States in 1882, as the family's live-in servant. How much of Wan's employment history got altered in translation to fiction can only be surmised. While the family at Temple Hill appears as representative of an older California lifestyle, according to the 1910 census Daggett's husband supported his family not as a rancher but as a Los Angeles real estate developer.[26] Despite her family's connection to the new Southern California economy, Daggett cast change—at least when it came to the social relations of production—in a critical, suspect light. *The Yellow Angel* was unapologetically didactic in arguing that the goal of domestic management was to transform a worker's moral character. The book's title referenced the well-known and widely read 1854 narrative poem "The Angel in the House," by the English author Coventry Patmore. In the late-Victorian era, the phrase "angel in the house" gained popular usage as shorthand for a woman's unwavering and selfless devotion to her husband, family, and domesticity.[27]

Sue, a "Yellow Angel," shows heaven-sent qualities that are captured in his devotion to his employer's family and his desire to please them at all costs. He displays these sentiments in gratitude for the love and education that the family at Temple Hill have imparted to him, which function as the basis for exchange between the parties. Sue is a student at the local mission school and the recipient of workplace lessons in Christianity, and these benefits "endeared him afresh to the hearts of his employers" (19). His improvement occurs within the confines of this Christian education, and not in terms of his realizing greater power over the contract of his labor or how he approached the Temple Hill family as a servant. Despite gaining a purportedly more enlightened perspective, he remains loyal and deferent as an employee. As the narrator puts it, "Occidental ideals hastened Celestial evolution, but had not ruined his cooking" (147). Outside the realm of fiction, employment postings that highlighted a household's religious integrity were often viewed with suspicion by servants. Writing in the early twentieth century, Rubinow recalled how "an old shrewd Irish servant girl (they are all girls, even if seventy years old and grandmothers)" told him that she " 'kept shy' " of advertisements that boasted of the morality of a prospective employer, as "she found out that the promise of a good home usually meant poor wages."[28] Chinese servants undoubtedly had similar reservations, although they were also more reliant on these situations since missionary employers were at least eager—unlike white households where prohibitions on the use of Chinese labor prevailed—to hire them.

The images that accompanied the publication of *The Yellow Angel* seem to rely on visual trickery to portray Sue's successful transformation from "heathen" to "civilized." Although the text includes no explanations, presumably the hand-drawn illustration and photograph shown here are a rendering and actual image of the Daggetts' real-life servant, Wan Quong. Further blurring the line between fact and fiction, in *The Yellow Angel* the images provide a visual complement to the changes that Sue undergoes. At the beginning of the novel, a drawing depicts Sue with a traditional Chinese queue and wearing a robe. In a photograph near the end of the book, Sue Chang (Wan Quong?) appears in a Western-style suit and haircut with his employers' child and dog. Whereas the "before" image is a drawn sketch—perhaps because Sue *never* dressed and styled his hair in customary Chinese fashion—in the "after" image Daggett presents photographic evidence.[29]

Working-class readers would have greeted the character of Sue Chang, an "angel" to the family at Temple Hill, with skepticism. It's doubtful that Chinese laborers would have agreed with his portrayal either. Among white women seeking to organize domestic labor along the lines of industrial work, depictions such as this encapsulated how employers invented status dependencies and embellished emotional attachments to undermine laborers' empowerment. In *Domestic Service*, Salmon acknowledged that while some employers wished to include servants in the cultural life of the household, as Sue was in the novel, such efforts were "doubtful remedies" when it came to the systemic problems that plagued the occupation as a whole. Integration of this sort could be seen only as "an attempt to restore the patriarchal relationship between employer and employee in a generation which looks with disfavor on paternalism in other forms of labor." Moreover, most servants

*HIS starched white sacklet and apron glistened in the California sunshine.*

Figure 6.1. Daggett, *The Yellow Angel*, 16.

wanted higher wages and more time off so that they could dine with their friends and not their employers.[30]

Daggett's portrayal of Sue's desire to be an intimate in the Temple Hill family implied Chinese laborers' motivations as workers were racially distinct from those of white laborers seeking greater independence. Sue's willingness to sacrifice material gain in exchange for receiving sentimental or moral wages is a recurring theme in the novel. Sue takes a job as a cook at a hotel where his brother works in San Bernardino, but his

"*HOW you think I look ?*"

Figure 6.2. Daggett, *The Yellow Angel*, 96.

time away from Temple Hill is brief. Although he earned higher wages at the hotel, the kitchen there is dirty, the food's quality is offensive, and the white waitresses he works with are unrelentingly cruel to him. Personally humiliated by his act of betrayal, Sue is relieved and humbled when he returns to Temple Hill and is welcomed back with open arms.[31] In contrast to what the novel presents, Chinese servants regularly left employment in private homes for work in hotels and boarding houses, and to cook in restaurants. There is no evidence that these workers, as a class, regretted leaving the sentimental embrace of white employers.

*The Yellow Angel* also provides commentary on Chinese servants' inclination to put aside family ties to blood relatives if properly absorbed into a caring household. Again, most servants chafed at this implication. In the novel, it is revealed that Sue, like many Chinese men working in the United States, has a wife and children in China who are barred from joining him in the United States. While the narrator expresses sympathy toward Sue and is a critic of the exclusion laws that have created this problem, she also implies that his sentimental attachment to the family at Temple Hill compensates. More troubling to the narrator is the fact that restrictive immigration laws infringe on employers' hiring needs. Upset over the difficulties Sue faces while leaving and reentering the United States, the narrator lashes out at white laborers and complains to her husband that "it isn't fair that an incompetent class who are simply dogs in the manger should be allowed to ruin the future of a great, grand state like California." When her husband suggests jokingly that she write to the president to voice her opinion, she snaps at him for making light of the situation: "if women do not understand the values of those who serve in the household who does?" (89–90).

The Yellow Angel does not delve into any in-depth discussion of Sue's fatherless family in China, which is revealing. If Sue was closely modeled on Wan, Daggett's real-life servant—then her inability to provide any details about his history suggests that she never bothered to learn much about her employee's life—even though she insisted that he was a beloved and respected member of the family. In contrast, in the novel Sue actively follows the lives of his employers' children as they leave to go to college, get married, and have their own children. He sends photographs of the narrator's grandchildren to his relatives in China, an act that delights his employers.[32]

In The Yellow Angel, Sue's service is juxtaposed with the narrator's discovery that Japanese servants make poor replacements. In this respect, Daggett contributed to the racialization of Japanese immigrants as closer to white—in their selfish aspirations—than the Chinese. The chapter "The Understudy" depicts the narrator's employment of a Japanese servant while Sue Chang is visiting his family in China, and the dire consequences that ensue. Initially, the nameless Japanese servant cooks wonderful meals and keeps a spotless kitchen in a manner comparable to Sue Chang. On the eve of a meal for some of Temple Hill's "prominent" neighbors, however, he quits suddenly without having given any notice, declaring that "I think I go learn be doctor" (53). The selfish

Japanese servant obsessed with his own personal advancement appears in contrast to Sue Chang, who would never leave on such short notice and damage his employers' social reputation in the process.

*The Yellow Angel's* depiction of the Japanese servant's opportunism reflected the more widely held belief that Japanese immigrants looked to get ahead whenever the opportunity arose, and did not properly pay their dues.[33] This was not unlike the accusations that white household employers leveled against Jewish and Italian immigrants back east. As sociologist Evelyn Nakano Glenn has argued, in response to the early twentieth-century decline in Chinese domestic laborers, "paeans of praise were sung in his memory." The nostalgic figure of the Chinese servant would become central to how California was represented to national audiences.[34] A 1907 article in the *Argonaut* noted that "a good many Japs take to domestic service, but only in a single instance have we ever seen a trace of that fine sprit of devotion and loyalty combined with integrity and good temper which so characteristically mark the Chinese in similar relationships." While both groups of laborers allegedly demonstrated servility, commentators contended that only the Chinese did so authentically. An article that appeared in *Good Housekeeping* stated that "the polite little Jap who serves your meals so daintily is using you, in nine cases out of ten, as a stepping stone to higher things."[35] In a special forum on "Oriental Exclusion" published by the *Annals of the American Academy of Political and Social Science* in 1909, the journalist and academic Chester Rowell remarked that "we find the Chinese fitting much better than the Japanese into the status which the white American prefers them both to occupy—that of biped domestic animals in the white man's service."[36] American commentators believed that the ambitions of the more aggressive and powerful Japanese state were reflected in emigrants' rejection of menial work. With China fragile and weak as a global power, such concerns did not apply to its subjects.

*The Yellow Angel* blithely ignored or dismissed the agency that Chinese laborers had demonstrated as migrant workers in the turn-of-the-century American service economy, and the tangible material gains they had won through the ability to demand continually higher wages as skilled cooks and servants. A different novel, not intent on producing Chinese racial difference as it related to domestic service, would have told a very different story.

## The Great Migration, Race, and Reform

Due to restrictive immigration laws, political economists and social scientists were aware that there were insufficient numbers of Chinese and Japanese men to satisfy demand for domestic labor. Whatever their racial fantasies about using these workers to stave off more substantive reforms to the occupation, they knew that scarcities posed a practical obstacle. According to national census figures for 1910, 49,355 Asian men worked in personal or domestic service. While this accounted for 27 percent of the population's wage-earning workforce, with only agricultural labor representing a higher percentage, the overall number of laborers doing this work remained relatively small. Moreover, despite the nostalgic insistence that Chinese and other Asian men remained committed to household service, the numbers tell a different story. Of the Asian men working in what census officials classified as domestic and personal service in 1910, roughly 19,000 were identified as being laundry owners, operatives, or managers, which was essentially identical to the number working as household servants. Within the category of household servant, cooks accounted for 68.5 percent of the jobs that Asian men held.[37]

At the start of the twentieth century, the demography of urban areas in the Northeast and Midwest was also beginning to change, which in turn opened up another front in respect to how reformers approached the servant problem. Historian Phyllis Palmer has argued that the steady growth of the black population in the North after 1900 meant that "housewives would not attack the problem of the organization of household work but would seek, instead, a labor force with no choice but to acquiesce."[38] In 1900, foreign-born white women accounted for 23 percent of women employed as servants; by 1920 this number would drop to 17.4 percent. More tellingly, whereas in 1900, 42.5 percent of white, foreign-born women who were in the labor force worked as servants, by 1920 that number was only 23.8 percent. In contrast, by 1920 black women accounted for 45.6 percent of women working as servants in the United States, and slightly fewer than half of all black women in the labor force worked as servants. The latter percentage was significantly higher when the agricultural labor of black women in the South was excluded. In the northern states of New York, Massachusetts, Pennsylvania, Ohio, and Illinois, the number of black women working as domestic servants increased from 58,000 in 1900 to 99,000 in 1920. The 99,000 black women working as servants in these states in 1920 accounted for 63 percent of the jobs held by black women in the northern labor force as a whole.[39] In comparison, in 1910, 561,008 foreign-born white women worked in personal or domestic service, and this number no longer greatly surpassed the 425,248 who worked in what census officials defined as "manufacturing and mechanical industries." Nationally, that same year only 67,987 black women worked in industrial trades, whereas 853,357 worked in personal or domestic service, mainly in the South.[40]

Southern black women voiced, whenever possible, their resistance to being labeled ideal servants. Their perspectives ought to have tempered northern white employers' excitement, as black migration from the South began to increase in volume, about how domestic service would be saved—yet again—from problems that white women brought to the profession. On January 25, 1912, the *Independent* published a provocative exposé titled "More Slavery at the South." The article presented in narrative form an edited interview that the newspaper's reporter had conducted with a black woman working as a domestic laborer in an unnamed Georgia city of approximately fifty thousand residents. The "Negro Nurse," who insisted on anonymity to avoid reprisals, explained how she had begun work as a general "housegirl" and subsequently moved through the ranks of domestic service from chambermaid to cook, before eventually becoming a nurse.

Although northern reformers like Frances Kellor stressed the need for protective societies that would defend black migrant women from urban dangers and predatory actors, the picture of naïveté and innocence that they painted relied on a racial understanding of blacks that emphasized their alleged simplicity as a people. Reformers failed to account for the myriad difficulties that black laborers had faced prior to migrating. Domestic service in the South, the "Negro Nurse" argued, generated working conditions in which black women were subject to constant verbal and physical harassment. "I believe nearly all white men take, and expect to take," she stated bluntly, "undue liberties with their colored female servants—not only the fathers, but in many cases the sons also."[41] She spoke from personal experience. In one incident her employer's husband had tried to kiss and grope her. When the nurse's husband confronted the white man about what had happened, he was physically assaulted, arrested, and fined twenty-five dollars, more than a month's wages, as a result. This was no small thing for the author to relay to the *Independent*'s white readers. Not only did her account make direct references to the rape and assault of black women by their white employers—a reversal of the prevailing discourse that identified black men as sexual predators—she also claimed that black domestic servants understood that by granting sexual favors without resistance they could potentially earn more.

"More Slavery at the South" also submitted a stark condemnation of southern paternalism. It sharply refuted whites' argument that blacks' desire to serve was somehow endemic to their race. At the time of the article's publication, the nurse's husband had passed away and she was a widow. Despite having children of her own to care for, she was pro-hibited by her employer from living outside the home. As a result, the nurse's eldest daughter had assumed responsibility for taking care of her younger siblings, and the nurse, by mandate of her employer, was allowed to visit her family only once every two weeks. Her children were prohibited from calling on their mom while she was at her employers' home under any circumstances. The nurse explained that when black servants and cooks took flour, soap, or sugar from their white employers' homes—commonly referred to as "pan-toting"—this did not represent thievery. Nor were these acts the relics of social relations carried over from slavery, as white social scientists often assumed. Rather, they were essential responses to low wages. As the nurse elaborated, taking home leftovers was "part of the oral contract, exprest or implied."[42] Black ser-vants won concessions where they could. The attempts of black servants in the South to organize and demand better working conditions and wages was difficult since there were hundreds of possible replacements among the poor, rural black population. In addition, those who quit ran the risk of being arrested for vagrancy, which often resulted in black men and women being sent to work as penal labor on one of Georgia's state-run farms.

Members of the *Independent*'s white readership were shocked and upset by the black nurse's message. One woman wrote from LaRue, Ohio, to state that the article had caused her to consider canceling her subscription, until she got the better of her emotions. The *Crisis*, the

NAACP's newspaper, had no doubts about the veracity of the article's claims and praised the *Independent* for showing that "the 'old, unhappy, far-off things' of slavery are not so far away after all."[43] "More Slavery at the South" refuted the commonly made argument that domestic service forged an intimate bond between black women and the white families that employed them, which transcended discriminatory hiring practices and black workers' aspirations for social mobility. In a national context, these arguments advanced the notion that an idiosyncratic feature of southern domestic life was the willingness of black servants to toil in premodern working conditions, inured to the stigma that marked domestic labor elsewhere. "More Slavery at the South" pierced this idyllic mythology. For the most part, however, the frank assessments contained within the article lacked the reach and audience to seriously dent the hegemonic, white public discourse of the period. Although the black media waged an active campaign against the "Mammy" stereotype and its racial implications, commercial figures like "Aunt Jemima" pushed in the other direction and breathed new life into the stereotype of black servility. White Americans faced increased black resistance to "Jim Crow" governance by the 1910s, and many were therefore eager to embrace representations of how things "used to be."[44]

Black servants' resolve that they be permitted to live separate from the white households where they worked, a point of conflict that dated back to Reconstruction, helped to usher in a key twentieth-century reform to domestic service that would benefit women from all backgrounds. The economist Rubinow, who later gained fame as a key architect of the original Social Security legislation, was one of only a few white commentators to acknowledge this. Living out allowed servants to escape their employers' expectation that they would be available to perform household labor at irregular hours and be on call at all times. For black domestic laborers who were married with their own families, living with their employers meant isolation from husbands and children, as the author of "More Slavery at the South" documented. Rubinow believed that making domestic service day labor was essential to improving the occupation's reputation. "Southern ladies will possibly be shocked at the suggestion that the unreliable colored servant girls are working for the progress of society," he noted, sarcastically. Yet, living out was "the strongest impetus to a normal regulation of the hours of labor; and the strongest foundation of the master's despotism, which extends over and beyond the working-hours, is destroyed thereby."[45] Black domestics in Washington relied on "penny saver" clubs, mutual benefit associations, and support from the city's black churches in order to raise enough money to rent their own accommodations and transition to day work.[46] Some white employers in the North welcomed living out for more racist reasons; they were reluctant to have black women living in the same house as them. Allegations that black servants conveyed diseases like tuberculosis between poor black communities and white middle-class homes also followed black migrants north.[47]

Depictions of black servants as childlike and blissful in their ignorance functioned to signify a continuing relationship to their slave past, and a commensurate inability to grasp concepts such as private ownership and formal wages. Collectively, such traits were posited as evidence of the retarded development of blacks as a race even if, under the right conditions, they could make black women (and men) valuable as servants. Rather than viewing black women migrants as veterans of southern labor struggles, reformers were often more concerned with whether black women's actions and behavior conformed to northern employers' expectations. Isabel Eaton, a white sociologist whose study of black domestic servants in Philadelphia accompanied the publication of W. E. B. Du Bois's *The Philadelphia Negro*, observed that "pilfering of food" was one of the most common complaints that white employers gave when assessing the performance of black servants. Another white employer told Eaton that the black servants she hired did not hesitate to take food home with them, but explained their actions by claiming that "they don't consider that stealing, and are perfectly honest about money." Still another concluded: "They are like children in temptation; they can't resist sweetmeats, but never take things of value."[48] Black sociologists, representing middle-class interests, produced similar analysis. Elizabeth Ross Haynes, who completed her master's in political science at Columbia University in 1923, noted in her thesis that employers in Washington, D.C., had offered "southern tradition" as an explanation in regard to incidents of theft by black domestics.[49] Acts that had defined black domestics' resistance to white supremacy and inadequate pay in the South—such as pan-toting—were recast as archaic behavior by northern white employers.

Repeating patterns that had predominated in earlier eras, both black and white northern reformers justified social control as the preferable alternative to excessive liberty, which they argued would ensnare gullible and unworldly black migrants, especially women, in sexual and economic exploitation. They emphasized controls that they felt would mitigate the dangers that accompanied a migratory workforce unmoored from the customs and cultures of their native region. The Urban League, which originated with the 1911 merger of the National League for the Protection of Colored Women, the Committee for Improving Industrial Conditions of Negroes in New York, and the Committee on Urban Conditions Among Negroes, devoted much of its early work to protecting black migrant laborers, especially women, from brokers it deemed corrupt. Befitting an organization that was founded in part by Frances Kellor, the Urban League focused on the dangers posed by interstate trafficking and recruitment into sex work.

Low wages and the structural precariousness that came with domestic labor, which affected even the most "moral" of wage seekers, rarely garnered the same attention. Black women's agency as migrants, despite the millions in remittances they sent back to the South and the amazing resilience they displayed, was framed by middle-class critics as disruptive rather than generative.[50] Mary White Ovington, the white cofounder and first executive secretary of the National Association for the Advancement of Colored People (NAACP), believed that the relative ease with which black women procured domestic work had led to a disproportionate ratio of black women to black men in New York. In 1911 she calculated that there were 123 black women to every 100 black men. This created a dangerous scenario where "in their hours of leisure the surplus women are known to play havoc with their neighbors' sons, even with their neighbors' husbands." Ovington was also concerned with the disruptive remaking of gender roles that she claimed threatened family stability. "Surplus Negro women, able to secure work," she argued, "support idle, able-bodied Negro men."[51] In the context of such assertions, the black middle class engaged in a "politics of respectability" in which servants were encouraged to avoid conflicts with employers, no matter how justified, and to rely on noncommercial brokers when looking for work. In 1899, the National Association of Colored Women's newspaper, for instance, praised a circular from the black Preachers Meeting of New York, which denounced employment agencies accused of giving black servants a bad name. Without any consideration of their abilities or experience, the circular categorically recommended New York's black pastors as the most reputable and capable brokers out there.[52]

There is some evidence that black sociologists were more attuned than their white peers to the structural forces that determined where black women worked. The black sociologists and married couple Elizabeth and George Haynes were acutely aware that discrimination was a central obstacle facing black domestic workers in the North and that black women, like their white counterparts, would prefer industrial work, clerical employment, or service in hotels and restaurants—if such opportunities were available.[53] The fact that in northern cities the majority of black men let alone women still had to work in private service jobs was evidence of just how prevalent discrimination was. In Philadelphia, until the Second World War 60 percent of gainfully employed black men worked in jobs classified as domestic service, as did 90 percent of all black women. Beginning in the 1910s, the Philadelphia chapter of the National Urban League began a campaign lobbying garment manufacturers to hire black women.[54]

White employers encountered fierce resistance to the integration of their workforces, even when they were not ideologically opposed to hiring black laborers. Ovington noted that in households wealthy enough to employ multiple servants, opposition to placing black female graduates of the Manhattan Trade School for Girls came not from employers, but from the white staff.[55] In her study of black domestic laborers in Philadelphia, Eaton observed that lighter-skinned black women would attempt to pass as white when seeking employment, in order to circumvent discrimination.[56] Historian Elizabeth Clark-Lewis, who conducted oral histories with black domestic laborers who worked in Washington in the first decades of the twentieth century, found that many felt that their white employers were especially exploitative in the tasks and assignments they gave them. They justified this division of labor by claiming that poor black migrants "were accustomed to intense, exhausting work."[57]

For black migrants heading north, jobs in domestic service were both economically essential and an unavoidable feature of a labor market that was impenetrably stratified by race. European immigrants had the choice to opt out of household work, and while a select number of commentators might interpret this act as selfish and in opposition to assimilative goals, it at least existed as an option. In a typical article of the period, the *Chicago Defender* celebrated the impact that World War I had had in suppressing immigration from Europe, and described the conflict as a "blessing" to black southerners. The article claimed that in the absence of European immigration, "Girls who found it difficult to find work in domestic service are now welcome to go in homes all over the country, and especially in the north, and reign as domestics." The newspaper had its own reasons for embracing a less-than-critical view of northern job markets, since increased migration resulted in revenue in the form of advertisements and subscriptions.[58] Outside these immediate interests, the newspaper adopted a pragmatic assessment of what migration meant relative to black economic gain, since remaining in the South was hardly the path to better wages. Free market proponents rely on comparative evaluations of this very nature to rationalize exploitation and discrimination, which are deemed acceptable sacrifices so long as worse scenarios can be imagined.

During World War I, when white women entered factory work in greater numbers due to male conscription, some black women seized the opportunity to earn better wages by going into vacated service positions in hotels and restaurants, which tended to pay better and came with greater autonomy than work in private households. This was only a temporary shift, however, and indicative of how racial and gender hierarchies governed labor markets simultaneously. When white women were displaced from the occupations they had claimed during the war by male soldiers returning home, they in turn displaced black women from the better service jobs. As historian Kim Phillips documents in Cleveland, black women there tried to avoid domestic service as much as possible, yet from 1915 to 1920—even during the war years—three-quarters of black women wage earners were still confined to this work.[59] White employers actively complied with efforts to maintain racially segmented labor markets and used discriminatory hiring practices to stave off, as a managerial tactic, the formation of solidarities across racial lines. In 1918, for example, when Congress passed a minimum wage law applying to women and child laborers in Washington, the response of the city's hotel owners was to fire their black housekeepers and waitresses and replace them with white women. Since hotels were compelled to pay more in wages, they made sure to demonstrate to the public that white laborers would be the beneficiaries.[60]

## "New Theories of the Social Situation": The 1917 Immigration Act and the Road to Quotas

In a November 1920 interview with the *New York Tribune*, P. A. Baker, superintendent of Ellis Island, explained to readers:

> It is possible that never again will the relation of master and servant in this country be what it was. . . . The aliens who are coming into the country, or are expected, have been influenced by new teachings. New theories of the social situation have also been produced in this country. Many are displaying aversion to being classified as servants who never protested before.

Baker aired these thoughts six months prior to Congress's May 1921 passage of the Emergency Quota Act, which, for the first time, restricted immigration from Europe on the basis of national origin rather than individual ineligibility. Queried as an expert, Baker was adamant that proposed limits on the number of European women allowed to enter the country would not exacerbate domestic labor scarcities. Italians, Jews, Slavs, and the other groups lumped together as "new immigrants," who were the main targets of the anticipated restrictions, refused this work anyway. The increase in the number of industrial jobs available to women meant that they were able to do so. Drastic changes were afoot. Baker explained that the American middle class had to prepare to raise a generation of women ready to survive without hired domestic labor. In his own home, his two daughters were being "educated to do their own housework."[61] Although nineteenth-century periodicals and newspapers had encouraged middle-class women to take a more active role in governing difficult Irish servants, and to improve their skills as household managers, most stopped well short of instructing these same women to train their daughters to sweep, scrub, and wait on their families.

Had Baker been more attentive to the political economy of the preceding decades, he might have been forced to acknowledge certain fallacies in his argument. His contention that immigrant women had "never protested before" when it came to accepting situations as servants was especially off base. In January 1893, Jonathan Weber, one of Baker's predecessors at Ellis Island, delivered a speech at the Cooper Union that had also addressed domestic service as integral to the public debate on immigration. Weber argued that in addition to whatever labor shortages that might occur, a guaranteed outcome of any attempt to restrict immigration would be the disruption of the social mobility that allowed Americanization to occur. As he expounded:

> The Holland-Dutch girl who passes through Ellis Island Station with wooden shoes upon her feet kicks them off in less than a week and puts on plain leather ones instead. Within a month she will wear high-heeled shoes with pointed toes, squeeze herself into a corset, an article she perhaps never saw before her arrival here, flourish a bustle and sport a parasol, and the chances are that within a year, some sensible fellow will have married and settled her in a cozy home, after which she will be . . . looking for a "green horn" to do her housework because she has become so Americanized that she is too delicate to do it herself, or because she is too busy with her piano lessons to afford the time.

Weber's gentle mockery of the immigrant's airs aside, his description makes clear that the path to Americanization that she has pursued—through marriage and the assumption of a role as wife and then presumably mother in her own home—was one to be praised.[62]

In 1893, Weber was still willing to bet on new European immigrants making up for any deficit of labor that the successful assimilation of older immigrants caused. His hypothetical Dutch girl is able to work on her own middle-class credentials and domesticity only because she can count on a "green horn" to do the drudge work. Speaking in 1920, Baker concluded that none of these points held anymore. The Eastern and Southern European immigrants arriving in industrial urban areas during the first two decades of the twentieth century exhibited a clear preference for factory jobs and subcontracted piecework completed in tenement workshops. Manufacturers recruited immigrant women to work in the garment industry, in cigar making, and in other trades where the employment of women laborers kept overall wages low, and purportedly drew upon their "natural" dexterity. Industrial jobs held greater appeal for many wage-earning women, though wages were typically equal to or lower than those found in domestic service, and did not include room and board as household employment did. The fact that Italian and Jewish immigrant women were more likely to immigrate with their families also influenced their occupational choices. Their parents wanted them to live at home and had the immediate authority to enforce this.[63]

Some commentators did persist in claiming that immigrant women's job selection was irrational. In May 1912, for instance, the *New York Times* published an article titled "New York Needs 100,000 Servants," in which Herman Robinson, the commissioner of licenses, lamented European women's decision-making process. One proprietor of an employment agency had related to Robinson how a prospective employer in Mount Vernon, New York—a suburb north of the city—had approached him looking for a woman to do general housework at the rate of six dollars a week, with room and board provided. Even though the standard factory wage for women averaged only five dollars a week, without room and board, the agent could not find any applicants willing to take the domestic job.[64] A letter to the editor of the *New York Tribune* in 1920 praised the racial science of the eugenicists Madison Grant and Lothrop Stoddard and argued that there was "no greater fallacy than the shibboleth of the 'melting pot.'" Among the evidence the author cited was the fact that new female immigrants "spurned" domestic service for factory work and other jobs, and, in making this choice, repudiated the opportunity to assimilate American middle-class values in a household setting. Industrialists benefitted from hiring immigrant labor, the author complained, but did nothing to stop the crime, anarchy, and illness that urban colonies of foreigners bred.[65]

* * *

Defining the social utility of domestic service became a primary focus in the enforcement of immigration laws. As chapter 4 discussed, the 1917 Immigration Act removed "personal servants" from the list of immigrants who were allowed to enter the United States under contract, even though it maintained this exemption for "domestic servants." When called on to interpret the revised statute in practice, immigration officials determined that the germane question was whether or not the service being performed could be considered essential to an employer's domestic rather than personal comfort, a line of reasoning that privileged families over individuals. When Gladys Taylor attempted to enter the United States from Canada shortly after the passage of the 1917 act, under contract to work as a child's nurse for an American family, she was initially denied entry. The denial was reversed by the commissioner general of immigration on the grounds that the work Taylor intended to do could be considered "essential to the welfare of numerous households." It was the opinion of the commissioner's legal counsel, A. W. Parker, that a nurse who attended to children could not be classified as superfluous or unnecessary labor. Defining what *was* superfluous or unnecessary, he listed "menials engaged to wait hand and foot upon persons who are old enough and physically able to attend to their personal wants."[66] Parker's parsing of what constituted legitimate consumer demand for contracted immigrant labor picked up the theme that congressional debates earlier in the decade had also hinged on. He was determined to insulate the bureaucracy from allegations that it was enabling, through its entry decisions, gratuitous forms of labor consumption.

Nurses themselves were adamant that their work was defined not only by its social utility, but also by their autonomy as laborers. In 1915, the social work magazine the *Survey* publicized a series of instances in which nurses coming from Canada or Europe had sought to enroll in hospital training schools, where they received both pay and on-the-job training, but had been denied admission into the United States on the grounds that they were contracted laborers. An editorial in the publication argued that it was the attitude of many immigrant nurses that they would rather be "barred out" than try to win entry by claiming that they were servants. Domestic service's reputation was such that the nurses were willing to sacrifice the possible right to admission in exchange for recognition of their professional status.[67] When the 1917 Immigration Act was finally passed over the veto of President Wilson, in response to these protests it included nurses among the classes of foreign laborers whose contract was now also exempted.

As a concept, utility was crisscrossed by numerous racial fault lines, which contradicted economic and social rationalizations as to what an immigrant servant might contribute. At times, this left officials to negotiate a labyrinthine set of conflicting assumptions. A decision made shortly after the passage of the 1917 act, for instance, permitted Nakagawa Ichi, a Japanese woman, to land in Seattle. Nakagawa had been hired as a nurse to accompany an infant child, whom an Issei couple living in Westfield, New Jersey, had adopted, from Japan. Nakagawa was originally barred on account of her being a personal servant rather than a domestic servant, but the decision was reversed by the acting commissioner general, Alfred Hampton, since "it would be illogical to hold that persons skilled in the care of young children are to be included in the parasitic class of servants in which valets, lady's maids, etc. are placed by some advanced thinkers." The notion of parasitic immigrants had been a frequent touch point in debates on the need to bar paupers, illiterates, and individuals destined to become public charges. Here, however, Hampton applied the term to acts of consumption deemed excessive to "common" conceptions of what represented socially beneficial labor. Racist biases about who should be encouraged to immigrate and settle also factored into his decision. Even if Nakagawa was permitted to land on the basis of her occupational exemption to the contract labor law, Hampton opined that the Japanese government had erred by issuing her a passport in the first place since, as a laborer, her migration was supposed to be restricted by the Gentlemen's Agreement of 1907 that the two countries had ratified. This was passed along to the State Department with instructions to clarify the matter with their Japanese counterparts, thereby denying any possible precedent to be used in the future.[68]

Since the late nineteenth century, nativists had argued that there was a correlation between illiteracy and other "negative" cultural and biological traits such as a predisposition to crime, the inability to assimilate, and racial inferiority.[69] The 1917 Immigration Act, responding to these concerns, introduced a literacy test that required immigrants over the age of sixteen to prove their reading capability, in the language of their choice, in order to be eligible for admission. Practical attempts to draw a correlation between illiteracy, "intelligence," and competency in domestic labor—and how they related to social utility more broadly conceived—were tenuous at best. With the ratification of the Nineteenth Amendment still three years away, literacy, as a measure of an immigrant's ability to vote and participate in formal politics independently, did not apply to women.[70] Henry H. Goddard, the New Jersey eugenicist who conducted tests on immigrants at Ellis Island in the years leading up to the 1917 act, had his assistant Miss Kite trace the work history of "R. D.," an Irish immigrant, after she was permitted to enter the country. R. D. had been flagged by officials at Ellis Island as illiterate and potentially "feeble-minded" when she arrived in 1916. Kite tracked down R. D. and found her working as a chambermaid at a military academy in Chester, Pennsylvania. A follow-up visit six months later revealed that she had left her position at the school, and had also been discharged from the private home where she was subsequently hired. Kite interviewed R. D.'s last employer, who attributed her dismissal to "certain obstinacy, [and] a determination to do her own way," which led the social worker to report that R. D.'s "mental state has directly to do with the intelligence and comes from a certain lack of power of comprehension."[71] This was a laughable correlation. Whereas Goddard and his assistants recorded R. D.'s resistance to her employer's attempts at managerial control as evidence of her wrongful admission, they could have just as easily placed her actions within the context of enduring workplace struggles between American servants and their employers.

Isaac Siegel, a Republican congressman from New York City, used the *New York Times* as a platform to urge Congress to waive the literacy test for immigrant women who pledged to work as servants. In what had by then become a type of tradition in debates concerning the crafting of immigration law, he was attuned to the ways in which household labor shortages could modify politicians' views on the need for indiscriminate restrictions. He added, however, a new racial dimension to this issue. In a 1920 interview, he noted that despite being illiterate, "black mammies" were considered the best class of American servants and that when compared to the possible entry of anarchists, "illiteracy is not the cloak of the danger we face in incoming immigrants."[72] Siegel was perhaps making a subtle jab at his southern Democrat counterparts in Congress who were the most fervent backers of restrictive legislation. Alternatively, Siegel may have been advancing the sincerely held liberal belief that immigration was inherently justified so long as demand existed. In this line of thinking, the market's demand for an immigrant's labor was the sole basis by which social utility was to be understood. Regardless, Siegel's comments were stripped of any language that tried to rationalize admission along the lines of more ambiguous understandings of culture, and instead he presented assimilation as a matter of economic function. The rejection of this logic, as evidenced by the eventual passage of quotas, demonstrates that restrictionists were committed to guarding a version of whiteness in which social qualities—such as educational attainment and a shared "Anglo-Saxon" culture—were values that distinguished members from others whose inclusion was predicated on economic function alone.

In 1921, Congress introduced "emergency" quotas that regulated the number of European immigrants permitted to enter the United States. Following precedent, the 1921 act allowed immigrants employed as servants to continue to enter in excess of the slots allotted to a given country. Since the 1921 act required immigrants to apply for visas prior to departing for the United States, European women seeking to enter as servants in excess of the quota had to enter into employment contracts in order to qualify. This functioned to make what was once an exemption a formal provision of admittance—at least until the 1924 Johnson-Reed Act was passed.[73] Leading up to the 1924 act, there were last-ditch efforts to use domestic labor to hold off quotas. Adolph Sabath, a Czech Jewish immigrant and Democratic congressman from Chicago's Fifth District, was perhaps the most outspoken opponent of quota restrictions in the House of Representatives. He had opposed the literacy test as well. During the debate on the 1924 act, Sabath went as far as to appeal to the eugenicist argument against immigration. He cited a letter from Augustine Davis, the president of Davis Equipment Corporation, who claimed that due to the decline in immigrant women willing to work as servants, American families now faced "race suicide." In all likelihood, Sabath knew that this was a farfetched claim based on the same troubling eugenicist logic that had targeted Jewish and other new immigrants as undesirable. But he appealed instead to employers' most dystopic fears of what labor shortages might bring. He tried, unsuccessfully, to convince his colleagues that the ability of the white middle classes to marry, own homes, and procreate was at stake.[74] When the Immigration Act of 1924 did become law, servants were no longer allowed to immigrate in excess of a nation's allotment, nor were they given preference—as skilled agricultural laborers were—within each nation's designated quota.

The discriminatory intentions of the 1924 act require contextualization. As historian Mae Ngai demonstrates, the 1924 act acknowledged the whiteness and potential citizenship of Southern and Eastern

European immigrants even if its logic claimed that these less desirable groups could be assimilated only in smaller numbers. Conversely, Asian immigrants who were ineligible to naturalize as citizens were restricted by the 1924 act altogether, and denied quotas outright.[75] This carried over to how nonimmigrant servants were treated as well. After the 1924 act went into effect, the European servants of American citizens were permitted to enter and stay in the United States for six months on visitor visas, without having to be indemnified by surety bonds—as was required for Chinese servants. It appears that there were some incidents where European women tried to deceive steamship and bureau officials into allowing them entry by claiming they were contracted as servants. Assunta Russo, who sought to enter without a quota visa in April 1925, was instructed by acquaintances in Italy to "falsify her statements regarding her employment as a domestic." She did this by claiming that she was destined for a man in Brooklyn who was to be her employer, which failed to win her admission.[76] Although details are murky, Russo's sources had the impression that claiming to be a contracted servant represented one way to potentially deceive bureau officials.

## Conclusion

Although it is not the focus of this chapter, it is important to note that at the turn of the century, a growing number of white commentators drawn from the ranks of feminism, Progressive Era reform movements, and socialism questioned the function of hired domestic labor altogether. They argued that new technological advancements, such as electric dishwashers and vacuum cleaners, could liberate households from dependencies on servants and, in theory, also free middle-class women from onerous labor and managerial duties that were taxing and socially unfulfilling. Smaller and better designed apartments would require less cleaning. A greater selection of prepared food products and a growth in affordable restaurants would make middle-class homes less reliant on cooks.[77] Rubinow, who concluded that domestic service would always carry a stigma, was among the reformers who wished for a future where servants would be "extinct as a dodo" and replaced by "scientific housekeeping." Kellor's "Housewife and Her Helper" column in the *Ladies' Home Journal* was another barometer of these changes. In October 1906 it was announced that it would alternate with a new column she would be writing: "The Woman Who Does Her Own Work."[78]

Among a significant subset of progressives and socialists, a belief in technological liberation went hand in hand with the argument that hired domestic labor could be obtained only when capitalist inequalities meant that there were vulnerable women workers who could be compelled into servitude in exchange for wages. This very point had been circulating since the mid-nineteenth century, when white immigrant women were encouraged to choose marital dependency over wage dependency. Edward Bellamy's immensely popular 1888 novel, *Looking Backward*, helped return this idea to the foreground. When the novel's main character, Julian West, falls into a coma in 1887 and awakes in Boston in 2000, he is shocked to discover that domestic service no longer exists as an occupation. As his hosts, the Leete family, patiently explain to him, because West and other late nineteenth-century Americans had "a boundless supply of serfs on whom you could impose all sorts of painful and disagreeable tasks," household employers had become "indifferent to devices to avoid the necessity of them." In Bellamy's imagined and utopic future, public kitchens and laundries and the automation of cleaning tasks had rendered private service no longer necessary. What remained of work once classified as domestic and private had been taken over by an industrial army, dignified in the labor they performed. When West expresses astonishment at seeing a waiter who has come to the Leetes' home, "serving so contentedly in a menial position," Edith Leete, who will become his wife, professes to have never heard the word "menial" before.[79]

Sources less enamored of the idea of social equality suggested that humans and machines could coexist as producers, and that servile work could fall more fully on the shoulders of racial minorities whom, as this chapter has explored, middle-class whites claimed were not motivated by the same aspirations to liberal freedom that informed the actions of white workers. A Gold Dust Washing Powder advertisement from 1893 argued that white women still toiling in household service had the right to demand that their domestic workplaces were up to date when it came to the latest technological and consumer innovations. It featured the tagline "Empty is the Kitchen—Bridget's Gone." The advertisement flipped earlier scripts in which "Bridget," the archetypical white, Irish servant, was to be blamed for being too picky in selecting where she wanted to work. Instead, the advertisement chastised middle-class employers for failing to keep up with the times. By not purchasing Gold Dust's superior product, they were allegedly driving away potential workers who did not want to perform the more arduous labor that less advanced cleaning products necessitated.

In 1903, the N.K. Fairbanks Company, Gold Dust Washing Powder's owners, would try out a different marketing approach. It shifted advertising resources to the branding of its infamous Gold Dust Twins, a set of racially caricatured black "pickaninnies" who were presented with the slogan: "Let the Gold Dust Twins Do Your Work." As the Gold Dust Twins' advertisements contended: "Dish washing is dreaded and

Figure 6.3. Gold Dust Washing Powder advertisement, *San Francisco Morning Call*, July 28, 1893.

avoided by everyone about the household," but the use of Gold Dust Washing Powder made it "play." As the product's depiction of happy black children insinuated, consumers would be transported to a racial realm where work deemed menial became tolerable.[80] The white middle-class public was unsure of whether it wanted to eliminate hired domestic service, elevate its working conditions, or relegate the labor to racial minorities.

Figure 6.4. Gold Dust Washing Powder advertisement, *Los Angeles Herald*, November 6, 1904.

# Epilogue

Put simply, the post-1924 history of domestic service is too complex and varied to cover here in any depth. Moreover, the place that household labor once occupied in the national discourse on domesticity and its relation to immigration and internal migration policies has changed considerably. Today, for instance, an immigrant woman can no longer land in the United States and state her intention to work in domestic service. Of course, this was a common experience for thousands of European women until 1924. Whether they were placed by the Castle Garden labor bureau or by federal immigration officials—or by one of the numerous commercial intelligence offices that dotted Lower Manhattan—unaccompanied immigrant women from Europe were essentially guaranteed work as servants, as long as they were physically able. After 1924, the United States would govern all authorized immigration through a system of "remote control," which endures today.[1] Immigrants are required to obtain visas before they emigrate, and can no longer take a calculated risk about their eligibility to enter—unless they are applying for asylum. The ethos of white settlerism and racial nation building that encouraged European women's discretionary admission no longer applies in what is now a postindustrial nation.

In similar terms, the popular craze for Chinese servants that enveloped white middle-class households after the completion of the transcontinental railroad in 1869 is a phenomenon also consigned to the past. Although the "production of difference" that Esch and Roediger reference remains a crucial component in labor management, it is no longer predicated on novel encounters with sources of racialized labor never before accessed.[2] Today one would be hard-pressed to find a political economist rambling on about how a new group of migrant laborers were primed to come to the rescue of American consumers. (There is fawning over machines, which, as chapter 3 argued, carries a type of racial history in its own right.) Discussions about how the employment of undocumented immigrants helps to keep down the costs of myriad goods and services that Americans purchase tend to be muted if vocalized at all.

I could continue—but I also want to call attention to continuities between the past and present. In particular, I want to suggest that the brokerage of domestic labor remains defined by what the state—at both its federal and local levels—has failed to accomplish. The federal government deserves special attention. It has failed to enact protections that would give domestic workers equal rights relative to other laborers. It has also fallen short in reforming immigration policies—an area of governance that is its sole domain—in order to help prevent the exploitation of domestic workers who are made vulnerable by their undocumented status. The combined absence of regulatory actions in these two areas has meant that domestic workers in the United States confront unique problems. Domestic workers' organizing campaigns and their simultaneous focus on workplace rights and legal status as inseparable political issues illustrate this point in practice.

## Brokering Live-In Servants: Post-1924 Sponsorship Strategies

In the immediate decades that followed the passage of the 1924 Immigration Act, household employers relied on the federal government to verify their credentials as refugee and immigrant sponsors. The employers who petitioned the state to serve in this capacity were keen to take advantage of sponsorship requirements to procure workers willing to live-in as servants. By 1940, only 5 percent of household servants still resided with their employers.[3] The ability to facilitate this working arrangement had become a luxury.

This explains in large part why household employers became involved in the resettlement of displaced persons during this period. Sponsorship provided a backdoor opportunity for the hire of live-in servants—at a time when middle-class households were unable to compete on the open market for the same labor. From the vantage point of the state, privileging household employers as sponsors of refugees was a policy decision rooted in custom. The government's sponsorship policies reflected the long-standing belief that domestic situations were ideal sites for the assimilation of populations requiring rehabilitation and uplift, who needed to be closely monitored and controlled.

The World War II incarceration of Japanese Americans occurred without due process and transformed detained internees into a captive labor supply. The racialization of Japanese Americans as a threat to national security resulted in the annulment of their civil liberties—including their freedom of contract—and enabled their compulsion into paid domestic work. On February 19, 1942, President Roosevelt signed Executive Order 9066, which authorized the forced military evacuation of Japanese families from their homes on the West Coast. More than 120,000 Japanese American citizens (Nisei) and immigrants of Japanese descent (Issei) were sent to ten internment camps in remote parts of the West and Arkansas, and held as detainees without charges being brought against them. In 1943, the War Relocation Authority (WRA), the federal agency that oversaw incarceration, introduced the "loyalty questionnaire" or application for leave clearance. If Issei and Nisei swore "unqualified allegiance to the United States," they became eligible for supervised work release, the equivalent of parole, to locations east of the Mississippi River. (They also became eligible for conscription into the armed forces.) Thirty-five thousand individuals, or approximately one-third of the total detained population, ended up being released to employers vetted and approved by the WRA.[4]

Household employers viewed work release and supervised resettlement as a potential windfall. Domestic situations helped to ameliorate the WRA's concerns that paroled internees would face housing discrimination or would cluster together in communities that re-created the segregation of the camps. Rumors of Japanese American internees' impending arrival in various locations stoked excitement over their possible use as servants. In November 1944, for instance, Ottis Peterson, the acting head of the Philadelphia WRA office, responded to an inquiry about the availability of Nisei domestics by stating that the office already had a backlog of more than a thousand requests.[5] Japanese Americans were restricted from jobs related to military production. They reported being denied jobs in clerical and professional work despite stellar qualifications. When Nisei women attempted to leave jobs as live-in servants for college, their employers often resisted. The sociologist

Evelyn Nakano Glenn cites one employer who told her Nisei domestic that "it was the maids' patriotic duty to remain on the job."[6] Relegated to domestic service, Nisei parolees expressed anger at being forced to take these jobs and, reflecting the work's post–Great Migration racialization, complained that they were treated similar to "colored servants."[7]

White households framed their acceptance of paroled Japanese American laborers in philanthropic terms that revitalized earlier eras' discourse of domestic uplift and liberal subject making. In Buffalo, New York, for instance, the wife of a "very busy physician" wrote to First Lady Eleanor Roosevelt to request her help in expediting the resettlement of a group of Nisei women to the area. The resettlement effort was being led by the YWCA, at local employers' urging. As the correspondent pleaded: "We feel we have a good home to offer the Japanese girl and a congenial atmosphere in which to make and [sic] new start and, in return, we should be most grateful for her help."[8] Putting aside why the women's labor was available to begin with or why a Japanese American woman would require a "new start," the prospective employer instead constructed a transactional scenario where domestic employment could help mold a "citizen"—in this case one who already had that status by birthright.

The post–World War II refugee crisis in Europe gave household employers another chance to sponsor live-in servants. In 1948, Congress passed the Displaced Persons Act, which allowed for two hundred thousand refugees living in camps in Germany and Austria to enter the United States in excess of quota limitations. The law mandated that refugees had to have work lined up and housing provided in order to prevent them from becoming public charges. As sponsors, household employers seeking live-in domestic servants were positioned to meet both of these requirements. In addition, the Displaced Persons Act included a ranking system where domestic workers received second preference for available visas, behind only agricultural laborers.[9] More than 14 percent of the sponsored refugees who received visas to enter the United States arrived as live-in servants.

Unlike paroled Nisei servants contracted to households, white European refugees did not have to receive federal approval when switching employers. Refugees were not required to commit to household service and their sponsors' employment on a long-term basis, as long as they did not become public charges. European refugees used the ranking system to their advantage. According to government reports, by the end of 1950, only 6.4 percent of the refugees who had arrived as servants remained in the occupation. Nonetheless, there were reported incidents where refugee servants—encountering the same struggles that all workers who entered as the legal dependents of employers faced—were held in what amounted to a state of bondage. One refugee woman was told that she had to remain under contract with her sponsor for more than a year, while another woman was informed that she had to work without wages. In both cases, the women were misled into thinking that they faced deportation if they refused to comply with their employers' orders.[10]

Growing demands for the restriction of immigration from the Western Hemisphere offered household employers a final opportunity to take advantage of the direct sponsorship of live-in servants. By order of the 1952 Walter-McCarran Act, each of Great Britain's colonies in the West Indies was limited to a quota of one thousand immigrants annually. Although the 1965 Immigration and Nationality Act for the first time limited immigration from other countries in the Western Hemisphere— namely Mexico—it had the effect of increasing the number of quotas that were available to now independent nations such as Jamaica, Trinidad and Tobago, and Barbados.[11] Until 1965, the only limitation on the issue of visas to other Western Hemisphere laborers had been whether or not they were deemed likely to become public charges. After 1965, employers seeking to sponsor immigrants on labor visas had to prove that the jobs they were offering did not "displace" American workers or lower an occupation's wage levels. This certification process was managed by regional offices of the Department of Labor.[12]

This new system for certifying immigrant labor represented a sea change in how immigration policy functioned as a whole. The United States could now determine which workers it wanted, at least when it came to the formal offer of visas.[13] Whereas contract immigration was once feared, since this system of importing labor allegedly empowered employers to undermine American workers' ability to earn higher wages—excepting the instances involving white women that this book has explored—by the second half of the twentieth century contracts in the form of visas were accepted as the best tool for the technocratic management of the labor supply.[14]

Enterprising household employers approached the labor certification process as an opportunity to contract live-in servants who remained unavailable in local employment markets. This created tension. Even before the ceiling on immigration from the Western Hemisphere went into effect in 1968, Department of Labor and immigration officials were already trying to find ways to curtail the number of visas being assigned to live-in servants. Reviving debates that had been taking place since the mid-nineteenth century, officials questioned whether immigrant servants could contribute to American society beyond satisfying households' immediate demand for their labor. Live-in servants were characterized as the types of immigrant workers who, despite fulfilling a labor need as defined by the market, did not purportedly add skills and—even more abstractly—attributes that would further the nation's preeminence. In December 1968, the Department of Labor released a report that tabulated that of the 93,324 visas it had issued in response to certified and approved jobs during the 1967 fiscal year, 34,336 went to service jobs, representing 37 percent of the total. Of the service jobs that were certified for the offer of visas, officials estimated, 88 to 95 percent were for positions as live-in servants. Jamaica and Trinidad and Tobago ranked first and second in terms of the countries of origin for service job visas, followed by England, Mexico, and Germany. Jamaica alone, officials highlighted, had sent 7,543 immigrants with these visas.

In addition to being concerned about the entry of "unskilled" and low-paid black immigrant workers, officials were also disturbed that employers were not actually receiving the labor that the federal government had brokered. A Department of Labor investigation in Chicago uncovered that within two months of having entered the United States, only two of the thirty women who had received visas to work as live-in servants remained in the homes they had been contracted to (the report did not indicate these women's countries of origin, or if they were from the Western or Eastern Hemisphere). The jobs these immigrants had left, investigators found, had been misrepresented in terms of working conditions and pay. But officials also suggested that immigrants had signed up for the positions for the sole purpose of getting visaed.

In response to these discoveries, in April 1968 the Department of Labor instituted a rule that immigrants applying for "maid" visas had to demonstrate to consular officials that they had at least one year of experience working as a live-in servant for pay in their native countries, under the assumption that these applicants were less likely to misrepresent their intentions. Stanley Ruttenberg, the assistant secretary of labor, explained that it was his sincere hope that the April rule would help eliminate issues with keeping visaed immigrants in the jobs they had applied to. This was preferable, he argued, to the introduction of a requirement that live-in servants "remain in that occupation for a period of time," which had also been proposed. Had this requirement been introduced, it would have compelled immigrants to remain in a job or be deported. This was a scenario that was unpalatable to the civil rights and Cold War–era federal government, which remained committed—on the surface at least—to defending workers' liberty of contract. As Ruttenberg concluded, optimistically, "If the measures we have taken are not successful in regulating the number of abuses in live-in maid cases, then other actions are possible, before we impose restrictions on alien workers which we do not impose on U.S. citizens."[15]

Ultimately, other actions were pursued. In October 1969, Department of Labor officials introduced a more stringent certification process for household employers trying to sponsor live-in servants. Under the new procedure, the department subjected employers to more rigorous evaluations as to whether the job they wanted filled actually necessitated live-in employees, or whether it instead might be categorized as work that could be done by day laborers hired from the existing American workforce. In addition, labor officials were instructed to scrutinize jobs that employers had presented as live-in servant positions, and, when possible, to reclassify them as nanny or professional caregiver jobs. These reclassifications forced employers to offer higher wages to the immigrant they were attempting to have visaed, or—as officials intended—to withdraw the request for certification altogether.[16] Through these measures the loophole through which Jamaicans and other West Indian migrants could enter as servants and then leave their jobs for other work was tightened considerably. In the 1968 calendar year, 25,419 immigrants came in with labor visas allotted to live-in household servants. By 1970 the number was only 10,479. Because household employers could not guarantee that black immigrant workers remained in service, they lost their privilege of sponsorship.[17]

* * *

The labor visas put in place by the 1965 Immigration Act had the distinct advantage of establishing a path to permanent immigration and citizenship. After 1976, when Western Hemisphere immigrants became subject to a visa preference and ranking system, applicants for live-in positions from those countries had to compete, at a considerable disadvantage, against skilled professionals also looking to emigrate. Although visas for professional caregiving occupations were made available at various points—today nursing and physical therapy, for instance, are granted automatic certification for job visas—in general "unskilled" workers hoping to immigrate fell into what is now called the Employment Third Preference (E3) or "other worker" category. During the 2015 fiscal year, the State Department issued only 2,029 visas to workers in the E3 category, which amounted to roughly 1.5 percent of the 134,388 visas allotted within the employment preference system as a whole.[18] Household employers who wish to be certified by the Department of Labor to hire immigrants as domestic workers have to contend with waits that can be more than a decade. They must also demonstrate through the labor certification process that such work cannot be completed by legal workers already in the United States. These are onerous hurdles from a household employer's standpoint, especially when documented and undocumented immigrants, who entered by other means, are readily available for hire.

The government-brokered sponsorship of live-in servants no longer provides a loophole within the permanent visa quota rankings, but it persists in other arenas. Today, U.S. immigration policy still contains various programs that are designed to benefit nonimmigrant visitors who wish to retain the services of assistants, family care providers, and domestics. There are whole classes of migrants arriving in the United States whose legal status to enter is directly tied to that of their employers. In 2015, slightly fewer than two thousand migrants classified as "attendants, servants, or personal employees" of A and G visa holders—those issued to diplomats, foreign government officials, and government employees of international organizations—were granted temporary admission.[19] This figure does not account for the B-1 visas issued to temporary visitors entering the United States for the purpose of business, which includes subclassifications pertaining to the "Nonimmigrant Who Is the Personal or Domestic Servant of a Nonimmigrant Employer" and to the "Nonimmigrant Domestic Servant of a U.S. Citizen," the latter for situations where an American employer is primarily stationed abroad. The State Department does not make available how many B-1 visa holders enter under these terms after receiving employment authorization, a process that entails, among other things, providing evidence that an "employer regularly employs personal and domestic servants and has done so for a period of years before coming to the United States."[20] As was the case during the era of Chinese exclusion, B-1 domestic workers are required to maintain employment relations with the employer whom they accompanied to the United States and receive pay only from this source—or face deportation.

In 2001 and 2007, Human Rights Watch and the American Civil Liberties Union (ACLU) published reports documenting what they considered to be significant abuses of household laborers classified as "migrant domestic workers," who had entered the United States on B-1, A-3, and G-5 visas. Respectively, these visas enable the entry of servants employed by visiting business professionals, domestic employees of diplomats, and household workers contracted to the personnel of international organizations. These abuses, as the ACLU summarizes, have manifested in the forms of violations of wage and hour requirements, constraints on domestics' freedom of movement, and physical, sexual, and emotional attacks. Federal policy—by focusing solely on ensuring the departure of migrant workers—bears responsibility for creating the status conditions that enable these abuses to occur.[21]

In contemporary debates about immigration reform, bonding features have continued to be attached to imagined guestworker programs that proponents say will reduce undocumented entries and overstays. The existing H-2B visa program, however—which in theory grants temporarily admitted guestworkers the same protections afforded to American workers—has been rife with abuses. In 2013, it was reported that H-2B Jamaican house and hotel cleaners hired by a company in Destin, Florida, to offer just one example, had the entirety of their wages stolen by their employer. This was done under the pretext of covering the cost of employer-provided housing.[22] The problems with the existing guestworker program have not deterred neoliberal reformers from suggesting that in the future guestworkers should be required to take out surety bonds upon entering the United States. Under such a policy, guestworkers would be financially liable for guaranteeing their own departure. Like with earlier bond programs, the logic is that this would shift the burdensome task of enforcement away from Immigration and Customs Enforcement.[23]

## In the Absence of Regulation . . .

As this book has documented, Progressive Era reformers were reluctant to view domestic service as an occupation worthy of improvement. Reforms to household labor relations, sociologists argued, would fail to benefit white laborers leaving the occupation in droves. The reimagined servant question of the first two decades of the twentieth century paved the way for what occurred in the 1930s. The major pieces of labor legislation passed during the New Deal—the Social Security Act and National Labor Relations Act (Wagner Act), both in 1935, as well as the 1938 Fair Labor and Standards Act (FLSA)—excluded domestic workers from their coverage. New Deal legislation coincided with a moment in American history when the involvement of black women in domestic work was reaching its apex, not only in the South but also in the urban North. Congress was against empowering black women and was also hesitant to regulate private middle-class homes as workspaces.[24] In 1950 the original Social Security Act was amended to include domestic workers, and in 1974 FLSA provisions governing minimum wages and maximum hours were extended to domestic workers as well. The Wagner Act's collective bargaining provisions still do not apply. As legal historian Risa Goluboff has argued, because the New Deal labor legislation failed to protect black agricultural and domestic laborers, in the 1940s and 1950s attorneys with the Civil Rights Section of the Department of Justice scrambled to close gaps in protections. Using the Thirteenth Amendment's prohibition on involuntary servitude, civil rights lawyers struggled to protect black domestic workers from peonage and other forms of compelled service.[25]

After 1924, the quota system and remote control made it virtually impossible for private employment agencies to broker or assist in the transnational migration of servants. As historian Emma Amador has documented, during the 1940s employment agencies targeted Puerto Rican women for recruitment into jobs in domestic service since they were not subject to immigration restrictions as colonial subjects. Commercial brokers treated the island's population as a labor supply that could be contracted without the impediments that visa requirements otherwise posed. Sent to the least desirable of jobs, Puerto Rican migrants in Chicago and other cities protested their treatment in an occupation that was virtually unregulated. They successfully convinced the Puerto Rican government, as a sending state, to become more involved in the process.[26]

The more substantial change that employment agencies underwent had to do with their increased involvement in staffing service jobs beyond the household. As the historical sociologist Erin Hatton has argued, after World War II entrepreneurs transformed employment agencies into businesses that catered to the ascendant "temp industry." Whereas employment agencies once brokered labor, as participants in the temp industry they hired workers and subcontracted their labor instead. In this redefined capacity, the new temp industry was at the forefront in allowing employers to sidestep collective bargaining agreements and other protections that workers had won by enabling them to hire temporary laborers who did not qualify for the same workplace rights.[27] Today, companies like Merry Maids, Molly Maid, and Maid Brigade operate with a similar model. They insulate employers from having to pay Social Security taxes and other benefits by offering servants as subcontracted labor. Even when intermediaries are not involved, household employers are encouraged to qualify domestic laborers as independent contractors rather than employees so as to avoid having to pay taxes.

The widespread presence of undocumented immigrant women in the United States has made vulnerability a built-in feature of the labor market. The availability of undocumented immigrant labor has been a boon to household employers, who benefit from access to a workforce that must be wary about how it exercises its liberty of contract. Since 1986, the number of immigrants classified as undocumented rose steadily, peaking at around twelve million in 2007. In 2012, researchers from the National Domestic Workers Alliance (NDWA) found that undocumented immigrant workers represented 36 percent of the more than two thousand participants surveyed, and that 85 percent of undocumented workers reported that they had refrained from complaining about job conditions and wage theft on account of their fear that their immigration status would be used to punish them. (As the NDWA notes, 36 percent is almost certainly a low figure, since undocumented workers are less likely to participate in these types of studies.) Undocumented workers also suffered regular wage penalties in terms of earnings, since their immigration status compelled them to be less selective in choosing jobs and in negotiating higher pay. They were also more likely to be found in jobs where especially strenuous labor was required and where toxic cleaning products were widely in use. Among the workers surveyed, undocumented laborers classified as nannies, caregivers, and housekeepers earned on average wages of ten dollars an hour, while documented counterparts in those same jobs earned twelve dollars.[28] As historian Eileen Boris argues, it is intersectional rather than coincidental that undocumented domestic workers are women of color. This reflects the larger trend in which state policies and social welfare have been mobilized to primarily benefit male, industrial, and white workers. "We cannot fully understand women and precarious labor without accounting for the ways that race, gender, and citizenship status," Boris notes, "work together."[29]

Domestic workers have no reason to expect employers to become more aware of what determines the fulfillment of household labor demands—even if there is ample evidence that this is a key step in reimagining how immigrant workers should be socially and politically incorporated. There are important arguments for economic participation being the baseline for civil protections. Law professor Hiroshi Motomura, for instance, asserts that the social contract—as a principle of liberal rule and an individual's relationship to the state—should apply to all immigrants consumed as labor. Undocumented immigrants enter the United States, Motomura argues, in response to the United States' "policy of acquiescing and tolerating immigration outside the law." This acquiescence is necessary to meet labor needs. Because unauthorized immigrants fulfill economic needs, their recruitment is tantamount to a type of contractual invitation to become "Americans in waiting"—whatever their legal status might be.[30] Libertarian philosophers like Michael Huemer have adopted a somewhat similar line of thinking in urging Americans to view their nation as a marketplace. As beneficiaries of this marketplace, American consumers have an ethical obligation to protect the undocumented immigrants who satisfy their labor demands from unjust intrusions on their safety and welfare.[31] As Aristide Zolberg argues, "strange bedfellows" have always been a feature of immigration policy debates. Open immigration proponents link the economic and cultural strains of classical liberalism and its multivalent notions of what it means to be a member of a free society.[32]

A positive sign in recent years has been the organizing and legislative successes of domestic workers themselves. This includes the passage of domestic workers' bills of rights in New York, Hawai'i, California, and, most recently, Massachusetts.[33] This suggests that immigrant and American-born domestic workers are by no means content to wait for employers, as the consumers of their labor, to lead the charge for reforms. Workers should provide the influential voices we listen to in respect to how immigration and domestic labor markets are to be regulated. Though they are not commodities, if human migrants are to be treated as such, they should at least be able to enter into transactions where they are fully empowered to sell their labor power in a just and protected manner.

# NOTES

## INTRODUCTION

1 "Late N. Greene Curtis," *Sacramento Daily Union*, September 9, 1897; "Death of N. Greene Curtis," *Sacramento Daily Union*, July 13, 1897; for Curtis's testimony before the congressional Pacific Railway Commission, see U.S. Congress, Senate, *Testimony Taken by the United States Pacific Railway Commission*, 50th Cong., 1st sess., 1887, Ex. Doc. 51, Part 6, 3027–36; and Charles Edward Russell, *Stories of the Great Railroads* (Chicago: Charles H. Kerr, 1912), 131–32.

2 "Funeral of Ye Gon Lun," *Sacramento Daily Union*, June 27, 1874; Ira M. Condit, *The Chinaman as We See Him: And Fifty Years of Work for Him* (Chicago: F. H. Revell, 1900), 181; "Tomb of Ye Gon Lun, " *Sacramento Daily Union*, August 29, 1874. On Chinese immigration and child labor, and white reformers' treatment of indenture and contract as problems rooted in race, see Wendy Rouse Jorae, *The Children of Chinatown: Growing Up Chinese American in San Francisco, 1850–1920* (Chapel Hill: University of North Carolina Press, 2009), 9–41, 78–109; Stacey Smith, *Freedom's Frontier: California and the Struggle over Unfree Labor, Emancipation, and Reconstruction* (Chapel Hill: University of North Carolina Press, 2013), 109–40; and Peggy Pascoe, *Relations of Rescue: The Search for Female Moral Authority in the American West, 1874–1939* (New York: Oxford University Press, 1993), 51–55.

3 Condit, "Ye Gon Lun," *New York Evangelist*, September 3, 1874; "Funeral of Ye Gon Lun," *Sacramento Daily Union*, June 27, 1874; and "A Chinese Bequest to a Mission," *New York Times*, July 26, 1874.

4 "Tomb of Ye Gon Lun," *Sacramento Daily Union*, August 29, 1874. On the exhumation of Chinese remains, see Wendy Rouse, " 'What We Didn't Understand': A History of Chinese Death Ritual in China and California," in *Chinese American Death Rituals*, ed. Sue Fawn Chung and Priscilla Wegars (Lanham, MD: AltaMira, 2005), 37–38. Limited funds, a lack of knowledge as to where immigrants were buried, and disinterest meant Chinese mutual associations' arrangements for the return of remains to China were not carried out in a comprehensive manner, even if this was often the perception that prejudiced white coverage of the practice gave.

5 Frederick Douglass, "Composite Nation," in *Lift Every Voice: African American Oratory, 1787–1900*, ed. Philip Sheldon Foner and Robert J. Branham (Tuscaloosa: University of Alabama Press, 1998), 493. I am grateful to Micki McElya for calling Douglass's speech to my attention and suggesting this connection. On the debates surrounding the 1870 Naturalization Act, see Najia Aarim-Heriot, *Chinese*

*Immigrants, African Americans, and Racial Anxiety in the United States, 1848–82* (Urbana: University of Illinois Press, 2003), 140–55.

6 On the roles that affect and intimacy play in the production of racial difference and in colonial governance, see Laura Wexler, *Tender Violence: Domestic Visions in the Age of U.S. Imperialism* (Chapel Hill: University of North Carolina Press, 2000), and Ann Laura Stoler, "Tense and Tender Ties: The Politics of Comparison in North American History and (Post)Colonial Studies," in *Haunted by Empire: Geographies of Intimacy in North American History*, ed. Stoler (Durham, NC: Duke University Press, 2006), 23–70, as well as the essays included in this edited volume.

7 Micki McElya, *Clinging to Mammy: The Faithful Slave in Twentieth-Century America* (Cambridge, MA: Harvard University Press, 2007), 5. On the inclusion of enslaved persons in white southern cemeteries, and the contested cultural meanings generated by this practice, see Mark Auslander, *The Accidental Slaveowner: Revisiting a Myth of Race and Finding an American Family* (Athens: University of Georgia Press, 2011), 128–50.

8 "A Chinese Bequest to a Mission," *New York Times*, July 26, 1874.

9 "Funeral of Ye Gon Lun," *Sacramento Daily Union*, June 27, 1874.

10 "To the Workingmen of Sacramento County" (advertisement), *Sacramento Daily Union*, September 1, 1877.

11 Jesse Benton Frémont, *A Year of American Travel* (New York: Harper & Brothers, 1878), 102–3.

12 *Christian Advocate*, November 23, 1882.

13 David R. Roediger and Elizabeth D. Esch, *The Production of Difference: Race and the Management of Labor in U.S. History* (New York: Oxford University Press, 2012), 8. For an introduction to how immigration and naturalization laws produced racial difference, see Ian Haney López, *White by Law: The Legal Construction of Race*, rev. ed. (New York: New York University Press, 2006). As this book argues, immigration policies developed in concert with strategies for labor management, and these two areas of governance were mutually constitutive when it came to the construction of ethnic and racial subjects.

   The relationship between representation and commodification has long been a focus in the history of slavery, and I build on this literature as well. See especially Walter Johnson, *Soul by Soul: Life Inside the Antebellum Slave Market* (Cambridge, MA: Harvard University Press, 1999), Stephanie Smallwood, "Commodified Freedom: Interrogating the Limits of Anti-slavery Ideology in the Early Republic," in *Whither the Early Republic: A Forum on the Future of the Field*, ed. John Lauritz Larson and Michael A. Morrison (Philadelphia: University of Pennsylvania Press, 2005), 139–48, and Nicholas Rinehart, "The Man That Was a Thing: Reconsidering Human Commodification in Slavery," *Journal of Social History* 49, no. 4 (Summer 2016): 1–23.

14 By contrast, historian Seth Rockman argues that in the early republic, "great demand for women's labor never exerted an upward pull on wage levels, and

if market forces had any impact on women's wages, it was to push them even further downward due to overcompetition in the few occupations where women clustered." Rockman, *Scraping By: Wage Labor, Slavery, and Survival in Early Baltimore* (Baltimore: Johns Hopkins University Press, 2009), 102.

15 Glenna Matthews, *"Just a Housewife": The Rise and Fall of Domesticity in America* (New York: Oxford University Press, 1989), 263–66.

16 Cited in Mary Cathryn Cain, "Race, Republicanism, and Domestic Service in the Antebellum United States," *Left History* 12, no. 2 (Fall/Winter 2007): 75.

17 Aristide R. Zolberg, *A Nation by Design: Immigration Policy in the Fashioning of America* (Cambridge, MA: Harvard University Press, 2009), 167. Political scientist John Torpey articulates this idea as states' efforts to "monopolize the legitimate means of movement." Torpey, *The Invention of the Passport: Surveillance, Citizenship and the State* (New York: Cambridge University Press, 2000), 6–10.

18 On the debates surrounding "white slavery" and the trafficking of women into sex work, see Jessica Pliley, "The Petticoat Inspectors: Women Boarding Inspectors and the Gendered Exercise of Federal Authority," *Journal of the Gilded Age and Progressive Era* 12, no. 1 (2013): 95–126; Gunther Peck, "Feminizing White Slavery in the United States: Marcus Braun and the Transnational Traffic in White Bodies, 1890–1910," in *Workers across the Americas: The Transnational Turn in Labor History*, ed. Leon Fink (New York: Oxford University Press, 2011), 221–44; Brian Donovan, *White Slave Crusades: Race, Gender, and Anti-vice Activism, 1887–1917* (Urbana: University of Illinois Press, 2006); Peck, "Making Sense of White Slavery and Whiteness," *Labor: Studies in Working-Class History of the Americas* 1, no. 2 (Summer 2004): 41–63; and David J. Langum, *Crossing over the Line: Legislating Morality and the Mann Act* (Chicago: University of Chicago Press, 1994). On fears that free labor would be undermined by the alleged trade in "coolie" labor, see Moon-Ho Jung, *Coolies and Cane: Race, Labor, and Sugar in the Age of Emancipation* (Baltimore: Johns Hopkins University Press, 2006), 11–38; Lisa Lowe, *The Intimacies of Four Continents* (Durham, NC: Duke University Press, 2015), 1–43; Edlie Wong, *Racial Reconstruction: Black Inclusion, Chinese Exclusion, and the Fictions of Citizenship* (New York: New York University Press, 2015); and Matthew Guterl, "After Slavery: Asian Labor, Immigration, and Emancipation in the United States and Cuba, 1840–1880," *Journal of World History* 14, no. 2 (June 2003): 209–41. As chapter 3 of this book addresses, depictions of Chinese immigrants as bonded labor had a racially informed view of their ability to contract. On *padrones* and similar complications and discursive ambiguities that accompanied portrayals of free yet trafficked European and Mexican labor, see Peck, *Reinventing Free Labor: Padrones and Immigrant Workers in the North American West, 1880–1930* (New York: Cambridge University Press, 2000) and Donna Gabaccia, "The 'Yellow Peril' and the 'Chinese of Europe': Global Perspectives on Race and Labor, 1815–1930," in *Migration, Migration History, History: Old Paradigms and New Perspectives*, ed. Jan Lucassen and Leo Lucassen (Bern: Peter Lang, 1997), 177–96.

19  Peck, "Feminizing White Slavery," 224; see also Adam McKeown, "How the Box
    Became Black: Brokers and the Creation of the 'Free' Migrant," *Pacific Affairs* 85
    (2012): 21–46.

20  On nineteenth-century changes to the governance of individuals, emphasizing the
    transition from status to contract, see Janet Halley, "What Is Family Law? A Gene-
    alogy Part I," *Yale Journal of Law & the Humanities* 23, no. 1 (2011): 1–95; Barbara
    Young Welke, *Law and the Borders of Belonging in the Long Nineteenth Century
    United States* (New York: Cambridge University Press, 2010); Amy Dru Stanley,
    *From Bondage to Contract: Wage Labor, Marriage, and the Market in the Age of
    Slave Emancipation* (New York: Cambridge University Press, 1998); and Carole
    Pateman, *The Sexual Contract* (Stanford, CA: Stanford University Press, 1988).

21  For an elaboration of this point in a more contemporary context, see Nancy Fra-
    ser, "From Redistribution to Recognition? Dilemmas of Justice in a 'Post-socialist'
    Age," *New Left Review*, no. 212 (1995): 68–93.

22  On the construction of northerners' free labor ideology in the post–Civil War
    period, and the dominant attitudes governing the parameters of what constituted
    acceptable forms of individual liberty, see Stanley, *From Bondage to Contract*;
    Jeffrey Sklansky, *The Soul's Economy: Market and Selfhood in American Thought,
    1820–1920* (Chapel Hill: University of North Carolina Press, 2002); James D.
    Schmidt, *Free to Work: Labor Law, Emancipation, and Reconstruction, 1815–1880*
    (Athens: University of Georgia Press, 1999); Alex Gourevitch, "Labor Republican-
    ism and the Transformation of Work," *Political Theory* 41, no. 4 (2013): 591–617;
    Cedric de Leon, *The Origins of Right to Work: Antilabor Democracy in Nineteenth-
    Century Chicago* (Ithaca, NY: Cornell University Press, 2015); Heather Cox Rich-
    ardson, *The Death of Reconstruction: Race, Labor, and Politics in the Post–Civil
    War North, 1865–1901* (Cambridge, MA: Harvard University Press, 2004); and
    Richardson, *West from Appomattox: The Reconstruction of America after the Civil
    War* (New Haven, CT: Yale University Press, 2008).

23  Robert J. Steinfeld, *Coercion, Contract, and Free Labor in the Nineteenth Century*
    (New York: Cambridge University Press, 2001), 8. See also Jan Lucassen, "Free
    and Unfree Labour before the Twentieth Century: A Brief Overview," and Stanley
    Engerman and Robert Steinfeld, "Labor—Free or Coerced? A Historical Reassess-
    ment of Differences and Similarities," both in *Free and Unfree Labour: The Debate
    Continues*, ed. Tom Brass and Marcel Van Der Linden (Bern: Peter Lang, 1997),
    45–56, 107–26; and Robert Miles, *Capitalism and Unfree Labor: Anomaly or Neces-
    sity?* (London: Tavistock, 1987).

24  Immanuel Wallerstein, "The Bourgeois(ie) as Concept and Reality," *New Left
    Review*, no. 167 (1988): 102.

25  On the use of pauper and penal institutions as suppliers of domestic labor in mid-
    nineteenth-century New York that is attentive to how race structured reformers'
    opinions of what constituted acceptable disciplinary compulsion, see Gunja Sen-
    Gupta, *From Slavery to Poverty: The Racial Origins of Welfare in New York, 1840–
    1918* (New York: New York University Press, 2010), 69–206. On the relationship

between black penal labor and domestic service in the American South, see Sarah Haley, *No Mercy Here: Gender, Punishment, and the Making of Jim Crow Modernity* (Chapel Hill: University of North Carolina Press, 2016). For a more theoretical overview of this subject, see Giovanni Procacci, "Social Economy and the Government of Poverty," in *The Foucault Effect: Studies in Governmentality*, ed. Graham Burchell, Colin Gordon, and Peter Miller (Chicago: University of Chicago Press, 1991), 151–68.

26 These experiences conform to what the historical sociologist Karl Polanyi calls "the great transformation." Free market capitalism—by destroying customary social relations—led to the commodification of labor as something to be sold on the market. Polanyi, *The Great Transformation: The Political and Economic Origins of Our Time*, 2nd ed. (Boston: Beacon, 2001).

27 Catharine Esther Beecher and Harriet Beecher Stowe, *The American Woman's Home: Or, Principles of Domestic Science: Being a Guide to the Formation and Maintenance of Economical, Healthful, Beautiful, and Christian Homes* (J.B. Ford, 1869), 328; Stowe, *Palmetto Leaves* (Boston: James R. Osgood, 1873), 314. On Stowe's views concerning household work and free labor ideology more generally, see Rachel N. Klein, "Harriet Beecher Stowe and the Domestication of Free Labor Ideology," *Legacy* 18, no. 2 (2001): 135–52.

28 Christopher Capozzola, "The Secret Soldiers' Union: Labor and Soldier Politics in the Philippine Scout Mutiny of 1924," in *Making the Empire Work: Labor and United States Imperialism*, ed. Daniel Bender and Jana Lipman (New York: New York University Press, 2015), 85–103. See also Evelyn Nakano Glenn, *Unequal Freedom: How Race and Gender Shaped American Citizenship and Labor* (Cambridge, MA: Harvard University Press, 2002), 14–16. On explicit forms of labor bondage that prevailed after the passage of the Thirteenth Amendment, see Leon Fink, *Sweatshops at Sea: Merchant Seamen in the World's First Globalized Industry, from 1812 to the Present* (Chapel Hill: University of North Carolina Press, 2014); Pete Daniel, *The Shadow of Slavery: Peonage in the South, 1901–69* (Urbana: University of Illinois Press, 1972); David M. Oshinsky, *Worse Than Slavery: Parchman Farm and the Ordeal of Jim Crow Justice* (New York: Free Press, 1997); and Alex Lichtenstein, *Twice the Work of Free Labor: The Political Economy of Convict Labor in the New South* (New York: Verso, 1996). Risa Goluboff's work, in contrast, examines peonage as a pressing concern of post–World War II civil rights advocacy. Risa L. Goluboff, *The Lost Promise of Civil Rights* (Cambridge, MA: Harvard University Press, 2010).

29 As the sociologist Jane Addams wrote of domestic service in 1896: "Both employers and employés, for the most part, hold moral conceptions and notions of duty which are tinged with feudalism." Addams, "A Belated Industry," *American Journal of Sociology* 1 (March 1896): 536.

30 Smith: "The labour of the menial servant . . . does not fix or realize itself in any particular subject or vendible commodity." From book 2, chapter 3 of *The Wealth of Nations*, in Adam Smith, *The Essential Adam Smith*, ed. Robert L. Heilbroner

(New York: Norton, 1986), 234. Karl Marx, *Grundrisse: Foundations of the Critique of Political Economy*, trans. Martin Nicolaus (New York: Random House, 1973), 208. With this formulation, historian Carolyn Steedman points out, Marx summarily dismissed the servants and service providers representing more than half of mid-nineteenth-century England's paid labor force from participation in the class struggle that he claimed drove history's course. Steedman, *Master and Servant: Love and Labour in the English Industrial Age* (New York: Cambridge University Press, 2007), 73.

31  For an overview of how debates about whether or not domestic work was productive labor exposed deep differences between feminist scholars and their orthodox Marxist colleagues, see Lise Vogel, "Historical-Critical Dictionary of Marxism: Domestic-Labour Debate," *Historical Materialism* 16, no. 2 (2008): 237–43. For a discussion of globalization and the more recent feminist critiques that have continued to challenge the idea that domestic labor is unproductive work undeserving of study within capitalist systems, see Silvia Federici, "The Reproduction of Labour-Power in the Global Economy, Marxist Theory and the Unfinished Feminist Revolution" (paper presented at the Crisis of Social Reproduction and Feminist Struggle seminar, University of California, Santa Cruz, January 27, 2009), caringlabor.wordpress.com; the collected essays by Federici in *Revolution at Point Zero: Housework, Reproduction, and Feminist Struggle* (Oakland: PM Press, 2012); and Mary Romero, *Maid in the USA*, 10th anniversary ed. (New York: Routledge, 2002), 47–75. See also Katrine Marcal, *Who Cooked Adam Smith's Dinner? A Story of Women and Economics* (New York: Pegasus Books, 2016).

32  For a discussion of the frequent critiques that surrounded nineteenth-century commercial intelligence offices specializing in domestic servants, see Faye E. Dudden, *Serving Women: Household Service in Nineteenth-Century America* (Middletown, CT: Wesleyan University Press, 1983), 79–87; Walter Licht, *Getting Work: Philadelphia, 1840–1950* (Cambridge, MA: Harvard University Press, 1992), 98–140; Vanessa H. May, *Unprotected Labor: Household Workers, Politics, and Middle-Class Reform in New York, 1870–1940* (Chapel Hill: University of North Carolina Press, 2011), 60–65; and Brian P. Luskey, "Special Marts: Intelligence Offices, Labor Commodification, and Emancipation in Nineteenth-Century America," *Journal of the Civil War Era* 3 (September 2013): 360–91.

33  Patience Price, "The Revolt in the Kitchen," *Godey's Lady's Book*, February 1868, 143–44.

34  There is a large body of literature that addresses idealized notions of what constituted "True Womanhood" and the "cult of domesticity." These ideas were first addressed in Barbara Welter, "The Cult of True Womanhood: 1820–1860," *American Quarterly* 18, no. 2 (1966): 151–74. For a discussion of the uses and misuses of the concept of "True Womanhood," see Mary Louise Roberts, "True Womanhood Revisited," and Nancy Hewitt, "Taking the True Woman Hostage," both in *Journal of Women's History* 14, no. 1 (2002): 150–55, 156–62; and Linda Kerber, "Separate Spheres, Female Worlds, Woman's Place: The Rhetoric of Women's History,"

*Journal of American History* 75, no. 1 (1988): 9–39. On the development of a bourgeois class with shared values and ideologies, see Sven Beckert, *The Monied Metropolis: New York City and the Consolidation of the American Bourgeoisie, 1850–1896* (New York: Cambridge University Press, 2001).

35 Jeanne Boydston, "The Woman Who Wasn't There: Women's Market Labor and the Transition to Capitalism in the United States," *Journal of the Early Republic* 16, no. 2 (July 1996): 183–206; Boydston, *Home and Work: Housework, Wages, and the Ideology of Labor in the Early Republic* (New York: Oxford University Press, 1990), esp. 120–41; and also, Carole Lasser, "The Domestic Balance of Power: Relations between Mistress and Maid in Nineteenth-Century New England," *Labor History* 28, no. 1 (1987): 5–22. Discussions of the concept of "help" and the mutuality and egalitarian working relationship it implied can be found in Matthews, *"Just a Housewife,"* 92–116, and Barbara Ryan, *Love, Wages, Slavery: The Literature of Servitude in the United States* (Urbana: University of Illinois Press, 2006), 15–44. On "republican motherhood" and its relationship to natural rights discourse and citizenship, see Linda Kerber, "The Republican Mother: Women and the Enlightenment—An American Perspective," *American Quarterly* 28, no. 2 (Summer 1976): 187–205. Following Daniel Rodgers, the goal in this book is to take seriously republicanism as an essential organizing concept of American political and social life, while also acknowledging that republicanism had many competing discursive uses. Rodgers, "Republicanism: the Career of a Concept," *Journal of American History* 79, no. 1 (June 1992): 11–38.

36 "The Princess Biddy; or 'Help' and 'Self-Help,'" *Putnam's Magazine* 14 (August 1869): 247.

37 On nineteenth-century domesticity's embrace of cultural imperialism, see Amy Kaplan, *The Anarchy of Empire in the Making of U.S. Culture* (Cambridge, MA: Harvard University Press, 2002), 23–50. For studies of domesticity that emphasize how its political economy was outward looking and actively commercial, see Roediger and Esch, *Production of Difference*, 108–14; Lori Merish, *Sentimental Materialism: Gender, Commodity Culture, and Nineteenth-Century American Literature* (Durham, NC: Duke University Press, 2000); Kristin L. Hoganson, *Consumers' Imperium: The Global Production of American Domesticity, 1865–1920* (Chapel Hill: University of North Carolina Press, 2007); and April Merleaux, *Sugar and Civilization: American Empire and the Cultural Politics of Sweetness* (Chapel Hill: University of North Carolina Press, 2015).

38 "Letters from the Fireside. That Old Question Again." *New York Observer*, November 16, 1865.

39 As historian William Leach documents, between 1870 and 1910 the number of workers employed in the service industry grew at a rate that was double that of industrial occupations. William R. Leach, *Land of Desire: Merchants, Power, and the Rise of a New American Culture* (New York: Vintage, 1994), 131.

40 David Roediger, *Wages of Whiteness* (New York: Verso, 1991), 133–56; Cain, "Race, Republicanism, and Domestic Service," 64–83.

41 E. L. Godkin, "The Coming of the Barbarian," *Nation*, July 15, 1869, 45.

42 Patrick Wolfe, "Settler Colonialism and the Elimination of the Native," *Journal of Genocide Research* 8, no. 4 (2006): 388. See also Scott Lauria Morgensen, *Spaces between Us: Queer Settler Colonialism and Indigenous Decolonization* (Minneapolis: University of Minnesota Press, 2011); and Mark Rifkin, *Manifesting America: The Imperial Construction of U.S. National Space* (New York: Oxford University Press, 2012). For an overview of settler colonialism as a concept, see Lorenzo Veracini, *Settler Colonialism* (London: Palgrave Macmillan, 2010).

43 Aziz Rana, *The Two Faces of American Freedom* (Cambridge, MA: Harvard University Press, 2010), 8–13.

44 "Ex-Gov. Seymour on the Coolie Question—Letter to the Working Men at Rochester," *New York Times*, August 6, 1870.

45 Michel Foucault writes in the *History of Sexuality* that biopower, and its praxis in racial and class biopolitics, was essential to capitalism and the legal superstructure that governed the social relations of capitalistic production. Biopolitics "acted as factors of segregation and social hierarchization . . . guaranteeing relationships of domination and effects of hegemony." Michel Foucault, *The History of Sexuality, Vol. 1: An Introduction*, trans. Robert Hurley, Reissue ed. (New York: Vintage, 1990), 140–41. On the ways in which service, deference, and economic submission to whites were imagined as qualities that defined citizenship and social membership in practice, beyond liberal theories of equality in natural rights, see Devon W. Carbado, "Racial Naturalization," *American Quarterly* 57, no. 3 (2005): 633–58; Glenn, *Unequal Freedom*, 18–55; and Etienne Balibar, "Racism and Nationalism," in Balibar and Immanuel Wallerstein, *Race, Nation, Class: Ambiguous Identities*, 2nd ed. (New York: Verso, 2011), 37–67.

46 Chinese immigrant cooks, if they were able to successfully raise capital, could open their own restaurants. See Yong Chen, *Chop Suey, USA: The Story of Chinese Food in America* (New York: Columbia University Press, 2014), 92–101. As historian Rebecca Sharpless documents, in the aftermath of the Civil War freed persons who possessed cooking skills were more likely to move from rural to urban areas with higher paying domestic jobs. Sharpless, *Cooking in Other Women's Kitchens: Domestic Workers in the South, 1865–1960* (Chapel Hill: University of North Carolina Press, 2010), 7.

47 As this book addresses, frustrated employers sometimes fantasized about boarding house life, even though temporary accommodations were often depicted as antithetical to the establishment of stable, middle-class domesticity, since living in these residencies meant that they would not be responsible for the hiring of servants. On servants in boarding houses, see Wendy Gamber, *The Boardinghouse in Nineteenth-Century America* (Baltimore: Johns Hopkins University Press, 2007), 55–62.

48 Frances Kellor, "The Housewife and Her Helper," *Ladies' Home Journal*, November 1906, 38. In 1900 Gail Laughlin observed that her surveys with employers and servants found significant differences in the hours on call and at work that each

party reported. Servants reported being on call an average of thirteen hours a day and at work twelve hours, whereas employers gave those numbers as twelve and nine, respectively. Laughlin, "Domestic Service," in U.S. Industrial Commission, *Report of the Industrial Commission on the Relations and Conditions of Capital and Labor Employed in Manufactures and General Business . . . etc.*, vol. 14 (Washington, DC: GPO, 1901), 756.

49 Dudden, *Serving Women*, 193–235; David M. Katzman, *Seven Days a Week: Women and Domestic Service in Industrializing America* (New York: Oxford University Press, 1978), 146–83.

50 For a social history of Irish servants in the United States that deals with these workers in isolation, see Margaret Lynch-Brennan, *The Irish Bridget: Irish Immigrant Women in Domestic Service in America, 1840–1930* (Syracuse, NY: Syracuse University Press, 2009).

51 On Irish servants as rebellious, politicized figures, see Andrew Urban, "Irish Domestic Servants, 'Biddy,' and Rebellion in the American Home, 1850–1900," *Gender & History* 21 (August 2009): 263–86; and Bronwen Walter, *Outsiders Inside: Whiteness, Place and Irish Women* (New York: Routledge, 2001), 64. Following historian Paul Kramer's argument, I use imperialism as a category of analysis rather than as a precise, defining term. This allows imperialism, as a concept, to be productive rather than deterministic in respect to thinking through relative positions of economic and political sovereignty. See Kramer, "Power and Connection: Imperial Histories of the United States in the World," *American Historical Review* 116, no. 5 (2011): 1348–91.

52 Chinese bodies, as a source of labor power, became the physical embodiment of finance capitalism and corporate rule that white workers could challenge only as abstractions. Chinese servants were not responsible for white Californians' economic woes. On this idea more theoretically conceived, see Iyko Day, *Alien Capital: Asian Racialization and the Logic of Settler Colonial Capitalism* (Durham, NC: Duke University Press, 2016).

53 See, for example, Tera W. Hunter, *To 'Joy My Freedom: Southern Black Women's Lives and Labors after the Civil War* (Cambridge, MA: Harvard University Press, 1997); and Elizabeth Clark-Lewis, *Living In, Living Out: African American Domestics in Washington, D.C., 1910–1940* (Washington, DC: Smithsonian Institution Press, 1994).

54 Mae Ngai, "Chinese Gold Miners and the 'Chinese Question' in Nineteenth-Century California and Victoria," *Journal of American History* 101, no. 4 (March 2015): 1082–1105, 1083.

55 Erika Lee, *At America's Gates: Chinese Immigration during the Exclusion Era, 1882–1943* (Chapel Hill: University of North Carolina Press, 2003), 24. See also Beth Lew-Williams, "Before Restriction Became Exclusion: America's Experiment in Diplomatic Immigration Control," *Pacific Historical Review* 83, no. 1 (February 2014): 24–56. See, as prominent works on the political history of exclusion, Elmer Sandmeyer, *The Anti-Chinese Movement in California* (1939, 1973; repr.,

Urbana: University of Illinois Press, 1991); Alexander Saxton, *The Indispensable Enemy: Labor and the Anti-Chinese Movement in California* (Berkeley: University of California Press, 1975); and Andrew Gyory, *Closing the Gate: Race, Politics, and the Chinese Exclusion Act* (Chapel Hill: University of North Carolina Press, 1998), 39–59. Whereas Sandmeyer and Saxton emphasize the racism of white workers as the cause that drove restrictions, Gyory blames politicians for making restriction a national issue, so as to avoid having to contend with class politics.

56 Daniel Kanstroom, *Deportation Nation: Outsiders in American History* (New York: Cambridge University Press, 2007), 107–30; Lucy E. Salyer, *Laws Harsh as Tigers: Chinese Immigrants and the Shaping of Modern Immigration Law* (Chapel Hill: University of North Carolina Press, 1995), 94–116; and Charles J. McClain, *In Search of Equality: The Chinese Struggle Against Discrimination in Nineteenth-Century America* (Berkeley: University of California Press, 1994), 191–219. See also José Jorge Mendoza, "Neither a State of Nature nor a State of Exception: Law, Sovereignty, and Immigration," *Radical Philosophy Review* 14, no. 2 (2011): 187–95.

57 Lee, *At America's Gates*, 48; Salyer, *Laws Harsh as Tigers*, 217–44.

58 As historian Kornel Chang states, "These dueling impulses—to reach outwards, collapse boundaries, and integrate formally disparate regions through boundless expansion, on the one hand, and to police movement across boundaries through bounded and delimited spaces, on the other—were formed dialectically constituting one of modernity's enduring paradoxes in which the global and national were fashioned together." Chang, *Pacific Connections: The Making of the U.S.-Canadian Borderlands* (Berkeley: University of California Press, 2012), 4.

59 See Smith, *Freedom's Frontier*, 206–30.

60 Kanstroom, *Deportation Nation*, 91–130.

61 On the origins of guestworker policies more generally, see Cindy Hahamovitch, "Creating Perfect Immigrants: Guestworkers of the World in Historical Perspective," *Labor History* 44, no. 1 (January 2003): 69–94; Hahamovitch, *No Man's Land: Jamaican Guestworkers in America and the Global History of Deportable Labor* (Princeton, NJ: Princeton University Press, 2011); Saskia Sassen, *Guests and Aliens* (New York: New Press, 1999); Kitty Calavita, *Inside the State: The Bracero Program, Immigration, and the I.N.S.* (New York: Routledge, 1992), and Mae Ngai, *Impossible Subjects: Illegal Aliens and the Making of Modern America* (Princeton, NJ: Princeton University Press, 2004), 96–126.

62 Walter Johnson, "On Agency," *Journal of Social History* 37, no. 1 (Fall 2003): 113–24. See also historian Seth Rockman's assertion that "the constraints and limits placed upon *choice*—that most cherished and defining characteristic of the American experience—frame the history of capitalism and its consequences for working people." Rockman, *Scraping By*, 12.

63 L. L. Dutcher to Griffing, February 20, 1867, Records of the Assistant Commissioner for the District of Columbia, Bureau of Refugees, Freedmen and Abandoned Lands, 1865–1869, RG 105, National Archives Microfilm Publications, no. M1055, roll 8, Letters Received.

64 Grace Greenwood, "A Tourist in the Far West," *New York Times*, February 9, 1878.
65 "In Matters of the Lutheran Emigrant House and Commissioner Williams,"
October 10, 1902, Series I, Ellis Island, William Williams Papers, Manuscripts and
Archives Division, New York Public Library; "Missionary Accused of Deceiving
Immigrants," *New York Times*, October 11, 1902; J. L. Neve, "Rev. Berkemeier and
Mr. Williams, the Commissioner of Immigration," *Lutheran Observer*, February
27, 1903, 262.

## CHAPTER 1. LIBERATING FREE LABOR

1 Gerard Moran puts the number of assisted emigrants to North America at
somewhere between 250,000 and 300,000. An additional 300,000 Irish individuals received assistance to go to Australia during the same time period. Moran,
*Sending Out Ireland's Poor: Assisted Emigration to North America in the Nineteenth
Century* (Dublin: Four Courts Press, 2004), 14–15. For a more celebratory account of Foster's assisted emigration work, which emphasizes charity rather than
political economy, see Ruth Ann Harris, "Where the Poor Many Is Not Crushed
Down to Exalt the Aristocrat: Vere Foster's Programme of Assisted Emigration
in the Aftermath of the Irish Famines," in *The Irish Worldwide: History, Heritage,
Identity, VI: The Meaning of the Famine*, ed. Patrick O'Sullivan (London: Leicester
University Press, 1997), 172–94. I use "Anglophone" to highlight the perceived affinities that nineteenth-century political economists attributed to English-speaking
societies and settlements, regardless of their sovereign affiliation. As destinations
for British, Irish, and European migrants, the United States, Canada, and Australia composed an Anglophone world, even if white arrivals to these destinations
represented a wide range of ethnic identities and did not speak English exclusively.
For further discussion of the term "Anglophone," on which my usage is based,
see James Belich, *Replenishing the Earth: The Settler Revolution and the Rise of the
Angloworld, 1783–1939* (New York: Oxford University Press, 2009), 58–59.
2 These figures are based on numbers that Foster provided. For the 1850s, see "Mr.
Vere Foster's Irish Female Emigration Fund, Under the Auspices of All the Clergy
of All Denominations in the West of Ireland," Easter 1883, Vere Foster Papers,
Public Relations Office of Northern Ireland (hereafter PRONI), D3618/D/10/11.
In his final circular soliciting monetary support, Foster claimed to have assisted
an additional 22,615 emigrants during the 1880s, from a total of 37,000 applications. He gave the average age of the female emigrant whose passage he financed
as twenty years and four months. "Mr. Vere Foster's Irish Female Emigration
Fund, Under the Auspices of All the Clergy of All Denominations in the West of
Ireland," November 1889, PRONI, D3618/D/10/14.
3 This expectation was stated to emigrants in a form that they received with their
ticket. Mary McNeill, *Vere Foster, 1819–1900: An Irish Benefactor* (Newton Abbot:
Institute of Irish Studies, Queen's University, Belfast, 1971), 83.
4 Between 1848 and 1900, Irish immigrants in North America would send $260
million in remittances back to Ireland. Of that amount, 90 percent came from the

United States, and 40 percent took the form of prepaid passage tickets, which immigrants sent to relatives and friends seeking to migrate. Historian Kerby Miller argues that even as remittances and reports of Irish success in the United States grew, most emigrants left Ireland due to economic and social changes that they believed compelled them to depart, even after the immediate threat of starvation had ebbed. Miller, *Emigrants and Exiles: Ireland and the Irish Exodus to North America* (New York: Oxford University Press, 1985), 353–426. While not the focus here, it is important to point out that Miller's argument that migrants equated emigration to exile has been the subject of much debate, especially in relationship to how the choice to emigrate might be gendered. Historian Hasia Diner, for instance, argues that many Irish women welcomed the opportunity to migrate, become wage earners, and escape the rural patriarchal society of Ireland. Diner, *Erin's Daughters in America*, 1–29. For similar views, see also Pauline Jackson, "Women in 19th Century Irish Emigration," *International Migration Review* 18, no. 4 (Winter 1984): 1004–20; and Carol Groneman, "Working-Class Immigrant Women in Mid-Nineteenth-Century New York," *Journal of Urban History* 4, no. 3 (May 1978): 255–73.

5 "Emigration. Address to the Industrious Poor and Their Friends in the United Kingdom, and More Especially in Ireland," December 1, 1851, PRONI, D3618/D/9/3. As historian Tyler Anbinder has documented, concerns about Irish pauper immigration peaked during the famine, when landowners were accused of ridding their estates of tenants on whom they no longer wanted to pay mandatory poor rates. Anbinder, "From Famine to Five Points: Lord Lansdowne's Irish Tenants Encounter North America's Most Notorious Slum," *American Historical Review* 107 (April 2002): 351–87; and "Lord Palmerston and the Irish Famine Emigration," *(Cambridge) Historical Journal* 44 (Summer 2001): 441–69. Anbinder notes that the Irish tenants who came to New York under these conditions did quite well relative to their poverty and the widespread opposition that their entry generated.

6 Harlon to Foster, May 9, 1862, PRONI, D3618/D/25/7.

7 On contests over clothing, see Diane M. Hotten-Somers, "Relinquishing and Reclaiming Independence: Irish Domestic Servants, American Middle-Class Mistresses, and Assimilation, 1850–1920," *Eire-Ireland* 36 (2001): 185–201.

8 Mary Frances Cusack, *Advice to Irish Girls in America, by the Nun of Kenmare* (New York: McGee, 1872), 26. On the Irish Catholic leadership's cautious approach toward promoting immigrant women's marriages, see Maureen Fitzgerald, *Habits of Compassion: Irish Catholic Nuns and the Origins of New York's Welfare System, 1830–1920* (Urbana: University of Illinois Press, 2006), 64–67.

9 No records for an unmarried woman named Mary Harlon appear in either the 1860 or the 1870 U.S. census. Nor does she appear—under her original surname—in New York City's registry of death certificates. Since Mary is a common name, it is impossible to determine whether an individual fitting Harlon's description married and took her husband's name. A twelve-year-old Mary Harlon born

in Ireland arrived in New York from Liverpool on the *Washington* on December 4, 1850. Foster also traveled on this ship. But that Harlon was accompanied by her mother and two infant sisters. Since none of these persons are referenced in her letters to Foster, it seems unlikely that this is *the* Mary Harlon. "Mary Harlon," in *New York, Irish Immigrant Arrival Records, 1846–1851*, Ancestry.com, accessed November 19, 2016.

10 Diary of Vere Foster's Trip to America, 1864, PRONI, D3618/D/6/10; Harlon to Foster, June 23, 1864, PRONI, D3618/D/25/8.

11 McNeill, *Vere Foster*, 45–59.

12 "Emigration" (a broadsheet copy of a letter from Foster to the directors of the American Emigrant's Friend Society, Philadelphia), PRONI, D3618/D/9/6.

13 "Ho! for California," *New York Times*, April 6, 1855. Despite an influx of migrants into the state during the late 1850s and 1860s, the *Times* reported that wages for servants had remained steady. "Wages and Labor in California," *New York Times*, April 21, 1867. On wage levels for servants in New York, see Diner, *Erin's Daughters in America*, 90; and Katzman, *Seven Days a Week*, 303–14.

14 Charles Loring Brace, *The New West; or, California in 1867–1868* (New York: G.P. Putnam, 1869), 348.

15 "Facts for Emigrants to California: A Circular Issued to Workingmen from the California Labor Exchange," William West to Hamilton Fish, July 6, 1869, National Archives and Records Administration, Department of State, Record Group 59, *Despatches from United States Consul, Dublin, Ireland, 1790–1906* (microform), vol. 7 (microform reel 7); *Freeman's Journal*, January 1, 1870.

16 Harlon to Foster, June 23, 1864, PRONI, D3618/D/25/8; Harlon to Foster, July 27, 1864, PRONI, D3618/D/25/9.

17 Harlon to Foster, December 20, 1864, PRONI, D3618/D/25/10. Harlon listed the McFarland home as her return address. On Walter McFarland's role in the construction and improvement of Fort Zachary Taylor, see Ames W. Williams, "Stronghold of the Straits: A Short History of Fort Zachary Taylor," *Tequesta* 14 (1954): 3–24.

18 Harlon to Foster, October 16, 1865, PRONI, D3618/D/25/11. See also Harlon to Foster, October 18, 1865, PRONI, D3618/D/25/12.

19 As historian Hidetaka Hirota documents, Massachusetts was aggressive in requiring shipmasters to take out bonds on Irish immigrants during the famine, whereas New York remained considerably more lax. In both ports, pauper immigrants were deported without court-issued warrants or judicial review of their cases during the 1850s. Hirota, "The Moment of Transition: State Officials, the Federal Government, and the Formation of American Immigration Policy," *Journal of American History* 99, no. 4 (2013): 1092–1108. See also Gerald L. Neuman, *Strangers to the Constitution* (Princeton, NJ: Princeton University Press, 1996), 19–43; and J. Matthew Gallman, *Receiving Erin's Children: Philadelphia, Liverpool, and the Irish Famine Migration, 1845–1855* (Chapel Hill: University of North Carolina Press, 2000), 32–34.

20 Anna Lowenhaupt Tsing, *The Mushroom at the End of the World: On the Possibility of Life in Capitalist Ruins* (Princeton, NJ: Princeton University Press, 2015), 63.

21 *New York Daily Tribune*, July 24, 1857. See also Adam Tuchinsky, *Horace Greeley's "New-York Tribune": Civil War–Era Socialism and the Crisis of Free Labor* (Ithaca, NY: Cornell University Press, 2009), 10–17. As the next chapter addresses, Greeley's support for assisted migration would wane during Reconstruction.

22 This thinking persisted until the end of the century. Restrictionists calling for numerical limitations on European immigration tended to distinguish between immigration that, as Henry Cabot Lodge put it in 1891, helped "to occupy or develop the vast territory and valuable resources of the Union," and what they believed were dangerous forms of urban concentration. Lodge, "The Restriction of Immigration," *North American Review*, January 1891, 32.

23 "The New York Labor Market: Female House-Servants," *Harper's Weekly*, July 4, 1857.

24 Cormac Ó Gráda, *Ireland's Great Famine: Interdisciplinary Perspectives* (Dublin: University College Dublin Press, 2006), 143–74, 158. See also David Noel Doyle, "The Irish as Urban Pioneers in the United States, 1850–1870," *Journal of American Ethnic History* 10, nos. 1/2 (October 1990): 36–59. In terms of quantifying the benefits of westward migration, and the advantages to be gained from labor and land markets in regions more recently settled by whites, economic historian Joseph Ferrie concludes that "half of all immigrant unskilled workers who move moved more than 400 miles between 1850 and 1860 moved up in occupational status." British and German migrants to the interior were more likely to become farm owners than were Irish settlers, corresponding to their great capital savings. Ferrie, *Yankeys Now: Immigrants in the Antebellum United States, 1840–1860* (New York: Oxford University Press, 1999), 147.

25 "Emigration," December 1, 1851, PRONI, D3618/D/9/3.

26 Clay Gish, "Rescuing the 'Waifs and Strays' of the City: The Western Emigration Program of the Children's Aid Society," *Journal of Social History* 33, no. 1 (1999): 121–41.

27 On nineteenth-century workers' legal efforts to recover withheld wages, see Peter Karsten, *Heart versus Head: Judge-Made Law in Nineteenth-Century America* (Chapel Hill: University of North Carolina Press, 1997), 157–89. Karsten actually concludes that judges in the Midwest and South were more sympathetic than previously assumed—although this did not change the limited possibilities for economic redress that servants working without contracts had. On character references, see Bruce Robbins, *The Servant's Hand: English Fiction from Below* (Durham, NC: Duke University Press, 1993), 36. These points are also discussed in greater detail in chapter 4.

28 Cited in McNeill, *Vere Foster*, 57.

29 Foster was a proponent of the 1849 Encumbered Estates Act, a parliamentary reform measure that gave courts the power to sell mortgaged estates on behalf of encumbered creditors. On the management of Irish landed estates, and

restrictions on their sale and subdivision both before and after the famine, see W. E. Vaughan, *Landlords and Tenants in Mid-Victorian Ireland* (New York: Clarendon Press, 1994).

30  This idea was most famously captured in Frederick Jackson Turner's 1893 declaration that "the existence of an area of free land, its continuous recession, and the advance of American settlement westward, explain American development." Turner, *The Frontier in American History* (New York: Henry Holt, 1921), 1. Historian Duncan Bell demonstrates that intellectuals and politicians on both sides of the Atlantic routinely referenced the overlapping imperial destinies of Great Britain, its settler colonies, and the United States. Bell, *The Idea of Greater Britain: Empire and the Future of World Order* (Princeton, NJ: Princeton University Press, 2007), 231–59.

31  On the ambiguous and situational relationship of Ireland and the Irish to British imperialism, see Kevin Kenny, "Ireland and the British Empire: An Introduction," in *Ireland and the British Empire*, ed. Kenny (New York: Oxford University Press, 2006), 1–26. See also the volume edited by Terrence McDonough, *Was Ireland a Colony? Economics, Politics, Ideology and Culture in the Irish Nineteenth Century* (Dublin: Irish Academic Press, 2005).

32  Belich, *Replenishing the Earth*, 9.

33  Part of the Black Star fleet, the *Washington* crammed more than 911 people into its berths. "Treatment of Emigrants on Passenger Ships" (clipping), *New York Daily Tribune*, n.d., PRONI, D3618/D/4/9.

34  During the trip, Foster—who hid his status as a nobleman and traveled in second class—brought these complaints to the captain of the *Washington* in the form of a petition signed by 120 of his fellow passengers. The captain responded by ordering a shipmate to physically assault Foster for challenging his authority. When he continued to protest, Foster was threatened with confinement by irons.

35  "Emigrant Ship 'Washington,'" Great Britain Parliament House of Commons, *Accounts and Papers of the House of Commons*, vol. 40 (London: House of Commons, 1851). Despite the parliamentary attention that conditions on the *Washington* received, the captain of the ship escaped prosecution.

36  See, for example, Lisa Chilton, *Agents of Empire: British Female Migration to Canada and Australia, 1860–1930* (Toronto: University of Toronto Press, 2007); Clare Midgley, *Feminism and Empire: Women Activists in Imperial Britain, 1790–1865* (New York: Routledge, 2007); Ellen Boucher, *Empire's Children: Child Emigration, Welfare, and the Decline of the British World, 1869–1967* (New York: Cambridge University Press, 2014), 23–52; Marie Ann Steiner, *Servants Depots in Colonial South Australia* (Adelaide: Wakefield Press, 2009); Robin Haines, "'The Idle and the Drunken Won't Do There': Poverty, the New Poor Law and Nineteenth-Century Government-Assisted Emigration to Australia from the United Kingdom," *Australian Historical Studies* 27, no. 108 (April 1997): 1–21; and Paula Hamilton, "'The Servant Class': Poor Female Migration to Australia in the Nineteenth Century," in *Poor Australian Immigrants in the Nineteenth Century*, ed. Eric Richards (Canberra: Australian National University, 1991).

37 "Emigration to North America," circular, March 31, 1852. PRONI, D3618/D/9/8; "Emigration to America," circular, April 1854. PRONI, D3618/D/9/14.

38 On British liberals' support of empire, see Theodore Koditshek, *Liberalism, Imperialism, and the Historical Imagination: Nineteenth Century Visions of a Greater Britain* (New York: Cambridge University Press), 2011; Uday Singh Mehta, *Liberalism and Empire* (Chicago: University of Chicago Press, 1999); and Catherine Hall, *Civilising Subjects: Metropole and Colony in the English Imagination, 1830–1867* (Chicago: University of Chicago Press, 2002). See also Eileen P. Sullivan, "Liberalism and Imperialism: J.S. Mill's Defense of the British Empire," *Journal of the History of Ideas* 44, no. 4 (1983): 599–617.

39 *Newry Examiner and Louth Advertiser*, March 2, 1857, cited in Marjorie Kohli, *The Golden Bridge: Young Immigrants to Canada, 1833–1939* (Toronto: Natural Heritage Books, 2003), 331.

40 On the ways in which primitive accumulation and the seizure of indigenous and common lands represent an invisible feature in the history of capitalism, see Michael Perelman, *The Invention of Capitalism: Classical Political Economy and the Secret History of Primitive Accumulation* (Durham, NC: Duke University Press, 2000) and John C. Weaver, *The Great Land Rush and the Making of the Modern World, 1650–1900* (Montreal: McGill-Queen's University Press, 2003). On these processes in the late nineteenth-century United States, see Karen Hansen, *Encounter on the Great Plains: Scandinavian Settlers and the Dispossession of Dakota Indians, 1890–1930* (New York: Oxford University Press, 2013), 1–28.

41 Ireland's relief policies were closely modeled on those in England, and reforms to the workhouse system there. In both places, changes to relief reflected the ascendancy of liberal political economy in the British Empire, and the belief that welfare had to be tied to wage-labor discipline. On these changes, see Polanyi, *Great Transformation*; Procacci, "Social Economy and the Government of Poverty"; and Jacques Donzelot, "The Mobilization of Society," in Burchell, Gordon, and Miller, *Foucault Effect*, 169–80. On similar changes to the governance of poverty in the United States, see Rockman, *Scraping By*, 158–93.

42 "Emigration," December 1, 1851, PRONI, D3618/D/9/3.

43 Moran, *Sending Out Ireland's Poor*, 142–58.

44 On the racial stereotypes British politicians and the media deployed in opposition to Irish self-governance, see L. Perry Curtis, Jr., *Apes and Angels: The Irishman in Victorian Caricature*, rev. ed. (Washington, DC: Smithsonian Institute Press, 1997), and Michael de Nie, *The Eternal Paddy: Irish Identity and the British Press, 1798–1882* (Madison: University of Wisconsin Press, 2004).

45 Foster, letter to his mother, *Farmer's Gazette*, 1852, PRONI, D3618/D/6/1–9. Foster's first trip to North America lasted from December 1850 until November 1851. He traveled throughout the United States and Canada, from New York to New Orleans to Minnesota and then back via Ontario to Québec. A series of nine

letters that he wrote to his mother during the trip were subsequently published in the Irish *Farmer's Gazette* in 1852. The clippings that PRONI has preserved do not, for the most part, include specific dates of publication.

46 Hughes to Foster, August 27, 1856, PRONI, D3618/D/3/2. Proposals calling for the establishment of Irish Catholic settler colonies in rural parts of the American West had circulated since the end of the eighteenth century. The 1850s witnessed a surge in these initiatives, inspired by the comparative successes that German immigrants had experienced in establishing themselves as western freeholders, and by the rise in nativism. Deirdre M. Moloney, *American Catholic Lay Groups and Transatlantic Social Reform in the Progressive Era* (Chapel Hill: University of North Carolina Press, 2002), 74–78. Hughes's willingness to support Foster's assisted emigration plans is particularly noteworthy given the archbishop's public feud with Thomas D'Arcy McGee, the Irish nationalist and journalist who convened the Irish Emigrant Aid Convention in Buffalo in February 1856. Hughes denounced McGee's scheme on the grounds that colonization contributed to the segregation of Irish Catholics from the rest of American society, while weakening the diaspora's urban power base. Henry J. Browne, "Archbishop Hughes and Western Colonization," *Catholic Historical Review* 36, no. 3 (October 1, 1950): 257–85.

47 *Canadian News*, September 3, 1856, cited in Kohli, *Golden Bridge*, 330.

48 "Emigration" (a broadsheet copy of a letter from Foster to the directors of the American Emigrant's Friend Society, Philadelphia), PRONI, D3618/D/9/6.

49 On the politics of respectability as practiced by black elites in the late nineteenth century, see Evelyn Brooks Higginbotham, *Righteous Discontent: The Women's Movement in the Black Baptist Church, 1880–1920* (Cambridge, MA: Harvard University Press, 1994).

50 Foster, letter to his mother, *Farmer's Gazette*, 1852, PRONI, D3618/D/6/1–9.

51 Cited in McNeill, *Vere Foster*, 83.

52 Foster, letter to his mother, *Farmer's Gazette*, July 1852, PRONI, D3618/D/6/1–9.

53 Foster, *Work and Wages; or, The Penny Emigrant's Guide to the United States and Canada*, 5th ed. (London: W. & F. G. Cash, 1855), 5.

54 Thomas Bouchi[?] to Foster, October 24, 1852, PRONI, D3618/D/8/6.

55 Belich, *Replenishing the Earth*, 229–60; William Cronon, *Nature's Metropolis: Chicago and the Great West* (New York: Norton, 1991), 55–96.

56 Foster's assistance between 1850 and 1857 coincided with an economic boom period in the region called the "Old Northwest," which ended with the Panic of 1857. Cities and towns such as Janesville welcomed the railroad, at least in its initial days, as a means to facilitate the import of new settlers. Overall, the white populations of Ohio, Indiana, Illinois, Michigan, and Wisconsin—where Foster sent many of his emigrants in the 1850s—would increase from roughly 250,000 people in 1815, to over six million by 1860. Belich, *Replenishing the Earth*, 225.

57 M. Justille McDonald, *History of the Irish in Wisconsin in the Nineteenth Century* (Washington, DC: Catholic University of America Press, 1954), 26, 62–66.

58  Boydston, "Woman Who Wasn't There," 204.

59  Foster, *Work and Wages*, 12–16.

60  Foster to the editor of *Irish American*, June 26, 1864 (clipping), PRONI, D3618/D/6/11; Amelia Ryerse Harris, "Diary of Amelia Ryerse Harris, July, 1864," in *The Eldon House Diaries: Five Women's Views of the 19th Century*, ed. Robin Harris and Terry Harris (Toronto: Champlain Society, 1994), 225–26.

61  "Female Emigration and Its Abuses," *Irish American*, August 29, 1857, PRONI, D3618/D/5/3; "Sea Monsters and Irish Victims," *Irish Vindicator*, August 15, 1857, PRONI, D3618/D/5/1; "Female Emigrants and Ship-Discipline," *New York Tablet*, August 22, 1857, PRONI, D3618/D/5/2. For a reprint of Smith's deposition, see "The Outcasts of Society," *Catholic Institute Magazine* 3, no. 2 (November 1857): 56.

62  "Morality on Shipboard," *New York Daily Tribune*, August 8, 1857; Handbill, August 4, 1857, PRONI, D3618/D/5/5.

63  Dilworth to Foster, January 23, 1855, PRONI, D3618/D/8/8.

64  Cited in McNeill, *Vere Foster*, 89.

65  On Farnham and the Women's Protective Emigration Society, see Jo Ann Levy, *Unsettling the West: Eliza Farnham and Georgiana Bruce Kirby in Frontier California* (Santa Clara, CA: Heyday Books, 2004), 155–64.

66  Elizabeth Phelps and Eliza Farnham, "Letter from New York," *California Farmer*, February 5, 1858; *New York Daily Tribune*, December 14, 1857.

67  Marilyn Irvin Holt, *The Orphan Trains: Placing Out in America* (Lincoln: University of Nebraska Press, 1994), 96–97; Elizabeth Phelps and Eliza Farnham, "Letter from Mrs. Eliza W. Farnham," *California Farmer*, April 9, 1858.

68  Farnham, "Women's Protective Emigration Society," *New York Daily Tribune*, January 19, 1858; "Girls for the West," *New York Daily Tribune*, February 17, 1858. On Catholic anxieties about religious conversions being a feature of the placing out system, see Fitzgerald, *Habits of Compassion*, 78–149.

69  "Help for Women with Small Children Wanted," 1857, PRONI, D3618/D/12/6.

70  Foster, *"Incidents of Travel in America": A Lecture Delivered by Vere Foster, Esq., in the Rosemary Street Lecture Hall, Belfast, on the 27th January, 1879* (Belfast, 1879), 10, PRONI, D3618/D/6/13.

71  Cited in Jean Harvey Baker, *Mary Todd Lincoln: A Biography* (New York: Norton, 2008), 107. Lincoln was more cautious when it came to nativism, and worked diligently to recruit Irish immigrants to the causes of free labor and soil. See Kevin Kenny, "Abraham Lincoln and the American Irish," *American Journal of Irish Studies* 10 (2013): 37–62.

72  Holt, *Orphan Trains*, 96–97.

73  See table 12, appendix, in Miller, *Emigrants and Exiles*, 581.

74  Fitzgerald, *Habits of Compassion*, 56.

75  "Population of the United States (by States and Territories) as Native and Foreign-Born, and of Foreign Parentage, at the Census of 1870," in *Ninth Census, Volume 1: The Statistics of the United States Population* (Washington, DC: GPO, 1872), 340 (table 6); Katzman, *Seven Days a Week*, 67.

76 William M. Bobo, *Glimpses of New York City* (Charleston: J. J. McCarter, 1852), 187–94, 191; Frederick Law Olmsted, *A Journey in the Seaboard Slave States: With Remarks on Their Economy* (New York: Dix & Edwards, 1856), 31.

77 Bobo, *Glimpses of New York City*, 192.

78 On Leech's "servantgalism" series, see Marion Harry Spielman, *The History of "Punch"* (London: Cassell, 1895), 422–23. In sympathetic American commentaries on the plight of the British and Irish working classes, the phrases "wage slavery" and "white slavery" were often used interchangeably. See, for instance, John C. Cobden, *The White Slaves of England* (Auburn, NY: Miller, Orton & Mulligan, 1854). For further elaboration of this point, see also Peck, "Making Sense of White Slavery and Whiteness," 41–63.

79 [Mother Mary Teresa] Austin Carroll, *Leaves from the Annals of the Sisters of Mercy* (New York: Catholic Publication Society, 1889), 3:177. Hanna Flynn was likely a composite figure used to describe the common experiences of Irish immigrant women rather than a specific individual. Fitzgerald, *Habits of Compassion*, 59–61.

80 For a more detailed examination of this point, see Urban, "Irish Domestic Servants."

81 E. L. Godkin, *Reflections and Comments, 1865–1895* (New York: Scribner's, 1895), 58. This essay was originally published in 1873 in Godkin's *Nation*, under the title "The Morals and Manners of the Kitchen." During Froude's visit to the United States, he engaged in a tempestuous exchange with the Irish-born priest Thomas Burke over whether Britain's forceful response to the 1867 Fenian uprisings in Ireland was justifiable. See Julia Markus, *J. Anthony Froude: The Last Undiscovered Victorian* (New York: Scribner's, 2005), 124–29.

On Irish servants' response to having to serve Froude, see William Henry Hurlbert, *Ireland under Coercion: The Diary of an American*, vol. 1 (Edinburgh: D. Douglas, 1888), 5. For media coverage of Irish servants' support for nationalist causes, see "The United States," *Times of London*, September 27, 1867; "News," *Times of London*, September 30, 1867; "The United States," *Times of London*, June 9, 1870; "American Opinion and Home Rule," *Times of London*, October 11, 1887; and "The Irish Parties: Mr. Parnell's Manifesto to the Irish Americans," *Times of London*, March 14, 1891. See also Niall Whelehan, *The Dynamiters: Irish Nationalism and Political Violence in the Wider World, 1867–1900* (New York: Cambridge University Press, 2012), 217–45.

82 "The Irish Declaration of Independence," *Puck*, May 9, 1883. Frederick Opper was the artist of the cartoon, although it is unclear if he wrote the accompanying commentary.

83 On the role that race played in the social construction of working women's gender, see Gail Bederman, *Manliness and Civilization: A Cultural History of Gender and Race in the United States, 1880–1917* (Chicago: University of Chicago Press, 1995), 25; and Cynthia Russett, *Sexual Science: The Victorian Construction of Womanhood* (Cambridge, MA: Harvard University Press, 1991), 144–48.

84 Robert Tomes, "Your Humble Servant," *Harper's Monthly*, June 1864, 57.

85 Carroll, *Leaves from the Annals of the Sisters of Mercy*, 3:179.

86 John Francis Maguire, *The Irish in America* (1868; repr., New York: Arno Press, 1969), 334–35.

87 During the 1860s and 1870s, Foster's interests gravitated toward efforts to improve the national school system in Ireland. Consistent with his liberal beliefs, Foster pushed for the creation of an Irish school system equal to those found in England and Scotland. Improved educational opportunities, Foster argued, were an essential riposte to the claims of nationalists that Ireland was the neglected and unjustly treated member of what was supposed to be a union of equals. Foster is estimated to have contributed funds to the renovation and improvement of upward of two thousand schools in Ireland, using his own money to supplement what he believed were inadequate government outlays. In the late 1860s, Foster also became involved in the creation of the Irish National Teachers' Organisation, a precursor to the Irish teachers' union. He became famous in this period for the eponymous copybooks that he produced and distributed, as a commercial venture, which offered tutorials on how to write in the cursive script. Foster would also publish drawing books for illustrators. McNeill, *Vere Foster*, 101–27, 149–80. See also Irish National Teachers' Organisation, Bangor Congress Committee, *A Short Biographical Study of Vere Foster, First President* (Belfast: Duffy Bros., 1956).

88 On the 1879 crisis in Ireland, and the rise of the Land League, see Barbara Lewis Solow, *The Land Question and the Irish Economy* (Cambridge, MA: Harvard University Press, 1971); Paul Bew, *Land and the National Question in Ireland, 1858–1882* (Atlantic Highlands, NJ: Humanities Press, 1979); Vaughan, *Landlords and Tenants*; and Donnacha Seán Lucey, *Land, Popular Politics and Agrarian Violence in Ireland: The Case of County Kerry* (Dublin: University College Dublin Press, 2011), 1–7. After the 1840s famine, there was an increase in the export of products like butter, beef, and mutton from midsized and large farms. The South and West of Ireland, which remained disproportionately divided into small farms and cottier tenancies, did not experience the same gains in production.

89 "Distress in the West of Ireland," *Northern Whig*, January 12, 1880, PRONI, D3618/D/13/1.

90 See the letters of application included in PRONI, D3618/D/14. On the multiple steps required for an emigrant to leave Ireland, see Anne O'Connell, "Take Care of the Emigrant Girls," *Eire/Ireland* 35, nos. 2/3 (2000–2001): 102–33.

91 *Freeman's Journal*, May 15, 1880; "Anti-Eviction Demonstration at Proughlish (Leitrim)," *Nation*, September 25, 1880; "Assisted Emigration" flyer, September 1880, annotated by "Captain Rock," PRONI, D3618/ D/13/3.

92 "A Returned Female Emigrant," *Freeman's Journal*, August 17, 1883.

93 "The Emigration Question," *Nation*, October 18, 1884.

94 Charlotte Grace O'Brien, "The Emigrant in New York," *Nineteenth Century*, October 1884, 546. On O'Brien's work in the field of migrant protection—where she often made arguments quite similar to Foster's—see Moloney, *American Catholic Lay Groups*, 91–100. Foster's response to O'Brien's criticisms is cited in McNeill, *Vere Foster*, 198.

95   Eric Foner, "Class, Ethnicity, and Radicalism in the Gilded Age: The Land League in Irish-America," in *Politics and Ideology in the Age of the Civil War* (New York: Oxford University Press, 1980), 150–200.

96   "To Regulate Immigration," 50th Cong., 2nd sess., House Report 3792, January 19, 1889.

97   "Government Emigration from Ireland," J. J. Piatt, U.S. Consul, Cork, to Department of State, July 25, 1883, National Archives and Records Administration, Department of State, Record Group 59, *Despatches from U.S. Consuls in Cork, 1800–1909* (microform), vol. 9 (microform reel 9); U.S. Congress, House of Representatives, *Testimony Taken by the Select Committee of the House of Representatives to Inquire into the Alleged Violation of the Laws Prohibiting the Importation of Contract Laborers, Paupers, Convicts, and Other Classes*, 50th Cong., 1st sess., 1888, Misc. Doc. 572, 10 (second section).

98   *Freeman's Journal*, November 23, 1882; "Mr. Vere Foster's Emigration Schemes: Alleged Extensive Frauds," *Kildare Observer*, November 25, 1882.

99   "Beaverline" (advertisement), *Kildare Observer*, March 17, 1883; for a sampling of the travel tickets Foster received, see PRONI, D3618/D/7.

100  Moran, *Sending out Ireland's Poor*, 183.

101  Foster to Gladstone, PRONI, T2111/37.

102  *1891 Immigration Act*, 51st Cong., 2nd sess., chap. 551, 26 Stat. 1084.

103  PRONI, D3618/D/29/2–4.

104  Stump to Foster, May 1, 1893, PRONI, D3618/D/29/5.

105  On the 1864 Act to Encourage Immigration, see Zolberg, *Nation by Design*, 168–75. On President Lincoln and the Republican Party's concerns about what constituted free migration, see Jason H. Silverman, *Lincoln and the Immigrant* (Carbondale: Southern Illinois University Press, 2015), 114–17.

## CHAPTER 2. HUMANITARIANISM'S MARKETS

1   On black Reconstruction-era migrations to the Midwest more generally, see Leslie Schwalm, *Emancipation's Diaspora: Race and Reconstruction in the Upper Midwest* (Chapel Hill: University of North Carolina Press, 2009).

2   Josiah Crawford to "Dear Sur," January 23, 1867, Records of the Assistant Commissioner for the District of Columbia, Bureau of Refugees, Freedmen and Abandoned Lands, 1865–1869, RG 105, National Archives Microfilm Publications (hereafter BRFAL-DC), no. M1055, roll 8, Letters Received (hereafter LR). Although I use the shortened "Freedmen's Bureau," the agency's full title, which includes refugees, highlights the federal government's concern with displacement. Bureau officials defended the agency by pointing to the assistance they offered white southerners, and by citing "refugees" as a race-neutral term.

3   "J. Crawford," in *1870 United States Federal Census* (database online) (Provo, UT: Ancestry.com, 2009). On the Union's wartime taxation, see W. Elliot Brownlee, *Federal Taxation in America: A Short History*, 2nd ed. (New York: Cambridge University Press, 2004), 31–36.

4 W. Sherman Savage, "Slavery in the West," in *African Americans on the Western Frontier*, ed. Monroe Lee Billington and Roger D. Hardway (Boulder: University of Colorado Press, 1998), 9–10; see also the appendix, 292. On the military transport and enlistment of enslaved and free black domestic labor, see Lea VanderVelde, *Mrs. Dred Scott: A Life on Slavery's Frontier* (New York: Oxford University Press, 2009).

5 Sojourner Truth, for instance, assisted black refugees' migration to Battle Creek, Michigan, and relied on the contacts and networks forged during her work with the Underground Railroad. She also called on established black residents of northern and western states to aid her plans whenever possible, since she trusted them to be attuned to the potential pitfalls of resettlement. Margaret Washington, *Sojourner Truth's America* (Urbana: University of Illinois Press, 2011), 322–23.

6 In the South vagrancy laws were used to bond black workers to their former plantations and slave owners. In the North, vagrancy laws targeted itinerant populations. Stanley, *From Bondage to Contract*, 98–137; Schmidt, *Free to Work*, 122–64.

7 On white free labor advocates' concept of the social debt that freed persons bore for their emancipation, see Saidiya V. Hartman, *Scenes of Subjection: Terror, Slavery, and Self-Making in Nineteenth-Century America* (New York: Oxford University Press, 1997), 125–63.

8 Hartman, *Scenes of Subjection*, 116–17, 121. See also Eric Foner, *Reconstruction: America's Unfinished Revolution, 1863–1877*, 3rd ed. (New York: Harper, 2002), 103–10; Julie Saville, *The Work of Reconstruction: From Slave to Wage Laborer in South Carolina 1860–1870* (New York: Cambridge University Press, 1996); and Schmidt, *Free to Work*, 93–121.

9 This is not to ignore that both black and white men served as valets and body servants before the war. But the war expanded the domestic labor that male servants performed. On the racialization of domestic labor in military contexts more generally, see Wexler, *Tender Violence*, 15–51.

10 Most historians focus on federal refugee policies first adopted in the aftermath of the Second World War. This clunky periodization does not account for various programs that administered to internally displaced persons, which date to the American Revolution. For an exploration that takes a more expansive genealogical approach to what has constituted the United States' refugee policies in different eras, see Evan Taparata, "No Asylum for Mankind: The Creation of Refugee Law and Policy in the United States, 1787–1924" (PhD diss., University of Minnesota, 2016).

11 I elaborate on this point in Andrew Urban, "Asylum in the Midst of Chinese Exclusion: Pershing's Punitive Expedition and the Columbus Refugees from Mexico, 1916–1921," *Journal of Policy History* 23 (Spring 2011): 204–29. The 1948 Displaced Persons Act, which introduced the first federal policy that provided wide-reaching statutory guidelines for the entry of migrants classified as refugees, included provisions that individuals and families seeking entry had to have

sponsors willing to provide employment and housing, as the epilogue to this book examines in greater detail.

12 The philosopher Giorgio Agamben argues that concentration and refugee camps represent spaces that geographically exemplify what he theorizes is the state of exception. Subject to sovereign rule, yet held distinct from the sovereign body, refugees are both the responsibility of the state yet outside its protections. Agamben, "Beyond Human Rights," in *Means Without End: Notes on Politics* (Minneapolis: University of Minnesota Press, 2000); see also Agamben, *Homo Sacer: Sovereign Power and Bare Life*, trans. Kevin Attell (Stanford, CA: Stanford University Press, 1998), 166–80. As theorist Ewa Plonowska Ziarek argues, one of the limits of Agamben's framing is that he does not explain how "the violent production of social death functions as a hidden territory not only of politics but also of commodity exchange," a point that is particularly relevant to the idea that refugees' and camp occupants' lack of formal or social citizenship makes them especially fungible as labor. Ziarek, "Bare Life on Strike: Notes on the Biopolitics of Race and Gender," *South Atlantic Quarterly* 107, no. 1 (December 2008): 96. See also Orlando Paterson, *Slavery and Social Death: A Comparative Study* (Cambridge, MA: Harvard University Press, 1982).

13 Chad Alan Goldberg, *Citizens and Paupers: Relief, Rights, and Race, from the Freedmen's Bureau to Workfare* (Chicago: University of Chicago Press, 2008), 31–75; Robert Harrison, *Washington during Civil War and Reconstruction: Race and Radicalism* (New York: Cambridge University Press, 2011), 105.

14 William Cohen, *At Freedom's Edge: Black Mobility and the Southern White Quest for Racial Control, 1861–1915* (Baton Rouge: Louisiana State University Press, 1991), 78–108; V. Jacque Voegeli, "A Rejected Alternative: Union Policy and the Relocation of Southern 'Contrabands' at the Dawn of Emancipation," *Journal of Southern History* 69, no. 4 (2003): 765–90.

15 SenGupta, *From Slavery to Poverty*, 57.

16 Dudden, *Serving Women*, 60; and Leslie Harris, *In the Shadow of Slavery: African Americans in New York City, 1626–1863* (Chicago: University of Chicago Press, 2003), 183. For a discussion of domestic labor in antebellum Baltimore, where employers relied on slaves they either leased or owned as well as free laborers, see Rockman, *Scraping By*, 100–131.

17 Kathleen Brown, "Body Work in the Antebellum United States," in Stoler, *Haunted by Empire*, 213–39.

18 Cited in Harris, *In the Shadow of Slavery*, 233–34.

19 Martin R. Delany, "Young Women," in *Martin R. Delany: A Documentary Reader*, ed. Robert S. Levine (Chapel Hill: University of North Carolina Press, 2003), 35.

20 Martin R. Delany, *The Condition, Elevation, Emigration, and Destiny of the Colored People of the United States* (Philadelphia, 1852).

21 Delany's vision aligned with that of white urban laborers, whose political activism in the 1850s took shape in groups like Young America, which

advocated for greater landowning opportunities. See Mark A. Lause, *Young America: Land, Labor, and the Republican Community* (Urbana: University of Illinois Press, 2005).

22  Harris, *In the Shadow of Slavery*, 232–33. For a broader exploration of Delany's philosophy on emigration, see Ethan J. Kytle, *Romantic Reformers and the Antislavery Struggle in the Civil War Era* (New York: Cambridge University Press, 2014), 159–205.

23  Isabella Furth, "Manifest Destiny, Manifest Domesticity, and the Leaven of Whiteness in *Uncle Tom's Cabin*," *Arizona Quarterly* 55, no. 2 (Summer 1999): 31–55.

24  Leon F. Litwack, *North of Slavery* (Chicago: University of Chicago Press, 1965), 72; Welke, *Law and the Borders of Belonging*, 48.

25  "The 'Contraband' Negros: What Shall We Do with Them?," *Independent*, July 18, 1861.

26  Horace James, *Annual Report of the Superintendent of Negro Affairs in North Carolina, 1864: With an Appendix Containing the History and Management of the Freedmen in This Department Up to June 1st, 1865* (Boston: W.F. Brown & Company, 1865), 46.

27  Kate Masur, " 'A Rare Phenomenon of Philological Vegetation': The Word 'Contraband' and the Meanings of Emancipation in the United States," *Journal of American History* 93, no. 4 (Spring 2007): 1056.

28  Capt. F. S. Winslow to M. C. Meigs, August 5, 1863, in *Freedom: Series 1, Volume 2: The Wartime Genesis of Free Labor: The Upper South: A Documentary History of Emancipation, 1861–1867*, ed. Ira Berlin et al. (New York: Cambridge University Press, 1993), 398.

29  U.S. Congress, Senate, *Message of the President of the United States Communicating a Letter Addressed to Him from a Committee of Gentlemen Representing the Freedman's Aid Societies of Boston, New York, Philadelphia, and Cincinnati, in Relation to the Freedmen under the Proclamation of Emancipation*, December 17, 1863, 38th Cong., 1st sess., 1863, S. Ex. Doc. 1, 5; American Freedmen's Inquiry Commission, *Records of the American Freedmen's Inquiry Commission, Final Report*, Senate Executive Document 53, 38th Cong., 1st sess., 1864.

30  Lewis C. Lockwood to Hon. Senator Wilson, January 29, 1862, in Berlin et al., *Freedom*, 112–13. On policies at Fortress Monroe more generally, see Willie Rose, *Rehearsal for Reconstruction: The Port Royal Experiment* (Athens: University of Georgia Press, 1999). On the tax at the Freedman's Village, see Micki McElya, *The Politics of Mourning: Death and Honor in Arlington National Cemetery* (Cambridge, MA: Harvard University Press, 2016), 74–77.

31  See, for example, Glenn David Brasher, *The Peninsula Campaign and the Necessity of Emancipation: African Americans and the Fight for Freedom* (Chapel Hill: University of North Carolina Press, 2014); and Christian Samito, *Becoming American Under Fire: Irish Americans, African Americans, and the Politics of Citizenship during the Civil War Era* (Ithaca, NY: Cornell University Press, 2009).

32  McElya, *Politics of Mourning*, 8.

33  Charles G. Leland, "Ana of the War. VI. The Contraband," *United States Service Magazine*, October 1865.

34  American Freedmen's Inquiry Commission, *Records of the American Freedmen's Inquiry Commission*, 22–23.

35  Cited in David Cecere, "Carrying the Home Front to War: Soldiers, Race, and New England Culture during the Civil War," in *Union Soldiers and the Northern Home Front: Wartime Experiences, Postwar Adjustments*, ed. Paul Alan Cimbala and Randall M. Miller (New York: Fordham University Press, 2002), 306; 317.

36  On the conscription of newly arrived Irish immigrants, see Scott Reynolds Nelson, "After Slavery: Forced Drafts of Irish and Chinese Labor in the American Civil War, or The Search for Liquid Labor," in *Many Middle Passages: Forced Migration and the Making of the Modern World*, ed. Emma Christopher, Cassandra Pybus, and Marcus Rediker (Berkeley: University of California Press, 2007), 150–64.

37  "The Scare Domestic," *New York Daily Tribune*, July 24, 1863; "Irish Servant Girls of New York," *Freeman's Journal*, August 14, 1863.

38  A copy of Oliver's correspondence was included in a letter that Lucy Chase, a missionary from Worcester, Massachusetts, received while stationed at Fort Monroe, Virginia. Oliver to C. B. Wilder, September 22, 1863, in *Dear Ones at Home: Letters from Contraband Camps*, ed. Henry Lee Swint (Nashville: Vanderbilt University Press, 1966), 87–88.

39  Cited in Harrison, *Washington during Civil War and Reconstruction*, 94; Mary Sears to O. O. Howard, March 24, 1867, BRFAL-DC, roll 8, LR; Janette Thomas Greenwood, *First Fruits of Freedom: The Migration of Former Slaves and Their Search for Equality in Worcester, Massachusetts, 1862–1900* (Chapel Hill: University of North Carolina Press, 2010), 120.

40  Harris, *In the Shadow of Slavery*, 285–86; Edwin G. Burrows and Mike Wallace, *Gotham: A History of New York City to 1898* (New York: Oxford University Press, 2000), 897.

41  Mary E. Dodge, "Our Contraband," *Harper's New Monthly Magazine*, August 1863, 396.

42  Masur, "'A Rare Phenomenon of Philological Vegetation,'" 1065, 1067.

43  Masur highlights the narrator's three Irish servants' racist opposition to Aggie's hiring as indicative of northern Democrats and Irish immigrants' reluctance to accept abolition as a war goal. While this is certainly true, Dodge's depictions of the Irish servants' actions also address workplace conflicts that existed before Aggie's arrival.

44  Dodge, "Our Contraband," 396–97.

45  Harriet Beecher Stowe, "The Chimney-Corner for 1866. Being a Family-Talk on Reconstruction," *Atlantic Monthly*, January 1866, 91. On Stowe's views concerning household work and free labor ideology more generally, see Klein, "Harriet Beecher Stowe."

46  Price, "Revolt in the Kitchen," 143–44.

47 This ignored, as historian Walter Johnson has shown, how enslaved persons were coerced and pressured to participate in marketing and selling their own labor, despite being unfree. Johnson, *Soul by Soul*, 162–88.

48 Oliver Otis Howard, "Circular no. 2," May 19, 1865, U.S. Congress, House of Representatives, in *Freedmen's Bureau. Message from the President of the United States, Transmitting Report of the Commissioner of the Bureau of Refugees, Freedmen, and Abandoned Lands*, 39th Cong., 1st sess., 1865, H. Exec. Doc. no. 11, 44.

49 Capt. Geo. A. Armes to Lieut. Col. John F. Marsh, September 6, 1865, and 2nd Lieut. Jas M. Johnston to Capt. Jacob F. Chur, July 19, 1866, both in *Freedom: A Documentary History of Emancipation, 1861–1867: Series 3, Volume 1: Land and Labor, 1866–1867*, ed. René Hayden et al. (Chapel Hill: University of North Carolina Press, 2013), 388, 433–34. On the efforts of freedwomen to avoid being hired by former masters, see Hunter, *To 'Joy My Freedom*, 21–43. See also Lewis C. Chartock, "A History and Analysis of Labor Contracts Administered by the Bureau of Refugees, Freedmen, and Abandoned Lands in Edgefield, Abbeville and Anderson Counties, South Carolina, 1865–1868" (PhD diss., Bryn Mawr College, 1974).

50 Foner, *Reconstruction*, 166–68; Laura Edwards, *Gendered Strife and Confusion: The Political Culture of Reconstruction* (Urbana: University of Illinois Press, 1998), 78.

51 Richardson, *Death of Reconstruction*, 6–7.

52 McElya, *Politics of Mourning*, 66–67.

53 Claude F. Oubre, *Forty Acres and a Mule: The Freedmen's Bureau and Black Land Ownership* (Baton Rouge: Louisiana State University Press, 1978), 81–93.

54 Oliver Otis Howard, "Report of the Commissioners of the Bureau of Refugees, Freedmen, and Abandoned Lands," in U.S. Congress, House of Representatives, *Freedmen's Bureau*, H. Exec. Doc. no. 11, 12.

55 Luskey, "Special Marts," 362.

56 Oliver S. St. John to Col. J. B. Kinsman, November 19, 1864, in Berlin et al., *Freedom: Series 1, Volume 2*, 204–6.

57 Solicitation by the New York and Brooklyn Freedmen's Employment Bureau, 1864, Collection of Brooklyn, N.Y., Civil War Relief Associations Records, Ephemera and Other Material, ARC.245, box 5, folder 7, Brooklyn Historical Society.

58 Carol Faulkner, *Women's Radical Reconstruction: The Freedmen's Aid Movement* (Philadelphia: University of Pennsylvania Press, 2007), 119.

59 "Letter from the Baltimore Association for the Moral and Educational Improvement of Colored People," *Pennsylvania Freedmen's Bulletin*, February 1865, 4–5.

60 C. H. Howard to Lewis Tappan, April 21, 1866, BRFAL-DC, roll 1, Letters Sent (hereafter LS).

61 Harrison, *Washington during Civil War and Reconstruction*, 61.

62 McElya, *Politics of Mourning*, 58–94.

63 C. H. Howard to Josephine Griffing, October 15, 1866, BRFAL-DC, roll 1, LS.

64 "Testimony by the Superintendent of Contrabands at Camp Barker before the American Freedmen's Inquiry Commission," in Berlin et al., *Freedom: Series 1, Volume 2*, 293.

65  Harrison, *Washington during Civil War and Reconstruction*, 67–68.

66  John Eaton to George B. Carse, June 16, 1865, and C. H. Howard to Anna Lowell, April 4, 1867, BRFAL-DC, roll 1, LS.

67  C. H. Howard to the Committee of the Industrial School, May 6, 1867, BRFAL-DC, roll 1, LS.

68  Joshua Rosenbloom, *Looking for Work, Searching for Workers: American Labor Markets during Industrialization* (New York: Cambridge University Press, 2002), 38. As William Cohen argues, black labor migrations during Reconstruction tended to follow interregional routes, with workers moving farther south and west within the former states of the Confederacy. See Cohen, *At Freedom's Edge*, 109–37. During the first two decades of the twentieth century, when black migration unassisted by the federal government became a more tangible and pressing concern, southern states attempted to criminalize the actions of labor brokers out of concerns that white planters would be deprived of sufficient labor. See William J. Breen, "Sectional Influences on National Policy: The South, the Labor Department, and the Wartime Mobilization, 1917–1918," in *The South Is Another Land: Essays on the Twentieth Century South*, ed. Bruce Clayton and John A. Salmond (Westport, CT: Greenwood, 1987), 69–84; and David E. Bernstein, *Only One Place of Redress: African Americans, Labor Regulations, and the Courts from Reconstruction to the New Deal* (Durham, NC: Duke University Press, 2001), 8–27.

69  Quoted in Harrison, *Washington during Civil War and Reconstruction*, 97.

70  John Grines to O. O. Howard, March 14, 1867, BRFAL-DC, roll 8, LR.

71  S. N. Clark to E. A. Merrell, February 27, 1867, and Clark to George W. Pratt, December 20, 1866, BRFAL-DC, roll 1, LS.

72  "Interview with the *Times* (London) Correspondent," April 12, 1866, in *The Papers of Andrew Johnson: February—July 1866*, vol. 10, ed. Paul Bergeron (Knoxville: University of Tennessee Press, 1967), 406–9; see also Harrison, *Washington during Civil War and Reconstruction*, 88.

73  C. H. Howard to Lewis Tappan, April 21, 1866, BRFAL-DC, roll 1, LS.

74  Clark to Pratt, December 20, 1866, BRFAL-DC, roll 1, LS.

75  U.S. Department of the Interior, *Register of Officers and Agents, Civil, Military, and Naval, in the Service of the United States, on the Thirtieth of September, 1867* (Washington, DC: GPO, 1868), 192. For 1870 income data, see Clarence D. Long, *Wages and Earnings in the United States: 1860–1890* (Princeton, NJ: Princeton University Press, 1960), 39–49.

76  Tilmon to Howard, February 6, 1867, BRFAL-DC, roll 7, LR; William Rogers to Tilmon, February 5, 1867, and Rogers to Tilmon, February 7, 1867, BRFAL-DC, roll 1, LS. See also Faulkner, *Women's Radical Reconstruction*, 124–25.

77  Of the 621 individuals sent to Cambridge, Elizabeth Pleck counted only 56 relocated migrants who remained in the area in 1870. Pleck, "Black Migration to Boston in the Late Nineteenth Century" (PhD diss., Brandeis University, 1973), 31–38. See also Faulkner, *Women's Radical Reconstruction*, 119–24.

78  L. L. Dutcher to Griffing, February 20, 1867, BRFAL-DC, roll 8, LR.

79 "L. L. Dutcher," in *1870 United States Federal Census* (database online) (Provo, UT: Ancestry.com, 2009).

80 Edward C. Knauer to A. P. Ketchum, April 3, 1867, BRFAL-DC, roll 8, LR.

81 McElya, *Politics of Mourning*, 90–91.

82 "American Seed Store" (advertisement), *Genesee Farmer*, January 1859, 70.

83 Bloss to Clark, March 12, 1867, BRFAL-DC, roll 8, LR.

84 Carleton Mabee, "Sojourner Truth Fights Dependence on Government: Moves Freed Slaves Off Welfare in Washington to Jobs in Upstate New York," *Afro-Americans in New York Life and History* 14 (January 1990): 7–26.

85 Spinner to Griffing, Josephine W. Griffing letters, Rare Book and Manuscript Library, Columbia University Library (hereafter RBML, Columbia), box 1.

86 Harrison, *Washington during Civil War and Reconstruction*, 89–90; Bureau of Refugees, Freedmen, and Abandoned Lands, *Annual Report of the Assistant Commissioner for the District of Columbia and West Virginia, for the Year Ending October 22, 1867* (Washington, DC: GPO, 1867), 12–13.

87 As Harrison notes, one of Griffing's main antagonists was John V. W. Vanderburgh, the local superintendent for the Washington office. Harrison, *Washington during Civil War and Reconstruction*, 83–84.

88 "Josephine Griffing," *Chicago Inter-Ocean*, April 16, 1887, Josephine W. Griffing letters, RBML, Columbia, box 1. For a focused (albeit somewhat outdated and hagiographic) look at Griffing's career, see Keith E. Melder, "Angel of Mercy in Washington: Josephine Griffing and the Freedmen, 1864–1872," *Records of the Columbia Historical Society, Washington, D.C.* 63/65 (1963): 243–72. See also Faulkner, *Women's Radical Reconstruction*, 83–99, 117–31.

89 Melder, "Angel of Mercy in Washington," 252.

90 National Freedman's Relief Association of the District of Columbia, *Third Annual Report of the National Freedman's Relief Association of the District of Columbia* (Washington, DC, 1865), 9.

91 Griffing to Howard, October 20, 1866, BRFAL-DC, roll 7, LR.

92 Greeley to Griffing, September 7, 1870, Josephine W. Griffing letters, RBML, Columbia, box 1. In 1872, Greeley's mounting antagonism toward Reconstruction and his belief that it had accomplished all it needed to as a federal program culminated in his nomination as the Democrats' candidate for president (he would die, having lost the popular vote, before the Electoral College voted). On Greeley's Reconstruction-era views, see Robert Kirkwood, "Horace Greeley and Reconstruction, 1865," *New York History* 40, no. 3 (1959): 270–80; Michael E. Woods, *Emotional and Sectional Conflict in the Antebellum United States* (New York: Cambridge University Press, 2014), 232–40; and Foner, *Reconstruction*, 503–11.

93 "The Freedmen of the Capital," *New York World*, February 25, 1870, RBML, Columbia, box 1.

94 On Ferguson and Sanxter, see Griffing, "An Appeal in Behalf of One [*sic*] of Washington's Slaves," *Washington Chronicle*, n.d., Griffing to Mott, April 22, 1870, Mott to Griffing, May 17, 1870, all in Josephine W. Griffing letters, RBML, Columbia, box 1.

95 Griffing, "Letter from Washington," *Greenwich Times*, Josephine W. Griffing letters, RBML, Columbia, box 1.

96 Minority of the Select Committee on Emancipation, *Report of the Minority of the Select Committee on Emancipation Relative to a Bill to Establish a Bureau of Freedman's Affairs*, January 20, 1864, 38th Cong., 1st sess., Report no. 2, 2.

97 On the discursive and legal construction of free subjects as a comparative endeavor during Reconstruction, see Smith, *Freedom's Frontier*, and Wong, *Racial Reconstruction*.

98 "Margaret Hosmer," in *Appleton's Cyclopedia of American Biography*, vol. 3, ed. James Grant Wilson and John Fiske (New York: D. Appleton, 1887), 286; Oscar Fay Adams, *A Dictionary of American Authors* (Boston: Houghton and Mifflin, 1897), 196.

99 On intertextuality, see Stuart Hall, "The Work of Representation," in *Representation: Cultural Representations and Signifying Practices*, ed. Jessica Evans Hall and Sean Nixon (Thousand Oaks, CA: Sage, 1997), 6; and Patricia Hill Collins, "Mammies, Matriarchs, and Other Controlling Images," in *Black Feminist Thought: Knowledge, Consciousness, and the Politics of Empowerment* (New York: Routledge, 2008), 76–107.

100 As Robin Kelley notes, "Quitting or threatening to quit just prior to an important social affair" was a strategy that black domestic workers frequently deployed to win better wages. Kelley, *Race Rebels: Culture, Politics, and the Black Working Class* (New York: Free Press, 1994), 18; Margaret Hosmer, "Mary Ann and Chyng Loo: Housekeeping in San Francisco," *Lippincott's Magazine*, October 1870, 354–55.

101 Margaret Hosmer, *You-Sing: The Chinaman in California. A True Story of the Sacramento Flood* (Philadelphia: Presbyterian Publication Society, 1868).

102 Hosmer, "Mary Ann and Chyng Loo," 355–57.

103 Ibid., 358–59.

## CHAPTER 3. CHINESE SERVANTS AND THE AMERICAN COLONIAL IMAGINATION

1 "The Chinese Question," *Wasp*, December 21, 1878.

2 *Commercial Herald*, November 29, 1877. As historian Joshua Paddison has documented, even though the restriction movement tried to portray whites as joined together in a united front against Chinese immigration, anti-Catholic nativism was resurgent in the 1870s. During this decade, more than 40 percent of San Francisco's population had been born in Europe, with Irish immigrants representing the largest single nationality within this number. Paddison, *American Heathens: Religion, Race, and Reconstruction in California* (Berkeley: University of California Press, 2012), 77–92. See also Robert Seager, "Some Denominational Reactions to Chinese Immigration to California, 1856–1892," *Pacific Historical Review* 28, no. 1 (1959): 49–66. Into the twentieth century, the identification of anti-Chinese policies with Irish Americans remained prominent. For instance, in 1902 the Chinese foreign legation to the United States referred to exclusionists as the "Irish party."

Michael H. Hunt, *The Making of a Special Relationship: The United States and China to 1914* (New York: Columbia University Press, 1983), 103–4.

3  Sing Lee, "The Irishman Must Go!," *Argonaut*, December 21, 1878.

4  F. A. Bee, *Opening Argument of F. A. Bee before the Joint Committee of the Two Houses of Congress on Chinese Immigration* (San Francisco, 1876), 33.

5  John Bonner, "Labor Question of the Pacific Coast," *Californian*, April 1892, 414. See also Chen, *Chop Suey, USA*, 61.

6  Hoganson, *Consumers' Imperium*, 11. Hoganson has argued that the late nineteenth-century growth in global commerce that Americans enjoyed repre- sented "an imperial buy in." Prior to the middle part of the twentieth century— with the exception of campaigns for tariffs against foreign manufactured goods— few white American wage laborers spent their time protesting the consumption and circulation of commodities that came from abroad, especially when they were the beneficiaries. See also Dana Frank, *Buy American: The Untold Story of Economic Nationalism* (Boston: Beacon, 1999), 33–55, and Woodruff D. Smith, "Complications of the Commonplace: Tea, Sugar, and Imperialism," *Journal of Interdisciplinary History* 23, no. 2 (1992): 259–78.

7  U.S. Congress, Joint Special Committee to Investigate Chinese Immigration, *Re- port of the Joint Special Committee to Investigate Chinese Immigration*, 44th Cong., 2nd sess., 1877, S. Rept. 689, 287. As Paul Kramer notes, in American republican thought, "empire was the tragic fate of republics that, in pursuit of expansion- ary power, crushed their own definitional freedom and virtue. The republic that became an empire had congealed irreversibly into something fundamentally unlike itself." Kramer, "Power and Connection," 1358. On the racial and political ideologies of Pacific World settler colonialism, see Marilyn Lake and Henry Reyn- olds, *Drawing the Global Colour Line: White Men's Countries and the International Challenge of Racial Equality* (Cambridge: Cambridge University Press, 2008).

8  Leach, *Land of Desire*, 131.

9  U.S. Congress, Joint Special Committee to Investigate Chinese Immigration, *Report*, 253. The economic historian Ping Qui, using official census records, tabulated that in 1880, 7,825 Chinese immigrants worked as servants statewide. Ping, *Chinese Labor in California, 1850–1880: An Economic Study* (Madison: State Historical Society of Wisconsin for the Department of History, University of Wis- consin, 1967), 126. On San Francisco's Chinese population, see George E. Waring, Jr., *Reports on the Social Statistics of Cities, Part II* (Washington, DC: GPO, 1887), 800. For the estimate of fourteen thousand Chinese servants, see Thomas Vivian, "John Chinaman in San Francisco," *Scribner's Monthly*, October 1876, 867.

10  Overall, Chinese immigrant laborers' role in building the modern American service economy has been understudied. For exceptions, see Paul C. P. Siu, *The Chinese Laundryman: A Study of Social Isolation*, ed. John Kuo Wei Tchen (New York: New York University Press, 1988), which was first completed as a disserta- tion in 1953. For a more recent study, see Heather R. Lee, "A Life Cooking for Others: The Work and Migration Experiences of a Chinese Restaurant Worker in

New York City, 1920–1946," in *Eating Asian America: A Food Studies Reader*, ed. Robert Ji-Song Ku, Martin F. Manalansan, and Anita Mannur (New York: New York University Press, 2013), 53–77; and Chen, *Chop Suey, USA*, 44–70.

11 Everett Hager Gordon, *An 1886 Chinese Labor Boycott in Los Angeles* (Pasadena, CA: Castle Press, 1982); Grace H. Stimson, *Rise of the Labor Movement in Los Angeles* (Berkeley: University of California Press, 1955), 60–67.

12 Lowe, *Intimacies of Four Continents*, 27; Jung, *Coolies and Cane*, 5. See also Wong, *Racial Reconstruction*. Historians have documented that in the case of Chinese labor migrations to the British West Indies, Cuba, and Peru, many workers were held in a state of multiyear indenture after being coerced or tricked into contracts while still in China. On the "coolie trade" to the Caribbean, see Evelyn Hu-DeHart, "Chinese Coolie Labour in Cuba in the Nineteenth Century: Free Labour or Neo-slavery?," *Slavery and Abolition* 14, no. 1 (April 1993): 67–83; Hu-DeHart, "La Trata Amarilla: The 'Yellow Trade' and the Middle Passage," in Christopher, Pybus, and Rediker, *Many Middle Passages*, 166–83; and Walton Look Lai, *Indentured Labor, Caribbean Sugar: Chinese and Indian Migrants to the British West Indies, 1838–1918* (Baltimore: Johns Hopkins University Press, 1993). Jung argues that prior to the Civil War, proslavery advocates pointed to the condition of Chinese and Indian contract laborers in British colonies to defend the allegedly more humane conditions of slavery (28–32).

13 For a prominent example of the historiography suggesting that Chinese immigrants arrived as bonded laborers, see Patricia Cloud and David W. Galenson, "Chinese Immigration and Contract Labor in the Late Nineteenth Century," *Explorations in Economic History* 24, no. 1 (1987): 22–42. For a critical rebuttal, see Charles McClain, "Chinese Immigration: A Comment on Cloud and Galenson," *Explorations in Economic History* 27, no. 3 (1990): 363–78; and Cloud and Galenson, "Chinese Immigration: Reply to Charles McClain," *Explorations in Economic History* 28, no. 2 (1991): 239–47. The overwhelming majority of Chinese laborers appear to have entered the United States without indentures to specific employers. They worked to satisfy debts because they had obligations to kinship, village, and other mutual networks and to commercial creditors—and not because they faced immediate violence. See Ngai, "Chinese Gold Miners," 1084 and n. 3; Elizabeth Sinn, *Pacific Crossing: California Gold, Chinese Migration, and the Making of Hong Kong* (Hong Kong: Hong Kong University Press, 2013), 45–53; Madeline Hsu, *Dreaming of Gold, Dreaming of Home: Transnationalism and Migration between the United States and South China, 1882–1943* (Stanford, CA: Stanford University Press, 2000), 16–54; and June Mei, "Socioeconomic Origins of Emigration: Guangdong to California, 1850–1882," *Modern China* 5 (October 1979): 463–501. On the financing of European transatlantic migration and the comparable debt obligations and relationships that European migrants entered into as part of the credit-ticket system, see Leslie Page Moch, *Moving Europeans: Migration in Western Europe since 1650*, 2nd ed. (Bloomington: Indiana University Press, 2009), 153–58; and Charles Tilly, "Transplanted Networks," in *Immigration*

*Reconsidered: History, Sociology, and Politics*, ed. Virginia Yans-McLaughlin (New York: Oxford University Press, 1990), 79–95.

14  C. C. Coffin, "China in Our Kitchens," *Atlantic Monthly*, June 1869, 749; "Table Talk," *Putnam's Magazine*, August 1869, 137; Abby Sage Richardson, "A Plea for Chinese Labor," *Scribner's Monthly*, July 1871, 290.

15  See, for instance, Delber McKee, *Chinese Exclusion versus the Open Door Policy, 1900–1906: Clashes over China Policy in the Roosevelt Era* (Detroit: Wayne State University Press, 1977), 15–27; Hunt, *Making of a Special Relationship*, 231–49; and Jennifer Snow, *Protestant Missionaries, Asian Immigrants, and Ideologies of Race in America, 1850–1924* (New York: Routledge, 2007), 55–88.

16  On nineteenth-century racial liberalism and the promotion of Christian universalism, see William R. Hutchison, *Errand to the World: American Protestant Thought and Foreign Missions* (Chicago: University of Chicago Press, 1993), 1–14; Timothy Tseng, "Ministry at Arms' Length: Asian Americans in the Racial Ideology of Mainline Protestants, 1882–1952" (PhD diss., Union Theological Seminary, 1994); Snow, *Protestant Missionaries*, 1–54; Paddison, *American Heathens*, 35–56; and Derek Chang, *Citizens of a Christian Nation: Evangelical Missions and the Problem of Race in the Nineteenth Century* (Philadelphia: University of Pennsylvania Press, 2010), 1–14. Chang and Snow emphasize how universalism often had the effect of exaggerating difference and casting it in a hierarchical light by exaggerating the "progress" that Asian and black Christians had to make in order to overcome their cultural limitations.

17  Lorenzo Sawyer dictations on "Chinese Question," Bancroft Library, University of California, Berkeley, BANC MSS C-D 321.

18  As the political scientist Aristide Zolberg documents, conflicts between protectionist "nativists" and free labor market "capitalists" have been a recurring theme in U.S. policy history and endure to the present. Zolberg, *Nation by Design*, 1–23. As argued here, state-coordinated guestworker programs originated as a compromise between these poles.

19  For theorizations of these processes more generally, see Edna Bonacich, "A Theory of Ethnic Antagonism: The Split Labor Market," *American Sociological Review* 37, no. 5 (1972): 547–59; and Scott Cummings, "White Ethnics, Racial Prejudice, and Labor Market Segmentation," *American Journal of Sociology* 85, no. 4 (1980): 938–50.

20  For sample indentures used to bring Chinese domestic servants over during the Gold Rush, see Jacob P. Leese Papers, California Historical Society, MS OV 10. After the Gold Rush, most migrants' passage tended to be financed by debt to lenders rather than formal indentures with predetermined employers. See Kwang Ki-Chaou's 1883 interview with Hubert Howe Bancroft. Kwang, "The Chinese in America," Bancroft Library, University of California, Berkeley, BANC MSS P-N 2. The traffic and commerce in Chinese women destined for sex work proved to be longer lasting. White Californians' belief that most Chinese women were enslaved as prostitutes, however, was an oversimplification. As historian Stacey Smith notes, "The claim that most Chinese women were enslaved prostitutes resulted

from whites' failure to recognize a range of household relationships—from polygamy to concubinage to domestic servitude—in which economic exchange in women might take place." Smith, *Freedom's Frontier*, 163. See also Judy Yung, *Unbound Feet: A Social History of Chinese Women in San Francisco* (Berkeley: University of California Press, 1995), 15–51.

21 *An Act to Prohibit the "Coolie Trade" by American Citizens in American Vessels*, 12 Stat. 340, chap. 27, 37th Cong., 2nd sess., February 19, 1862, 340–41. As Jung documents, the 1862 act, which was first drafted as a bill prior to the start of the Civil War, received support from anti-slavery activists in Congress. Jung, *Coolies and Cane*, 33–38. On the proposed 1852 California legislation calling for the enforcement of labor contracts, see Liping Zhu, *A Chinaman's Chance: The Chinese on the Rocky Mountain Mining Frontier* (Boulder: University of Colorado Press, 2000), 23.

22 These accounts were compiled in the appendices to J. Tyrwhitt Brooks, M.D. [pseud.], *California. Four Months among the Gold-Finders, Being the Diary of an Expedition from San Francisco to the Gold Districts* (Paris: A. and W. Galignani, 1849), 124, 128. On native Californians and bonded child labor, see Smith, *Freedom's Frontier*, 20–21.

23 "A Letter from Lo-Chum-Qui—Curious Document," *Daily Alta California*, June 23, 1853.

24 "Hardships of Servant Hire," *Sacramento Daily Union*, June 25, 1859.

25 Ngai, "Chinese Gold Miners," 1082–1105.

26 Susan Johnson, *Roaring Camp: The Social World of the California Gold Rush* (New York: Norton, 2000), 99–140.

27 On the role of Chinese labor in the construction of the transcontinental railroad, see Alexander Saxton, "The Army of Canton in the High Sierra," *Pacific Historical Review* 35, no. 2 (1966): 141–52; Paul Ong, "The Central Pacific Railroad and Exploitation of Chinese Labor," *Journal of Ethnic Studies* 13, no. 2 (Summer 1985): 119–24; and Richard White, *Railroaded: The Transcontinentals and the Making of Modern America* (New York: Norton, 2012), 293–304. On the transition of Chinese laborers away from railroad work, see June Mei, "Socioeconomic Developments among the Chinese in San Francisco, 1848–1906," in *Labor Immigration under Capitalism: Asian Workers in the United States before World War II*, ed. Lucie Cheng and Edna Bonacich (Berkeley: University of California Press, 1984), 370–401; and Sucheng Chan, *This Bittersweet Soil: The Chinese in California Agriculture, 1860–1910* (Berkeley: University of California Press, 1986), 45.

28 U.S. Congress, Joint Special Committee to Investigate Chinese Immigration, *Report*, 666–88.

29 A. W. Loomis, "How Our Chinamen Are Employed," *Overland Monthly* 2 (March 1869): 232–33.

30 On the debates surrounding Chinese immigrants and the 1870 Naturalization Act, see Aarim-Heriot, *Chinese Immigrants*, 140–55; and Paddison, *American Heathens*, 11–31.

31 Agoston Haraszthy, "Chinese for Labor," *Pacific Expositor*, December 1860, 263.

32  Fanny Stevenson, "My China Boys," *Lippincott's Magazine*, March 1881, 261.

33  In 1877, for instance, the firms of King and Merritt and Pierce and Company were listed in the *City Directory* in the section titled "Employment Offices—Chinese," alongside four Chinese-owned businesses. Henry Langley, *Langley's San Francisco Directory for 1877* (San Francisco: Francis, Valentine, 1877), 955.

34  *Boston Daily Advertiser*, October 26, 1874; "Ways That Are Dark," *San Francisco Evening Bulletin*, April 11, 1881; and A. D. Richardson, "John," *Atlantic Monthly*, December 1869, 745.

35  As K. Scott Wong argues, nineteenth- and early twentieth-century sources written by Chinese migrants in the United States almost always reflected the perspective of the intellectual, religious, and merchant elite. Their opinions were framed, in part, as repudiations of the myriad attacks on Chinese immigrants' ability to assimilate and contribute to the United States. Wong, "The Transformation of Culture: Three Chinese Views of America," *American Quarterly* 48 (June 1996): 201–32. On the social mobility and transgressions of boundaries that uniquely marked the experiences of the Chinese immigrant elite, see Kenneth H. Marcus and Yong Chen, "Inside and Outside Chinatown: Chinese Elites in Exclusion Era California," *Pacific Historical Review* 80 (August 2011): 369–400.

36  Huie Kin, *Reminiscences* (Peiping: San Yu Press, 1932), 16–35, 28. Food historian Andrew Coe points out that white Americans had an aversion to the more authentic Chinese dishes that immigrant cooks might have prepared, since they believed the cuisine was "odd, smelly, and repulsive" and filled with mysterious ingredients. Coe, *Chop Suey: A Cultural History of Chinese Food in the United States* (New York: Oxford University Press, 2009), 134.

37  Huie, *Reminiscences*, 31.

38  Ira M. Condit, *English and Chinese Reader, with a Dictionary* (New York: American Tract Society, 1882), 40–41.

39  Chen, *Chop Suey, USA*, 66–68.

40  File 14517/2–6, Chinese Arrival Files, San Francisco, Records of the U.S. Immigration and Naturalization Service, RG 85, National Archives, Pacific Region, San Bruno, CA.

41  U.S. Congress, Joint Special Committee to Investigate Chinese Immigration, *Report*, 1174.

42  Cited in Chen, *Chop Suey, USA*, 44.

43  On the role that perceptions of Chinese immigrants' sexuality and gendered behavior played as factors in exclusion, see Eithne Luibhéid, *Entry Denied: Controlling Sexuality at the Border* (Minneapolis: University of Minnesota Press, 2002), 31–54; Nayan Shah, *Contagious Divides: Epidemics and Race in San Francisco's Chinatown* (Berkeley: University of California Press, 2001), 77–104; and Jennifer Ting, "Bachelor Society: Deviant Heterosexuality and Asian American Historiography," in *Privileging Positions: The Sites of Asian American Studies*, ed. Gary Y. Okihiro et al. (Pullman: Washington State University Press, 1995), 271–80. For a broader theoretical examination of how the state constructed sexuality as a

category to be used in determining immigrants' eligibility for entry in the early twentieth century, see Margot Canaday, *The Straight State: Sexuality and Citizenship in Twentieth-Century America* (Princeton, NJ: Princeton University Press, 2011), 19–54.

44 Karen J. Leong, "'A Distinct and Antagonistic Race': Constructions of Chinese Manhood in the Exclusionist Debates, 1869–1878," in *Across the Great Divide: Cultures of Manhood in the American West*, ed. Matthew Basso, Laura McCall, and Dee Garceau (New York: Routledge, 2001), 131–48, 143. See also Robert Lee, *Orientals: Asian Americans in Popular Culture* (Philadelphia: Temple University Press, 1999), 83–105; and, from a more theoretical standpoint, David L. Eng, *Racial Castration: Managing Masculinity in Asian America* (Durham, NC: Duke University Press, 2001), 1–34.

45 On the frequent turnover attributed to white servants' marriages in California, see Edward Young, Department of the Treasury, Bureau of Statistics, *Special Report on Immigration; Accompanying Information for Immigrants Relative to the Prices and Rentals of Land, the Staple Products, Facilities of Access to Market, Cost of Farm Stock, Kind of Labor in Demand in the Western and Southern States, etc., etc.* (Washington, DC: GPO, 1871), 183.

46 Prentice Mulford, "Glimpses of John Chinaman," *Lippincott's Magazine*, February 1873, 224; Harriet Elizabeth Prescott Spofford, *The Servant Girl Question* (Boston: Houghton, Mifflin, 1881), 166.

47 On the background and policy history of the Page Act, see George Peffer, *If They Don't Bring Their Women Here: Chinese Female Immigration before Exclusion* (Champaign: University of Illinois Press, 1999); and Adam McKeown, "Transnational Chinese Families and Chinese Exclusion, 1875–1943," *Journal of American Ethnic History* 18, no. 2 (1999): 73–110.

48 Henry Grimm, *"The Chinese Must Go." A Farce in Four Acts* (San Francisco: A. Bancroft, 1879), 3.

49 "California," *Friend's Review*, January 31, 1880.

50 Sarah Henshaw, "California Housekeepers and Chinese Servants," *Scribner's Monthly*, August 1876, 739.

51 Spofford, *Servant Girl Question*, 167.

52 As Gordon Chang argues, this was a common theme in Americans' and Europeans' depictions of China's "mystique," and a rationale for imperial interventions. See Chang, *Fateful Ties: A History of America's Preoccupation with China* (Cambridge, MA: Harvard University Press, 2015), 49–89.

53 Industrial employers also compared Chinese immigrant workers to machines. In 1903, for instance, Edmund Smith called his new machine for eviscerating and cleaning salmon for canning the "iron chink" in reference to its speed and reliability. Carlos Arnaldo Schwantes, *Hard Traveling: A Portrait of Work Life in the New Northwest* (Lincoln: University of Nebraska Press, 1999), 117.

54 Mary Mapes Dodge, "Miss Maloney on the Chinese Question," *Scribner's Monthly*, January 1871, 350–52.

55 Mulford, "Glimpses of John Chinaman," 224.

56 "Chinese Servants. Some of Johnny's Sayings and Doings" (reprint of *New York Post* article), *Atlanta Constitution*, September 12, 1874.

57 Lee Chew, "The Biography of a Chinaman," *Independent*, February 19, 1903, 423. See also K. Scott Wong, "Cultural Defenders and Brokers: Chinese Responses to the Anti-Chinese Movement," in *Claiming America: Constructing Chinese American Identities during the Exclusion Era*, ed. Wong and Sucheng Chan (Philadelphia: Temple University Press, 1998), 3–40, and Helen H. Jun, "Black Orientalism: Nineteenth-Century Narratives of Race and U.S. Citizenship," *American Quarterly* 58, no. 4 (2006): 1047–66.

58 On the "family wage" and its relationship to industrial homework, see Eileen Boris, *Home to Work: Motherhood and the Politics of Industrial Homework in the United States* (New York: Cambridge University Press, 1994), 81–124; and Stanley, *From Bondage to Contract*, 175–217.

59 John Kuo Wei Tchen, *New York before Chinatown: Orientalism and the Shaping of American Culture, 1776–1882* (Baltimore: Johns Hopkins University Press, 1999), 75–79.

60 The "coming man" was the title for a series of lithographs and accompanying articles that appeared in *Frank Leslie's Illustrated Newspaper* in 1870. The "coming man" referenced both the potential that white capitalists saw in the work ethic of Chinese laborers, and the belief that Chinese immigrants—as "heathens" and unfree subjects—might be elevated to independent manhood through their exposure to Christianity and American progress. Philip P. Choy, Lorraine Dong, and Marlon K. Hom, *Coming Man: 19th Century American Perceptions of the Chinese* (Seattle: University of Washington Press, 1994), 21–24.

61 A. M., "A Glimpse of San Francisco," *Lippincott's Magazine* (June 1870): 647; Spofford, *Servant Girl Question*, 181. The term "John Chinaman" was not unique to domestic service—it was a generic moniker used to describe any male Chinese immigrant, regardless of his occupation. All Chinese immigrants were "John Chinamen" in that they were interchangeable and indistinguishable as individual workers. Tchen, *New York before Chinatown*, 174. According to the *Oxford English Dictionary*, the name "John Chinaman" originated with early nineteenth-century British sailors, who were not interested in learning how to pronounce Chinese names, and generically called the various Chinese interlocutors they encountered "John." *Oxford English Dictionary*, s.v. "John Chinaman," www.oed.com (accessed July 20, 2016).

62 These accounts were excerpted in California newspapers. "The Chinese," *Daily Alta California*, July 16, 1869; "The Chinese Question," *California Farmer*, August 5, 1869. Jung, *Coolies and Cane*, 181–220.

63 On the North Adams strike and the contracted Chinese laborers, see Anthony Lee, *A Shoemaker's Story: Being Chiefly about French Canadian Immigrants, Enterprising Photographers, Rascal Yankees, and Chinese Cobblers in a Nineteenth-Century Factory Town* (Princeton, NJ: Princeton University Press, 2008), and

Frederick Rudolph, "Chinamen in Yankeedom: Anti-unionism in Massachusetts in 1870," *American Historical Review* 53, no. 1 (October 1947): 1–29.

64 "The New Invasion," *New York Daily Tribune*, September 23, 1870; William Shanks, "Chinese Skilled Labor," *Century*, September 1871, 497. See also Daniel Liestman, "Chinese Labor at the Passaic Steam Laundry in Belleville," *New Jersey History* 112, nos. 1–2 (1994): 21–33.

65 *Christian Union*, November 5, 1870.

66 *Boston Daily Advertiser*, November 4, 1870. The *Advertiser* article explaining the failure of Palmer's intelligence office appeared a day before the *Christian Union* article lauding the venture was published. For "Ah" Young's comments on the difficulties in convincing Chinese workers to migrate east, see "Table Talk," *Appleton's Journal of Popular Literature, Science, and Art*, December 3, 1870, 679.

67 Francis A. Walker, "Our Domestic Service," *Scribner's Monthly*, December 1875, 278.

68 Workingman's Party of California, *Chinatown Declared a Nuisance* (San Francisco, 1880).

69 "Chinamen Coming East," *New York Times*, March 4, 1880.

70 "The Chinese in New York," *New York Times*, March 6, 1880; S.H.P., letter to the editor, *New York Herald*, March 14, 1880.

71 On Chinese invasion fiction as a genre, see Wong, *Racial Reconstruction*, 124–74.

72 Plays and musical theater performed in yellowface represented another medium in which conflicts between Irish women and Chinese men were staged. See Krystyn R. Moon, *Yellowface: Creating the Chinese in American Popular Music and Performance, 1850s–1920s* (New Brunswick, NJ: Rutgers University Press, 2004), 45, 54.

73 "Chinese Emigration," *New York Times*, March 20, 1880.

74 In response to Kalloch's threat, members of San Francisco's commercial elite formed the Citizens Protective Union, which caused the pragmatic mayor to retreat from his position. The Protective Union's council claimed in a letter to residents of San Francisco that while "the whole people of California recognize the evils of Chinese emigration," the methods of the current agitation had "brought dishonor upon American civilization." "San Francisco Troubles," *New York Times*, March 10, 1880.

75 See Lee Chew's narrative, which documents this process. Chew, "Biography of a Chinaman," 417–23.

76 Esther Baldwin, "The Chinese Question in the United States," *Gospel in All Lands*, March 15, 1883, 125; *Christian Union*, April 20, 1882.

77 Fuzhou was formerly romanized as Foochow. "Death of a Missionary," *Christian Advocate and Journal*, April 11, 1861. On the prominent role that health concerns played in American missionaries' lives in nineteenth-century China, and how this contributed to a "martyr complex," see Jessie G. Lutz, "Attrition among Protestant Missionaries in China, 1807–1890," *International Bulletin of Missionary Research* 36, no. 1 (2012): 22–27.

78 Quoted in Frances J. Baker, *The Story of the Woman's Foreign Missionary Society of the Methodist Episcopal Church, 1869–1895* (Cincinnati: Curts & Jennings, 1895), 412. On the Baldwins' backgrounds, see also Frances Elizabeth Willard and Mary Ashton Rice Livermore, *American Women: Fifteen Hundred Biographies with over 1,400 Portraits* (New York: Mast, Crowell & Kirkpatrick, 1897), 48; and Tchen, *New York before Chinatown*, 185–86. Baldwin wrote under her husband's name— "Mrs. S.L. Baldwin"—in her published books and articles.

79 Jane Hunter, *The Gospel of Gentility: American Women Missionaries in Turn-of-the-Century China* (New Haven, CT: Yale University Press, 1989), 165. This is not to dismiss historian Ryan Dunch's argument that Chinese Christians actively negotiated and determined the terms of their participation in missionary communities. Dunch challenges earlier accounts of Chinese Christians that depicted them as "culturally or psychologically dominated by Western missionaries" (xvii). One of Dunch's subjects, the Methodist journalist and political reformer Huang Niashang, for instance, coauthored a series of articles with Esther Baldwin denouncing foot binding. Dunch, *Fuzhou Protestants and the Making of a Modern China, 1857–1927* (New Haven, CT: Yale University Press, 2001), 33–34.

80 Stephen L. Baldwin, "Foo-chow," *Frank Leslie's Popular Monthly*, November 1884, 536–45.

81 W. S. Robinson, "Mrs. Esther E. Baldwin," in *Minutes of the Newark Conference of the Methodist Episcopal Church; Held in the Central Methodist Episcopal Church, Newark, New Jersey; March 30 to April 3, 1919* (Newark, 1919), 91. I am grateful to Frances Bristol, reference archivist for the General Commission on Archives and History of the United Methodist Church, for providing me with this source. Esther Baldwin, *Must the Chinese Go? An Examination of the Chinese Question* (New York: H.B. Elkins, 1890), 63. In the 1880 federal census, Fong Ka Ku, a forty-three-year-old Chinese-born male, is listed as living in the Baldwin residence at 1106 Broad Street in Newark. *1880 United States Federal Census*, Ancestry. com (accessed July 24, 2016); original source: Tenth Census of the United States, 1880 (NARA microfilm publication T9, 1,454 rolls), Records of the Bureau of the Census, Record Group 29, National Archives, Washington, DC, roll 778, p. 284A. In a separate article that she published in the *Independent*, Baldwin would cite her servant "Wo," although this appears to be the same individual—for some reason referred to by a different name—given the timing of the events she recounts. Baldwin, "My Experience," *Independent*, July 27, 1882.

82 In-text page citations refer to the 1890 edition of Baldwin, *Must the Chinese Go?*

83 Allison Sneider argues that in subsequent decades white suffragists—in a parallel move—would use imperialism to create a political space to present claims about their own racial fitness to vote. Sneider, *Suffragists in an Imperial Age: U.S. Expansion and the Woman Question, 1870–1929* (New York: Oxford University Press, 2008). See also Vincente Rafael, "Colonial Domesticity: White Women and United States Rule in the Philippines," *American Literature* 67 (December 1995): 639–66; and Mary Renda, "Doing Everything: Religion, Race, and Empire

in the U.S. Protestant Women's Missionary Enterprise, 1812–1960," in *Competing Kingdoms: Women, Mission, Nation, and the American Protestant Empire, 1812–1960*, ed. Barbara Reeves-Ellington, Kathryn Kish Sklar, and Connie A. Shemo (Durham, NC: Duke University Press, 2010), 367–90.

84  Both of the earlier prefaces were included in the third edition. Baldwin, *Must the Chinese Go?*, 2–3.

85  "Petitions and Memorials," 49th Cong., 1st sess., *Congressional Record* 17, pt. 6: 6036. Baldwin's 1901 letter is cited in McKee, *Chinese Exclusion*, 28, 49.

86  George Frederick Seward, *Chinese Immigration, in Its Social and Economical Aspects* (New York, 1881), 125.

87  Ann Jane Sinclair to Mary Ann Graham, December 1879, Sinclair Letters, PRONI, D1497/4/2. I am grateful to historian Kerby Miller for providing me with a copy of this letter.

88  Martha Mabie Gardner, "Working on White Womanhood: White Working Women in the San Francisco Anti-Chinese Movement, 1877–1890," *Journal of Social History* 33, no. 1 (Autumn 1999): 73–95.

89  *In re Tiburcio Parrott*, 1 F. 481 (C.C.D. Cal. 1880). On the legal background to the case, see McClain, *In Search of Equality*, 79–92. See also Paul Kens, "Civil Liberties, Chinese Laborers, and Corporations," in *Law in the Western United States*, ed. Gordon Morris Bakken (Norman: University of Oklahoma Press, 2001), 499–502.

90  *Yick Wo v. Hopkins*, 118 U.S. 356 (1886). The legal historian Gabriel Chin argues that *Yick Wo* and similar cases should not be interpreted as attempts to defend the American civil rights of Chinese immigrants, and emphasizes instead that the Supreme Court decision in *Yick Wo* rested primarily on its understanding of Chinese immigrants' treaty rights. Chin, "Unexplainable on Grounds of Race: Doubts about Yick Wo," *University of Illinois Law Review* 2008 (2008): 1359. For a critical response to Chin, which argues that *Yick Wo* represented a lost opportunity to more vigorously enforce the Fourteenth Amendment in a manner that protected minority groups from racial discrimination, see David Bernstein, "Revisiting Yick Wo v. Hopkins," *University of Illinois Law Review* 2008 (2008): 1393.

91  A. J. Hanson, "The Chinaman in America," *Methodist Review*, September 1892, 712.

92  Senator Morgan, speaking on S. 3304, on July 20, 1888, 50th Cong., 1st sess., *Congressional Record* 19, pt. 7: 6572.

93  "Oregon Appeal for Chinese," *New York Times*, July 13, 1905; U.S. Immigration Commission, *Reports of the Immigration Commission: Immigrants in Industries (In Twenty-Five Parts). Part 25: Japanese and Other Immigrant Races in the Pacific Coast and Rocky Mountain States*, 61st Cong., 2nd sess., Doc. no. 633, 1911, 175; and "Oregon Appeal for Chinese," *New York Times*, July 13, 1905.

94  Hubert Howe Bancroft, *New Pacific* (1900; rev. ed., New York: Bancroft Company, 1912), 434–35.

95  Hubert Howe Bancroft, *Retrospection: Political and Personal* (New York: Bancroft Company, 1912), 345–59. Although Bancroft used the phrase "Asiatics" indiscriminately, it is clear that he meant Chinese immigrants specifically. Elsewhere in the

text Bancroft distinguished Chinese from Japanese immigrants, and argued that the Japanese immigrant "is captious, clamorous of his rights, and would like to become the equal or superior of the white race" (357).

96  D. S. Cowan to Charles S. Fairchild, Secretary of the Treasury, August 30, 1888, National Archives and Records Administration, Washington, DC, Record Group 85, Custom Case Files no. 3358d, 1877–1891 (hereafter NARA, Custom Case Files no. 3358d), box 2, folder 12.

## CHAPTER 4. CONTROLLING AND PROTECTING WHITE WOMEN

1  U.S. Bureau of Immigration, *Annual Report of the Commissioner-General of Immigration to the Secretary of Commerce and Labor for the Fiscal Year Ended June 30, 1911* (Washington, DC: GPO, 1912), 12–13. A legal challenge to the twenty-five-dollar requirement was eventually brought before the District Court for the Southern District of New York in 1909. Williams agreed to rehear the cases of the plaintiffs who were denied admission due to the rule rather than risk an adverse precedent. Vincent J. Cannato, *American Passage: The History of Ellis Island* (New York: Harper, 2009), 195–204.

2  On the treatment of immigrants at Ellis Island as media and anthropological spectacles, see Anna Pegler-Gordon, *In Sight of America: Photography and the Development of U.S. Immigration Policy* (Berkeley: University of California Press, 2010), 107–12; and Amy L. Fairchild, *Science at the Borders: Immigrant Medical Inspection and the Shaping of the Modern Industrial Labor Force* (Baltimore: Johns Hopkins University Press, 2003), 83–118. For a focused account of Ellis Island's daily operation and administration, see Ronald H. Bayor, *Encountering Ellis Island: How European Immigrants Entered America* (Baltimore: Johns Hopkins University Press, 2014).

3  *Saturday Evening Post* clipping, Series I, Ellis Island, William Williams Papers, Manuscripts and Archives Division, New York Public Library (hereafter cited as Williams Papers). The citation to the original article is Arthur Train, "Shall He Go Back? Trying to Get through the Gate at Ellis Island," *Saturday Evening Post*, March 5, 1910, 15–17, 47.

4  Stephen Graham, *With Poor Immigrants to America* (New York: Macmillan, 1914), 46–47. See also Deirdre M. Moloney, *National Insecurities: Immigrants and U.S. Deportation Policy since 1882* (Chapel Hill: University of North Carolina Press, 2012), 28–50.

5  J. F. Goulburn [sp?] to Williams, March 10, 1910, Williams Papers.

6  Zolberg, *Nation by Design*, 193–98; Gwendolyn Mink, *Old Labor and New Immigrants in American Political Development* (Ithaca, NY: Cornell University Press, 1986); and Kitty Calavita, *U.S. Immigration Law and the Control of Labor* (London: Academic Press, 1984).

7  See Hirota, "Moment of Transition."

8  *1882 Immigration Act (An Act to Regulate Immigration)*, 22 Stat. 214 (1882): sec. 2; *1891 Immigration Act (An Act in Amendment to the Various Acts Relative to*

*Immigration and the Importation of Aliens under Contract or Agreement to Perform Labor)*, 26 Stat. 1084: sec. 1.

9 For further elaboration of this point, see Canaday, *Straight State*, 25.

10 "Laws against poverty and those regulating morality wove easily through one another," historian Martha Gardner notes. Gardner, *The Qualities of a Citizen: Women, Immigration, and Citizenship, 1870–1965* (Princeton, NJ: Princeton University Press, 2005), 91.

11 Peck, "Feminizing White Slavery." On middle-class officials and reformers' overly simplistic understanding of sex trafficking, see also Pliley, "Petticoat Inspectors"; and Moloney, *National Insecurities*, 53–68.

12 Dudden, *Serving Women*, 79–86; Licht, *Getting Work*, 135–37.

13 On accusations that employment agencies falsified laborers' credentials and engaged in outright fraud against employers, see May, *Unprotected Labor*, 24–26.

14 "Intelligence Offices—Blood Suckers," *New York Times*, July 26, 1855. On licensing and penalties, see "The Mayor's Office—Model Intelligence Offices," *New York Times*, September 7, 1862. As historian Brian Luskey documents, New York's Common Council required proprietors of intelligence offices to pay a twenty-five-dollar licensing fee and demonstrate their good character as early as 1823. Luskey, "Special Marts," 365. Enforcement however remained lax until the twentieth century.

15 Friedrich Kapp, *Immigration and the Commissioners of Emigration of the State of New York* (New York: Nation Press, 1870), 85–104; Richard J. Purcell, "The New York Commissioners of Emigration and Irish Immigrants: 1847–1860," *Studies: An Irish Quarterly Review* 37, no. 145 (1948): 29–42. For the original 1847 act and its amended versions, see New York (State) Commissioners of Emigration, *Annual Reports of the Commissioners of Emigration of the State of New York: From the Organization of the Commission, May 5, 1847, to 1860, Inclusive: Together with Tables and Reports, and Other Official Documents* (Commissioners of Emigration, 1861), appendix.

16 The *Passenger Cases* refer to two bundled cases, *Smith v. Turner; Norris v. Boston*, 48 U.S. 283 (1849). On the *Passenger Cases'* relationship to rulings on the federal government's legal jurisdiction over fugitive slaves, and the use of the Commerce Clause to justify its oversight of immigration, see Tony Freyer and Daniel Thomas, "The *Passenger Cases* Reconsidered in Transatlantic Commerce Clause History," *Journal of Supreme Court History* 36 (2011): 216–35. *Henderson v. Mayor of City of New York*, 92 U.S. 259 (1875) was adjudicated by the Supreme Court only a year before the case of *Chy Lung v. Freeman*, 92 U.S. 275 (1876), which denied California, as a state, the right to levy bonds designed to limit Chinese immigration.

17 Kapp, *Immigration and the Commissioners of Emigration*, 115–17; Commissioners of Emigration, *Annual Reports of the Commissioners of Emigration of the State of New York*, 74 (Fifth Annual Report for the Year 1851); "Immigration," *New York Times*, September 12, 1865; and Commissioners of Emigration, "Annual Report of the Commissioner of Emigration of the State of New York 1877, for the Year

Ending December 31, 1877," 8, in New York Senate, *Documents of the Senate of the State of New York. One Hundred and First Session, 1878*, vol. 1, nos. 1–22 (Albany: Jerome B. Parmenter, 1878). Historian Joshua Rosenbloom argues that by the Civil War the labor exchange had "become little more than an 'intelligence office' supplying domestic servants to the New York market," the inference being that the importance of this service paled in comparison to the placement of male industrial laborers. Rosenbloom, *Looking for Work*, 71.

18 Versions of the Irish Emigrant Society and German Emigrant Society had been organized and reorganized under different names since the late eighteenth century, before taking a more permanent form in the 1840s. See Robert Ernst, *Immigrant Life in New York City, 1825–1863* (Port Washington, NY: Ira J. Friedman, 1965), 32–36; Richard J. Purcell, "The Irish Emigrant Society of New York," *Studies: An Irish Quarterly Review* 27, no. 108 (1938): 583–99; and John Fahey, "James Irwin: Irish Emigrant Agent, New York City, 1846–1858," *New York History* 93, no. 3 (2012): 219–45.

19 Cited in Ernst, *Immigrant Life in New York City*, 30.

20 "The New York Labor Market," *Harper's Weekly*, July 4, 1857; "Immigration," *New York Times*, September 12, 1865.

21 "Immigration at New York and the Labor Supply," *Bradstreet's*, April 1, 1882, 194.

22 Committee on Commerce and Navigation, "Report of the Committee on Commerce and Navigation upon the Affairs of the Commissioners of Emigration of New York City, no. 143, in Assembly, April 10, 1872," in New York Assembly, *Documents of the Assembly of the State of New York. Ninety-Fifth Session—1872*, vol. 10 (Albany: Argus Company, 1872). The main charge of corruption centered on Michael Nolan, a lawyer who apparently received kickbacks from the steamship companies in exchange for reducing the commutation fee they were supposed to pay from $2.50 to $1.50. Nolan, who had served with the Irish American General Patrick Henry Jones during the Civil War, would also be the focal point of the 1875 investigation. Mark Dunkelman, *Patrick Henry Jones: Irish American, Civil War General, and Gilded Age Politician* (Baton Rouge: Louisiana State University Press, 2015), 130–40.

23 The letter writer gave his or her name as "One Who Knows." "More Abuses at Castle Garden," *New York Times*, July 3, 1871.

24 "Report of the Committee of Investigation into the Affairs of the Commissioners of Emigration and Quarantine, no. 33, in Assembly, January 28, 1876," in New York Assembly, *Documents of the Assembly of the State of New York. Ninety-Ninth Session—1876*, vol. 4 (Albany: Werd, Parsons, 1876), 129–37.

25 "John E. Develin's Death," *New York Times*, February 24, 1888.

26 "Report of the Committee of Investigation into the Affairs of the Commissioners of Emigration and Quarantine," in New York Assembly, *Documents—1876*, 178.

27 On the increased application of the "employment at will" doctrine to cases that involved wage workers after the Civil War, see Christopher L. Tomlins, *Law, Labor, and Ideology in the Early American Republic* (New York: Cambridge University

Press, 1993), 261–90; and Jay M. Feinman, "The Development of the Employment at Will Rule," *American Journal of Legal History* 20 (1976): 118–35.

28 "Affairs at the State Capital," *New York Herald*, April 11, 1858; "Servants Suits," *New York Times*, February 13, 1860; and "Albany. Legislative Work Yesterday," *New York Times*, January 20, 1876.

29 Laughlin, "Domestic Service," 757–58, and Felice Batlan, *Women and Justice for the Poor: A History of Legal Aid, 1863–1945* (New York: Cambridge University Press, 2015), 39. See also May, *Unprotected Labor*, 67–70. By 1910, the Legal Aid Society had adopted a policy of refusing assistance to servants who left without giving notice. In her 1923 book, *The Immigrant's Day in Court*, the sociologist Kate Holladay Claghorn observed that this policy was followed by legal aid societies across the country, since their middle-class supporters and financial backers claimed that providing assistance in these cases was "distinctly undermining the character of the working classes." Batlan also notes that it was common for the male attorneys who staffed legal aid societies to be condescending to the female servants who approached them with workplace grievances, since many failed to take the occupation seriously. Claghorn, *The Immigrant's Day in Court* (New York: Carnegie Foundation, 1923), 482, and Batlan, *Women and Justice for the Poor*, 114–22.

30 John Fabian Witt, "Rethinking the Nineteenth-Century Employment Contract, Again," *Law and History Review* 18, no. 3 (2000): 55.

31 Mrs. H. W. [Eunice White] Beecher, *Motherly Talks with Young Housekeepers: Embracing Eighty-Seven Brief Articles on Topics of Home Interest, and about Five Hundred Choice Receipts for Cooking, Etc.* (New York: J.B. Ford, 1873), 248–49.

32 Commissioners of Emigration, "Annual Report of the Commissioners of Assembly. No. 26. In Assembly, February 16, 1882," in New York Assembly, *Documents of the Assembly of the State of New York. One Hundred and Fifth Session, 1882*, vol. 2 (Albany: Weed, Parsons, 1882), 8.

33 Erickson, *American Industry and the European Immigrant, 1860–1885* (Cambridge, MA: Harvard University Press, 1957), 95–97.

34 Commissioners of Emigration, "Annual Report of the Commissioner of Emigration of the State of New York 1877," 8, in New York Senate, *Documents*; and "Annual Report of the Commissioners of Emigration. February 11, 1884," 39–40 (available online through the Columbia University Library digitized texts collection).

35 "European Emigrants—Constant Demand for Their Labor," *San Francisco Daily Evening Bulletin*, July 21, 1881.

36 Rosenbloom, *Looking for Work*, 72–73.

37 "Would Keep the Bureau. But Mr. Stephenson Says It Is a Pesthouse," *New York Times*, February 16, 1888; "Not the Labor Bureau's Fault," *New York Times*, February 18, 1888.

38 U.S. Congress, House of Representatives, *Report of the Select Committee on Immigration and Naturalization, and Testimony Taken by the Committee on Immigration of the Senate and the Select Committee on Immigration and Naturalization*

*of the House of Representatives under Concurrent Resolution of March 12, 1890, Reported to the House by Mr. Owen, of Indiana, January 15, 1891,* 51st Cong., 2nd sess., 1891, Report no. 3472, 161.

39  U.S. Congress, House of Representatives, *Testimony Taken by the Select Committee of the House of Representatives to Inquire into the Alleged Violation of the Laws Prohibiting the Importation of Contract Laborers, Paupers, Convicts, and Other Classes,* 50th Cong., 1st sess., 1888, Misc. Doc. 572, 273; 533–34.

40  "One More Chance for Life. The Labor Bureau at Castle Garden to be Investigated," *New York Times,* February 22, 1888; "Not Much Harmony," *New York Times,* June 1, 1888; "Hot Words at a Meeting. Lack of Harmony at Castle Garden," *New York Times,* August 30, 1889.

41  U.S. Congress, House of Representatives, *Testimony Taken by the Select Committee,* 286–89; 301–5.

42  Ibid., 533.

43  U.S. Congress, House of Representatives, *Report of the Select Committee on Immigration and Naturalization,* 169.

44  Terrence Powderly, for instance, after serving as head of the Knights of Labor from 1879 to 1893, held the position of Commissioner General of Immigration from 1897 to 1902, where he led efforts to ramp up the enforcement of Chinese restriction laws. Powderly, the child of Irish immigrants who grew up in Pennsylvania coal country, was also a fervent supporter of Irish nationalist causes. See Delber McKee, " 'The Chinese Must Go!' Commissioner General Powderly and Chinese Immigration, 1897–1902," *Pennsylvania History: A Journal of Mid-Atlantic Studies* 44, no. 1 (January 1977): 37–51, and Ely M. Janis, *A Greater Ireland: The Land League and Transatlantic Nationalism in Gilded Age America* (Madison: University of Wisconsin Press, 2015), 132–33.

45  For a summary of these changes, see U.S. Citizenship and Immigration Services History (UCSIS) Office and Library, "Overview of INS History" (2012), www.uscis.gov (accessed December 27, 2016).

46  On the implementation of these deportation procedures and post-entry enforcement of the "likely to become a public charge" provision, see Kanstroom, *Deportation Nation,* 124–32; and Dorothee Schneider, *Crossing Borders: Migration and Citizenship in the Twentieth-Century United States* (Cambridge, MA: Harvard University Press, 2011), 123–28.

47  On the harassment that Chinese immigrants faced as a formal enforcement imperative, see Lee, *At America's Gates,* 47–74; and Adam McKeown, "Ritualization of Regulation: The Enforcement of Chinese Exclusion in the United States and China," *American Historical Review* 108, no. 2 (April 2003): 377–403.

48  *Act of March 3,* 1893 (27 Stat. 570): sec. 2.

49  On immigration to Philadelphia, see Frederic Miller, "Immigration through the Port of Philadelphia," in *Forgotten Doors: The Other Ports of Entry to the United States,* ed. M. Mark Stolarik (Philadelphia: Balch Institute Press, 1998), 37–54.

50  As historian Deirdre Moloney argues, social anxieties about immigrant women's economic independence and associated sexual and social freedoms, which they gained through their participation in industrial work, encouraged immigration officials to promote marriage. Moloney, *National Insecurities*, 30. See also Kathy Peiss, *Cheap Amusements: Working Women and Leisure in Turn-of-the-Century New York* (Philadelphia: Temple University Press, 1986), 110–14; and Joanne J. Meyerowitz, *Women Adrift: Independent Wage Earners in Chicago, 1880–1930* (Chicago: University of Chicago Press, 1991), 21–42.

51  Gardner, *Qualities of Citizen*, 100–108.

52  On conditions in the Pacific Mail Steamship Company detention shed, see Lee, *At America's Gates*, 124–27.

53  Kate Kerghrin, May 18, 1896, in *Department of Commerce and Labor, Bureau of Immigration and Naturalization. Records of the Special Boards of Inquiry, District no. 4 (Philadelphia), Immigration and Naturalization Service, 1893–1909*, Records of the Immigration and Naturalization Service, 1787–2004, Record Group 85, National Archives at Washington, DC. These records have been digitized by Ancestry.com and are accessible online. See Ancestry.com, *Philadelphia, Pennsylvania, Immigration Records, Special Boards of Inquiry, 1893–1909* (hereafter *Records of the Special Boards of Inquiry, Philadelphia*).

54  Nellie Sullivan, May 10, 1896, *Records of the Special Boards of Inquiry, Philadelphia*. For Philadelphia landing numbers, see U.S. Bureau of Immigration, *Annual Report of the Commissioner-General of Immigration to the Secretary of the Treasury for the Fiscal Year Ended June 30, 1896* (U.S. Government Printing Office, 1896), 39–41.

55  Lizzie and Maggie Farrell, November 5, 1900, *Records of the Special Boards of Inquiry, Philadelphia*.

56  Mary Waterhouse, November 12, 1900, *Records of the Special Boards of Inquiry, Philadelphia*. Laughlin, "Domestic Service," 747–49.

57  U.S. Bureau of Immigration, *Annual Report of the Commissioner-General of Immigration to the Secretary of the Treasury*, 40.

58  Mary Rolands, October 2, 1899, *Records of the Special Boards of Inquiry, Philadelphia*.

59  Letters relating to Adeline Porter, folder 3, 1897, 02–04–02.4, Letters and Telegrams Received Concerning Status and Treatment of Immigrants, 1892–1903, Record Group 85, National Archives at Philadelphia.

60  Ellis Island's early years were marked by numerous problems having to do with the new facilities. Most notably, from June 1897 to December 1900, the processing of immigrants relocated to the Battery Barge Office, next to the old Castle Garden, after a fire destroyed Ellis Island's original wooden structures.

61  McSweeney's investigation by Commissioner General Powderly and the Treasury Department was kept secret from the public. Hans P. Vought, *The Bully Pulpit and the Melting Pot: American Presidents and the Immigrant, 1897–1933* (Macon, GA: Mercer University Press, 2004), 37–38; "Report of Investigating Committee

at New York Immigrant Station," June 1900, file 51424/2, Subject Correspondence Files of the Immigration and Naturalization Service, National Archives and Records Administration, Washington, DC, Record Group 85 (hereafter Subject Correspondence Files, NARA); Cannato, *American Passage*, 117–19.

62 Senner to Powderly, May 17, 1897, file 13595, Subject Correspondence Files, NARA; Edward Alfred Steiner, *On the Trail of the Immigrant* (New York: Revell, 1906), 80.

63 Cannato, *American Passage*, 149–64. Williams resigned from his first term in office in December 1904 because he could not tolerate sharing authority with Joe Murray, an Irish American machine politician who followed McSweeney.

64 Pliley, "Petticoat Inspectors."

65 Sargent marked the letter "personal," suggesting that he was conscious that his articulation of these views would generate questions about the bureau's commitment to fairness. Sargent to Williams, October 6, 1902, Williams Papers.

66 U.S. Congress, House of Representatives, *Regulation of Immigration of Aliens. Letter from the Secretary of Labor Transmitting Comments, Data, and Suggestions on a Bill (H.R. 6060) to Regulate the Immigration of Aliens to and the Residence of Aliens in the United States, February 2, 1914*, 63rd Cong., 2nd sess., 1914, House Doc. 689, 4.

67 Memorandum 19695, September 22, 1903, Williams to the Supervising Inspector, Williams Papers, emphasis original.

68 "Ellis Island, Its Organization and Some of Its Work," December 1912, 26, Williams Papers; Bayor, *Encountering Ellis Island*, 79.

69 Frances Kellor, "Protection of Immigrant Women," *Atlantic Monthly*, February 1908, 250–51.

70 "Reasons Why the Austro-Hungarian Home Has Been Debarred from Ellis Island," n.d., Williams Papers.

71 Hajos to Williams, December 19, 1904, Williams Papers.

72 For these provisions, see *1885 Contract Labor Law (An Act to Prohibit the Importation and Migration of Foreigners and Aliens under Contract or Agreement to Perform Labor in the United States, Its Territories, and the District of Columbia)*, 23 Stat. 332, exceptions in sec. 5; *1891 Immigration Act*, secs. 1 and 3; and *1917 Immigration Act (An Act to Regulate the Immigration of Aliens to and the Residence of Aliens in the United States)*, 39 Stat. 874, sec. 3. The other exceptions to the Foran Act were cases where officials determined that "skilled labor" could not be obtained domestically and, by occupation, actors, artists, lecturers, and singers. In 1892, the U.S. Supreme Court overturned the debarment of an English minister recruited and contracted to work in a New York Episcopal church, ruling unanimously that legislators had intended for the statute to only cover professions requiring manual labor. *Church of the Holy Trinity v. United States*, 143 U.S. 457 (1892).

73 Rendigs Fels, "The American Business Cycle of 1879–85," *Journal of Political Economy* 60, no. 1 (1952): 60–67; Gabaccia, " 'Yellow Peril' and the 'Chinese of Europe.' "

74 Calavita, *U.S. Immigration Law and the Control of Labor*, 44–72. As Calavita points out, the process of drafting the Foran Act was precipitated by the petitions of skilled glass workers organized under the Federation of Organized Trades and Labor Unions (the predecessor of the AFL), who were concerned about the importation of European tradesmen. Calavita argues that even though the Knights of Labor eventually got behind the act, due to the ability of corporations to hire strikebreakers domestically, it had little effect on the union's organizing campaigns. See also Erickson, *American Industry and the European Immigrant*, 148–66; and Edward Hutchinson, *Legislative History of American Immigration Policy: 1798–1965* (Philadelphia: University of Pennsylvania Press, 1981), 89–92.

75 *1885 Contract Labor Law*, H.R. 2550, 48th Cong., 2nd sess., *Congressional Record* 16, pt. 2: 1624, 1631, and 1634. On the social construction of race in the Foran Act debates, see also Mink, *Old Labor and New Immigrants*, 108–11; and Calavita, *U.S. Immigration Law and the Control of Labor*, 61.

76 *Congressional Record* 16, pt. 2: 1621. Four days later, Willard Saulsbury, a Democrat from Delaware, unsuccessfully attempted to further amend the bill so as to exempt agricultural laborers from restrictions on importation as well. Saulsbury argued that since the bill was designed to prevent corporations from importing large numbers of foreign workers, in order to lower wages, it should not extend to small farmers wishing to bring in laborers during times of worker scarcity. *Congressional Record* 16, pt. 2: 1787. When the Senate amendments to the bill were reintroduced into the House of Representatives, they were accepted without debate. *Congressional Record* 16, pt. 2: 2032.

77 "An Act to Regulate the Immigration of Aliens to and the Residence of Aliens in the United States," HR 6060, 63rd Cong., 2nd sess., *Congressional Record* 51, pt. 3: 2827.

78 *1917 Immigration Act*, HR 10384, 64th Cong., 1st sess., *Congressional Record* 53, pt. 5: 4942.

79 Ibid., 4890.

80 Ibid., 4947–48.

81 The reference to the July 1907 Attorney General ruling comes from an undated memo in file 52481/5, Subject Correspondence Files, NARA.

82 Keefe to Williams, May 15, 1911, Subject Correspondence Files, NARA.

83 Thomas Owen to Bureau of Immigration, December 13, 1916; Parker to Owen, December 28, 1916, Subject Correspondence Files, NARA.

84 Charles Barnes, Director, New York Bureau of Employment to Commissioner General of Immigration, December 2, 1915; Hampton, Acting Commissioner General of Immigration to Barnes, December 7, 1915, Subject Correspondence Files, NARA.

85 E. B. Barnes to the Commissioner General of Immigration, February 28, 1911; Larned to Barnes, March 4, 1911, Subject Correspondence Files, NARA.

86 Sutro to Secretary of Department of Commerce and Labor, September 27, 1912; Sutro to Commissioner General of Immigration, September 30, 1912; Keefe to

Sutro, October 1, 1912; Keefe to Williams, October 3, 1912; Edwin Woods to Williams, October 8, 1912; Williams to Keefe, October 9, 1912; Keefe to Sutro, October 11, 1912, Subject Correspondence Files, NARA.

87  Canada, Department of the Interior, "Office of the High Commissioner of Canada, Immigration, November 4, 1905," in *Sessional Paper no. 25, Annual Report for the Department of the Interior for the Year 1905–1906* (Ottawa: S.E. Dawson, 1906); Minister of Interior, *Canada Wants Domestic Servants* (Ottawa, 1909); and F. C. Blair, Secretary of Immigration, to Gladys Potts, September 6, 1919, in House of Commons, *Reports from Commissioners, Inspectors and Others* (London, 1919).

88  On employment agencies' relationship to various establishments associated with commerce in what reformers viewed as vice, see Frances Kellor, *Out of Work: A Study of Employment Agencies: Their Treatment of the Unemployed, and Their Influence upon Homes and Businesses* (New York: G. P. Putnam's Sons, 1904), 77–103. While *Out of Work* dealt with unemployment as it affected both men and women, a whole chapter (6, pp. 118–51) was devoted to intelligence offices specializing in placing women in domestic positions. Grace Abbott, a social worker with Hull House and one of the founders of the Immigrant Protective League, reached similar conclusions to Kellor in her own study. See Grace Abbott, "The Chicago Employment Agency and the Immigrant Worker," *American Journal of Sociology* 14, no. 3 (1908): 289–305.

89  Ellen Fitzpatrick, *Endless Crusade: Women Social Scientists and Progressive Reform* (New York: Oxford University Press, 1990), 131.

90  For a more detailed discussion of Kellor's educational background and connections to different reform agencies, see ibid., 58–80, 130–65.

91  Elizabeth Banks, "Out of Work," *New York Times*, December 10, 1904.

92  *1891 Immigration Act*, 26 Stat. 1084: sec. 3.

93  Kellor, *Out of Work*, 70–76, 72.

94  Ibid., 72–73.

95  Fitzpatrick, *Endless Crusade*, 136–37; Rosenbloom, *Looking for Work*, 58; and May, *Unprotected Labor*, 96–105. As May notes, Kellor envisioned using the Intermunicipal Research Committee to get the New York employment agency law copied and implemented in other states where there were branches. For the full text of the 1904 act, see New York State, *Laws of the State of New York Passed at the One Hundred and Twenty-Seventh Session of the Legislature, Begun January Sixth, 1904, and Ended April Fifteenth, 1904, in the City of Albany*, vol. 2 (Albany: J.B. Lyon Company, 1904), chap. 432, 1053–58; and, for the amended 1906 act, New York State, *Laws of the State of New York Passed at the One Hundred and Twenty-Ninth Session of the Legislature, Begun January Third, 1906, and Ended May Third, 1906, in the City of Albany*, vol. 1 (Albany: J.B. Lyon Company, 1906), chap. 327, 831–38.

96  Kellor, "The Housewife and Her Helper," *Ladies' Home Journal*, February 1906, 32.

97  Kellor, "The Housewife and Her Helper," *Ladies' Home Journal*, May 1906, 30.

98  On the tensions between liberal pluralism and Anglo-Saxon chauvinism within the Progressive movement, see Rivka Shpak Lissak, *Pluralism and Progressives:*

*Hull House and the New Immigrants, 1890–1919* (Chicago: University of Chicago Press, 1989).

99 Kellor, "The Immigrant Woman," *Atlantic Monthly*, September 1907, 404.

100 On the Supreme Court peonage cases, see Michael J. Klarman, *From Jim Crow to Civil Rights: The Supreme Court and the Struggle for Racial Equality* (New York: Oxford University Press, 2006), 61–97. Legal scholar Aziz Huq points out that the constitutional issue that justices adjudicated was due process pertaining to liberty of contract rather than a broader defense of minority civil rights. Huq, "Peonage and Contractual Liberty," *Columbia Law Review* 101 (2001): 351.

101 Kellor, *Out of Work: A Study of Unemployment*, rev. ed. (New York: G. P. Putnam's Sons, 1915), 226–27.

102 Kellor, *Immigration and the Future* (New York: George H. Doran, 1920), 38.

## CHAPTER 5. BONDED CHINESE SERVANTS

1 On this period in the history of the U.S. naval base at Guantánamo, see Jonathan M. Hansen, *Guantánamo: An American History* (New York: Hill & Wang, 2011), 146–93.

2 Kathleen M. López, *Chinese Cubans: A Transnational History* (Chapel Hill: University of North Carolina Press, 2013), 15–81. Considered Cuban territory due to the unique terms of its lease, the base at Guantánamo was not and is not subject to American immigration or labor laws. For a longer history of the naval base's reliance on service workers recruited from around the world, see Jana Lipman, *Guantánamo: A Working-Class History between Empire and Revolution* (Berkeley: University of California Press, 2008), 191–227.

3 All of the materials pertaining to "Ah" See and Sing Lee come from file 54472/6, Subject Correspondence Files, NARA.

4 In 2016, this would be roughly equivalent to seven thousand dollars.

5 These details were explained in a memorandum that Fay drafted in July 1923.

6 For a more extensive discussion of this point, see Lee, *At America's Gates*, 77–109.

7 As historian Beth Lew-Williams argues, the original 1882 act "was weak both by accident and by design," since policymakers were uncertain as to what powers they had to disregard existing treaty obligations with China. Lew-Williams, "Before Restriction Became Exclusion," 27.

8 On unauthorized Chinese immigration, see Lee, *At America's Gates*, 111–46; Estelle T. Lau, *Paper Families: Identity, Immigration Administration, and Chinese Exclusion* (Durham, NC: Duke University Press, 2007), 33–66; and Patrick Ettinger, "'We Sometimes Wonder What They Will Spring on Us Next': Immigrants and Border Enforcement in the American West, 1882–1930," *Western Historical Quarterly* 37 (Summer 2006): 159–81.

9 For further elaboration of this point, see Tony Ballantyne and Antoinette Burton, "Introduction: The Politics of Intimacy in an Age of Empire," in *Moving Subjects: Gender, Mobility, and Intimacy in an Age of Global Empire*, ed. Ballantyne and Burton (Champaign: University of Illinois Press, 2009), 1–30. The United States'

emergence as an imperial power was also undergirded by the transport of workers to sites where its sovereign rule was being imposed. See Julie Greene, *The Canal Builders: Making America's Empire at the Panama Canal* (New York: Penguin, 2009); and Greene, "Movable Empire: Labor, Migration, and U.S. Global Power during the Gilded Age and Progressive Era," *Journal of the Gilded Age and Progressive Era* 15, no. 1 (January 2016): 4–20.

10  Madeline Y. Hsu, *The Good Immigrants: How the Yellow Peril Became the Model Minority* (Princeton, NJ: Princeton University Press, 2015), 23–54; Paul Kramer, "Empire Against Exclusion in Early 20th Century TransPacific History," *Nanzan Review of American Studies* 33 (2011): 13–32; and Kramer, "Is the World Our Campus? International Students and U.S. Global Power in the Long Twentieth Century," *Diplomatic History* 33 (November 2009): 775–806.

11  Bonds were also required for touring, nonimmigrant Chinese laborers such as opera and theatrical performers. See Nancy Yunhwa Rao, "Transnationalism and Everyday Practice: Cantonese Opera Theatres of North America in the 1920s," *Ethnomusicology Forum* 25, no. 1 (January 2016): 107–30.

12  On the types of imperial communities in China that exceptions to prohibitions on the entry of laborers were designed to benefit, see Sherman Cochran, *Encountering Chinese Networks: Western, Japanese, and Chinese Corporations in China, 1880–1937* (Berkeley: University of California Press, 2000); and Robert Bickers and Christian Henriot, eds., *New Frontiers: Imperialism's New Communities in East Asia, 1842–1953* (Manchester: Manchester University Press, 2000).

13  See, for an overview of what due process protections to pursue liberty of contract meant to workers, Steinfeld, *Coercion, Contract, and Free Labor*, 253–89.

14  McKeown, "Ritualization of Regulation."

15  See, as works that provide important theoretical and anthropological context to this point, Aihwa Ong, *Neoliberalism as Exception: Mutations in Citizenship and Sovereignty* (Durham, NC: Duke University Press, 2006); Ong, *Flexible Citizenship: The Cultural Logics of Transnationality* (Durham, NC: Duke University Press, 1999); Anne McNevin, *Contesting Citizenship: Irregular Migrants and New Frontiers of the Political* (New York: Columbia University Press, 2011); Andrew Linklater, *Critical Theory and World Politics: Citizenship, Sovereignty and Humanity* (New York: Routledge, 2007); Saskia Sassen, "Local Actors in Global Politics," *Current Sociology* 52, no. 4 (July 2004): 649–70; and Arjun Appadurai, *Modernity at Large: Cultural Dimensions of Globalization* (Minneapolis: University of Minnesota Press, 1996).

16  For an overview of the precarity and vulnerability that undocumented immigrants' status produces, see David Bacon, *Illegal People: How Globalization Creates Migration and Criminalizes Immigrants* (Boston: Beacon, 2008), 1–22; and Aviva Chomsky, *Undocumented: How Immigration Became Illegal* (Boston: Beacon, 2014), 113–51.

17  *Case of the Chinese Cabin Waiter*, 13 Fed. 286 (1882), 289. Field was also a U.S. Supreme Court judge at the time. He rode "circuit" and served in dual capacity.

18  Kitty Calavita, "Chinese Exclusion and the Open Door with China: Structural Contradictions and the 'Chaos' of Law, 1882–1910," *Social & Legal Studies* 10 (2001): 209.

19  Robert A. Wilson, "Diplomatic Immunity from Criminal Jurisdiction: Essential to Effective International Relations," *Loyola of Los Angeles International and Comparative Law Journal* 7 (1984): 113.

20  See Lew-Williams, "Before Restriction Became Exclusion."

21  *Treaty between the United States and China, Concerning Immigration. Concluded November 17, 1880; Ratification Advised by the Senate May 5, 1881; Ratified by the President May 9, 1881; Ratification Exchanged July 19, 1881; Proclaimed October 5, 1881,* 22 Stat. 826, art. 2; *An Act to Execute Certain Treaty Stipulations Relating to Chinese (1882 Chinese Restriction Act),* 22. Stat. 58, secs. 8 and 13.

22  *Official Opinions of the Attorneys-General of the United States, Advising the President and Heads of Departments in Relation to Their Official Duties, etc.,* 51st Cong., 1st sess., Mis. Doc. no. 238, 1890, 542–43. When he issued his opinion in 1887, Garland included the full text of Brewster's 1884 decision on the matter.

23  "Chinese Female Nurses," *Daily Alta California,* February 24, 1887.

24  Pacific Mail Steamship Company to Manning, February 26, 1887, and Manning to Pacific Mail Steamship Company, March 3, 1887, NARA, Custom Case Files no. 3358d, box 5, folder 1.

25  [Untitled editorial], *Daily Alta California,* February 27, 1887.

26  The circular was printed under the headline "A Treasury Ruling," *Daily Alta California,* March 10, 1887.

27  *In re Chung Toy Ho,* 42 Fed. 398 (1890).

28  On the discrimination Chinese immigrants faced as participants and witnesses in criminal proceedings more generally, see John R. Wunder, "Chinese in Trouble: Criminal Law and Race on the Trans-Mississippi West Frontier," *Western Historical Quarterly* 17, no. 1 (January 1986): 25–41.

29  American Consulate-General, Canton, China to Department of State, January 2, 1907, file 53266/75, Subject Correspondence Files, NARA.

30  On illegal Chinese immigration and immigrants' views of their actions, see Lee, *At America's Gates,* 189–207.

31  *Ex Parte Chun Woi San,* 230 Fed. 538 (1914), file 53552/7, Subject Correspondence Files, NARA.

32  As historian Lucy Salyer argues, the 1905 boycott of American goods in China and mounting diplomatic pressure represented turning points that caused President Roosevelt to rein in the Bureau of Immigration's most grievous abuses. Salyer, *Laws Harsh as Tigers,* 162–69. See also Lee, *At America's Gates,* 68–74.

33  File 54081/8, Subject Correspondence Files, NARA.

34  See Chang, *Pacific Connections,* 2–3, for further articulation of this point.

35  Affidavit of Anderson, October 9, 1883, and Affidavit of Maddocks, July 17, 1883, NARA, Custom Case Files no. 3358d, box 4, folder 4.

36 Christian G. Fritz, "A Nineteenth Century 'Habeas Corpus Mill': The Chinese before the Federal Courts in California," *American Journal of Legal History* 32, no. 4 (1988): 347–72; Salyer, *Laws Harsh as Tigers*, 20.What became the Northern District of California existed as a single district for all of California until 1886, when a separate Southern District was established.

37 *Chew Heong v. United States*, 112 U.S. 536 (1884). As the controlling decision in the case, Field departed from all three of his colleagues and denied Chew Heong permission to land. When the case went to the U.S. Supreme Court, he became one of the two dissenting opinions. Fritz, "A Nineteenth Century 'Habeas Corpus Mill,'" 363–69.

38 As had been the case previously, the United States tried to establish this through treaty first. When treaty negotiations with China concerning laborers' right to return stalled, however, Congress passed the unilateral legislation. Lew-Williams, "Before Restriction Became Exclusion," 48–49.

39 Goddard to Department of the Treasury, October 22, 1889, and Treasury to Goddard, October 24, 1889, Custom Case Files no. 3358d, box 5, folder 2, NARA.

40 Marie Allen Kimball, "Chinese House Servants," *Chautauquan*, May 1893, 207–8.

41 "Dodging the Law," *Morning Call*, March 31, 1893.

42 Elizabeth Bales, "The Chinese through an Official Window," *Overland Monthly* 22 (August 1893): 138–47, 140.

43 The Chinese Six Companies did post placards in the Chinatowns of cities such as San Francisco and Portland, warning residents that they would face "penalties" if they disobeyed organized resistance to the law and registered with government officials. But opposition among Chinese immigrants and American-born citizens was widespread even before these warnings were promulgated. For a discussion of the campaign to resist registration, see Jean Pfaelzer, *Driven Out: The Forgotten War Against Chinese Americans* (Berkeley: University of California Press, 2008), 291–335.

44 "Wise Speaks Out," *Morning Call*, July 28, 1893; "Chinese Tricks," *Morning Call*, September 16, 1893.

45 Grace Chang, *Disposable Domestics: Immigrant Women Workers in the Global Economy* (Cambridge, MA: South End Press, 2000), 110–13.

46 "After His Hat," *Morning Call*, September 27, 1893; "Still at Large," *Morning Call*, September 28, 1893; "He May Disburse," *Morning Call*, September 30, 1893.

47 File 13893/9–4, Chinese Arrival Files, San Francisco, Records of the U.S. Immigration and Naturalization Service, RG 85, National Archives, Pacific Region, San Bruno, CA. On language skills as a factor in immigration officials' determinations of whether Chinese immigrants and American-born citizens were eligible to enter, see Lee, *At America's Gates*, 107–9.

48 Anita Rupprecht, "Excessive Memories: Slavery, Insurance and Resistance," *History Workshop Journal* 64, no. 1 (2007): 6–28; James Oldham, "Insurance Litigation Involving the *Zong* and Other British Slave Ships, 1780–1807," *Journal of Legal History* 28, no. 3 (2007): 319–28; and Sharon Ann Murphy, "Securing Human

Property: Slavery, Life Insurance, and Industrialization in the Upper South," *Journal of the Early Republic* 25, no. 4 (2005): 615–52.

49 "Report of Wm. J. Gavigan, Special Counsel, San Francisco, August 8, 1888," in San Francisco Board of Supervisors, *San Francisco Municipal Reports Fiscal Year 1887–88, Ending June 30, 1888* (San Francisco: W. M. Hinton, 1888), 800–809; "No More Bail Bonds," *Daily Alta California*, July 11, 1890; "Bail in Chinese Cases," *Daily Alta California*, July 12, 1890; and, for Wallace's statement, "Chinese Bondsmen," *Daily Alta California*, July 23, 1890.

50 "Chinese Exclusion," *Morning Call*, February 2, 1891; "Chinese Sureties," *Morning Call*, February 13, 1892.

51 *Immigration Act*, 22 Stat. 214 (1882): sec. 3; *Immigration Act*, 34 Stat. 898 (1907): sec. 20.

52 López, *Chinese Cubans*, 149–51; Grace Delgado, *Making the Chinese Mexican: Global Migration, Localism, and Exclusion in the U.S.-Mexico Borderlands* (Stanford, CA: Stanford University Press, 2012), 75–79. On alleged incidents of unauthorized entry committed by Chinese laborers in transit, see U.S. Congress, House of Representatives, *Compilation from the Records of the Bureau of Immigration of Facts Concerning the Enforcement of the Chinese Exclusion Acts*, 59 Cong., 1st sess., 1906, House Doc. 847, 79–90.

53 "Chinese Laborers—Transit through the United States," in *Synopsis of the Decisions of the Treasury Department on the Construction of the Tariff, Navigation, and Other Laws, for the Year Ended December 31, 1889* (Washington, DC: GPO, 1890), 368–71.

54 Windom to Blaine, November 26, 1889, and Tsui Kwo Yin to Blaine, December 16, 1889, in Department of State, *Papers Relating to the Foreign Relations of the United States* (Washington, DC: GPO, 1890), 146; 149–50. These rules did not apply to in-transit passengers transferring between ships.

55 Bureau of Immigration, *Laws, Treaty and Regulations Relating to the Exclusion of Chinese* (Washington, DC: GPO, 1902), 49–50; Robert Chao Romero, *The Chinese in Mexico, 1882–1940* (Tucson: University of Arizona Press, 2012), 32–34.

56 For further elaboration of this point, see Andrew Urban, "Enforcing the Inequalities of Global 'Free' Trade: Chinese Sailors, Immigration Restrictions, and the Right to Land in U.S. Ports, 1882–1930" (paper, Labor and Empire Conference, University of California, Santa Barbara, November 2014); and Justin Jackson, " 'The Right Kind of Men': Flexible Capacity, Chinese Exclusion, and the Imperial Politics of Maritime Labor Reform in the United States, 1898–1905," *Labor* 10, no. 4 (Winter 2013): 39–60.

57 *In re Ah Kee*, 22 Fed. 519 (1884).

58 Hager to Manning, July 26, 1888, NARA, Custom Case Files no. 3358d, box 9, folder 3.

59 Despite accusations of substitutions, maritime labor required training and experience, and Chinese laborers could not be recruited at random to go to sea. Mae Ngai, *The Lucky Ones: One Family and the Extraordinary Invention of Chinese America* (Princeton, NJ: Princeton University Press, 2012), 150–52, 173–88.

60 Dan Hardy, "Cushman Rice: The Man Who Was Gatsby?," *Writing in the Margins*, Spring 2008, 4–5.

61 File 56/930, box 279, Chinese Exclusion Acts Case Files, 1880–1960, Immigration and Naturalization Service, Record Group 85, National Archives and Records Administration–Northeast Region (New York) (hereafter cited as NARA, CECF, NY).

62 Adam M. McKeown, *Melancholy Order: Asian Migration and the Globalization of Borders* (New York: Columbia University Press, 2008), 11.

63 U.S. Bureau of Immigration, *Annual Report of the Commissioner-General of Immigration* (Washington, DC: GPO, 1922), 143.

64 Wexler, *Tender Violence*, 15–51.

65 File 54783/42, Subject Correspondence Files, NARA.

66 File 54472/3, Subject Correspondence Files, NARA.

67 Sibray to Colby, June 11, 1920, file 54686/4, Subject Correspondence Files, NARA.

68 Thomas Sammons, American Consulate-General, Canton to Bureau of Immigration, Seattle, WA, January 31, 1919, file 54594/53, Subject Correspondence Files, NARA.

69 Thomas Keating to Bureau of Immigration, Washington, February 6, 1920, file 54783/5, Subject Correspondence Files, NARA.

70 File 54174/16, Subject Correspondence Files, NARA.

71 File 14/3616, box 109, NARA, CECF, NY.

72 "Orders Doctor Hardy's Servant Back to China," *St. Louis Republic*, November 1, 1904; Ngai, *Lucky Ones*, 112.

73 File 54783/15. The use of surety bonds by vacationing white Canadians who wished to travel with their Chinese servants seems to have been relatively common. See also files 54424/97, 97A, and 97B, Subject Correspondence Files, NARA.

74 File 54686/53, Subject Correspondence Files, NARA.

75 File 53725/77, Subject Correspondence Files, NARA.

76 File 55817/206, Subject Correspondence Files, NARA.

77 File 54875/23, Subject Correspondence Files, NARA.

78 File 54783/104, Subject Correspondence Files, NARA.

79 Alexandra Minna Stern, "Buildings, Boundaries, and Blood: Medicalization and Nation-Building on the U.S.-Mexico Border, 1910–1930," *Hispanic American Historical Review* 79, no. 1 (1999): 41–81.

80 For a discussion of the dynamics that contemporary cross-border workers face, see Alena Semuels, "Crossing the Mexican-American Border, Every Day," *Atlantic*, January 25, 2016.

81 On the railroads as agents of U.S. imperialism, see Daniel Lewis, *Iron Horse Imperialism: The Southern Pacific of Mexico, 1880–1951* (Tucson: University of Arizona Press, 2007).

82 File 55127/47, Subject Correspondence Files, NARA.

83 File 54424/92, Subject Correspondence Files, NARA.

84 On nonimmigrant laborers and their governance today, see Philip Kretsedemas, "The Limits of Control: Neo-liberal Policy Priorities and the US Non-immigrant

Flow," *International Migration* 50 (February 1, 2012): 1468–2435; and Payal Banerjee, "Transnational Subcontracting, Indian IT Workers, and the U.S. Visa System," *Women's Studies Quarterly* 38, nos. 1–2 (2010): 89–110.

85 As part of the *bracero* program, employers were mandated to take out what were commonly called performance or compliance bonds, to ensure guestworkers' "ultimate departure." See Public Law 45, April 29, 1943 (H.J. Res. 96); Barbara A. Driscoll, *The Tracks North: The Railroad Bracero Program of World War II* (Austin: University of Texas Press, 1999), 99–100; and Calavita, *Inside the State*, 20, 43. Ngai uses the term "imported colonialism" to describe the status of guestworkers who were not only bonded to employers but also, after the New Deal, excluded from protections that federal and state labor laws offered citizens. Ngai, *Impossible Subjects*, 129.

## CHAPTER 6. RACE AND REFORM

1 On Opper's hostility toward Irish servants, see Maureen Murphy, "Bridget and Biddy: Images of the Irish Servant Girl in *Puck* Cartoons, 1880–1890," in *New Perspectives on the Irish Diaspora*, ed. Charles Fanning (Carbondale: Southern Illinois University Press, 2000), 152–75. As American studies scholar M. Alison Kibler documents, by the first decade of the twentieth century, popular uses of the "Biddy" stereotype had become less publicly acceptable. In 1907, Irish American protesters successfully halted productions of the theatrical performance *The Irish Servant Girls*, a long-running satirical show in which male actors donned women's clothing to depict a masculine and blundering version of "Biddy." See Kibler, *Censoring Racial Ridicule: Irish, Jewish, and African American Struggles over Race and Representation, 1890–1930* (Chapel Hill: University of North Carolina Press, 2015), 51–81.

2 "The Home Club," *Outlook*, February 12, 1898, 451.

3 On domestic labor as a strategy for governing native peoples, and as a form of coercive market assimilation, see Jane Simonson, *Making Home Work: Domesticity and Native American Assimilation in the American West, 1860–1919* (Chapel Hill: University of North Carolina Press, 2006); Victoria Haskins, "'The Matter of Wages Does Not Seem to Be Material': Native American Domestic Workers' Wages under the Outing System in the United States, 1880s–1930s," in *Towards a Global History of Domestic and Caregiving Workers*, ed. Dirk Hoerder, Elise van Nederveen Meerkerk, and Silke Neunsinger (Leiden: Brill, 2015), 323–45; and Robert A. Trennert, "Educating Indian Girls at Nonreservation Boarding Schools, 1878–1920," *Western Historical Quarterly* 13, no. 3 (1982): 271–90.

4 "Southern Servant Girls," *Brooklyn Eagle*, April 23, 1900; *Gonzáles v. Williams*, 192 U.S. 1 (1904); Chang, *Pacific Connections*, 77. See also Sam Erman, "Meanings of Citizenship in the U.S. Empire: Puerto Rico, Isabel Gonzalez, and the Supreme Court, 1898–1905," *Journal of American Ethnic History* 27, no. 4 (2008): 5–33. On mid-twentieth-century contract domestic labor migrations from Puerto Rico to the continental United States, see Emma Amador, "Organizing Puerto Rican

Domestics: Resistance and Household Labor Reform in the Puerto Rican Diaspora after 1930," *ILWCH: International Labor and Working Class History* 88 (Fall
2015): 67–86.

5  Lucy Maynard Salmon, *Domestic Service* (1897; repr., New York: Macmillan, 1901),
174–75.

6  "Southern Servant Girls," *Brooklyn Eagle*, April 23, 1900. On efforts to block the
recruitment and contract of black southern laborers into northern jobs, see Bernstein, *Only One Place of Redress*, 8–27; and Cohen, *At Freedom's Edge*, 248–73.

7  Andrew Zimmerman, *Alabama in Africa: Booker T. Washington, the German
Empire, and the Globalization of the New South* (Princeton, NJ: Princeton Uni-
versity Press, 2010), 205–6, 222–36. As historian Touré Reed addresses, the Urban
League, which originated with the 1911 merger of the National League for the
Protection of Colored Women (founded by Frances Kellor), the Committee for
Improving Industrial Conditions of Negroes in New York, and the Committee on
Urban Conditions Among Negroes, has often been misinterpreted as primarily
indebted to Booker T. Washington's efforts at the Tuskegee Institute. Reed argues
instead that northern reformers were more indebted to the sociological theories
of assimilation advanced by the Chicago School of Sociology. Reed, *Not Alms but
Opportunity: The Urban League & the Politics of Racial Uplift, 1910–1950* (Chapel
Hill: University of North Carolina Press, 2008), 11–26. Criminologists frequently
drew connections between the legacies of slavery and what they believed was the
natural propensity of black women to engage in criminal actions after migrating
to the North. See Cheryl Hicks, *Talk with You Like a Woman: African American
Women, Justice, and Reform in New York, 1890–1935* (Chapel Hill: University of
North Carolina, 2010), 125–58; and Kali Gross, *Colored Amazons: Crime, Violence,
and Black Women in the City of Brotherly Love, 1880–1910* (Durham, NC: Duke
University Press, 2006). For a critique of the historical scholarship that has
depicted black migrants to the North as "premodern," see also Ira Berlin, *The
Making of African America: The Four Great Migrations* (New York: Viking, 2010),
152–200.

8  Kellor, "Immigrant Woman," 401; I. M. Rubinow, "The Problem of Domestic
Service," *Journal of Political Economy* 14, no. 8 (1906): 507.

9  Katzman, *Seven Days a Week*, 61.

10  Joseph A. Hill, *Women in Gainful Occupations, 1870–1920. A Study of the Trend of
Recent Changes in the Numbers, Occupational Distribution and Family Relationship of Women Reported in the Census as Following a Gainful Occupation* (Washington, DC, 1929), 35.

11  See Ruth Schwartz Cowan's discussion of alternative modes for organizing household production in *More Work for Mother: The Ironies of Household Technology
from the Open Hearth to the Microwave* (New York: Basic Books, 1985), 102–50.

12  On the role of social science and technocratic expertise in empowering the
Progressive Era middle class and providing it with authority, see, most notably,

Robert Wiebe, *The Search for Order, 1877–1920* (New York: Hill & Wang, 1966). On the specific role of women social scientists, see Fitzpatrick, *Endless Crusade.*

13  Addams, "Belated Industry," 543.

14  May, *Unprotected Labor*, 13–14.

15  Salmon, *Domestic Service*, 140–66. See also Katzman, *Seven Days a Week*, 266–80.

16  Addams, "Belated Industry," 539; Addams, *Newer Ideals of Peace* (New York: Macmillan, 1907), 199–200.

17  Mary Roberts Smith, "Domestic Service: The Responsibility of Employers," *Forum* 27 (August 1899): 682. While working toward her graduate degree at Stanford, Coolidge went by Mary Roberts Smith, using the surname of her first husband. In 1906, after divorcing and remarrying, she would change her name to Mary Roberts Smith Coolidge. For the sake of clarity here, I refer to her as Coolidge throughout. For Coolidge's biography, see Mary Jo Deegan, "Introduction," in Coolidge, *Why Women Are So* (1912; repr., Amherst, NY: Humanity Books, 2004), 7–23.

18  Coolidge, *Chinese Immigration* (New York: Henry Holt, 1909), 252.

19  Historian Louise Michele Newman describes Coolidge as an "evolution feminist." Newman, *White Women's Rights: The Racial Origins of Feminism in the United States* (New York: Oxford University Press, 1999), 152–59.

20  In his historiographical review and foreword to the reprint of Elmer Sandmeyer's book *The Anti-Chinese Movement in California*, Roger Daniels argues that Coolidge was a "WASP historian" whose antipathy toward the anti-Chinese movement was caught up in her own "class biases." Daniels, "Foreword," in Sandmeyer, *Anti-Chinese Movement in California*, 3.

21  J. R. Commons, "Chinese Immigration," *Political Science Quarterly* 26, no. 1 (1911): 151.

22  Salmon, *Domestic Service*, 177.

23  "With the Authors," *Los Angeles Times*, September 21, 1913. The second half of *The Yellow Angel* contained three separate short stories not discussed here, which also featured Chinese characters learning about Christianity.

24  The book's national reception was something that the *Los Angeles Times* noted in its admiring review. "Yellow Angel," *Los Angeles Times*, February 22, 1914.

25  Mary Sue Daggett, *The Yellow Angel* (Chicago: Browne & Howell, 1914) (dedication). In-text page citations refer to this edition.

26  "Mary Stewart Daggett," in *1910 United States Federal Census* (database online) (Provo, UT: Ancestry.com, 2009).

27  On Coventry Patmore's original poem, see Ian Anstruther, *Coventry Patmore's Angel: A Study of Coventry Patmore, His Wife Emily and the Angel in the House* (London: Haggerston Press, 1992).

28  Rubinow, "Problems of Domestic Service," 512.

29  Before-and-after pictures were common features in accounts of racial uplift. See, for example, Wexler, *Tender Violence*, 94–126; and Eric Margolis and Jeremy

Rowe, "Images of Assimilation: Photographs of Indian Schools in Arizona," *History of Education* 33, no. 2 (2004): 199–230.

30 Salmon, *Domestic Service*, 171.

31 Daggett, *Yellow Angel*, 83–104.

32 Ibid., 29.

33 At the height of Japanese immigration to the United States, between 1904 and 1907, in the San Francisco area alone approximately four thousand Japanese men worked as servants or "houseboys." Many Japanese servants were students who did domestic work on a temporary, part-time basis. Evelyn Nakano Glenn, *Issei, Nisei, War Bride: Three Generations of Japanese American Women in Domestic Service* (Philadelphia: Temple University Press, 1986), 107.

34 Well into the twentieth century, Chinese servants would continue to appear as symbols of the old West and as figures whose loyalty to early white settlers—as providers of services—defined an almost heroic partnership. See, for instance, the cook Lee in John Steinbeck's novel *East of Eden* (1952), and Hop Sing, the cook and servant in the television series *Bonanza* (1959–1973).

35 Excerpts from the *Argonaut* article were reprinted in "Orientals in the West," *New York Daily Tribune*, September 15, 1907; Jean Faison, "The Virtues of the Chinese Servant," *Good Housekeeping*, March 1906, 280.

36 Chester Rowell, "Chinese and Japanese Immigrants—A Comparison," *Annals of the American Academy of Political and Social Science* 34, no. 2 (1909): 3.

37 Alba M. Edwards, Census Bureau, *Population: Comparative Occupation Statistics for the United States, 1870–1940*, part 2 (Washington, DC: GPO, 1943), table 13, 158; table 14, 165.

38 Phyllis Palmer, *Domesticity and Dirt: Housewives and Domestic Servants in the United States, 1920–1945* (Philadelphia: Temple University Press, 1989), 134.

39 George J. Stigler, *Domestic Servants in the United States: 1900–1940*, Occasional Paper no. 24 (New York: National Bureau of Economic Research, 1946), 7, 9.

40 Edwards, Census Bureau, *Population*, 165.

41 A Negro Nurse, "More Slavery at the South," *Independent*, January 25, 1912, 198.

42 Ibid., 199.

43 C. Rawley, "Self-Control," *Independent*, May 30, 1912, 1163; Jessie Fauset, "What to Read," *Crisis* 3, no. 6 (April 1912): 262. On the efforts of black activists to reveal the myths surrounding rape and race in the South, see McElya, *Clinging to Mammy*, 160–206, and Hazel Carby, *Reconstructing Womanhood: The Emergence of the Afro-American Woman Novelist* (New York: Oxford University Press, 1989), 20–39.

44 See McElya, *Clinging to Mammy*, 207–52.

45 Rubinow, "Problem of Domestic Service," 515.

46 Clark-Lewis, *Living In, Living Out*, 123–46.

47 Hunter, *To 'Joy My Freedom*, 187–219. Household employers' concerns about the spread of disease were not exclusive to black servants. Advances in scientific knowledge regarding germ theory and the spread of contagions made domestic

laborers more susceptible to fears that they were carriers of illness who might infect the families who employed them. See, for example, Judith Walzer Leavitt, *Typhoid Mary: Captive to the Public's Health* (New York: Beacon, 1997).

48  Isabel Eaton, *A Special Report on Domestic Service* (Boston: Ginn, 1889), 486. Eaton's report was included as part of W. E. B. Du Bois's *The Philadelphia Negro: A Social Study*. On this partnership, see Mary Jo Deegan, "W. E. B. Du Bois and the Women of Hull-House, 1895–1899," *American Sociologist* 19, no. 4 (1988): 301–11.

49  Haynes's thesis was published by the *Journal of Negro History*. Elizabeth Ross Haynes, "Negroes in Domestic Service in the United States: Introduction," *Journal of Negro History* 8, no. 4 (1923): 412–13.

50  See, for instance, Carole Marks, "The Bone and Sinew of the Race: Black Women, Domestic Service and Labor Migration," *Marriage and Family Review* 19 (1993): 149–73.

51  See Mary White Ovington, *Half a Man: The Status of the Negro in New York* (New York: Longmans, Green, 1911), 148. Ovington's interpretation was indebted to the observations and arguments made by the Howard University professor Kelly Miller, whose book *Race Adjustment: Essays on the Negro in America* (1908) included a discussion of "surplus negro women" in northern cities. W. E. B. Du Bois also addressed the imbalance of sexes among the black community in the North. See Hicks, *Talk with You Like a Woman*, 29–31.

52  *National Association Notes* 2, no. 10 (March 1891), Records of NACWC, reel 23, slide 284.

53  Haynes, "Negroes in Domestic Service," 392. See also Enobong Branch, *Opportunity Denied: Limiting Black Women to Devalued Work* (New Brunswick, NJ: Rutgers University Press, 2011), 49–96.

54  Licht, *Getting Work*, 125–26.

55  Ovington, *Half a Man*, 162–63.

56  Eaton, *Special Report on Domestic Service*, 467.

57  Clark-Lewis, *Living In, Living Out*, 111.

58  "World's Great War a Mighty Blessing," *Chicago Defender*, August 5, 1916. On the *Defender*'s role as a booster of migration, see Ethan Michaeli, *The Defender: How the Legendary Black Newspaper Changed America* (Boston: Houghton Mifflin Harcourt, 2016), 61–79.

59  Kimberley L. Phillips, *AlabamaNorth: African-American Migrants, Community, and Working-Class Activism in Cleveland, 1915–45* (Urbana: University of Illinois Press, 1999), 76.

60  Haynes, "Negroes in Domestic Service," 414–15. The DC minimum wage law was overturned in 1923 by the Supreme Court Case *Adkins v. Children's Hospital*, which asserted that the 1918 law infringed upon employers' freedom of contract. See Joan G. Zimmerman, "The Jurisprudence of Equality: The Women's Minimum Wage, the First Equal Rights Amendment, and *Adkins v. Children's Hospital*, 1905–1923," *Journal of American History* 78, no. 1 (1991): 188–225.

61 Arnold D. Prince, "Returning Tide of Immigrants Brings No House Servants," *New York Tribune*, January 25, 1920. The "returning tide" referenced the resumption of immigration after it had been stopped by the First World War.

62 "Speech by Jno. B. Weber, Commissioner of Immigration, Port of New York, at Cooper Union, New York City, January 4, 1893," in Committee on Immigration and Naturalization, Committee Papers, "Protection of American labor and endorsement of the Law of Domicile and Restriction of Immigration" (HR53A-F17.1), box 101, Record Group 233, National Archives, Washington, DC.

63 In his classic work on the subject, John Higham differentiates between nativist and "Know Nothing" ideologies that sought to restrict the immigration of Irish Catholics in the mid-nineteenth century, and nativist ideologies informed by theories of racial science that held sway between 1880 and World War II. While anti-Catholic attitudes persisted among groups like the Ku Klux Klan and the Midwestern-based American Protective Association, by the end of the nineteenth century many restrictionists viewed Irish and German Catholics as members of "superior" Northern and Western European races. Higham, *Strangers in the Land: Patterns of American Nativism, 1860–1925* (New Brunswick, NJ: Rutgers University Press, 1955). On the occupational preferences that "new" immigrants displayed, see Donna Gabaccia, *From the Other Side: Women, Gender, and Immigrant Life in the U.S., 1820–1990* (Bloomington: Indiana University Press, 1994), 45–52.

64 "New York Needs 100,000 Servants," *New York Times*, May 5, 1912.

65 A. D., "Is the Melting Pot a Fallacy?" *New York Tribune*, November 20, 1920. As historian Daniel Bender notes, "When observers of America's growing cities talked about immigrant 'colonies,' they truly meant places and sites of conquest, not simply close-knit and growing communities." Bender, *American Abyss: Savagery and Civilization in the Age of Industry* (Ithaca, NY: Cornell University Press, 2009), 71. Immigration historians have long addressed assimilation as a spatial issue, as the widespread use of metaphors such as "uprooted" and "transplanted" indicates. For a historiographical review of how scholars have theorized assimilation in the United States, see Russell A. Kazal, "Revisiting Assimilation," *American Historical Review* 100 (April 1995): 437–71.

66 A. W. Parker, "In re Gladys Taylor, Aged 21. Supplemental Memorandum for the Assistant Secretary," October 9, 1917, file 54261/196, Subject Correspondence Files, NARA.

67 Untitled editorial, *Survey*, n.d., clipping in file 52481/5, Subject Correspondence Files, NARA.

68 Alfred Hampton, Assistant Commissioner-General of Immigration, "In re Nakagawa Ichi. Aged 29. Memorandum for the Assistant Secretary," June 25, 1917, file 54261/196, Subject Correspondence Files, NARA.

69 On the long lead-up to the passage of the literacy test, and the positions of various interest groups, see Claudia Goldin, "The Political Economy of Immigration Restriction in the United States, 1890 to 1921," in *The Regulated Economy:*

A *Historical Approach to Political Economy*, ed. Claudia Goldin and Gary Libecap (Chicago: University of Chicago Press, 1994), 225–39.

70  See also Jeanne D. Petit, *Men and Women We Want: Gender, Race, and the Progressive Era Literacy Test Debate* (Rochester: University of Rochester Press, 2010), 31–58.

71  These findings were reported in Goddard, "Mental Tests and the Immigrant," *Journal of Delinquency* 2, no. 5 (September 1917): 264–65. On Goddard's work more generally, see Stephen Jay Gould, *The Mismeasure of Man*, rev. ed. (New York: Norton, 1996), 188–204.

72  Siegel, despite his stance in the *Times*, does not appear to have officially brought this matter before Congress. "Why Not Import Your Servant?," *New York Times*, April 25, 1920. See also McElya, *Clinging to Mammy*, 215–17.

73  *1921 Emergency Quota Law (An Act to Limit the Immigration of Aliens into the United States)*, 42 Stat. 5, sec. 2 (d).

74  Sabath on March 4, 1923, 67th Cong., 4th sess., *Congressional Record* 64, pt. 6: 5680.

75  *1924 Immigration Act (An Act to Limit the Immigration of Aliens into the United States, and for Other Purposes)*, 43 Stat. 669; Mae Ngai, "The Architecture of Race in American Immigration Law: A Reexamination of the Immigration Act of 1924," *Journal of American History* 86, no. 1 (June 1999): 67–92.

76  On visitors' visas given to European servants accompanying returning American citizens, see, for example, Edwin Shaughnessy, Deputy Commissioner of Immigration to District Director, Ellis Island, February 15, 1939, file 55800/500. For Russo's story, see James Parker, Attorney for the Italia America Shipping Corp. to the Commissioner General of Immigration, April 30, 1925, file 55395/665. Both files come from the Subject Correspondence Files, NARA.

77  Cowan, *More Work for Mother*, 103–9. As Cowan contends, for many middle-class women, the decrease in the number of live-in servants available for hire, combined with heightened expectations for cleanliness and comfort that new commercial technologies and services created, increased their individual workloads (154–60). Historian Faye Dudden argues that technological solutions were more appealing to household employers than experts' recommendations that families reform labor relations in their own homes. Dudden, "Experts and Servants: The National Council on Household Employment and the Decline of Domestic Service in the Twentieth Century," *Journal of Social History* 20, no. 2 (1986): 269–90.

78  Rubinow, "Household Service as a Labor Problem," *Journal of Home Economics* 3 (April 1911): 132; Frances Kellor, "The Woman Who Does Her Own Work," *Ladies' Home Journal*, October 1906, 34.

79  Edward Bellamy, *Looking Backward, 2000–1887* (1888; repr., Boston: Bedford Books, 1995), 87, 105–6. Upton Sinclair's Helicon Hall, a commune in which members did all of the domestic labor, was one experiment in part based on Bellamy's text. Sinclair proudly recounted how the author Sinclair Lewis was one of the commune's servants. Upton Sinclair, "My Private Utopia," *Nation*, July 11, 1928.

80  On the use of black racial stereotypes in turn-of-the-century advertising, see Velma Maia Thomas, "Your Advertisement Troubles Me: Atlanta's Gold Dust

Twins," *Atlanta Studies*, July 27, 2015; McElya, *Clinging to Mammy*, 15–37; and Marilyn Kern-Foxworth, *Aunt Jemima, Uncle Ben, and Rastus: Blacks in Advertising, Yesterday, Today, and Tomorrow* (Westport, CT: Greenwood, 1994).

## EPILOGUE

1 On remote control, see Aristide Zolberg, "The Archeology of Remote Control," in *Migration Control in the North Atlantic World: The Evolution of State Practices in Europe and the United States from the French Revolution to the Inter-war Period*, ed. Andreas Fahrmeier, Olivier Faron, and Patrick Weil (New York: Berghahn Books, 2003), 195–222.

2 Roediger and Esch, *Production of Difference*.

3 Martha J. Bailey and William J. Collins, "The Wage Gains of African-American Women in the 1940s," *Journal of Economic History* 66, no. 3 (2006): 745n18.

4 On internment, the application for leave clearance, and work resettlement, see Ngai, *Impossible Subjects*, 175–201; Brian Masaru Hayashi, *Democratizing the Enemy: The Japanese American Internment* (Princeton, NJ: Princeton University Press, 2004); Allan W. Austin, "Eastward Pioneers: Japanese American Resettlement during World War II and the Contested Meaning of Exile and Incarceration," *Journal of American Ethnic History* 26, no. 2 (January 2007): 58–84; and Charlotte Brooks, "In the Twilight Zone between Black and White: Japanese American Resettlement and Community in Chicago, 1942–1945," *Journal of American History* 86, no. 4 (2000): 1655–87.

5 Peterson to Harry Kessler, November 14, 1944, Records of the War Relocation Authority, Record Group 210 (hereafter WRA Records), entry 16, file 71.900F, box 488.

6 Evelyn Nakano Glenn, "From Servitude to Service Work: Historical Continuities in the Racial Division of Paid Reproductive Labor," *Signs* 18, no. 1 (1992): 14.

7 Brooks, "In the Twilight Zone," 1664–73. As was the case during World War I, black women continued to face job discrimination, despite industrial labor shortages caused by the United States' entry into the conflict. During World War II, black women's overall representation in both private household and commercial service work increased, despite a commensurate spike in wartime industrial jobs. On the employment discrimination black women encountered during World War II, see Jacqueline Jones, *Labor of Love, Labor of Sorrow: Black Women, Work, and the Family from Slavery to the Present*, 2nd ed. (New York: Basic Books, 2009), 199–207.

8 Kimball to Mrs. Franklin D. Roosevelt, March 17, 1943, WRA Records, entry 16, file 71.900F, box 487.

9 *1948 Displaced Persons Act (An Act to Authorize for a Limited Period of Time the Admission into the United States of Certain European Displaced Persons for Permanent Residence, and for Other Purposes)*, 62 Stat. 1009: secs. 2(c) and 6(b).

10 Gardner, *Qualities of a Citizen*, 206–7.

11 On the guestworker programs that were used to recruit labor from the British West Indies as work-arounds to the 1952 quota restrictions, see Hahamovitch, *No*

*Man's Land,* 117–22. On the 1965 Immigration Act and its architecture, see Ngai, *Impossible Subjects,* 227–64. For more specific discussions of how the 1965 act affected different immigrant groups and aspects of American life, see the essays in Gabriel J. Chin and Rose Cuison Villazor, eds., *The Immigration and Nationality Act of 1965: Legislating a New America* (New York: Cambridge University Press, 2015).

12 Edith Lowenstein, "The Act of October 3, 1965 to Amend the Immigration and Naturalization Act; and for Other Purposes," *Interpreter Releases* 43, no. 6 (February 3, 1966): 32. The certification provision relating to the availability of American workers and wage levels was first introduced in the 1952 Walter-McCarran Act but not actually enforced until the middle part of the 1960s, when *braceros* began applying for visas rather than entering as guestworkers. David North, "The Immigration of Non-professional Workers to the United States," *International Migration Review* 6, no. 1 (Spring 1972): 66.

13 Ngai, *Impossible Subjects,* 238.

14 How labor certification decisions were made was apparently quite opaque. As one observer complained, not only did employers lack basic instructions and guidelines explaining the process, "most aggravating of all, when the government decides that you cannot have that maid (or irrigator or carpenter), it sends you a cold form." Cited in Peter Rodino, "The Impact of Immigration on the American Labor Market," *Rutgers Law Review* 27 (1973–74): 247.

15 Quoted in Edith Lowenstein, "Review of the Operation of the Immigration and Nationality Act as Amended by the Act of October 3, 1965, Part III: Labor Department," *Interpreter Releases* 45, no. 50 (December 30, 1968): 372.

16 Edith Lowenstein, "Labor Department Struggles with Live-in Maid Problem," *Interpreter Releases* 46, no. 45 (November 20, 1969): 273–76. See also the helpful discussion in Gardner, *Qualities of a Citizen,* 212–19.

17 North, "Immigration of Non-professional Workers," 67.

18 U.S. State Department, "Immigrant Visas Issued and Adjustments of Status, Table V (Part 2), Fiscal Year 2015," travel.state.gov (accessed August 13, 2016). For a theoretical focus on how state policies have contributed to the globalization of care work in recent decades, see Joya Misra, Jonathan Woodring, and Sabine N. Merz, "The Globalization of Care Work: Neoliberal Economic Restructuring and Migration Policy," *Globalizations* 3, no. 3 (September 1, 2006): 317–32; and Eleonore Kofman, "Rethinking Care through Social Reproduction: Articulating Circuits of Migration," *Social Politics: International Studies in Gender, State & Society* 19, no. 1 (March 1, 2012): 142–62, among a large and growing body of scholarly literature.

19 U.S. State Department, "Table XVI(B) Nonimmigrant Visas Issued by Classification (Including Border Crossing Cards), Fiscal Years 2011–2015," travel.state.gov (accessed August 7, 2016).

20 Department of Homeland Security, U.S. Citizenship and Immigration Services, "Instructions for I-765, Application for Employment Authorization," www.uscis.gov (accessed August 7, 2016).

21  Human Rights Watch, "Hidden in the Home: Abuse of Domestic Workers with Special Visas in the United States" (2001), www.hrw.org (accessed August 7, 2016); ACLU, "Trafficking and Exploitation of Migrant Domestic Workers by Diplomats and Staff of International Organizations in the United States" (2007), www .aclu.org (accessed August 7, 2016). More recently, the *Boston Globe* published an investigative article documenting many of the same issues, and the conditions akin to slavery that servant guestworkers are sometimes held in. Beth Healy and Megan Woolhouse, "For Some Domestic Workers, a Life of Isolated Servitude," *Boston Globe*, September 6, 2015. See also Alex Tizon, "My Family's Slave," *Atlantic Monthly*, June 2017, and Premilla Nadasen's critical response to this article, "Interrogating the Master Narrative of 'My Family's Slave,'" *Black Perspectives*, June 2, 2017, www.aaihs.org (accessed June 7, 2017).

22  Addie Hampton, "Jamaican Guestworkers Protest Alleged Abuse from Panhandle Employer," *WMBB News*, September 4, 2013. This and numerous other violations of the H-2B visa law have been compiled by the advocacy group National Guestworker Alliance, www.guestworkeralliance.org.

23  For proposals that call for guestworkers indemnifying their own departure, see Alex Nowrasteh, with the Cato Institute, "How to Make Guest Worker Visas Work," *Policy Analysis*, January 31, 2013; and Maurice Schiff, "When Migrants Overstay Their Legal Welcome: A Proposed Solution to the Guest-Worker Program" (IZA Discussion Paper no. 1401, November 2004).

24  On race and the drafting of the National Labor Relations Act, see Juan Perea, "The Echoes of Slavery: Recognizing the Racist Origins of the Agricultural and Domestic Worker Exclusion from the National Labor Relations Act," *Ohio State Law Journal* 72 (2011): 95. For a longer history of private household employers' resistance to regulation, see May, *Unprotected Labor*, 106–45. For a good summary of how domestics remain excluded from different federal statutory protection, including new civil rights and Occupational Safety and Health Administration (OSHA) rules, see National Domestic Workers Alliance, "Employment Protections for Domestic Workers: An Overview of Federal Law," www.domesticworkers.org (accessed August 11, 2016).

25  Goluboff, *Lost Promise of Civil Rights*, 141–73.

26  Amador, "Organizing Puerto Rican Domestics."

27  Erin Hatton, *The Temp Economy: From Kelly Girls to Permatemps in Postwar America* (Philadelphia: Temple University Press, 2011).

28  Linda Burnham and Nik Theodore, National Domestic Workers Alliance, *Home Economics: The Invisible and Unregulated World of Domestic Work* (New York, 2012), xii, 12, 20–21. On the vulnerability of undocumented workers more broadly, see Torrie Hester, "Deportability and the Carceral State," *Journal of American History* 102, no. 1 (2015): 141–51; Shannon Gleeson, *Conflicting Commitments: The Politics of Enforcing Immigrant Worker Rights in San Jose and Houston* (Ithaca, NY: Cornell University Press, 2012); Nicholas De Genova, *Working the Boundaries:*

*Race, Space, and "Illegality" in Mexican Chicago* (Durham, NC: Duke University Press, 2005); and Bacon, *Illegal People.*

29 Eileen Boris, "Force and Shadow in the Making of Precarity: Racialized Bodies and State Power," *Kalfou* 2, no. 2 (Fall 2015): 307.

30 Hiroshi Motomura, "Who Belongs? Immigration Outside the Law and the Idea of Americans in Waiting," *UC Irvine Law Review* 2 (2012): 374; and Motomura, *Americans in Waiting: The Lost Story of Immigration and Citizenship in the United States* (New York: Oxford University Press, 2006), 176–80. For a well-rounded debate on the legal philosophies undergirding open and restrictive immigration policies, see the essays in Carol M. Swain, ed., *Debating Immigration* (New York: Cambridge University Press, 2007).

31 Michael Huemer, "Is There a Right to Immigrate?," *Social Theory and Practice* 36, no. 3 (2010): 429–61.

32 Zolberg, *Nation by Design*, 14–23.

33 On domestic worker organizing, past and present, domestically and internationally, see May, *Unprotected Labor*, 146–82; Eileen Boris and Premilla Nadasen, "Domestic Workers Organize!," *WorkingUSA: The Journal of Labor and Society* 11 (December 2008): 413–43.

# INDEX

## ABOUT THE AUTHOR

Andrew Urban is Assistant Professor of American Studies and History at Rutgers University. His next project explores the history of Seabrook Farms, an agribusiness and company town in southern New Jersey that recruited incarcerated Japanese Americans, guestworkers from the British West Indies, and European refugees during the 1940s.